The O'Leary Series

Microsoft® Excel 2002

Introductory Edition

The O'Leary Series

Microsoft® Excel 2002

Introductory Edition

Timothy J. O'Leary

Arizona State University

Linda I. O'Leary

Information Technology

McGraw-Hill Irwin

Boston Burr Ridge, IL Dubuque, IA Madison, WI New York
San Francisco St. Louis Bangkok Bogotá Caracas Kuala Lumpur
Lisbon London Madrid Mexico City Milan Montreal New Delhi
Santiago Seoul Singapore Sydney Taipei Toronto

McGraw-Hill Higher Education

A Division of The McGraw-Hill Companies

MICROSOFT® Excel 2002, INTRODUCTORY EDITION
Published by McGraw-Hill/Irwin, an imprint of the McGraw-Hill Companies, Inc. 1221 Avenue of the Americas, New York, NY, 10020. Copyright © 2002 by the McGraw-Hill Companies, Inc. All rights reserved.

Some ancillaries, including electronic and print components, may not be available to customers outside the United States.

Disclaimer: This book is designed to help you improve your computer use. However, the author and publisher assume no responsibility whatsoever for the uses made of this material or for decisions based on their use, and make no warranties, either expressed or implied, regarding the contents of this book, its merchantability, or its fitness for any particular purpose.

Neither the publisher nor anyone else who has been involved in the creation, production, or delivery of this product shall be liable for any direct, incidental, or consequential damages, such as, but not limited to, loss of anticipated profits or benefits or benefits resulting from its use or from any breach of warranty. Some states do not allow the exclusion or limitation of direct, incidental, or consequential damages, so the above disclaimer may not apply to you. No dealer, company, or person is authorized to alter this disclaimer. Any representation to the contrary will not bind the publisher or author.

This book is printed on acid-free paper.

domestic   3 4 5 6 7 8 9 0 QPD/QPD 0 9 8 7 6 5 4 3 2
international   1 2 3 4 5 6 7 8 9 0 QPD/QPD 0 9 8 7 6 5 4 3 2 1

ISBN 0-07-247241-3

Publisher: *George Werthman*
Sponsoring editor: *Dan Silverburg*
Developmental editor: *Sarah Wood*
Senior marketing manager: *Paul Murphy*
Senior project manager: *Jean Hamilton*
Manager, new book production: *Melonie Salvati*
Media producer: *David Barrick*
Freelance design coordinator: *Gino Cieslik*
Lead supplement coordinator: *Marc Mattson*
Photo research coordinator: *David A. Tietz*
Cover & interior design: *Maureen McCutcheon*
Cover image: *Digitalvision*
Typeface: *10.5/13 New Aster*
Compositor: *Rogondino & Associates*
Printer: *Quebecor World Dubuque Inc.*

Library of Congress Control Number 2001095804

INTERNATIONAL EDITION ISBN 0-07-112358-X

www.mhhe.com

Information Technology

Information Technology at McGraw-Hill/Irwin

At McGraw-Hill Higher Education, we publish instructional materials targeted at the higher education market. In an effort to expand the tools of higher learning, we publish texts, lab manuals, study guides, testing materials, software, and multimedia products.

At McGraw-Hill/Irwin (a division of McGraw-Hill Higher Education), we realize that technology has created and will continue to create new mediums for professors and students to use in managing resources and communicating information to one another. We strive to provide the most flexible and complete teaching and learning tools available as well as offer solutions to the changing world of teaching and learning.

McGraw-Hill/Irwin is dedicated to providing the tools for today's instructors and students to successfully navigate the world of Information Technology.

- **Seminar Series**   McGraw-Hill/Irwin's Technology Connection seminar series offered across the country every year demonstrates the latest technology products and encourages collaboration among teaching professionals.

- **McGraw-Hill/Osborne**   This division of The McGraw-Hill Companies is known for its best-selling Internet titles, *Internet & Web Yellow Pages* and the *Internet Complete Reference*. For more information, visit Osborne at **www.osborne.com**.

- **Digital Solutions**   McGraw-Hill/Irwin is committed to publishing digital solutions. Taking your course online doesn't have to be a solitary adventure, nor does it have to be a difficult one. We offer several solutions that will allow you to enjoy all the benefits of having your course material online.

- **Packaging Options**   For more information about our discount options, contact your McGraw-Hill/Irwin Sales representative at 1-800-338-3987 or visit our web site at **www.mhhe.com/it**.

APPROVED COURSEWARE

What does this logo mean?

It means this courseware has been approved by the Microsoft® Office User Specialist Program to be among the finest available for learning *Microsoft Word 2002, Microsoft Excel 2002, Microsoft Access 2002,* and *Microsoft PowerPoint 2002*. It also means that upon completion of this courseware, you may be prepared to become a Microsoft Office User Specialist.

What is a Microsoft Office User Specialist?

A Microsoft Office User Specialist is an individual who has certified his or her skills in one or more of the Microsoft Office desktop applications of Microsoft Word, Microsoft Excel, Microsoft PowerPoint®, Microsoft Outlook® or Microsoft Access, or in Microsoft Project. The Microsoft Office User Specialist Program typically offers certification exams at the "Core" and "Expert" skill levels.* The Microsoft Office User Specialist Program is the only Microsoft approved program in the world for certifying proficiency in Microsoft Office desktop applications and Microsoft Project. This certification can be a valuable asset in any job search or career advancement.

More Information:

To learn more about becoming a Microsoft Office User Specialist, visit www.mous.net

To purchase a Microsoft Office User Specialist certification exam, visit www.DesktopIQ.com

To learn about other Microsoft Office User Specialist approved courseware from McGraw-Hill/Irwin, visit http://www.mhhe.com/catalogs/irwin/cit/mous/index.mhtml

---

* The availability of Microsoft Office User Specialist certification exams varies by application, application version and language. Visit www.mous.net for exam availability.

Microsoft, the Microsoft Office User Specialist Logo, PowerPoint and Outlook are either registered trademarks or trademarks of Microsoft Corporation in the United States and/or other countries.

Who benefits from Microsoft, Office User Specialist certification?

Employers

Microsoft Office User Specialist ("MOUS") certification helps satisfy employers' needs for qualitative assessments of employees' skills. Training, coupled with MOUS certification, offers organizations of every size, the ability to enhance productivity and efficiency by enabling their employees to unlock many advanced and laborsaving features in Microsoft Office applications. MOUS certification can ultimately improve the bottom line.

Employees

MOUS certification demonstrates employees' productivity and competence in Microsoft Office applications, the most popular business applications in the world. Achieving MOUS certification verifies that employees have the confidence and ability to use Microsoft Office applications in meeting and exceeding their work challenges.

Instructors

MOUS certification validates instructors' knowledge and skill in using Microsoft Office applications. It serves as a valuable credential, demonstrating their potential to teach students these essential applications. The MOUS Authorized Instructor program is also available to those who wish to further demonstrate their instructional capabilities.

Students

MOUS certification distinguishes students from their peers. It demonstrates their efficiency in completing assignments and projects, leaving more time for other studies. Improved confidence toward meeting new challenges and obstacles is yet another benefit. Achieving MOUS certification gives students the marketable skills necessary to set them apart in the competitive job market.

To learn more about MOUS certification, visit www.mous.net

To purchase a MOUS certification exam, visit www.DesktopIQ.com

Brief Contents

Detailed Contents

Lab 3 — Managing and Analyzing a Workbook EX3.1

Working Together: Linking, Embedding, and E-mailing EXWT1.1

Lab 4 — Using Solver, Creating Templates, and Evaluating Scenarios EX4.1

Lab

5 Using Data Tables, Creating Macros, and Designing Onscreen Forms EX5.1

Lab

6 Creating and Using Lists and Web Pages EX6.1

Acknowledgments

The new edition of The O'Leary Series has been made possible only through the enthusiasm and dedication of a great team of people. Because the team spans the country, literally from coast to coast, we have utilized every means of working together including conference calls, FAX, e-mail, and document collaboration. We have truly tested the team approach and it works!

Leading the team from McGraw-Hill/Irwin are George Werthman, Publisher and Alexandra Arnold, Developmental Editor. Their renewed commitment, direction, and support have infused the team with the excitement of a new project.

The production staff is headed by Jean Hamilton, Project Manager, whose planning and attention to detail has made it possible for us to successfully meet a very challenging schedule. Members of the production team include: Gino Cieslik, Designer; Pat Rogondino, Compositor; Susan Defosset, Copy Editor; Melonie Salvati, Production Supervisor; Marc Mattson, Supplement Coordinator; and David Barrick, Media Producer. We would particularly like to thank Pat and Susan—team members for many past editions—whom we can always depend on to do a great job.

Finally, we are particularly grateful to a small but very dedicated group of people who helped us develop the manuscript. Colleen Hayes, Susan Demar, and Kathy Duggan have helped on the last several editions and continue to provide excellent developmental and technical support. To Steve Willis and Carol Cooper who provide technical expertise, youthful perspective, and enthusiasm, my thanks for helping get the manuscripts out the door and meeting the deadlines.

Preface

Introduction

The 20th century not only brought the dawn of the Information Age, but also rapid changes in information technology. There is no indication that this rapid rate of change will be slowing— it may even be increasing. As we begin the 21st century, computer literacy will undoubtedly become prerequisite for whatever career a student chooses. The goal of the O'Leary Series is to assist students in attaining the necessary skills to efficiently use these applications. Equally important is the goal to provide a foundation for students to readily and easily learn to use future versions of this software. This series does this by providing detailed step-by step instructions combined with careful selection and presentation of essential concepts.

About the Authors

Tim and Linda O'Leary live in the American Southwest and spend much of their time engaging instructors and students in conversation about learning. In fact, they have been talking about learning for more than 25 years. Something in those early conversations convinced them to write a book, to bring their interest in the learning process to the printed page. Today, they are as concerned as ever about learning, about technology, and about the challenges of presenting material in new ways, both in terms of content and the method of delivery.

A powerful and creative team, Tim combines his years of classroom teaching experience with Linda's background as a consultant and corporate trainer. Tim has taught courses at Stark Technical College in Canton, Ohio, Rochester Institute of Technology in upper New York state, and is currently a professor at Arizona State University in Tempe, Arizona. Tim and Linda have talked to and taught students from ages 8 to 80, all of them with a desire to learn something about computers and the applications that make their lives easier, more interesting, and more productive.

About the Book

Times are changing, technology is changing, and this text is changing, too. Do you think the students of today are different from yesterday? There is no doubt about it—they are. On the positive side, it is amazing how much effort students will put toward things they are convinced are relevant to them. Their effort directed at learning application programs and exploring the Web seems at times limitless. On the other hand, students can often be shortsighted, thinking that learning the skills to use the application is the only objective. The mission of the series is to build upon and extend this interest by not only teaching the specific application skills but by introducing the concepts that are common to all applications, providing students with the confidence, knowledge, and ability to easily learn the next generation of applications.

What's New in This Edition?

- **Introduction to Computer Essentials**—A brief introduction to the basics of computer hardware and software (Appears in Office XP, Volume I only).

- **Introduction to Windows 2000**—Two hands-on labs devoted to Windows 2000 basics (Appears in Office XP, Volume I only).

- **Introduction to the WWW: Internet Explorer and E-mail**—Hands-on introductions for using Internet Explorer to browse the WWW and using e-mail (Appears in Office XP, Volume I only).

- **Topic Reorganization**—The text has been reorganized to include main and subtopic heads by grouping related tasks. For example, tasks such as changing fonts and applying character effects appear under the "Formatting" topic head. This results in a slightly more reference-like approach, making it easier for students to refer back to the text to review. This has been done without losing the logical and realistic development of the case.

- **Clarified Marginal Notes**—Marginal notes have been enhanced by more clearly identifying the note content with box heads and the use of different colors.

  Additional Information—Brief asides with expanded discussion of features.

  Having Trouble?—Procedural tips advising students of possible problems and how to overcome.

  Another Method—Alternative methods of performing a procedure.

- **Larger Screen Figures**—Make it easier to identify elements and read screen content.

- All **Numbered Steps** and bullets appear in left margin space making it easy not to miss a step.

- A **MOUS (*Microsoft Office User Specialist*) Skills** table, appearing at the end of each lab, contains page references to MOUS skills learned in the lab.

- **Two new References** are included at the end of each text.

  Data File List—Helps organize all data and solution files.

  MOUS (*Microsoft Office User Specialist*) Skills—Links all MOUS objectives to text content and end-of-chapter exercises.

Same Great Features as the Office 2000 Series

- **Relevant Cases**—Four separate running cases demonstrate the features in each application. Topics are of interest to students—At Arizona State University, over 600 students were surveyed to find out what topics are of interest to them.

- **Focus on Concepts**—Each chapter focuses on the concepts behind the application. Students learn the essentials, so they can succeed regardless of the software package they might be using.

- **Steps**—Numbered procedural steps clearly identify each hands-on task needed to complete the step.

- **Screens**—Plentiful screen illustrations illustrate the completion of each numbered step to help students stay on track.

- **Callouts**—Meaningful screen callouts identify the results of the steps as well as reinforce the associated concept.

- **End-of-Chapter Material**

   Terminology—Questions and exercises test recall of the basic information and terminology in the lab.

   - Screen Identification
   - Matching
   - Multiple Choice

   Concepts—Questions and exercises review students' understanding of concepts and ability to integrate ideas presented in different parts of the lab.

   - Fill-In
   - Discussion Questions

   Hands-On Practice Exercises—Students apply the skills and concepts they learned to solve case-based exercises. Many cases in the practice exercises tie to a running case used in another application lab. This helps to demonstrate the use of the four applications across a common case setting. For example, the Adventure Travel Tours case used in the Word labs is continued in practice exercises in Excel, Access, and PowerPoint.

   - Step-by-Step
   - On Your Own
   - On The Web

- **Rating System**—The 3-star rating system identifies the difficulty level of each practice exercise in the end-of-chapter materials.

- **Working Together Labs**—At the completion of the brief and introductory texts, a final lab demonstrates the integration of the MS Office applications and the WWW.

Instructor's Guide

We understand that, in today's teaching environment, offering a textbook alone is not sufficient to meet the needs of the many instructors who use our books. To teach effectively, instructors must have a full complement of supplemental resources to assist them in every facet of teaching from preparing for class, to conducting a lecture, to assessing students' comprehension. *The O'Leary Series* offers a fully-integrated supplements package and Web site, as described below.

Instructor's Resource Kit

The **Instructor's Resource Kit** contains a computerized Test Bank, an Instructor's Manual, and PowerPoint Presentation Slides. Features of the Instructor's Resource Kit are described below.

- **Instructor's Manual**   The Instructor's Manual contains lab objectives, concepts, outlines, lecture notes, and command summaries. Also included are answers to all end-of chapter material, tips for covering difficult materials, additional exercises, and a schedule showing how much time is required to cover text material.

- **Computerized Test Bank**   The test bank contains over 1,300 multiple choice, true/false, and discussion questions. Each question will be accompanied by the correct answer, the level of learning difficulty, and corresponding page references. Our flexible Diploma software allows you to easily generate custom exams.

- **PowerPoint Presentation Slides**   The presentation slides will include lab objectives, concepts, outlines, text figures, and speaker's notes. Also included are bullets to illustrate key terms and FAQs.

Online Learning Center/Web Site

Found at **www.mhhe.com/oleary**, this site provides additional learning and instructional tools to enhance the comprehension of the text. The OLC/Web Site is divided into these three areas:

- **Information Center**   Contains core information about the text, supplements, and the authors.

- **Instructor Center**   Offers instructional materials, downloads, additional exercises, and other relevant links for professors.

- **Student Center**   Contains data files, chapter competencies, chapter concepts, self-quizzes, flashcards, projects, animations, additional Web links, and more.

Skills Assessment

SimNet (Simulated Network Assessment Product) provides a way for you to test students' software skills in a simulated environment. SimNet is available for Microsoft Office 97, Microsoft Office 2000, and Microsoft Office XP. SimNet provides flexibility for you in your course by offering:

- Pre-testing options
- Post-testing options
- Course placement testing
- Diagnostic capabilities to reinforce skills
- Proficiency testing to measure skills
- Web or LAN delivery of tests.
- Computer-based training tutorials (new for Office XP)
- MOUS preparation exams

For more information on skills assessment software, please contact your local sales representative, or visit us at **www.mhhe.com/it**.

Digital Solutions to Help You Manage Your Course

PageOut is our Course Web Site Development Center that offers a syllabus page, URL, McGraw-Hill Online Learning Center content, online exercises and quizzes, gradebook, discussion board, and an area for student Web pages.

Available free with any McGraw-Hill/Irwin product, PageOut requires no prior knowledge of HTML, no long hours of coding, and a way for course coordinators and professors to provide a full-course web site. PageOut offers a series of templates—simply fill them with your course information and click on one of 16 designs. The process takes under an hour and leaves you with a professionally designed Web site. We'll even get you started with sample web sites, or enter your syllabus for you! PageOut is so straightforward and intuitive, it's little wonder why over 12,000 college professors are using it. For more information, visit the PageOut Web site at **www.pageout.net**.

Online courses are also available. Online Learning Centers (OLCs) are your perfect solutions for Internet-based content. Simply put, these Centers are "digital cartridges" that contain a book's pedagogy and supplements. As students read the book, they can go online and take self-grading quizzes or work through interactive exercises. These also provide students appropriate access to lecture materials and other key supplements.

Online Learning Centers can be delivered through any of these platforms:

McGraw-Hill Learning Architecture (TopClass)

Blackboard.com

Ecollege.com (formerly Real Education)

WebCT (a product of Universal Learning Technology)

McGraw-Hill has partnerships with WebCT and Blackboard to make it even easier to take your course online. Now you can have McGraw-Hill content delivered through the leading Internet-based learning tool for higher education. At McGraw-Hill, we have the following service agreements with WebCT and Blackboard:

Instructor Advantage Instructor Advantage is a special level of service McGraw-Hill offers in conjuction with WebCT designed to help you get up and running with your new course. A team of specialists will be immediately available to ensure everything runs smoothly through the life of your adoption.

Instructor Advantage Plus Qualified McGraw-Hill adopters will be eligible for an even higher level of service. A certified WebCT or Blackboard specialist will provide a full day of on-site training for you and your staff. You will then have unlimited e-mail and phone support through the life of your adoption. Please contact your local McGraw-Hill representative for more details.

Technology Connection Seminar Series

McGraw-Hill/Irwin's Technology Connection seminar series offered across the country every year demonstrates the latest technology products and encourages collaboration among teaching professionals.

Computing Essentials

Available alone, or packaged with the O'Leary Series, *Computing Essentials* offers a unique, visual orientation that gives students a basic understanding of computing concepts. *Computing Essentials* is one of the few books on the market that is written by a professor who still teaches the course every semester and loves it! While combining current topics and technology into a highly illustrated design geared to catch students' interest and motivate them in their learning, this text provides an accurate snapshot of computing today. When the book is bundled with software application lab manuals, students are given a complete representation of the fundamental issues surrounding the personal computing environment.

The text includes the following features:

- **A "Learn By Doing" approach** encourages students to engage in activity that is more interactive than the traditional learning pattern students typically follow in a concepts course. The exercises, explorations, visual orientation, inclusion of screen shots and numbered steps, and integrated internet references combine several methods to achieve an interactive learning environment for optimum reinforcement.

- **Making IT Work For You** sections visually demonstrate how technology is used in everyday life. Topics covered include how find a job online and how to protect a computer against viruses. These "gallery" style boxes combine text and art to take students step-by-step through technological processes that are both interesting and useful. As an added bonus, the *CE 2001-2002 Making IT Work Video Series* has been created to compliment the topics presented throughout the text.

- **On the Web Explorations** appear throughout the margins of the text and encourage students to go to the Web to visit several informative and established sites in order to learn more about the chapter's featured topic.

- **On the Web Exercises** present thought-provoking questions that allow students to construct articles and summaries for additional practice on topics relevant to that chapter while utilizing Web resources for further research. These exercises serve as additional reinforcement of the chapter's pertinent material while also allowing students to gain more familiarity with the Web.

- **A Look to the Future** sections provide insightful information about the future impact of technology and forecasts of how upcoming enhancements in the world of computing will play an important and powerful role in society.

- **Colorful Visual Summaries**, appearing at the end of every chapter, provide dynamic, graphical reviews of the important lessons featured in each chapter for additional reinforcement.

- **End-of-Chapter Review** material follows a three-level format and includes exercises that encourage students to review terms, concepts, and applications of concepts. Through matching, true/false, multiple choice, short answer completion, concept matching, and critical thinking questions, students have multiple review opportunities.

PowerWeb

PowerWeb is an exciting new online product available from McGraw-Hill. A nominally priced token grants students access through our web site to a wealth of resources—all corresponding to computer literacy. Features include an interactive glossary; current events with quizzing, assessment, and measurement options; Web survey; links to related text content; and WWW searching capability via Northern Lights, an academic search engine. Visit the PowerWeb site at **www.dushkin.com/powerweb**.

Interactive Companion CD-ROM

This free student CD-ROM, designed for use in class, in the lab, or at home by students and professors alike, includes a collection of interactive tutorial labs on some of the most popular and difficult topics in information technology. By combining video, interactive exercises, animation, additional content, and actual "lab" tutorials, we expand the reach and scope of the textbook. The lab titles are listed below.

- Binary Numbers
- Basic Programming
- Computer Anatomy
- Disk Fragmentation
- E-mail Essentials
- Multimedia Tools
- Workplace Issues (ergonomics/privacy/security)
- Introduction to Databases
- Programming II
- Network Communications
- Purchasing Decisions
- User Interfaces
- File Organization
- Word Processing and Spreadsheets
- Internet Overview
- Photo Editing
- Presentation Techniques
- Computer Troubleshooting
- Programming Overview
- SQL Queries

Student's Guide

As you begin each lab, take a few moments to read the **Case Study** and the **Concept Overview**. The case study introduces a real-life setting that is interwoven throughout the entire lab, providing the basis for understanding the use of the application. Also, notice the **Additional Information**, **Having Trouble?**, and **Another Method** boxes scattered throughout the book. These tips provide more information about related topics, help to get you out of trouble if you are having problems and offer suggestions on other ways to perform the same task. Finally, read the text between the steps. You will find the few minutes more it takes you is well worth the time when you are completing the practice exercises.

Many learning aids are built into the text to ensure your success with the material and to make the process of learning rewarding. The pages that follow call your attention to the key features in the text.

Creating and Editing a Document

LAB 1

Objectives appear at the beginning of the lab and identify the main features you will be learning.

objectives

After completing this lab, you will know how to:

1.	Develop a document as well as
2.	Insert and delete text and blank
3.	Display formatting marks.
4.	Use AutoCorrect, AutoText, and Auto
5.	Use automatic spelling and gramma
6.	Save, close, and open files.
7.	Select text.
8.	Undo and redo changes.
9.	Change fonts and type sizes.
10.	Bold and color text.
11.	Change alignment.
12.	Insert, size, and move pictures.
13.	Preview and print a document.

Each lab begins with a **Case Study**, which introduces a real-life setting that is interwoven throughout the lab, providing the basis for understanding the use of the application.

Case Study

Adventure Travel

As a recent college graduate, you have accepted a job as advertising coordinator for Adventure Travel, a specialty travel company that organizes active adventure vacations. The company is headquartered in Los Angeles and has locations in other major cities throughout the country. You are responsible for coordination of the advertising program for all locations. This includes the creation of many kinds of promotional materials: brochures, flyers, form letters, news releases, advertisements, and a monthly newsletter. You are also responsible for creating Web pages for the company Web site.

Adventure Travel is very excited about four new tours planned for the upcoming year. They want to promote them through informative presenta

tions held throughout the country. Your first job as advertising coordinator will be to create a flyer advertising the four new tours and the presentations about them. The flyer will be modified according to the location of the presentation.

The software tool you will use to create the flyer is the word processing application Word 2002. It helps you create documents such as letters, reports, and research papers. In this lab, you will learn how to enter, edit, and print a document while you create the flyer (shown left) to be distributed in a mailing to Adventure Travel clients.

Using Word Wrap

Now you will continue entering more of the paragraph. As you type, when the text gets close to the right margin, do not press ←Enter to move to the next line. Word will automatically wrap words to the next line as needed.

concept 6

Word Wrap

6   The **word wrap** feature automatically decides where to end a line and wrap text to the next line based on the margin settings. This saves time when entering text, as you do not need to press ←Enter at the end of a full line to begin a new line. The only time you need to press ←Enter is to end a paragraph, to insert blank lines, or to create a short line such as a salutation. In addition, if you change the margins or insert or delete text on a line, the program automatically readjusts the text on the line to fit within the new margin settings. Word wrap is common to all word processors.

> The **Concepts** that are common to all applications are emphasized— providing you with the confidence, knowledge, and ability to easily learn the next generation of applications.

❶ ● Press →.

● **Type:** about some of the earth's greatest unspoiled habitats and to find out how you can experience the adventure of a lifetime.

Your screen should be similar to Figure 1.22

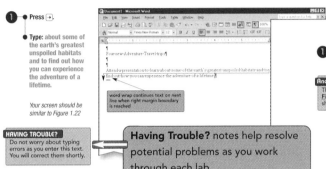

> word wrap continues text on next line when right margin boundary is reached

HAVING TROUBLE?
Do not worry about typing errors as you enter this text. You will correct them shortly.

> **Having Trouble?** notes help resolve potential problems as you work through each lab.

The program has wrapped the text that would overlap the beginning of the next line. You will continue the par a second sentence.

❶ ● Click ☒ Close Window in the menu bar.

Another Method
The menu equivalent is File/Close and the keyboard shortcut is Ctrl + F4.

Your screen should be similar to Figure 1.28

> **Another Method** notes offer additional ways to perform a procedure.

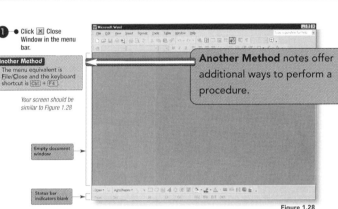

> Empty document window

> Status bar indicators blank

Figure 1.28

Because you did not make any changes to the document since saving it, the document window is closed immediately. If you had made additional changes, Word would ask if you wanted to save the file before closing it. This prevents the accidental closing of a file that has not been saved first. Now the Word window displays an empty document window, and the status bar indicators are blank because there are no open documents.

Opening a File

You asked your assistant to enter the remaining information in the flyer for you while you attended the meeting. Upon your return, you find a note from your assistant on your desk. The note explains that he had a little trouble entering the information and tells you that he saved the revised file as Flyer2. You want to open the file and continue working on the flyer.

❶ ● Move to Z (second line of paragraph below tour list).

● Drag to the right until all the text including the space before the word "locations" is highlighted.

HAVING TROUBLE?
Hold down the left mouse button while moving the mouse to drag.

Additional Information
When you start dragging over a word, the entire word including the space after it is automatically selected.

Your screen should be similar to Figure 1.41

> Clear **Step-by-Step Instructions** detail how to complete a task, or series of tasks.

> text, including ending space, selected

> **Additional Information** notes offer brief asides with expanded coverage of content.

Figure 1.41

The cha [...] be mod [...] remove [...]

> **Screen captures** and **callouts** to features show how your screen should look at the completion of a step.

> Location to open files

> Changes dialog box view

Figure 1.29

❷ ● Press Delete.

You also decide to delete the entire last sentence of the paragraph. You can quickly select a standard block of text. Standard blocks include a sentence, paragraph, page, tabular column, rectangular portion of text, or the entire document. The following table summarizes the techniques used to select standard blocks.

To Select	Procedure
Word	Double-click in the word.
Sentence	Press Ctrl and click within the sentence.
Line	Click to the left of a line when the mouse pointer is ⇗.
Multiple lines	Drag up or down to the left of a line when the mouse pointer is ⇗.
Paragraph	Triple-click on the paragraph or double-click to the left of the paragraph when the mouse pointer is a ⇗.
Multiple paragraphs	Drag to the left of the paragraphs when the mouse pointer is ⇗.
Document	Triple-click or press Ctrl and click to the left of the text when the mouse pointer is ⇗.
	Use Edit/Select All or the keyboard shortcut Ctrl + A.

> **Tables** provide quick summaries of toolbar buttons, key terms, and procedures for specific tasks.

concept summary

Each lab ends with a **Concept Summary** that reinforces the concepts presented throughout.

LAB 1
eating and Editing a Document

Template (WD1.7)
A template is a document file that includes predefined settings that are used as a pattern to create many common types of documents.

Automatic Grammar Check (WD1.18)
The automatic grammar-checking feature advises you of incorrect grammar as you create and edit a document, and proposes possible corrections.

Auto Text and Auto Complete (WD1.20)
The AutoText feature includes entries, such as commonly used phrases, that can be quickly inserted into a document. If the AutoComplete feature is on, a ScreenTip appears as you type the first four characters of an AutoText entry, suggesting the remainder of the AutoText entry you may want to use.

AutoCorrect (WD1.21)
The AutoCorrect feature makes some basic assumptions about the text you are typing and, based on these assumptions, automatically identifies and/or corrects the entry as you type.

A **Key Terms** section, a **MOUS Skills** guide, and a **Command Summary** table provide a list of page-referenced terms and keyboard and toolbar shortcuts, which can be a useful study aid.

Terminology is reinforced through **Screen Identification**, **Matching**, **Multiple Choice**, and **True/False** questions.

WD1.64
Word 20

lab review

LAB 2
Organizing Your Work

key terms

alignment	WN1.53	end-of-file marker	WN1.5	picture	WN1.55
AutoComplete	WN1.20	font	WN1.46	points	WN1.46
AutoCorrect	WN1.2	font size	WN1.46	ruler	WN1.5
automatic grammar check	WN1.8	format	WN1.	sans serif font	WN1.46
automatic spelling check	WN1.23	formatting mark	WN1.3	select	WN1.4
AutoText	WN1.20	Formatting toolbar	WN1.5	selection rectangle	WN1.5
character formatting	WN1.45	global template	WN1.7	serif font	WN1.46
clip art	WN1.55	graphic	WN1.55	sizing handles	WN1.5
cursor	WN1.5	Insert mode	WN1.3	SmartTag	WN1.27
custom dictionary	WN1.23	insertion point	WN1.5	source program	WN1.55
default	WN1.7	main dictionary	WN1.23	Standard toolbar	WN1.5
drawing object	WN1.55	Normal template	WN1.7	template	WN1.7
Drawing toolbar	WN1.6	object	WN1.55	TrueType	WN1.47
edit	WN1.	Overtype mode	WN1.3	typeface	WN1.46
embedded object	WN1.55	paragraph formatting	WN1.45	word wrap	WN1.26

MOUS Skills

The Microsoft Office User Specialist (MOUS) certification program is designed to measure your proficiency in performing basic tasks using the Office 2002 applications. Getting certified demonstrates that you have the skills and provides a valuable industry credential for employment. After completing this lab, you have learned the following Word Microsoft Office User Specialist skills:

Skill	Description	Page
Inserting and	Insert text	39
Modifying text	Use spelling and grammar checking	23
	Apply and modify character formats	45
		45
		45
...ment)	53
		61
		61
		63
		55

Terminology

screen identification

In the following Word screen, letters identify important elements. Enter the correct term for each screen element in the space provided.

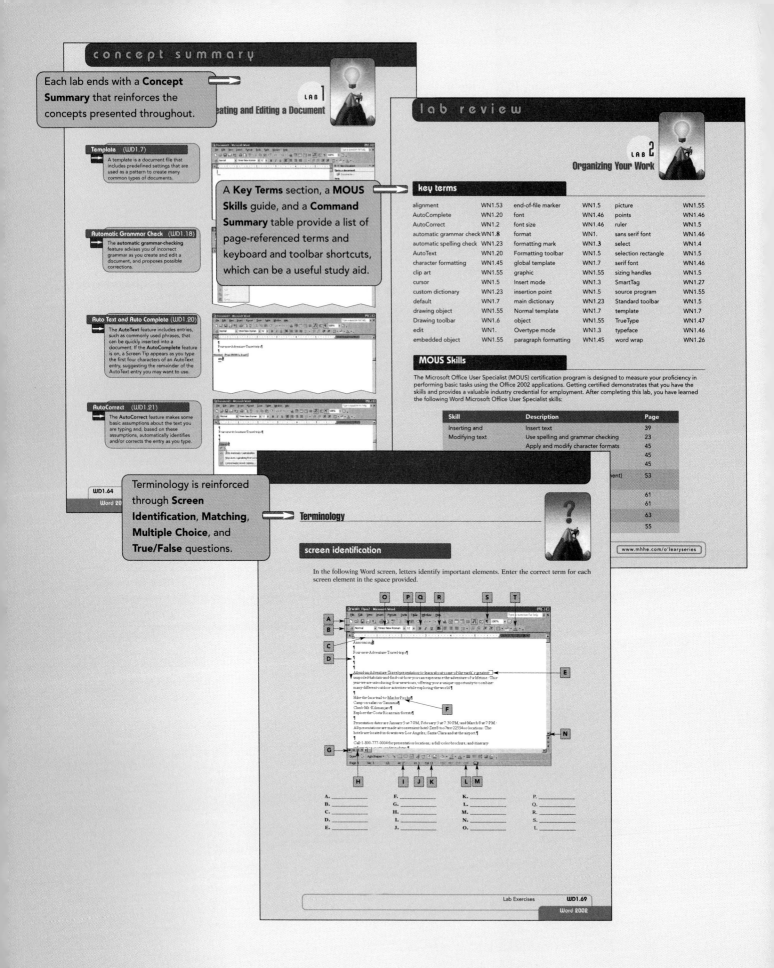

A. _____
B. _____
C. _____
D. _____
E. _____
F. _____
G. _____
H. _____
I. _____
J. _____
K. _____
L. _____
M. _____
N. _____
O. _____
P. _____
Q. _____
R. _____
S. _____
t. _____

Lab Exercises WD1.69
Word 2002

Concepts

Fill-in questions

1. A small blue box appearing under a word or character indicates that the _____ feature was applied.

2. If a word is underlined with purple dots, this indicates a(n) _____.

3. The _____ feature displays each page of your document in a reduced size so you can see the page layout.

4. To size a graphic evenly, click and drag the _____ in one corner of the graphic.

5. It is good practice to use only _____ types of fonts in a document.

6. When you use _____, new text replaces existing text as you type.

7. The _____ sits on the right side of the window and contains buttons and icons to help you perform common tasks, such as opening a blank document.

8. Use _____ when you want to keep your existing document with the original name and make a copy with a new name.

9. The _____ window displays a reduced view of how the current page will appear when printed.

10. The _____ feature includes entries, such as commonly used phrases, that can be quickly inserted into a document.

discussion questions

1. Discuss several uses you may have for a word processor. Then e2002lain the steps you would follow to create a document.

2. Discuss how the AutoCorrect and Spelling and Grammar Checker features help you as you type. ...es of corrections does the AutoCorrect feature make?

   ...ow word wrap works. What happens when text is added? What happens when text is

   ...ree ways you can select text. Discuss when it would be appropriate to use the different

   ...ow the Undo and Redo features work. What are some advantages of these features?

   ...ow graphics can be used in a document. What should you consider when adding graphics ...ment? Can the use of a graphic change the reader's response to a document?

Concepts are reinforced in **Fill-In** and **Discussion** questions.

Hands-On Exercises

rating system

★ Easy
★★ Moderate
★★★ Difficult

step-by-step

★ **Writing a Memo**

1. Universal Industries is starting a casual Friday policy. Ms. Jones, the Vice President of Human Resources, has sent a memo informing employees of this new policy. Your completed memo is shown here.

   a. Open a blank Word document and create the memo with the following text. Press Tab twice ater you type colons (:) in the To, From, Date, and RE lines. This will make the information following the colons line up evenly. Enter a blank line below the RE line and between paragraphs.

   To: [Your Name]
   From: Ms. Jones
   Date: [Current date]
   RE: Business Casual Dress Code

   Effective next Friday, business casual will be allowed in the corporate facility on Fridays and the day before a holiday break. Business casual is sometimes difficult to interpret. For men, it is a collared shirt and tailored trousers. For women, it is a pantsuit or tailored trousers or skirt. Business casual is not jeans, t-shirts, or exercise clothes. A detailed dress code will be available on the company intranet.

   Thank you for your cooperation in this matter.

   CSJ/xxx

   b. Correct any spelling and grammar errors that are identified.
   c. Change the font for the entire memo to14 pt.
   d. Change the alignment of the memo body to justified.
   e. Insert a blank line under the Date line and insert the AutoText reference line "RE:".
   f. Press Tab and type "Business Casual Dress Code".
   g. Save the document as Dress Code on your data disk.
   h. Preview and print the document.

Hands-on Exercises develop critical thinking skills and offer step-by-step practice. These exercises have a rating system from easy to difficult, and test your ability to apply the knowledge you have gained in each lab.

Introduction to Microsoft Office XP

What is Office XP?

Microsoft Office XP is a suite of applications that can be used individually and that are designed to work together seamlessly. The applications include tools used to create, discuss, communicate, and manage projects. If you share a lot of documents with other people, these features facilitate access to common documents. This version has expanded and refined the communication and collaboration features and integration with the World Wide Web. In addition, several new interface features are designed to make it easier to perform tasks and help users take advantage of all the features in the applications.

The Office XP suite is packaged in different combinations of components. The major components and a brief description are provided in the following table.

Component	Description
Word 2002	Word processor
Excel 2002	Spreadsheet
Access 2002	Database manager
PowerPoint 2002	Presentation graphics
Outlook 2002	Desktop information manager
FrontPage 2002	Web page authoring
Publisher	Desktop publishing
SharePoint	Team Web sites

The four main components of Office XP—Word, Excel, Access, and PowerPoint—are described in more detail in the following sections.

Word 2002

Word 2002 is a word processing software application whose purpose is to help you create text-based documents. Word processors are one of the most flexible and widely used application software programs. A word processor can be used to manipulate text data to produce a letter, a report, a memo, an e-mail, message or any other type of correspondence. Two documents you will produce in the first two Word labs, a letter and flyer, are shown here.

February 18, 2001

Dear Adventure Traveler,

Imagine hiking and paddling your way through the rain forests of Costa Rica under the stars in Africa, or following in the footsteps of the ancient Inca as you backp the Inca trail to Machu Picchu. Turn these dreams of adventure into memories you w forever by joining Adventure Travel Tours on one of our four new adventure tours.

To tell you more about these exciting new adventures, we are offerin presentations in your area. These presentations will focus on the features and cultu region. We will also show you pictures of the places you will visit and activities participate in, as well as a detailed agenda and package costs. Plan on attending o following presentations:

Date	Time	Location	Room
January 5 ----- 7:00 PM ----------- Town Center Hotel ------- Room 284B
February 3 ---- 7:30 PM ----------- Airport Manor ------------- Conference Room A
March 8 ------- 7:00 PM ----------- Country Inn ---------------- Mountainside Room

In appreciation of your past patronage, we are pleased to offer you a 10% disco price of any of the new tour packages. You must book the trip at least 60 days pr departure date. Please turn in this letter to qualify for the discount.

Our vacation tours are professionally developed solely for your enjoyment. W almost everything in the price of your tour while giving you the best possible value dollar. All tours include:

- Professional tour manager and local guides
- All accommodations and meals
- All entrance fees, excursions, transfers and tips

We hope you will join us this year on another special Adventure Travel Tour Your memories of fascinating places and challenging physical adventures should li long, long time. For reservations, please see your travel agent, or contact Adventure Tr at 1-800-777-0004. You can also visit our new Web site at www.AdventureTravelTours

Best regards,

Student Name

A letter containing a tabbed table, indented paragraphs, and text enhancements is quickly created using basic Word features.

Announcing
New Adventure Travel Tours

This year we are introducing four new tours, offering you a unique opportunity to combine many different outdoor activities while exploring the world.

Hike the Inca trail to Machu Picchu
Camp on safari in Tanzania
Climb Mt. Kilimanjaro
Explore the Costa Rican rain forests

Attend an Adventure Travel presentation to learn about some of the earth's greatest unspoiled habitats and find out how you can experience the adventure of a lifetime.

Presentation dates and times are January 5 at 7 PM, February 3 at 7:30 PM, and March 8 at 7 PM. All presentations are held at convenient hotel locations located in downtown Los Angeles, Santa Clara and at the airport.

Call us at 1-800-777-0004 for presentation locations, a full color brochure, and itinerary information, costs, and tour dates.

Visit Our
Web site at
AdventureTravelTours.com

A flyer incorporating many visual enhancements such as colored text, varied text styles, and graphic elements is both eye-catching and informative.

The beauty of a word processor is that you can make changes or corrections as you are typing. Want to change a report from single spacing to double spacing? Alter the width of the margins? Delete some paragraphs and add others from yet another document? A word processor allows you to do all these things with ease.

Word 2002 includes many group collaboration features to help streamline how documents are developed and changed by group members. You can also create and send e-mail messages directly from within Word using all its features to create and edit the message. You can also send an entire document as your e-mail message, allowing the recipient to edit the document directly without having to open or save an attachment.

Word 2002 is also closely integrated with the World Wide Web, detecting when you type a Web address and automatically converting it to a hyperlink. You can also create your own hyperlinks to locations within documents, or to other documents, including those at external locations such as a Web site or file server. Its many Web-editing features, including a Web Page Wizard that guides you step by step, help you quickly create a Web page. You will see how easy it is when you create the Web page shown below in the Working Together tutorial.

A Web page created in Word and displayed in the Internet Explorer browser.

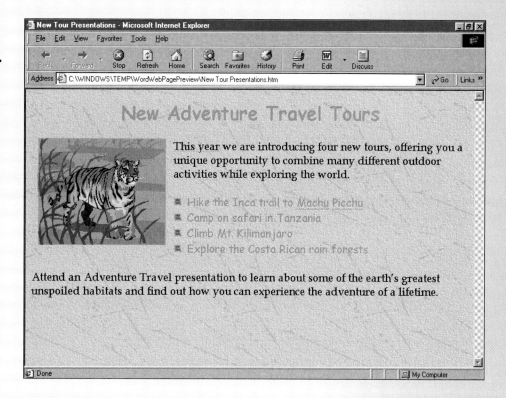

Excel 2002

Excel 2002 is an electronic worksheet that is used to organize, manipulate, and graph numeric data. Once used almost exclusively by accountants, worksheets are now widely used by nearly every profession. Marketing professionals record and evaluate sales trends. Teachers record grades and calculate final grades. Personal trainers record the progress of their clients. Excel includes many features that not only help you create a well-designed worksheet, but one that produces accurate results. Formatting features include visual enhancements such as varied text styles, colors, and graphics. Other features help you enter complex formulas and identify and correct formula errors. You can also produce a visual display of data in the form of graphs or charts. As the values in the worksheet change, charts referencing those values automatically adjust to reflect the changes.

Excel also includes many advanced features and tools that help you perform what-if analysis and create different scenarios. And like all Office XP applications, it is easy to incorporate data created in one application into another. Two worksheets you will produce in Labs 2 and 3 of Excel are shown here.

A worksheet showing the quarterly sales forecast containing a graphic, text enhancements, and a chart of the data is quickly created using basic Excel features.

A large worksheet incorporating more complex formulas, visual enhancements such as colored text, varied text styles, and graphic elements is both informative and attractive.

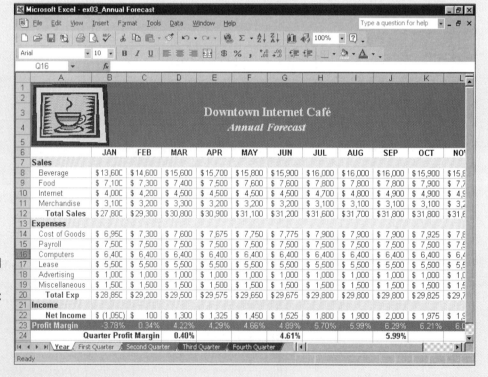

You will see how easy it is to analyze data and make projections using what-if analysis and what-if graphing in Lab 3 and to incorporate Excel data in a Word document as shown in the figures below.

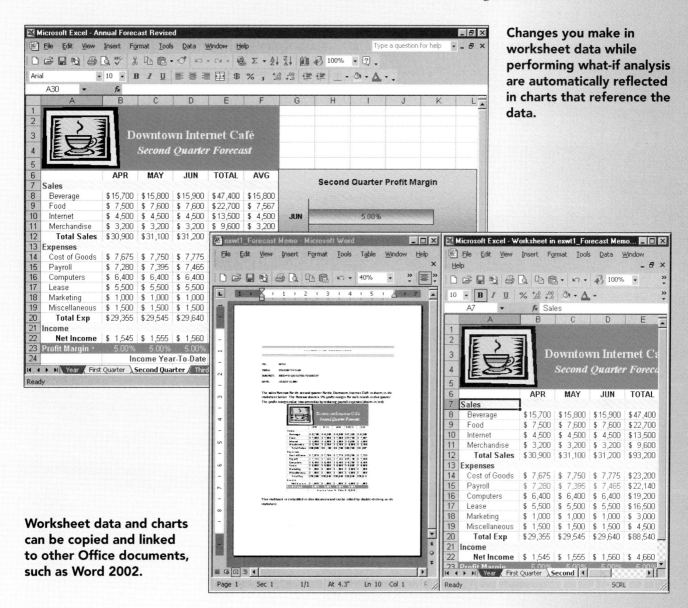

Changes you make in worksheet data while performing what-if analysis are automatically reflected in charts that reference the data.

Worksheet data and charts can be copied and linked to other Office documents, such as Word 2002.

Access 2002

Access 2002 is a relational database management application that is used to create and analyze a database. A database is a collection of related data. In a relational database, the most widely used database structure, data is organized in linked tables. Tables consist of columns (called fields) and rows (called records). The tables are related or linked to one another by a common field. Relational databases allow you to create smaller and more manageable database tables, since you can combine and extract data between tables.

The program provides tools to enter, edit, and retrieve data from the database as well as to analyze the database and produce reports of the output. One of the main advantages of a computerized database is the ability to quickly add, delete, and locate specific records. Records can also be easily rearranged or sorted according to different fields of data, resulting in multiple table arrangements that provide more meaningful information for different purposes. Creation of forms makes it easier to enter and edit data as well. In the Access labs you will create and organize the database table shown below.

A relational database can be created and modified easily using basic Access features.

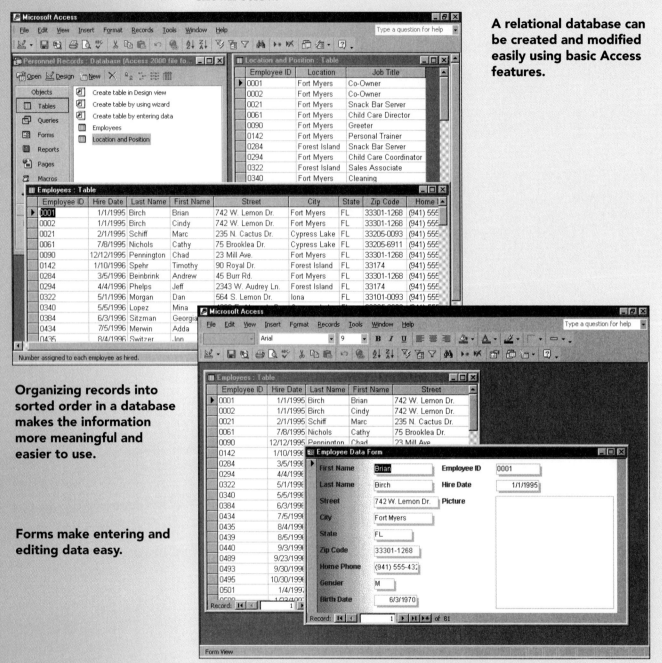

Organizing records into sorted order in a database makes the information more meaningful and easier to use.

Forms make entering and editing data easy.

Another feature is the ability to analyze the data in a table and perform calculations on different fields of data. Additionally, you can ask questions or query the table to find only certain records that meet specific conditions to be used in the analysis. Information that was once costly and time-consuming to get is now quickly and readily available. This information can then be quickly printed out in the form of reports ranging from simple listings to complex, professional-looking reports in different layout styles, or with titles, headings, subtotals, or totals.

A database can be queried to locate and display only specified information.

A professional-looking report can be quickly generated from information contained in a database.

PowerPoint 2002

PowerPoint 2002 is a graphics presentation program designed to help you produce a high-quality presentation that is both interesting to the audience and effective in its ability to convey your message. A presentation can be as simple as overhead transparencies or as sophisticated as an on-screen electronic display. In the first two PowerPoint labs you will create and organize the presentation shown on the next page.

A presentation consists of a series of pages or "slides" presenting the information you want to convey in an organized and attractive manner.

When running an onscreen presentation, each slide of the presentation is displayed full-screen on your computer monitor or projected onto a screen.

Common Office XP Features

Additional Information

Please read the Before You Begin and Instructional Conventions sections in the Overview to Word 2002 (WDO.4) before starting this section.

Now that you know a little about each of the applications in Microsoft Office XP, we will take a look at some of the features that are common to all Office applications. This is a hands-on section that will introduce you to the features and allow you to get a feel for how Office XP works. Although Word 2002 will be used to demonstrate how the features work, only common features will be addressed. These features include using menus, the Office Assistant and Office Help, task panes, toolbars, and starting and exiting an application. The features that are specific to each application will be introduced individually in each lab.

Starting an Office Application

There are several ways to start an Office application. One is to use the New Office Document command on the Start menu and select the type of document you want to create. Another is to use the Documents command on the Start menu and select the document name from the list of recently used documents. This starts the associated application and opens the selected document at the same time. The two most common ways to start an Office XP application are by choosing the application name from the Start menu or by clicking a desktop shortcut for the program if it is available.

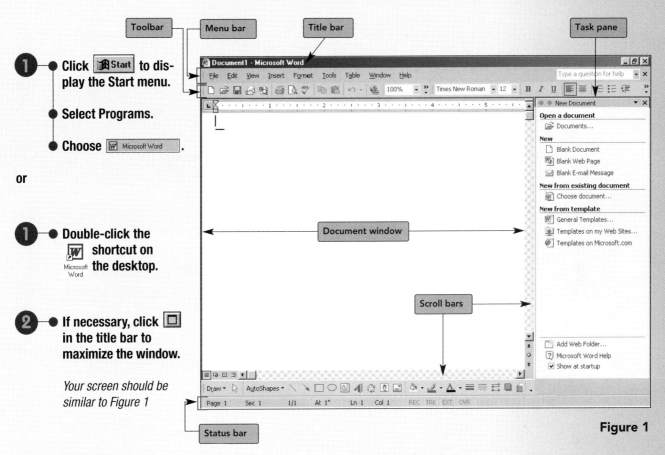

1
● Click **Start** to display the Start menu.

● Select Programs.

● Choose **W** Microsoft Word.

or

1
● Double-click the **W** Microsoft Word shortcut on the desktop.

2
● If necessary, click □ in the title bar to maximize the window.

Your screen should be similar to Figure 1

Figure 1

Additional Information

Application windows can be sized, moved, and otherwise manipulated like any other windows on the desktop. Refer to your text or, if available, to the *Introduction to Windows 2000* labs for information about working with windows.

The Word program is started and displayed in a window on the desktop. The left end of the application window title bar displays the file name followed by the program name, Microsoft Word. The right end of the title bar displays the ▬ Minimize, ▣ Restore, and ☒ Close buttons. They perform the same functions and operate in the same way as in Windows 98 and 2000.

The **menu bar** below the title bar displays the application's program menu. The right end displays the document window's ☒ Close button. As you use the Office applications, you will see that the menu bar contains many of the same menus, such as File, Edit, and Help. You will also see several menus that are specific to each application.

The **toolbars** located below the menu bar contain buttons that are mouse shortcuts for many of the menu items. Commonly, the Office applications will display two toolbars when the application is first opened: Standard and Formatting. They may appear together on one row (as in Figure 1), or on separate rows.

The large center area of the program window is the **document window** where open application files are displayed. Currently, there is a blank Word document open. The **task pane** is displayed on the right side of the document window. Task panes provide quick access to features as you are using the application. As you perform certain actions, different task panes automatically open. In this case, since you just started an application, the New Document task pane is automatically displayed, providing different ways to create a new document or open an existing document.

The **status bar** at the bottom of the window displays location information and the status of different settings as they are used. Different information is displayed in the status bar for different applications.

On the right and bottom of the document window, are vertical and horizontal scroll bars. A **scroll bar** is used with a mouse to bring additional lines of information into view in a window. The vertical scroll bar is used to move up or down, and the horizontal scroll bar moves side to side in the window.

As you can see, many of the features in the Word window are the same as in other Windows applications. The common user interface makes learning and using new applications much easier.

Using Menus

A **menu** is one of many methods you can use to accomplish a task in a program. When opened, a menu displays a list of commands.

 Click File to open the File menu.

Your screen should be similar to Figure 2

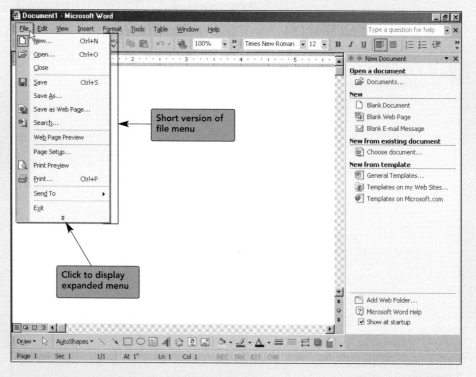

Figure 2

When an Office program menu is first opened, it may display a short version of commands. The short menu is a personalized version of the menu that displays basic and frequently used commands and hides those used less often. An expanded version will display automatically after the menu is open for a few seconds (see Figure 3).

Your screen should be similar to Figure 3

Expanded File menu

Previously hidden commands are displayed

Shortcut key

Indicates a dialog box will be displayed

Indicates a submenu will be displayed

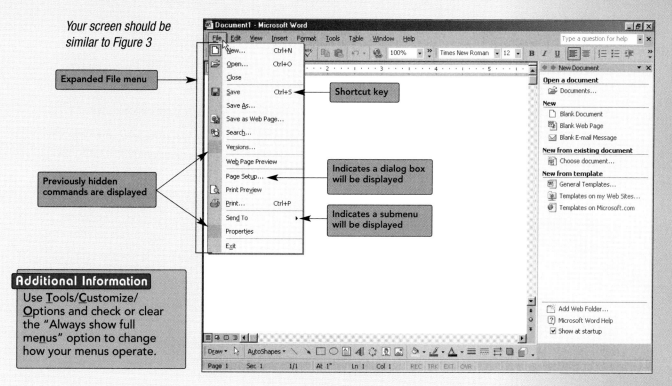

Additional Information

Use Tools/Customize/Options and check or clear the "Always show full menus" option to change how your menus operate.

Figure 3

When the menu is expanded the hidden commands are displayed. Once one menu is expanded, others are expanded automatically until you choose a command or perform another action.

2 ● Point to each menu in the menu bar to see the full menu for each.

● Point to the File menu again.

Many commands have images next to them so you can quickly associate the command with the image. The same image appears on the toolbar button for that feature. Menus may include the following features (not all menus include all features):

Feature	Meaning
Ellipsis (...)	Indicates a dialog box will be displayed
▶	Indicates a submenu will be displayed
Dimmed	Indicates the command is not available for selection until certain other conditions are met
Shortcut key	A key or key combination that can be used to execute a command without using the menu
Checkmark	Indicates a toggle type of command. Selecting it turns the feature on or off. A checkmark indicates the feature is on.

Once a menu is open, you can select a command from the menu by pointing to it. A colored highlight bar, called the **selection cursor**, appears over the selected command.

3 ● **Point to the Send To command to select it and display the submenu.**

Your screen should be similar to Figure 4

Figure 4

Then to choose a command, you click on it. When the command is chosen, the associated action is performed. You will use a command in the Help menu to access the Microsoft Office Assistant and Help features.

Note: If your screen displays the Office Assistant character as shown in Figure 5, skip step 4.

4 ● **Point to Help.**

● **Click Show the Office Assistant to choose the command.**

Your screen should be similar to Figure 5

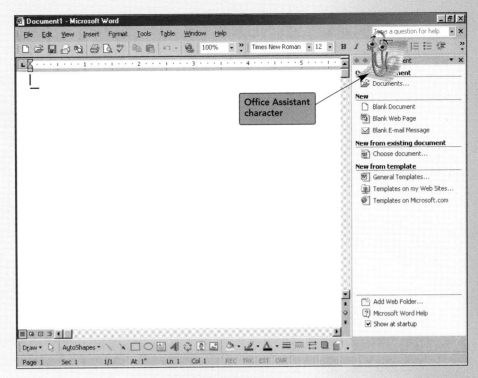

Figure 5

HAVING TROUBLE?

If the Assistant does not appear, this feature has been disabled. If this is the case, choose <u>H</u>elp/Microsoft Word <u>H</u>elp or press F1 and skip to the section "Using Help."

The command to display the Office Assistant has been executed, and the Office Assistant character is displayed. The default Assistant character is Clippit shown in Figure 5. Because there are eight different characters from which you can select, your screen may display a different Assistant character.

Using the Office Assistant

When the Office Assistant is on, it automatically suggests help topics as you work. It anticipates what you are going to do and then makes suggestions on how to perform a task. In addition, you can activate the Assistant at any time to get help on features in the Office application you are using. Clicking on the Assistant character activates it and displays a balloon in which you can type the topic you want help on. You will ask the Office Assistant to provide information on the different ways you can get help while using the program.

1 ● **Click on the Office Assistant character to activate it.**

● **Type** *How do I get help?* **in the text box.**

● **Click** Search .

Another Method

You could also press ⏎Enter to begin the search.

Your screen should be similar to Figure 6

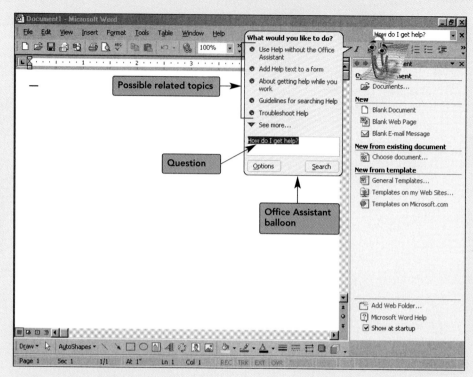

Possible related topics

Question

Office Assistant balloon

Figure 6

The balloon displays a list of related topics from which you can select.

2 ● **Select "About getting help while you work."**

Additional Information

Clicking See more... displays additional topics.

Your screen should be similar to Figure 7

Selected topic

Help program opens and displays information on selected topic

Two open windows

Figure 7

Another Method

You can also choose Help/Microsoft Word Help, or click ? or press F1 to start Help.

The Help program opens and displays the selected topic. Because Word Help is a separate program within Office, it appears in its own window. The Help window overlaps the Word window so that it is easy to read the information in Help while referring to the application window. The taskbar displays a button for both open windows.

Now that Help is open, you no longer need to see the Assistant. To access commands to control the Office Assistant, you will display the object's shortcut menu by right-clicking on the Assistant character. **Shortcut menus** display the most common menu options related to the selected item only.

3 ● **Right-click the Assistant to display the shortcut menu.**

● **Choose Options.**

● **Click Use the Office Assistant to clear the option.**

● **Click   OK   .**

● **Click ▢ to maximize the Help window.**

● **If necessary, click ◁▤ to display the Tabs frame.**

Your screen should be similar to Figure 8

Figure 8

Using Help

In the Help window, the toolbar buttons help you use different Help features and navigate in Help.

The Help window is divided into two vertical frames. **Frames** divide a window into separate, scrollable areas that can display different information. The left frame in the Help window is the Tabs frame. It contains three folder-like tabs, Contents, Answer Wizard, and Search, that provide three different means of getting Help information. The open tab appears in front of the other tabs and displays the available options for the feature. The right frame is the content frame where the content for the selected topic is displayed.

1 ● Click the **C**ontents tab to open it.

HAVING TROUBLE?

If you cannot see the Contents tab, click the ◀ tab scroll button to bring it into view.

Your screen should be similar to Figure 9

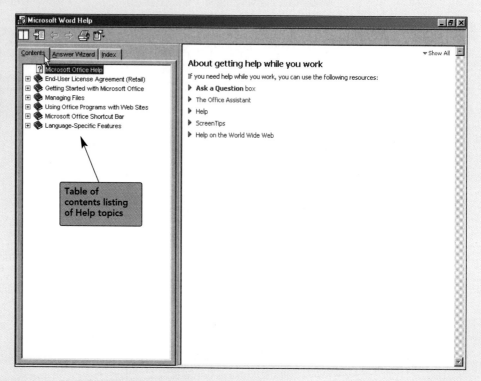

Figure 9

Using the Contents Tab

The Contents tab displays a table of contents listing of topics in Help. Clicking on an item preceded with a ⊞ opens a "chapter," which expands to display additional chapters or specific Help topics.

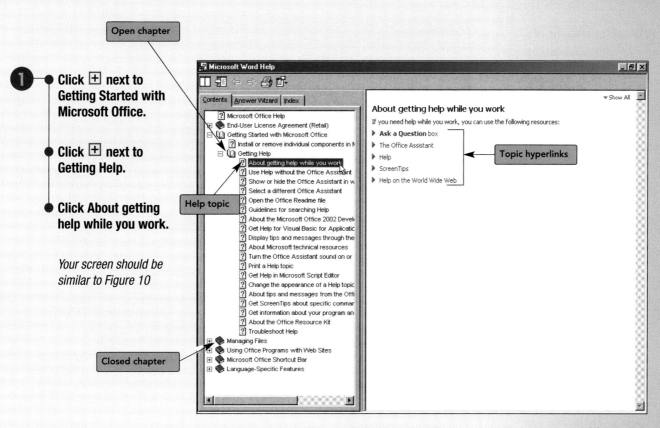

1 ● Click ⊞ next to Getting Started with Microsoft Office.

● Click ⊞ next to Getting Help.

● Click About getting help while you work.

Your screen should be similar to Figure 10

Open chapter

Help topic

Closed chapter

Topic hyperlinks

Figure 10

You have opened two chapters and selected a Help topic. Open chapters are preceded with a 📖 icon and topics with a ？ icon.

Using a Hyperlink

The Help topic tells you about five resources you can use to get help. Each resource is a **hyperlink** or connection to additional information in the current document, in online Help, or on the Microsoft Office Web site. It commonly appears as colored or underlined text. Clicking the hyperlink accesses and displays the information associated with the hyperlink. A hyperlink preceded with a ▶ indicates clicking the link will display additional information about the topic.

1 ● Click the "Ask a Question box" hyperlink.

● Click the "The Office Assistant" hyperlink.

Your screen should be similar to Figure 11

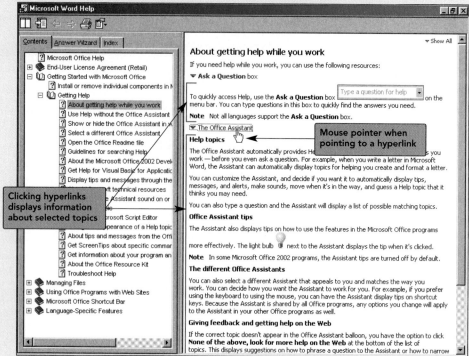

Figure 11

Additional Information

Clicking the scroll arrows scrolls the text in the frame line by line, and dragging the scroll box up or down the scroll bar moves to a general location within the frame area.

The content frame displays additional information about the two selected topics. Now, because there is more information in the content frame than can be displayed at one time, you will need to use the vertical scroll bar to scroll the additional information into the frame as you read the Help information. Also, as you are reading help, you may see text that appears as a hyperlink. Clicking on the text will display a definition of a term.

2 ● Using the scroll bar, scroll the content frame to read the information on this topic.

● Click the "shortcut keys" hyperlink.

Your screen should be similar to Figure 12

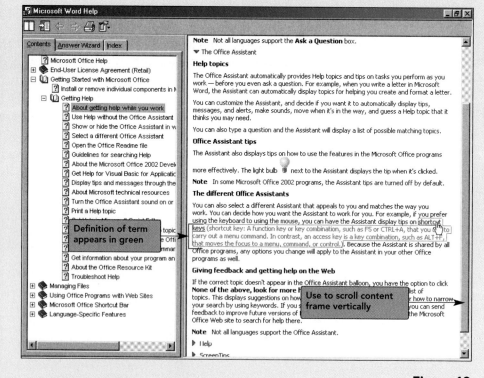

Figure 12

Scrolling the frame displays the information at the bottom of the frame while the information at the top of the frame is no longer visible. The end of the Help information is displayed in the frame. A definition of the term "shortcut keys" is displayed in green text.

Click on the definition to clear it.

Click on the Use Help without the Office Assistant topic in the Contents tab.

Additional Information

Pointing to a topic in the content frame that is not fully visible displays the full topic in a ScreenTip box.

Your screen should be similar to Figure 13

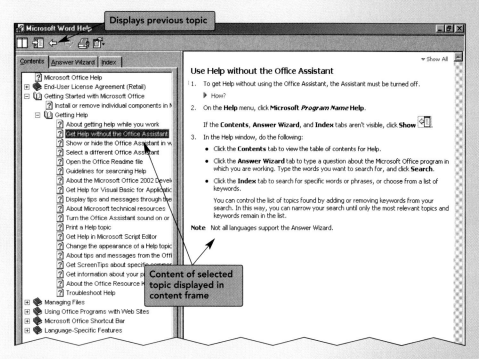

Figure 13

The content frame now displays the Help information about the selected topic. To quickly return to the previous topic,

Click ⬅ Back.

Your screen should be similar to Figure 14

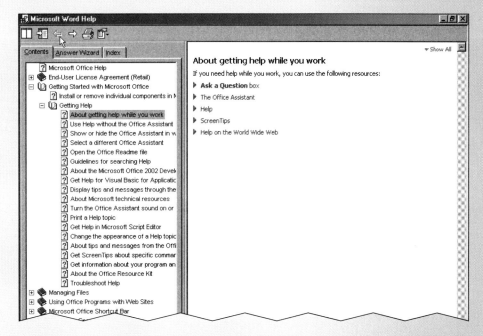

Figure 14

The topic is redisplayed as it originally appeared, without the topic selections expanded.

Using the Index Tab

To search for Help information by entering a word or phrase for a topic, you can use the Index tab.

①──● Open the Index tab.

HAVING TROUBLE?
If the Index tab is not visible in the frame, click the ▶ scroll button to display it.

Your screen should be similar to Figure 15

Enter word or phrase to locate

Alphabetical list of keywords

Figure 15

The Index tab consists of a text box where you can type a word or phrase that best describes the topic you want to locate. Below it is a list box displaying a complete list of Help keywords in alphabetical order. You want to find information about using the Index tab.

2 • Type **index** in the text box.

• Click [Search].

Your screen should be similar to Figure 16

19 Help topics containing keyword "index"

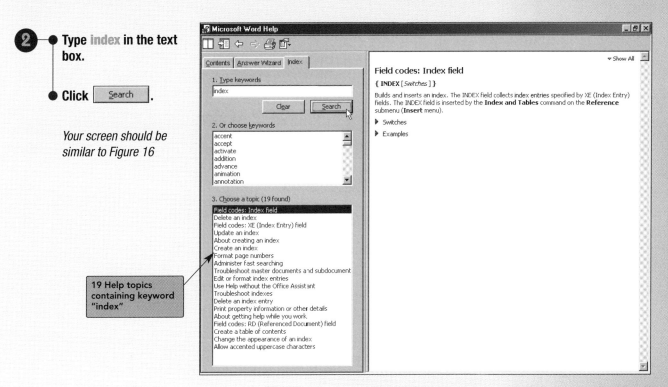

Figure 16

The topic list displays 19 Help topics containing this word, and the content frame, displays the information on the first topic. However, many of the located topics are not about the Help Index feature. To narrow the search more, you can add another word to the keyword text box.

3 • Click in the text box.

• Type **help** following the word "index."

• Click [Search].

Your screen should be similar to Figure 17

Two topics contain both keywords

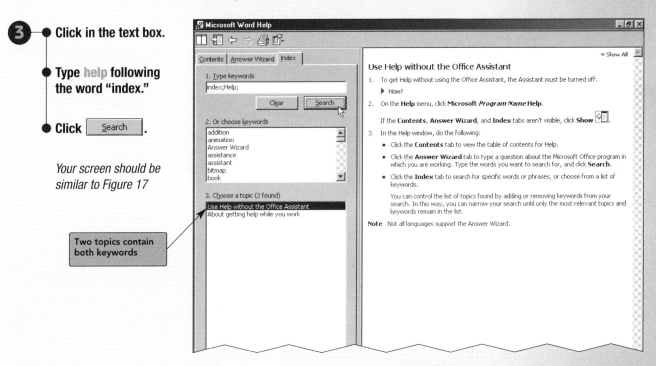

Figure 17

Now only two topics were located that contain both keywords. The first topic in the list is selected and displayed in the content frame.

Using the Answer Wizard

Another way to locate Help topics is to use the Answer Wizard tab. This feature works just like the Office Assistant and the Answer box to locate topics. You will use this method to locate information on toolbars.

1 ● **Open the Answer Wizard tab.**

● **Type** How do I use toolbars? **in the text box.**

● **Click** Search **.**

Your screen should be similar to Figure 18

Topics related to your search

Additional Information
The search term does not need to be worded as a question. It can also be a word or phrase.

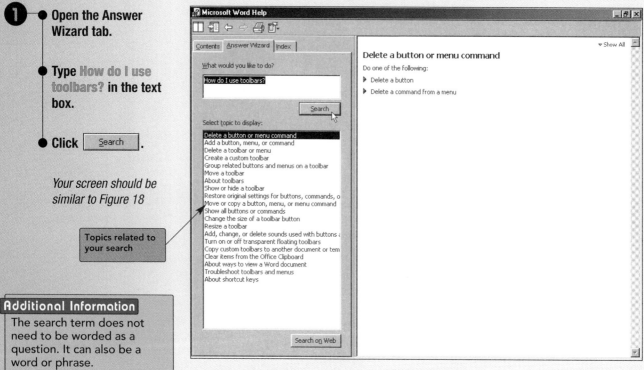

Figure 18

The topic list box displays all topics that the Answer Wizard considers may be related to the question you entered.

2 ● **Select "About toolbars" from the topic list.**

● **Click Show All.**

Your screen should be similar to Figure 19

Selected topic

Selected topic is displayed in Content frame

Displays/hides all topic information

Topic information fully displayed

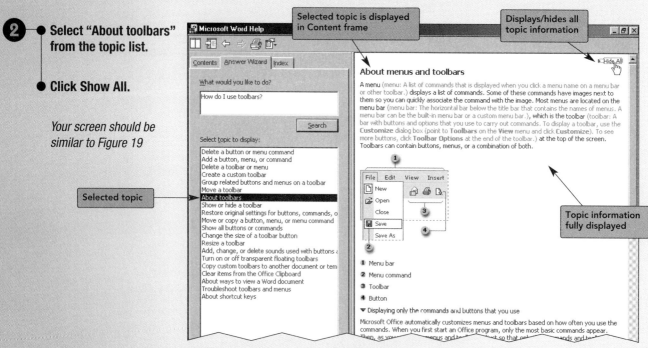

Figure 19

All topics are expanded and definitions displayed.

3 ● Read the information about this topic.

● Click ☒ to close Help.

Your screen should be similar to Figure 20

Figure 20

The Help window is closed, and the Word window is displayed again.

HAVING TROUBLE?

Your system must have an Internet connection to access the Microsoft Office Web site. If you do not have that, skip this section.

Getting Help on the Web

A final source of Help information is the Microsoft Office Web site. If a Help topic begins with "Web," clicking it takes you to the Web site and displays the topic in your Help window. You can also connect directly to this site from any Office application using the Help menu.

1 ● Choose **Help**/Office on the **Web**.

● If necessary, enter your user information and make the appropriate selections to connect to the Internet.

● If necessary, click United States.

Your screen should be similar to Figure 21

Figure 21

The browser application on your system is started and displays the Microsoft Office Web site. Now you could select any of the hyperlinks to further explore the site.

2 ● Read the information on this page.

● Click ☒ Close to close the browser.

● If necessary, disconnect from the Internet.

The Word application window is displayed again.

Using Toolbars

While using Office XP, you will see that many toolbars open automatically as different tasks are performed. Toolbars initially display the basic buttons. Like menus, they are personalized automatically, displaying those buttons you use frequently and hiding others. The More Buttons ⟩ button located at the end of a toolbar displays a drop-down button list of those buttons that are not displayed. When you use a button from this list, it then is moved to the toolbar, and a button that has not been used recently is moved to the More Buttons list.

Initially, Word displays two toolbars, Standard and Formatting, on one row below the menu bar (see Figure 22). The Standard toolbar contains buttons that are used to complete the most frequently used menu commands. The Formatting toolbar contains buttons that are used to change the appearance or format of the document.

> **HAVING TROUBLE?**
> Your screen may display different toolbars in different locations. This is because the program displays the settings that were in effect when it was last exited.

1 • **Right-click on any toolbar to display the shortcut menu.**

Your screen should be similar to Figure 22

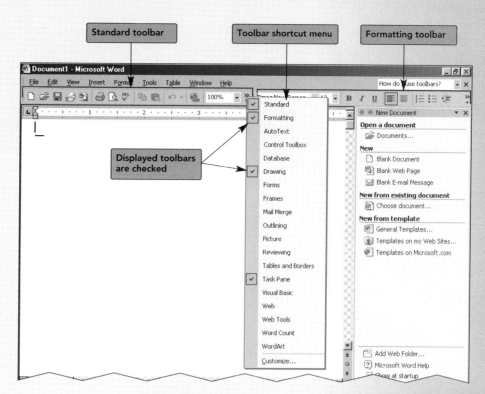

Standard toolbar   **Toolbar shortcut menu**   **Formatting toolbar**

Displayed toolbars are checked

Figure 22

Additional Information
The Customize option can be used to change features of toolbars and menus.

The toolbar shortcut menu displays a list of toolbar names. The Formatting, Standard, and Task Pane options should be checked, indicating they are displayed. Clicking on a toolbar from the list will display it on-screen. Clicking on a checked toolbar will hide the toolbar.

2 • **Click Task Pane to clear the checkmark.**

Your screen should be similar to Figure 23

Docked toolbars display move handle

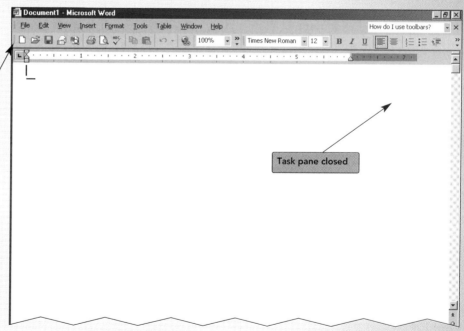

Task pane closed

Figure 23

The task pane is closed. When a toolbar is open, it may appear docked or floating. A docked toolbar is fixed to an edge of the window and displays a vertical bar ▮ called the move handle, on the left edge of the toolbar. Dragging this bar up or down allows you to move the toolbar. If multiple toolbars share the same row, dragging the bar left or right adjusts the size of the toolbar. If docked, a toolbar can occupy a row by itself, or several can be on a row together. A floating toolbar appears in a separate window.

3 ● Drag the move handle of the Standard toolbar into the document window.

Another Method

You can also double-click the top or bottom edge of a docked toolbar to change it to a floating toolbar.

Your screen should be similar to Figure 24

Figure 24

The Standard toolbar is now floating and can be moved to any location in the window by dragging the title bar. If you move it to the edge of the window, it will attach to that location and become a docked toolbar. A floating toolbar can also be sized by dragging the edge of toolbar.

4 ● Drag the title bar of the floating toolbar to move it to the row below the Formatting toolbar.

● Move the Formatting toolbar below the Standard toolbar.

Your screen should be similar to Figure 25

Additional Information

You can permanently display the toolbars on two rows using Tools/Customize/Options or by choosing Customize/Options from the toolbar shortcut menu and selecting "Show Standard and Formatting toolbars on two rows."

Figure 25

The two toolbars now occupy two rows. To quickly identify the toolbar buttons, you can display the button name by pointing to the button.

Point to any button on the Standard toolbar.

Your screen should be similar to Figure 26

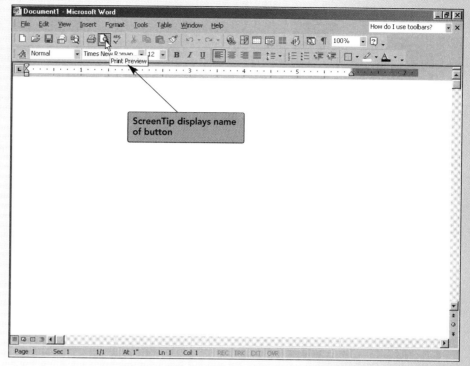

ScreenTip displays name of button

Figure 26

A ScreenTip containing the button name appears next to the mouse pointer.

Exiting an Office Application

The Exit command on the File menu can be used to quit most Windows programs. Alternatively, you can click the ☒ Close button in the program window title bar.

Click ☒ Close.

The program window is closed and the desktop is visible again.

lab review

Starting an Office Application

key terms

document window   I.10
frame   I.16
hyperlink   I.17
menu   I.10
menu bar   I.9
scroll bar   I.10
selection cursor   I.12
shortcut menu   I.15
status bar   I.10
task pane   I.10
toolbar   I.9

command summary

Command	Shortcut	Button	Action
Start/Programs			Opens program menu
File/Exit	Alt + F4		Exits Office program
View/Toolbars			Hides or displays toolbars
View/Task Pane			Hides or displays task pane
Tools/Customize/Options			Changes settings associated with toolbars and menus
Help/Microsoft Word Help	F1	?	Opens Help window
Help/Show the Office Assistant			Displays Office Assistant

Overview to Excel 2002

What Is an Electronic Spreadsheet?

The electronic spreadsheet, or worksheet, is an automated version of the accountant's ledger. Like the accountant's ledger, it consists of rows and columns of numerical data. Unlike the accountant's ledger, which is created on paper using a pencil and a calculator, the electronic spreadsheet is created by a computer system running spreadsheet application software.

In contrast to word processing, which manipulates text, spreadsheet programs manipulate numerical data. The first spreadsheet program, VisiCalc, was introduced in 1979. Since then spreadsheets have evolved into a powerful business tool that has revolutionized the business world.

The electronic spreadsheet eliminates the paper, pencil, and eraser. With a few keystrokes, the user can quickly change, correct, and update the data. Even more impressive is the spreadsheet's ability to perform calculations from very simple sums to the most complex financial and mathematical formulas. The calculator is replaced by the electronic spreadsheet. Analysis

A chart of the first quarter sales visually shows sales trends

A worksheet for the Downtown Internet Café Annual Forecast

of data in the spreadsheet has become a routine business procedure. Once requiring hours of labor and/or costly accountants' fees, data analysis is now available almost instantly using electronic spreadsheets.

Nearly any job that uses rows and columns of numbers can be performed using an electronic spreadsheet. Typical uses include the creation of budgets and financial planning for both business and personal situations.

Excel 2002 Features

Spreadsheet applications help you create well-designed spreadsheets that produce accurate results. These programs not only make it faster to create spreadsheets, they also produce professional-appearing results. Their advantages include the ability to quickly edit and format data, perform calculations, create charts, and print the spreadsheet.

The Microsoft Excel 2002 spreadsheet program uses a workbook file that contains one or more worksheets. Each worksheet can be used to organize different types of related information. Numeric or text data is entered into the worksheet in a location called a cell. These entries can then be erased, moved, copied, or edited. Formulas can be entered that perform calculations using data contained in specified cells. The results of the calculations are displayed in the cell containing the formula.

The design and appearance of the worksheet can be enhanced in many ways. There are several commands that control the format or display of a cell. For instance, numeric entries can be displayed with dollar signs or with a set number of decimal places. Text or label entries can be displayed centered or left- or right-aligned to improve the spreadsheet's appearance. You can further enhance the appearance of the worksheet by changing the type style and size and by adding special effects such as bold, italic, borders, boxes, drop shadows, and shading to selected cells. Columns and rows can be inserted and deleted. The cell width can be changed to accommodate entries of varying lengths.

You can change the values in selected cells and observe their effect on related cells in the worksheet. This is called what-if or sensitivity analysis. Questions that once were too expensive to ask or took too long to answer can now be answered almost instantly and with little cost. Planning that was once partially based on instinct has been replaced to a great extent with facts. However, any financial planning resulting from the data in a worksheet is only as accurate as that data and the logic behind the calculations.

You can also produce a visual display of data in the form of graphs or charts. As the values in the worksheet change, charts referencing those values automatically adjust to reflect the changes. You can also enhance the appearance of a graph by using different type styles and sizes, adding three-dimensional effects, and including text and objects such as lines and arrows.

Case Study for Excel 2002 Labs

The Downtown Internet Café is a new concept in coffeehouses, combining the delicious aromas of a genuine coffeehouse with the fun of using the Internet. You are the new manager for the coffeehouse and are working with the owner, Evan, to develop a financial plan for the next year.

Lab 1: Your first project is to develop a forecast for the Café for the first quarter. You will learn to enter numbers, perform calculations, copy data, label rows and columns, and format entries in a spreadsheet using Excel 2002.

Lab 2: After creating the first quarter forecast for the Downtown Internet Café, you have decided to chart the sales data to make it easier to see the trends and growth patterns. You also want to see what effect a strong advertising promotion of the new Café features will have on the forecasted sales data.

Lab 3: You have been asked to revise the workbook to include forecasts for the second, third, and fourth quarters. Additionally, the owner wants you to create a composite worksheet that shows the entire year's forecast and to change the data to achieve a 5 percent profit margin in the second quarter.

Working Together: Your analysis of sales data for the first quarter has shown a steady increase in total sales. Evan, the Café owner, has asked you for a copy of the forecast that shows the growth in Internet sales if a strong sales promotion is mounted. You will include the worksheet and chart data in a memo to the owner.

Before You Begin

To the Student

The following assumptions have been made:

- Microsoft Excel 2002 has been properly installed on your computer system.

- You have the data files needed to complete the series of Excel 2002 Labs and practice exercises. These files are supplied by your instructor.

- You have completed the McGraw-Hill Windows 98 or 2000 Labs or you are already familiar with how to use Windows and a mouse.

To the Instructor

A complete installation of Office XP is required in which all components are installed and are available to students while completing the labs.

Please be aware that the following settings are assumed to be in effect for the Excel 2002 program. These assumptions are necessary so that the screens and directions in the labs are accurate.

- The New Workbook Task Pane is displayed when Excel is started (Use Tools/Options/View).

- The ScreenTips feature is active (Use Tools/Customize/Options/Show ScreenTips on toolbar).

- The Status bar is displayed (Use Tools/Options/View).

- The horizontal and vertical scroll bars are displayed (Use Tools/Options/View).

- The Paste Options and Show Insert Options buttons are displayed (Use Tools/Options/Edit).

- The Standard and Formatting toolbars are displayed on separate rows (Tools/Customize/Options).

- Full menus are always displayed (Tools/Customize/Options).

- The Normal view is on; Zoom is 100 percent (Use View/Normal; View/ Zoom/100%).

- The Office Clipboard is displayed automatically. (Click Options on the Office Clipboard task pane and select Show Office Clipboard Automatically.)

- The Office Assistant feature is not on (Right-click on the Assistant character, choose Options and clear the Use the Office Assistant option.)

- All default settings for a new workbook are in effect.

In addition, all figures in the labs reflect the use of a standard VGA display monitor set at 800 by 600. If another monitor setting is used, there may be more or fewer rows and columns displayed in the window than in the figures. The 800 by 600 setting displays rows 1 through 27 and columns A through L. This setting can be changed using Windows setup.

Microsoft Office XP Shortcut Bar

The Microsoft Office XP Shortcut bar (shown below) may be displayed automatically on the Windows desktop. Commonly, it appears in the right side of the desktop; however, it may appear in other locations, depending upon your setup. The Shortcut bar on your screen may also display different buttons. This is because the Shortcut bar can be customized to display other toolbar buttons.

The Office Shortcut bar makes it easy to open existing documents or to create new documents using one of the Microsoft Office XP applications. It can also be used to send e-mail, add a task to a to-do list, schedule appointments, or access Office Help.

Instructional Conventions

Hands-on instructions you are to perform appear as a sequence of numbered black steps. Within each step, a series of bullets identifies the specific actions that must be performed. Step numbering begins over within each main topic heading throughout the lab.

Command sequences you are to issue appear following the word "Choose." Each menu command selection is separated by a /. If the menu command can be selected by typing a letter of the command, the letter will appear underlined and bold. Items that need to be selected will follow the word "Select" and will appear in black text. You can select items with the mouse or directional keys. (See Example A).

Example A

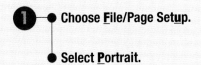

Commands that can be initiated using a button and the mouse appear following the word "Click." The icon (and the icon name if the icon does not include text) is displayed following Click. The menu equivalent and keyboard shortcut appear in a margin note when the action is first introduced. (See Example B).

Example B

> **Another Method**
> The menu equivalent is
> **File/Open** and the keyboard
> shortcut is Ctrl + O.

Information you are asked to type appears in blue and bold. (See Example C). File names appear in blue.

Example C

Creating and Editing a Worksheet

objectives

After completing this lab, you will know how to:

1.	Enter, edit, and clear cell entries.
2.	Save, close, and open workbooks.
3.	Specify ranges.
4.	Copy and move cell entries.
5.	Enter formulas and functions.
6.	Adjust column widths.
7.	Change cell alignment.
8.	Format cells.
9.	Insert rows.
10.	Insert and size a ClipArt graphic.
11.	Enter and format a date.
12.	Preview and print a worksheet.

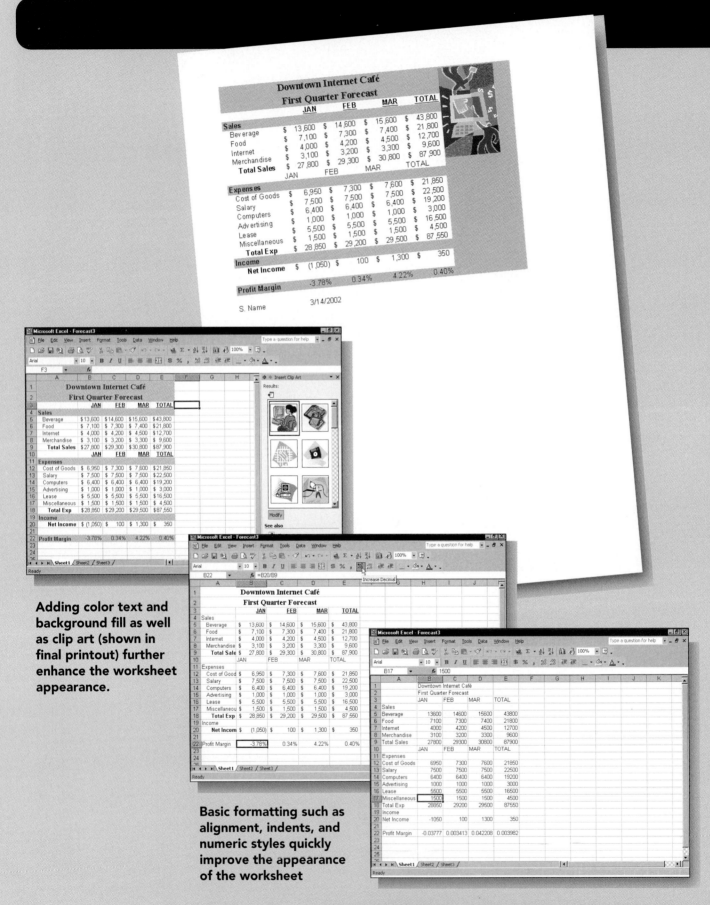

Adding color text and background fill as well as clip art (shown in final printout) further enhance the worksheet appearance.

Basic formatting such as alignment, indents, and numeric styles quickly improve the appearance of the worksheet

Enter labels, numbers, and formulas to create the basic structure of a worksheet.

Downtown Internet Café

You are excited about your new position as manager and financial planner for a local coffeehouse. Evan, the owner, has hired you as part of a larger effort to increase business at the former Downtown Café. Evan began this effort by completely renovating his coffeehouse, installing Internet hookups and outlets for laptops, and changing its name to the Downtown Internet Café. You and Evan expect to increase sales by attracting Internet-savvy café-goers, who, you hope, will use the Downtown Internet Café as a place to meet, study, or just relax.

Evan wants to create a forecast estimating sales and expenses for the first quarter. As part of a good business plan, you and Evan need a realistic set of financial estimates and goals.

In this lab, you will help with the first quarter forecast by using Microsoft Excel 2002, a spreadsheet application that can store, manipulate, and display numeric data. You will learn to enter numbers, perform calculations, copy data, and label rows and columns as you create the basic structure of a worksheet for the Downtown Internet Café. You will then learn how to enhance the worksheet using formatting features and by inserting a ClipArt graphic as shown here.

The following concepts will be introduced in this lab:

1	**Template**	A template is a workbook file that includes predefined settings that can be used as a pattern to create many common types of workbooks.
2	**Text and Numeric Entries**	The information or data you enter in a cell can be text, numbers, or formulas.
3	**AutoCorrect**	The AutoCorrect feature makes some basic assumptions about the text you are typing and, based on these assumptions, automatically corrects the entry.
4	**Column Width**	The size or width of a column controls how much information can be displayed in a cell.
5	**Copy and Move**	The contents of worksheet cells can be duplicated (copied) or moved to other locations in the worksheet or between worksheets, saving you time by not having to recreate the same information.
6	**Range**	A selection consisting of two or more cells on a worksheet is a range.
7	**Formulas**	A formula is an equation that performs a calculation on data contained in a worksheet.
8	**Relative Reference**	A relative reference is a cell or range reference in a formula whose location is interpreted in relation to the position of the cell that contains the formula.
9	**Functions**	Functions are prewritten formulas that perform certain types of calculations automatically.
10	**Recalculation**	Whenever a number in a referenced cell in a formula changes, Excel automatically recalculates all formulas that are dependent on the changed value.
11	**Alignment**	Alignment settings allow you to change the horizontal and vertical placement and the orientation of an entry in a cell.
12	**Fonts**	Fonts consist of typefaces, point sizes, and styles that can be applied to characters to improve their appearance.
13	**Number Formats**	Number formats affect how numbers look onscreen and when printed.
14	**Styles**	A style consists of a combination of formats that have been named and that can be quickly applied to a selection.
15	**Graphics**	A graphic is a non-text element or object, such as a drawing or picture that can be added to a document.

Exploring Excel 2002

As part of the renovation of the Downtown Internet Café, new computers and the most current versions of software programs were installed, including the latest version of the Microsoft Office suite of applications, Office XP. You are very excited to see how this new and powerful application can help you create professional budgets and financial forecasts.

Starting Excel 2002

You will use the spreadsheet application Excel 2002 included in the Office suite to create the first quarter forecast for the Café.

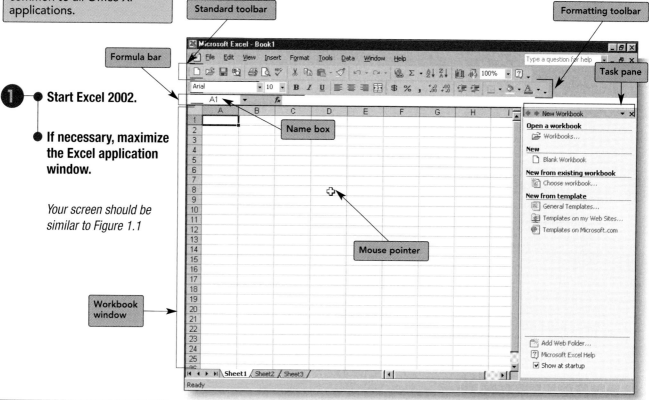

Figure 1.1

1 ● Start Excel 2002.

● If necessary, maximize the Excel application window.

Your screen should be similar to Figure 1.1

After a few moments, the Excel application window is displayed.

Exploring the Excel Window

The Excel window title bar displays the program name, Microsoft Excel, followed by Book1, the name of the open file. The menu bar below the title bar displays the Excel program menu. It consists of nine menus that provide access to the commands and features you will use to create and modify a worksheet.

The toolbars, normally located below the menu bar, contain buttons that are mouse shortcuts for many of the menu items. The **Standard toolbar** contains buttons that are used to complete the most frequently used menu commands. The **Formatting toolbar** contains buttons that are used to change the appearance or format of the document. Excel includes 23 different toolbars. Many of the toolbars appear automatically as you use different features. Your screen may display other toolbars if they were on when the program was last exited.

Below the toolbars is the formula bar. The **formula bar** displays entries as they are made and edited in the workbook window. The **Name box**, located at the left end of the formula bar, provides information about the selected item. The Edit Formula button is used to create or edit a formula.

The **task pane** is displayed on the right side of the window. There are eight different task panes that display depending on the task being performed. Since you just started Excel, the New Workbook task pane is automatically displayed providing different ways to create a new workbook or open an existing workbook.

The large area to the left of the task pane is the **workbook window**. A **workbook** is an Excel file that stores the information you enter using the program in worksheets. You will learn about the different parts of the workbook window and worksheets shortly.

The mouse pointer can appear as many different shapes. The mouse pointer changes shape depending upon the task you are performing or where the pointer is located on the window. Most commonly it appears as a ↖ or ✛. When it appears as a ✛, it is used to move to different locations in the workbook window and when it appears as a ↖, it is used to select items.

● Move the mouse pointer into the center of the workbook window to see it appear as ✛.

● Move the mouse pointer to the menu bar to see it appear as ↖.

Workbook window

Your screen should be similar to Figure 1.2

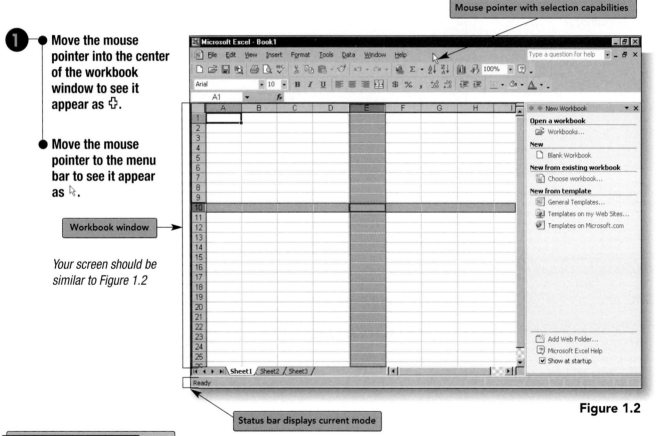

Mouse pointer with selection capabilities

Status bar displays current mode

Figure 1.2

The status bar at the bottom of the Excel window displays information about various Excel settings. The left side of the status bar displays the current mode or state of operation of the program, in this case, Ready. When Ready is displayed, you can move around the workbook, enter data, use the function keys, or choose a command. As you use the program, the status bar displays the current mode. The modes will be discussed as they appear throughout the labs.

Finally, your screen may display the Office Assistant. This feature provides quick access to online Help.

Exploring the Workbook Window

The workbook window displays a new blank workbook file containing three blank sheets. A sheet is used to display different types of information, such as financial data or charts. Whenever you open a new workbook, it displays a worksheet.

A **worksheet**, also commonly referred to as a **spreadsheet**, is a rectangular grid of **rows** and **columns** used to enter data. It is always part of a workbook and is the primary type of sheet you will use in Excel. The worksheet is much larger than the part you are viewing in the window. The worksheet actually extends 256 columns to the right and 65,536 rows down.

The **row numbers** along the left side and the **column letters** across the top of the workbook window identify each worksheet row and column. The intersection of a row and column creates a **cell**. Notice the heavy border, called the **cell selector**, surrounding the cell located at the intersection of column A and row 1. The cell selector identifies the **active cell**, which is the cell your next entry or procedure affects. Additionally, the Name box in the

Name box

formula bar displays the **reference**, consisting of the column letter and row number of the active cell. The reference of the active cell is A1.

Each sheet in a workbook is named. The default names are Sheet1, Sheet2, and so on, displayed on **sheet tabs** at the bottom of the workbook window. The name of the **active sheet**, which is the sheet you can work in, appears bold. The currently displayed worksheet in the workbook window, Sheet1, is the active sheet.

1 ● **Click the Sheet2 tab.**

Another Method

You can also press Ctrl + Page Down to move to the next sheet and Ctrl + Page Up to move to the previous sheet.

Your screen should be similar to Figure 1.3

Blank worksheet in Sheet 2

Active sheet

Close task pane

Tab scroll buttons

Sheet tabs

Figure 1.3

An identical blank worksheet is displayed in the window. The Sheet2 tab letters are bold, the background is highlighted, and it appears in front of the other sheet tabs to show it is the active sheet.

The sheet tab area also contains **tab scroll buttons**, which are used to scroll tabs right or left when there are more worksheet tabs than there is available space. You will learn about these features throughout the labs.

2 ● **Click the Sheet1 tab to make it the active sheet again.**

● **Click ⊠ in the task pane title bar to close the task pane.**

Another Method
The View/Task Pane command can also be used to hide the task pane.

Your screen should be similar to Figure 1.4

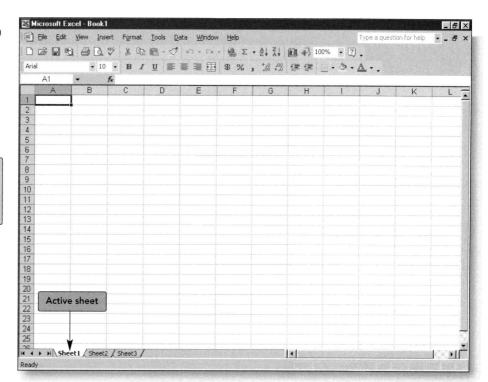

Active sheet

Figure 1.4

With the task pane closed, the workbook window is now the full width of the application window space, allowing much more of the worksheet to be displayed.

Moving around the Worksheet

Another Method
You can use the directional keys in the numeric keypad (with NumLock off) or, if you have an extended keyboard, you can use the separate directional keypad area.

Either the mouse or the keyboard can be used to move the cell selector from one cell to another in the worksheet. To move using a mouse, simply point to the cell you want to move to and click the mouse button. Depending upon what you are doing, using the mouse to move may not be as convenient as using the keyboard, in which case the directional keys can be used. You will use the mouse, then the keyboard to move the cell selector.

1 ● **Click cell B3.**

● **Press → (3 times).**

● **Press ↓ (4 times).**

Your screen should be similar to Figure 1.5

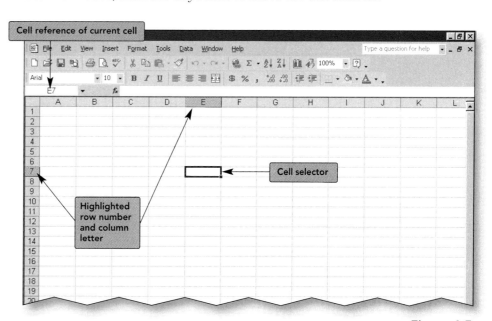

Cell reference of current cell

Cell selector

Highlighted row number and column letter

Figure 1.5

The cell selector is now in cell E7, making this cell the active cell. The Name box displays the cell reference. In addition, the row number and column letter appear highlighted to further identify the location of the active cell.

As you have learned, the worksheet is much larger than the part you are viewing in the window. To see an area of the worksheet that is not currently in view, you need to scroll the window. Either the keyboard or the mouse can be used to quickly scroll a worksheet. Again, both methods are useful depending upon what you are doing. The key and mouse procedures shown in the tables that follow can be used to move around the worksheet.

Keys	Action
Page Down	Moves cell selector down one full window
Page Up	Moves cell selector up one full window
Alt + Page Down	Moves cell selector right one full window
Alt + Page Up	Moves cell selector left one full window
Ctrl + Home	Moves cell selector to upper-left corner cell of worksheet
Home	Moves cell selector to beginning of row
End →	Moves cell selector to last-used cell in row
End ↓	Moves cell selector to last-used cell in column

Mouse	Action
Click scroll arrow	Scrolls worksheet one row/column in direction of arrow
Click above/below scroll box	Scrolls worksheet one full window up/down
Click right/left of scroll box	Scrolls worksheet one full window right/left
Drag scroll box	Scrolls worksheet multiple windows up/down or right/left

In addition, if you hold down the arrow keys, the Alt + Page Up or Alt + Page Down keys, or the Page Up or Page Down keys, you can quickly scroll through the worksheet. When you use the scroll bar, however, the cell selector does not move until you click on a cell that is visible in the window.

You will scroll the worksheet to see the rows below row 25 and the columns to the right of column L.

Press [Page Down] **(3 times).**

Press [Alt] **+** [Page Down] **(3 times).**

Your screen should be similar to Figure 1.6

HAVING TROUBLE?

Your screen may display more or fewer rows and columns depending on your screen and system settings.

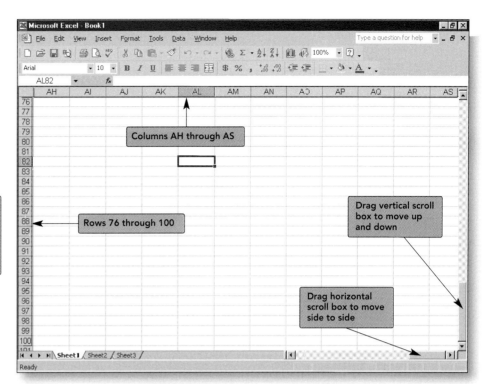

Figure 1.6

The worksheet scrolled downward and left three full windows and the window displays rows 76 through 100 and columns AH through AS of the worksheet. The cell selector is in cell AL82. As you scroll the worksheet using the keyboard, the cell selector also moves.

It is even more efficient to use the scroll bar to move long distances.

Slowly drag the vertical scroll box up the scroll bar until row 1 is displayed.

Slowly drag the horizontal scroll box left along the scroll bar until column A is displayed.

Additional Information

The position of the scroll box indicates the relative location of the area you are viewing within the worksheet and the size of the scroll box indicates the proportional amount of the used area.

Your screen should be similar to Figure 1.7

Figure 1.7

Notice that the Name box displays the cell selector location as AL82. When you use the scroll bar to scroll the worksheet, the cell selector does not move.

4 ● Practice moving the cell selector around the worksheet using each of the keys presented in the table on page EX1.10.

● Press ⌈Ctrl⌉ + ⌈Home⌉ to move to cell A1.

Another Method

You can also type a cell address in the Name box to move to that location.

Your screen should be similar to Figure 1.8

Figure 1.8

You can use the mouse or the keyboard with most of the exercises in these labs. As you use both the mouse and the keyboard, you will find that it is more efficient to use one or the other in specific situations.

Creating New Workbooks

Now that you are familiar with the parts of the workbook and how to move around, you are ready to create a worksheet showing the forecast for the first three months of operation for the Downtown Internet Café.

Using the Default Workbook Template

When you first start Excel, a new blank Excel workbook is opened. It is like a blank piece of paper that already has many predefined settings. These settings, called **default** settings, are generally the most commonly used settings and are stored as a workbook template.

concept 1

Templates

1 A workbook **template** is a file that includes predefined settings that can be used as a pattern to create many common types of workbooks. Every Excel workbook is based on a template. The default settings for a basic blank workbook are stored in the Book.xlt template file. Whenever you create a new workbook using this template, the same default settings are used.

Many other templates are available within Excel and on the Microsoft Internet site that are designed to help you create professional-looking workbooks. They include templates that create different styles of balance sheets, expense statements, loan amortizations, sales invoices, and timecards. You can also design and save your own workbook templates.

You will use the default workbook template to create the worksheet for the Café. As you create a new workbook, the development progresses through several stages.

Developing a Workbook

Workbook development consists of four steps; planning, entering and editing, testing, and formatting. The objective is to create well-designed worksheets that produce accurate results and are clearly understood, adaptable, and efficient.

Step	Description
1. Plan	Specify the purpose of the workbook and how it should be organized. This means clearly identifying the data that will be input, the calculations that are needed to achieve the results, and the output that is desired. As part of the planning step, it is helpful to sketch out a design of the worksheet to organize the worksheet's structure. The design should include the worksheet title and row and column headings that identify the input and output. Additionally, sample data can be used to help determine the formulas needed to produce the output.
2. Enter and edit	Create the structure of the worksheet using Excel by entering the worksheet labels, data, and formulas. As you enter information, you are bound to make errors that need to be corrected or edited, or you will need to revise the content of what you have entered to make it clearer or to add or delete information.
3. Test	Test the worksheet for errors. Several sets of real or sample data are used as the input, and the resulting output is verified. The input data should include a full range of possible values for each data item to ensure the worksheet can function successfully under all possible conditions.
4. Format	Enhance the appearance of the worksheet to make it more readable or attractive. This step is usually performed when the worksheet is near completion. It includes many features such as boldface text, italic, and color.

As the complexity of the worksheet increases, the importance of following the design process increases. Even for simple worksheets like the one you will create in this lab the design process is important.

During the planning phase, you have spoken with the Café manager regarding the purpose of the workbook and the content in general. The primary purpose is to develop a forecast for sales and expenses for the next year. Evan first wants you to develop a worksheet for the first quarter forecast and then extend it by quarters for the year. After reviewing past budgets and consulting with Evan, you have designed the basic layout for the first quarter forecast for the Café as shown below.

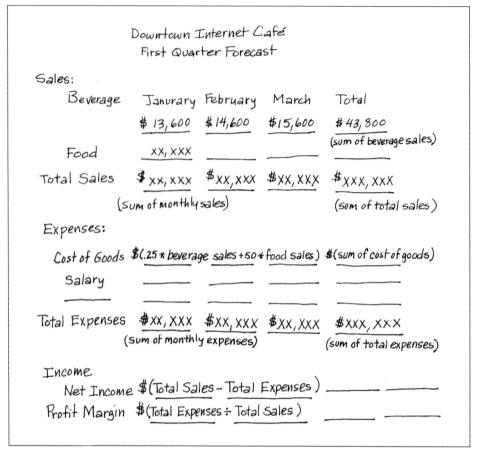

Downtown Internet Café
First Quarter Forecast

Sales:

	January	February	March	Total
Beverage	$ 13,600	$14,600	$15,600	$ 43,800 (sum of beverage sales)
Food	XX,XXX	____	____	
Total Sales	$ XX,XXX	$ XX,XXX	$ XX,XXX	$ XXX,XXX (sum of total sales)
	(sum of monthly sales)			

Expenses:

Cost of Goods	$(.25 * beverage sales + 50 * food sales)			$(sum of cost of goods)
Salary	____	____	____	____
Total Expenses	$XX,XXX	$XX,XXX	$XX,XXX	$XXX,XXX (sum of total expenses)
	(sum of monthly expenses)			

Income
Net Income $(Total Sales - Total Expenses) ____ ____
Profit Margin $(Total Expenses ÷ Total Sales) ____ ____

Entering and Editing Data

Now that you understand the purpose of the workbook and have a general idea of the content, you are ready to begin entering the data. You enter data by moving to the cell where you want the data displayed and typing the entry using the keyboard.

As you can see, the budget contains both descriptive text entries and numeric data. These are two types of entries you can make in a worksheet.

concept 2

Text and Numeric Entries

2 The information or data you enter in a cell can be text, numbers, or formulas. **Text** entries can contain any combination of letters, numbers, spaces, and any other special characters. **Number** entries can include only the digits 0 to 9 and any of the special characters, + − ( ) , . / $ % Σ =. Number entries can be used in calculations. An entry that begins with an equal sign (=) is a **formula**. Formula entries perform calculations using numbers or data contained in other cells. The resulting value from formulas is a **variable** value because it can change if the data it depends on changes. In contrast, a number entry is a **constant** value. It does not begin with an equal sign and does not change unless you change it directly by typing in another entry.

Entering Text

First you will enter the worksheet headings. Row and column **headings** are entries that are used to create the structure of the worksheet and describe other worksheet entries. Generally, headings are text entries. The column headings in this worksheet consist of the three months (January through March) and a total (sum of entries over three months) located in columns B through E. To enter data in a worksheet, you must first select the cell where you want the entry displayed. The column heading for January will be entered in cell B2.

1 ● Move to B2.

● Type J.

Your screen should be similar to Figure 1.9

Figure 1.9

Several changes have occurred in the window. As you type, the entry is displayed both in the active cell and in the formula bar. An insertion point appears in the active cell and marks your location in the entry. Two new buttons, ⊠ and ☑, appear in the formula bar. They can be used with a mouse to complete your entry or cancel it.

Notice also that the mode displayed in the status bar has changed from Ready to Enter. This notifies you that the current mode of operation in the worksheet is entering data. To continue entering the heading,

2 ● **Type** anuary.

HAVING TROUBLE?

If you make an error while typing the entry, use Backspace to erase the characters back to the error. Then retype the entry correctly.

Your screen should be similar to Figure 1.10

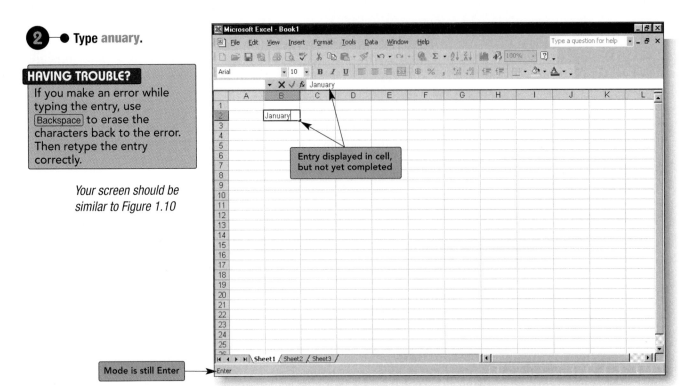

Figure 1.10

Although the entry is displayed in both the active cell and the formula bar, you need to press the ←Enter key or click ☑ to complete your entry. If you press Esc or click ☒, the entry is cleared and nothing appears in the cell. Since your hands are already on the keyboard, it is quicker to press ←Enter than it is to use the mouse to click ☑.

3 ● **Press** ←Enter.

Your screen should be similar to Figure 1.11

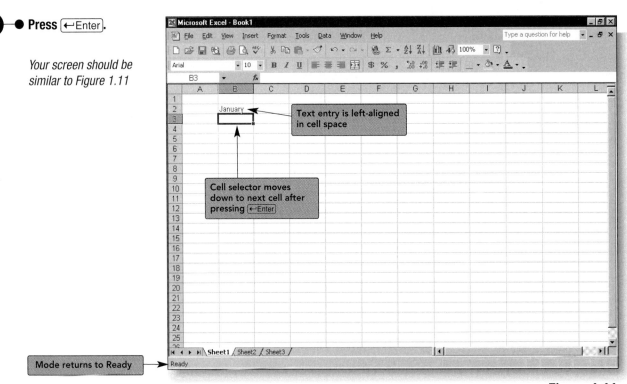

Figure 1.11

The entry January is displayed in cell B2, and the mode has returned to Ready. In addition, the cell selector has moved to cell B3. Whenever you use the [←Enter] key to complete an entry, the cell selector moves down one cell.

Notice that the entry is positioned to the left side of the cell space. The positioning of cell entries in the cell space is called **alignment**. This is a default setting included in the default workbook template you are using. You will learn more about this feature later in the lab.

Clearing an Entry

After looking at the entry, you decide you want the column headings to be in row 3 rather than in row 2. This will leave more space above the column headings for a worksheet title. The [Delete] key can be used to clear the contents from a cell. To remove the entry from cell B2 and enter it in cell B3,

1 ● **Move to B2.**

● **Press** [Delete].

Another Method

The menu equivalent is Edit/Clear/Contents. Clear Contents is also an option on the shortcut menu.

● **Move to B3.**

● **Type January.**

● **Click** ☑.

Your screen should be similar to Figure 1.12

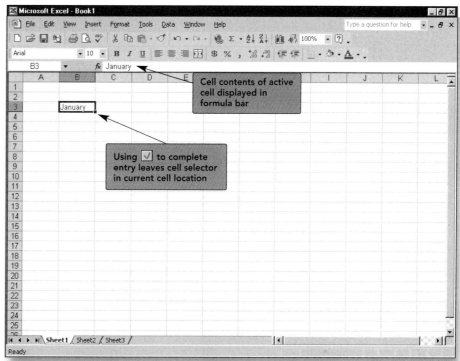

Figure 1.12

The cell selector remains in the active cell when you use ☑ to complete an entry. Because the cell selector is positioned on a cell containing an entry, the contents of the cell are displayed in the formula bar.

Editing an Entry

You would like to change the heading from January to JAN. An entry in a cell can be entirely changed in the Ready mode or partially changed or edited in the Edit mode. To use the Ready mode, you move the cell selector to the cell you want to change and retype the entry the way you want it to appear. As soon as a new character is entered, the existing entry is cleared.

Generally, however, if you need to change only part of an entry, it is quicker to use the Edit mode. To change to Edit mode, double-click on the cell whose contents you want to edit.

Double-click B3.

HAVING TROUBLE?

The mouse pointer must be ✛ when you double-click on the cell.

Another Method

Pressing the F2 key will also change to Edit mode. The insertion point is positioned at the end of the entry.

Your screen should be similar to Figure 1.13

Figure 1.13

The status bar shows that the new mode of operation is Edit. The insertion point appears in the entry, and the mouse pointer changes to an I-beam when positioned on the cell. The mouse pointer can now be used to move the insertion point in the entry by positioning the I-beam and clicking.

In addition, in the Edit mode, the following keys can be used to move the insertion point:

Key	Action
Home	Moves insertion point to beginning of entry
End	Moves insertion point to end of entry
→	Moves insertion point one character right
←	Moves insertion point one character left

Additional Information

You can also use Ctrl + Delete to delete everything to the right of the insertion point.

Once the insertion point is appropriately positioned, you can edit the entry by removing the incorrect characters and typing the correct characters. The Delete key erases characters at the insertion point, and the Backspace key erases characters to the left of the insertion point. You will change this entry to JAN.

2 ● **If necessary, move the insertion point to the end of the entry.**

● **Press** [Backspace] **(4 times).**

● **Press** [Home]**.**

● **Press** [→]**.**

● **Press** [Caps Lock]**.**

● **Press** [Insert]**.**

● **Type** A**.**

Your screen should be similar to Figure 1.14

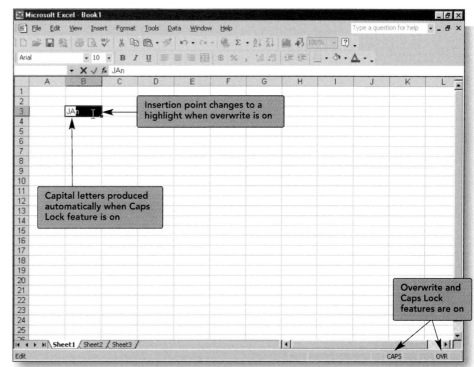

Figure 1.14

The four characters at the end of the entry were deleted using [Backspace]. Turning on the Caps Lock feature produced an uppercase letter A without having to hold down [⇧Shift]. Finally, by pressing [Insert] the program switched from inserting text to overwriting text as you typed. The insertion point changes to a highlight to show the character will be replaced. The status bar displays CAPS and OVR to let you know these features are on.

Additional Information

The Caps Lock indicator light on your keyboard is lit when this feature is on.

3 ● **Type** N**.**

● **Press** [←Enter]**.**

Your screen should be similar to Figure 1.15

Additional Information

Overwrite is automatically turned off when you leave Edit mode or if you press [Insert] again.

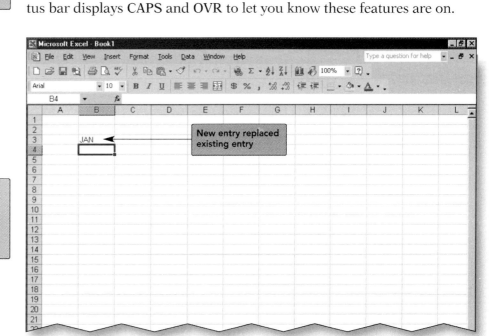

Figure 1.15

The new heading JAN is entered into cell B3, replacing January. As you can see, editing will be particularly useful with long or complicated entries.

Next, you will enter the remaining three headings in row three. You can also complete an entry by moving to any other worksheet cell.

4 ● **Move to C3.**

● **Type FEB.**

● **Press** → **or** Tab ⇆ **or click D3.**

● **Complete the column headings by entering MAR in cell D3 and TOTAL in cell E3.**

● **When you are done, turn off** Caps Lock **.**

Your screen should be similar to Figure 1.16

Figure 1.16

The column headings are now complete for the first quarter.

Using AutoCorrect

As soon as you complete an entry in a cell, Excel checks the entry for accuracy. This is part of the automatic correcting feature of Excel.

concept 3

AutoCorrect

3 The **AutoCorrect** feature makes some basic assumptions about the text you are typing and, based on these assumptions, automatically corrects the entry. The AutoCorrect feature automatically inserts proper capitalization at the beginning of sentences and in the names of days of the week. It will also change to lowercase letters any words that were incorrectly capitalized due to the accidental use of the Caps Lock key. In addition, it also corrects many common typing and spelling errors automatically.

One way the program automatically makes corrections is by looking for certain types of errors. For example, if two capital letters appear at the beginning of a word, the second capital letter is changed to a lowercase letter. If a lowercase letter appears at the beginning of a sentence, the first letter of the first word is capitalized. If the name of a day begins with a lowercase letter, the first letter is capitalized.

Another way the program makes corrections is by checking all entries against a built-in list of words that are commonly spelled incorrectly or typed incorrectly. If it finds the entry on the list, the program automatically replaces the error with the correction. For example, the typing error "aboutthe" is automatically changed to "about the" because the error is on the AutoCorrect list. You can also add words that you want to be automatically corrected to the AutoCorrect list. Words you add are added to the list on the computer you are using and will be available to anyone who uses the machine after you.

Above the column headings, in rows 1 and 2, you want to enter a title for the worksheet. While entering the title, you will intentionally misspell two words to demonstrate how the AutoCorrect feature works.

Move to B1.

Type Downtown Internet Cafe.

Press [Enter].

Type Firts Quater Forecast.

Press [Enter].

Your screen should be similar to Figure 1.17

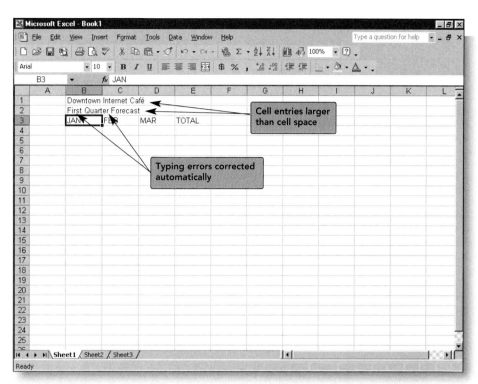

Figure 1.17

Additional Information

Excel automatically adds an accent over the e in Café if the feature to recognize French words is enabled.

The two typing errors were automatically corrected when you completed the entry. When a text entry is longer than the cell's column width, Excel will display as much of the entry as it can. If the cell to the right is empty, the whole entry will be displayed. If the cell to the right contains an entry, the overlapping part of the entry is not displayed.

Next, the row headings need to be entered into column A of the worksheet. The row headings and what they represent are shown on the next page.

Heading	Represents
Sales	
Beverage	Income from sales of drinks (espresso, gourmet coffee, cold drinks)
Food	Income from sales of sandwiches and salads
Internet	Income from Internet connection time charges
Merchandise	Income from sales of Café tee shirts, mugs, and so forth
Total Sales	Sum of all sales
Expenses	
Cost of Goods	Cost of beverage and food items sold
Salary	Personnel expenses
Computers	Monthly payment for computer hardware
Lease	Monthly lease expense
Miscellaneous	Monthly expenses for T1 line, phone, electricity, water, trash removal, etc.
Income	
Net Income	Total sales minus total expenses
Profit Margin	Net income divided by total sales

2 ● **Complete the row headings for the Sales portion of the worksheet by entering the following headings in the indicated cells:**

Cell	Heading
A4	Sales
A5	Beverage
A6	Food
A7	Internet
A8	Merchandise
A9	Total Sales

HAVING TROUBLE?
Remember to press [Enter] or an arrow key to complete the last entry.

Your screen should be similar to Figure 1.18

Figure 1.18

Entering Numbers

Next, you will enter the expected beverage sales numbers for January through March into cells B5 through D5. As you learned earlier, number entries can include the digits 0 to 9 and any of these special characters: + − ( ), . / $ % Σ =. When entering numbers, it is not necessary to type the comma to separate thousands or the currency ($) symbol. You will learn about adding these symbols shortly.

You will enter the expected beverage sales for January first.

● Move to **B5**.

● Type 13600.

● Press ↵Enter.

Additional Information

You can use the number keys above the alphabetic keys or the numeric keypad area to enter numbers. If you use the numeric keypad, the Num Lock key must be on.

Your screen should be similar to Figure 1.19

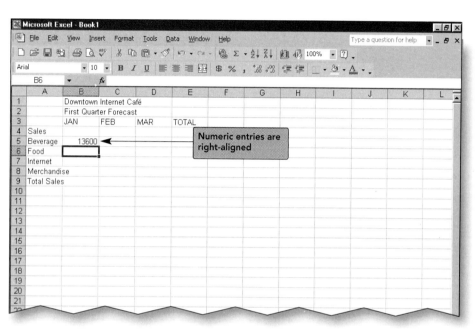

Figure 1.19

Unlike text entries, Excel displays number entries right-aligned in the cell space by default.

● In the same manner, enter the January sales numbers for the remaining items using the values shown below.

Cell	Number
B6	7100
B7	3600
B8	3100

● Move to **A8**.

Your screen should be similar to Figure 1.20

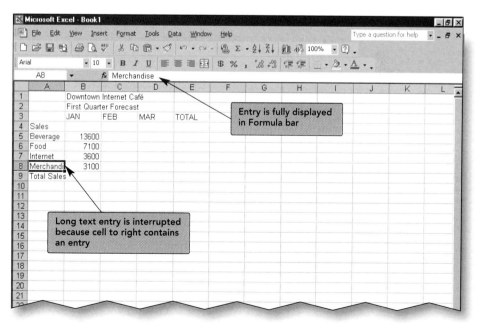

Figure 1.20

After entering the numbers for January in column B, any long headings in column A were cut off or interrupted. Notice that the entry in cell A8 is no longer completely displayed. It is a long text entry and because the cell to the right (B8) now contains an entry, the overlapping part of the entry is shortened. However, the entire entry is fully displayed in the Formula bar. Only the display of the entry in the cell has been shortened.

Changing Column Widths

To allow the long text entries in column A to be fully displayed, you can increase the column's width.

concept 4

Column Width

4 The size or width of a column controls how much information can be displayed in a cell. A text entry that is larger than the column width will be fully displayed only if the cells to the right are blank. If the cells to the right contain data, the text is interrupted. On the other hand, when numbers are entered in a cell, the column width is automatically increased to fully display the entry.

The default column width setting in the default workbook template is 8.43. The number represents the average number of digits that can be displayed in a cell using the standard type style. The column width can be any number from 1 to 255.

When the worksheet is printed, it appears as it does currently on the screen. Therefore, you want to increase the column width to display the largest entry. Likewise, you can decrease the column width when the entries in a column are short.

Dragging the Column Boundary

Additional Information
You can also adjust the size of any row by dragging the row divider line or by using Format/Row/Height.

The column width can be quickly adjusted by dragging the boundary line located to the right of the column letter. Dragging it to the left decreases the column width, while dragging it to the right increases the width. As you drag, a temporary column reference line shows where the new column will appear and a ScreenTip displays the width of the column.

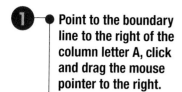

1 ● Point to the boundary line to the right of the column letter A, click and drag the mouse pointer to the right.

HAVING TROUBLE?

Make sure the mouse pointer changes to ⟺ before you drag the column boundary line to size the column.

● When the ScreenTip displays 15.00, release the mouse button.

Another Method

The menu equivalent is Format/Column/Width.

Your screen should be similar to Figure 1.21

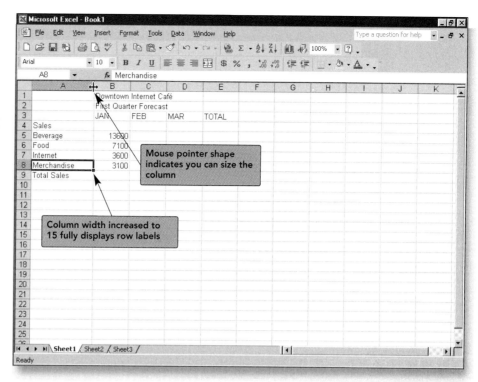

Figure 1.21

Now, however, the column width is wider than needed.

Using AutoFit

Another way to change the column width is to automatically adjust the width to fit the column contents.

1 ● Double-click the A column boundary line.

HAVING TROUBLE?

Make sure the mouse pointer changes to ⟺ before you double-click on the column boundary line.

Another Method

The menu equivalent is Format/Column/AutoFit Selection.

Your screen should be similar to Figure 1.22

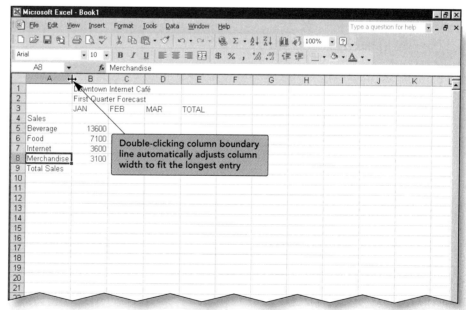

Figure 1.22

The column width is sized to just slightly larger than the longest cell contents.

Saving, Closing, and Opening Workbooks

You have a meeting you need to attend shortly, so you want to save your work to a file and close the file. As you enter and edit data to create a new workbook, the changes you make are immediately displayed onscreen and are stored in your computer's memory. However, they are not permanently stored until you save your work to a file on a disk. Once a workbook is saved as a file, it can be closed and opened again at a later time to be further edited.

As a backup against the accidental loss of work due to power failure or other mishap, Office XP includes an AutoRecover feature. When this feature is on, as you work you may see a pulsing disk icon briefly appear in the status bar. This indicates the program is saving your work to a temporary recovery file. The time interval between automatic saving can be set to any period you specify; the default is every 10 minutes. When you start up again, the recovery file is automatically opened containing all changes you made up to the last time it was saved by AutoRecover. You then need to save the recovery file. If you do not save it, it is deleted when closed. While AutoRecover is a great feature for recovering lost work, it should not be used in place of regularly saving your work.

Saving a New Workbook

You will save the work you have done so far on the workbook. The Save or Save As commands on the File menu are used to save files. The Save command or the 🖫 Save button will save the active file using the same file name by replacing the contents of the existing file with the document as it appears on your screen. The Save As command allows you to save a file with a new file name or to a new location. This leaves the original file unchanged.

Additional Information

When a workbook is saved for the first time, either Save or Save As can be used.

1 ● Choose **File/Save As**.

Your screen should be similar to Figure 1.23

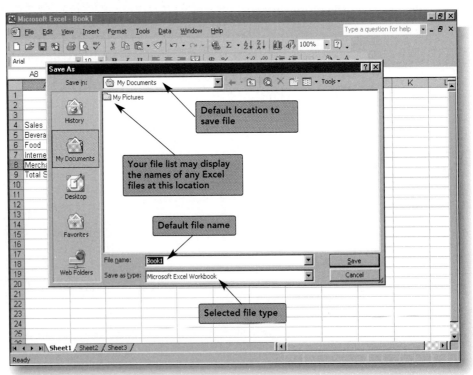

Figure 1.23

This Save As dialog box is used to specify the location to save the file and the file name. The Save In drop-down list box displays the default folder as the location where the file will be saved, and the File Name text box displays the proposed file name. The file list box displays the names of any Excel workbook files in the default location. Only Excel workbook files are listed, because the selected file type in the Save As Type list box is Excel Workbook. First you need to change the location where the file will be saved.

2 ● **Open the Save In drop-down list box.**

● **Select the appropriate location to save the file.**

HAVING TROUBLE?

If you are saving to a floppy disk and an error message is displayed, check that your disk is properly inserted in the drive and click ⬚ OK ⬚.

Your screen should be similar to Figure 1.24

Additional Information

If your system uses Windows NT, My Network Places is Network Neighborhood; in Windows 98, it is Web Folders.

Additional Information

If your dialog box displays the extension, this is a function of your Windows setup.

Additional Information

In addition to the .xls file type, Excel workbooks can also be saved in several different file formats that have different file extensions depending upon the format.

Additional Information

Windows documents can have up to 215 characters in the file name. Names can contain letters, numbers, and spaces; the symbols \, /, ?, :, *, ", < and > cannot be used.

Figure 1.24

If the location you are saving to does not contain other Excel files, your file list will be empty as shown here. Otherwise, your file list may display Excel file names. You can also select the location to save your file from the Places bar along the left side of the dialog box. The icons bring up a list of recently accessed files and folders, the contents of the My Documents and Favorites folder, the Windows desktop, and folders that reside on a network or Web through My Network Places. Selecting a folder from one of these lists changes to that location. You can also click the ⬚ button in the toolbar to return to folders that were previously opened.

Next, you need to enter a file name and specify the file type. The File Name box displays the default file name, Book1. The Save as Type box displays Excel workbook as the default format in which the file will be saved. Workbooks are identified by the file extension .xls. The file type you select determines the file extension that will be automatically added to the file name when the file is saved. You will change the file name to Forecast.

New file name

3 ● Triple-click in the File
Name text box to high-
light the file name.

● Type Forecast.

● Click [Save] or
press [Enter].

Additional Information
The file name can be entered
in either uppercase or
lowercase letters and will
appear exactly as you type it.

*Your screen should be
similar to Figure 1.25*

Additional Information
The file name in the title bar
may display the workbook
file extension, .xls.

Closes workbook file

	A	B	C	D	E
1		Downtown Internet Café			
2		First Quarter Forecast			
3		JAN	FEB	MAR	TOTAL
4	Sales				
5	Beverage	13600			
6	Food	7100			
7	Internet	3600			
8	Merchandise	3100			
9	Total Sales				

Figure 1.25

The new file name is displayed in the application window title bar. The worksheet data that was on your screen and in the computer's memory is now saved at the location you specified in a new file called Forecast.

Closing a Workbook

You are now ready to close the workbook file.

1 ● Click Close Window (in the menu bar).

Another Method
The menu equivalent is
File/Close.

Because you did not make any changes to the document since saving it, the document window is closed immediately and the Excel window displays an empty workspace. If you had made additional changes, Excel would ask if you wanted to save the file before closing it. This prevents the accidental closing of a file that has not been saved first.

Note: If you are running short on lab time, this is an appropriate place to end your session.

Opening an Existing Workbook

Additional Information
You can also quickly open a
recently used file by selecting
it from the list of file names
displayed at the bottom of
the File menu and at the top
of the New Workbook task
pane.

After attending your meeting, you continued working on the Café forecast. To see what has been done so far, you will open the workbook file named ex01_Forecast2.

1 ● Choose **View/Task Pane.**

● Click 📂 **More Workbooks (in the task pane).**

Another Method

The menu equivalent is **File/Open** and the keyboard shortcut is Ctrl + O. You can also click 📂 Open in the Standard toolbar.

Additional Information

The **File/New** command or ⬜ Blank Workbook on the New Workbook task pane opens a blank new workbook.

Your screen should be similar to Figure 1.26

Figure 1.26

In the Open dialog box, you specify the location and name of the file you want to open. The Look In drop-down list box displays the last specified location, in this case the location where you saved the Forecast workbook. The large list box displays the names of all Excel workbooks with the file extensions displayed in the Files of type box. As in the Save As dialog box, the Places bar can be used to quickly access recently used files. When selecting a file to open, it may be helpful to see a preview of the file first. To do this, you can change the dialog box view.

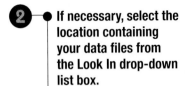

2 • If necessary, select the location containing your data files from the Look In drop-down list box.

• Open the Views drop-down list.

• Choose Preview.

• Select ex01_Forecast2.

Your screen should be similar to Figure 1.27

Figure 1.27

A preview of the selected file is displayed in the right pane of the dialog box. To return the view to the list of file names and open this file,

Additional Information

To see a preview, the workbook must be saved with the Save preview picture option selected under File/Properties. You will learn about this feature in Lab 2.

3 • Open the Views drop-down list.

• Choose List.

• Select ex01_Forecast2.

• Click Open.

Another Method

You could also double-click the file name to both select it and choose Open.

Your screen should be similar to Figure 1.28

Figure 1.28

The workbook is opened and displayed in the workbook window. The workbook contains the additional sales values for February and March, the expense row headings, and several of the expense values for the month of January.

Duplicating Cell Contents

Next, you want to enter the estimated expenses for salary, computers, lease, and miscellaneous for February and March. They are the same as the January expense numbers. Because these values are the same, instead of entering the same number repeatedly into each cell you can quickly copy the contents of one cell to another. You also want to move information from one location in the worksheet to another.

concept 5

Copy and Move

5 The contents of worksheet cells can be duplicated (copied) or moved to other locations in the worksheet or between worksheets, saving you time by not having to retype the same information. An entry that is copied leaves the original, called the **source** or **copy area**, and inserts a duplicate at a new location, called the **destination** or **paste area**. A selection that is moved is removed or cut from the original location in the source and inserted at the destination.

When a selection is moved or copied, the selection is stored in the system Clipboard, a temporary Windows storage area in memory. The system Clipboard contents are then inserted at the new location specified by the location of the insertion point.

Office XP also includes an Office Clipboard that can store up to 24 items that have been cut or copied. This allows you to insert multiple items from various Office files and paste all or part of the collection of items into another file.

Using Copy and Paste

When using Copy and Paste, you first use the Copy command to copy the cell contents to the system Clipboard. Then you move to the new location where you want the contents copied and use the Paste command to insert the system Clipboard contents into the selected cells. Be careful when pasting to the new location because any existing entries are replaced.

To use the Copy command, you first must select the cell or cells in the source containing the data to be copied. You will copy the value in cell B12 into cells C12 and D12.

1 ● Move to B12.

● Click 📋 Copy.

Another Method

The menu equivalent is
Edit/Copy and the shortcut
key is Ctrl + C. Copy is also
available on the shortcut
menu.

*Your screen should be
similar to Figure 1.29*

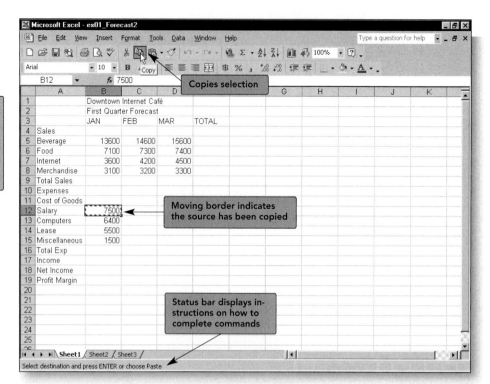

Figure 1.29

A moving border identifies the source and indicates that the contents have
been copied to the system Clipboard. The instructions displayed in the status bar tell you to select the destination where you want the contents
copied. You will copy it to cell C12.

2 ● Move to C12.

● Click 📋 Paste.

Another Method

The menu equivalent is
Edit/Paste and the shortcut
key is Ctrl + V. Paste is also
available on the shortcut
menu.

*Your screen should be
similar to Figure 1.30*

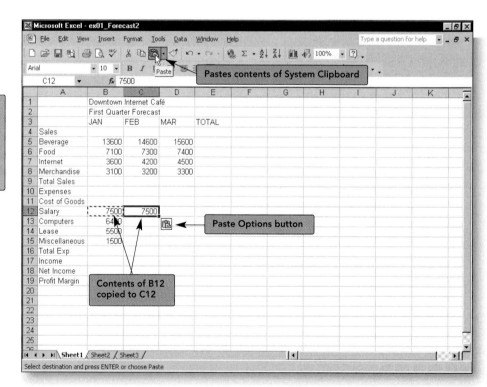

Figure 1.30

The contents of the system Clipboard are inserted at the specified destination location. Each time the paste command is used, the 📋 Paste Options

button is available. Clicking on the button opens the Paste Options menu that allows you to control how the information you are pasting is inserted.

3 ● Click 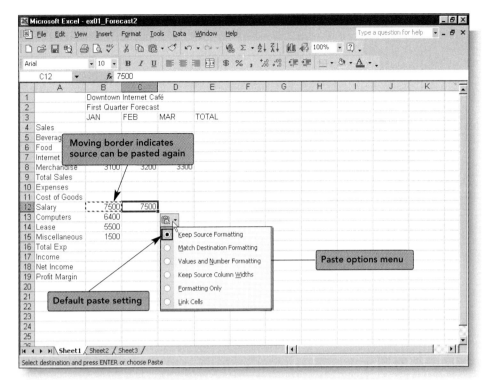 Paste Options.

Your screen should be similar to Figure 1.31

Figure 1.31

The selected option, Keep Source Formatting, will insert the copy exactly as it appears in the source. This is the default paste setting and is appropriate for this and most situations.

4 ● Click outside the menu to close it.

The moving border is still displayed indicating the system Clipboard still contains the copied entry. Now you can complete the data for the Salary row by pasting the value again from the system Clipboard into cell D12. While the moving border is still displayed, you can also simply press ←Enter to paste. However, as this method clears the contents of the system Clipboard immediately, it can only be used once.

5 Move to D12.

Press ↵Enter.

Your screen should be similar to Figure 1.32

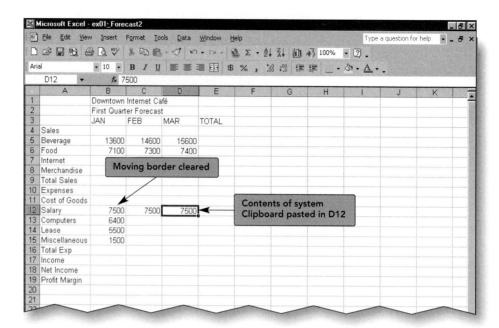

Figure 1.32

The contents of the system Clipboard are inserted at the specified destination location and the moving border is cleared indicating the system Clipboard is empty.

Selecting a Range

Now you need to copy the Computers value in cell B13 to February and March. You could copy and paste the contents individually into each cell. It is much faster, however, to select a paste area that consists of multiple cells, called a range, and paste the contents to all cells in the selection at once.

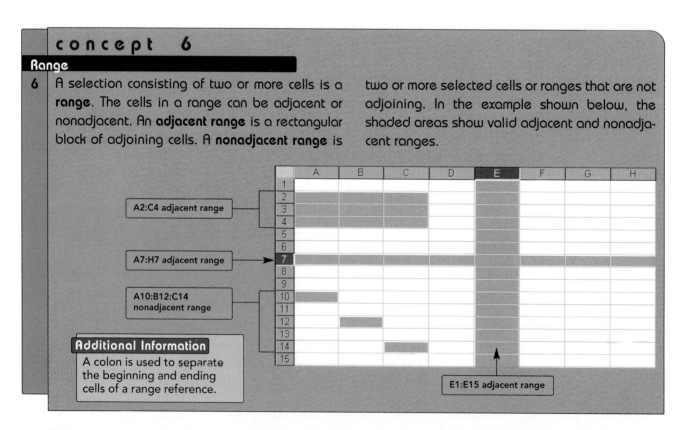

concept **6**

Range

6 A selection consisting of two or more cells is a **range**. The cells in a range can be adjacent or nonadjacent. An **adjacent range** is a rectangular block of adjoining cells. A **nonadjacent range** is two or more selected cells or ranges that are not adjoining. In the example shown below, the shaded areas show valid adjacent and nonadjacent ranges.

A2:C4 adjacent range

A7:H7 adjacent range

A10:B12:C14 nonadjacent range

Additional Information

A colon is used to separate the beginning and ending cells of a range reference.

E1:E15 adjacent range

To complete the data for the Computer row, you want to copy the value in cell B13 to the system Clipboard and then copy the system Clipboard contents to the adjacent range of cells C13 through D13. To select an adjacent range, drag the mouse from one corner of the range to the other. If the range is large, it is often easier to select the range by clicking on the first cell of the range, then hold down ⇧Shift while clicking on the last cell of the range.

- **Move to B13.**

- **Click 🖻 Copy.**

- **Drag to select the range of cells C13:D13.**

Another Method

You can also hold down Shift and use the directional keys to select a range.

- **Click 🖺 Paste.**

Your screen should be similar to Figure 1.33

Figure 1.33

The destination range is highlighted and identified by a dark border surrounding the selected cells. The entry copied from cell B13 was pasted into the selected destination range. Also notice the AutoCalculate button in the status bar is now active. This button displays the sum of values in a selected range of cells. It can also display the average, count, minimum, or maximum values in a range by selecting the appropriate option from the button's shortcut menu.

Also, because this is the second consecutive copy you have performed in the workbook, the Office Clipboard task pane automatically opened. As items are copied, an entry representing the copied item is displayed in the

Clipboard gallery. The newest item appears at the top of the gallery. Each entry includes an icon representing the source Office program and a portion of copied text. Because the previous item you copied was cleared from the System Clipboard, only one item is displayed in the gallery. You can click an item in the gallery to paste it or use Paste All to paste all items in the gallery.

Using the Fill Handle

Next you will copy the January Lease expenses to cells C14 through D14 and Miscellaneous expenses to cells C15 through D15. You can copy both values at the same time across the row by first specifying a range as the source. Another way to copy is to drag the **fill handle**, the black box in the lower-right corner of the selection.

1 ● Drag to select cells B14:B15.

● Point to the fill handle and when the mouse pointer is a ✛, drag the mouse to extend the selection to cells C14:D15.

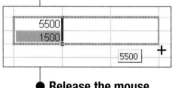

● Release the mouse button.

Another Method

The menu equivalent is Edit/Fill/Right or Ctrl + R.

Your screen should be similar to Figure 1.34

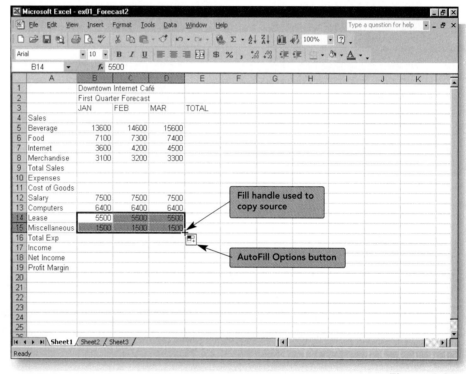

Figure 1.34

The range of cells to the right of the source is filled with the same value as in the source cell. The Fill command does not copy the source to the system Clipboard and therefore an item for the copied selection does not appear in the Office Clipboard task pane gallery. Because the Office Clipboard task pane is no longer needed, it closes automatically. Additionally, you cannot paste the source multiple times. The AutoFill Options button menu commands can be used to modify how the fill operation was performed.

Inserting Copied Cells

You also decide to include another row of month headings above the expense columns to make the worksheet data easier to read. To do this quickly, you can insert copied data between existing data. To indicate where to place the copied text, you move the cell pointer to the upper-left cell of the area where you want the selection inserted and specify the direction you want to shift the surrounding cells.

1 ● Copy the contents of cells A3:E3.

● Move to A10.

● Choose **I**nsert/Copied C**e**lls.

● If necessary, select Shift Cells Down from the Insert Paste dialog box.

Insert Paste

Insert
- ○ Shift cells **r**ight
- ◉ Shift cells **d**own

[OK] [Cancel]

● Click [OK] on the Task Pane to close it.

● Press (Esc) to clear the moving border.

Your screen should be similar to Figure 1.35

Additional Information

You can insert cut selections between existing cells by choosing Cut C**e**lls from the Insert menu.

Additional Information

Holding down (Ctrl) while dragging a selection copies it to the new location.

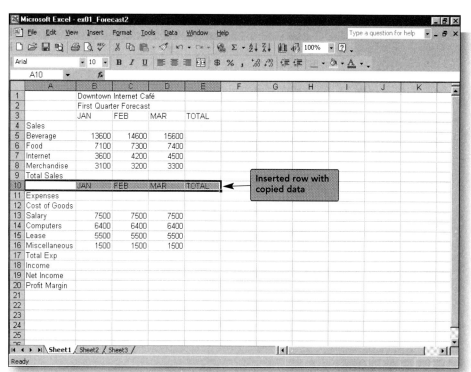

Figure 1.35

The copied data is inserted into the existing row (10) and all entries below are moved down one row.

Moving Entries

You also decide the profit margin row of data would stand out more if a blank row separated it from the net income row. You could remove the cell contents using Edit/Cut and then paste the contents from the system Clipboard into the new location. Alternatively, you can drag the cell border to move the cell contents. Dragging is quickest and most useful when the distance between cells is short and they are visible within the window, whereas Cut and Paste is best for long-distance moves.

1 ● Move to cell A20.

● Point to the border of the selection and when the mouse pointer shape is 🔺, drag the selection down one row to cell A21 and release the mouse button.

Additional Information

As you drag, an outline of the cell selection appears and the mouse pointer displays the cell reference to show its new location in the worksheet.

● Choose File/Save As and save the changes you have made to the workbook as Forecast3.

Your screen should be similar to Figure 1.36

Figure 1.36

The cell contents was moved into cell A21 and cleared from the original cell.

Review of Copying and Moving Methods

To review, you have learned three methods to copy or move an entry:

1. Use the Copy, Cut and Paste commands: Edit/Copy (Ctrl + C) or 📋, Edit/Cut (Ctrl + X) or ✂, and Edit/Paste (Ctrl + V) or 📋.

2. Use the Edit/Fill command: Right, Left, Up, or Down or drag the fill handle.

3. Drag the cell border of the selection to move. Hold down Ctrl while dragging a selection to copy.

When you use the Copy and Cut commands, the contents are copied to the system Clipboard and can be copied to any location in the worksheet, another workbook, or another application multiple times. When you use Edit/Fill or drag the fill handle, the destination must be in the same row or column as the source, and the source is not copied to the system Clipboard. Dragging the cell border to move or copy also does not copy the source to the system Clipboard.

Working with Formulas

The remaining entries that need to be made in the worksheet are formula entries.

concept 7

Formulas

7 A formula is an equation that performs a calculation on data contained in a worksheet. A formula always begins with an equal sign (=) and uses the following arithmetic **operators** to specify the type of numeric operation to perform: + (addition), – (subtraction), / (division), * (multiplication), % (percent), ^ (exponentiation).

In a formula that contains more than one operator, Excel calculates the formula from left to right and performs the calculation in the following order: percent, exponentiation, multiplication and division, and addition and subtraction (see Example A). If a formula contains operators with the same precedence (for example, addition and subtraction), they are again evaluated from left to right. The order of precedence can be overridden by enclosing the operation you want performed first in parentheses (see Example B). When there are multiple sets of parentheses, Excel evaluates them working from the innermost set of parentheses out.

| Example A: | =5*4–3 | Result is 17 (5 times 4 to get 20, and then subtract 3 for a total of 17) |
| Example B: | =5*(4–3) | Result is 5 (4 minus 3 to get 1, and then 1 times 5 for a total of 5) |

The values on which a numeric formula performs a calculation are called **operands**. Numbers or cell references can be operands in a formula. Usually cell references are used, and when the numeric entries in the referenced cell(s) change, the result of the formula is automatically recalculated.

Entering Formulas

The first formula you will enter will calculate the total Beverage sales for January through March (cell E5) by summing the numbers in cells B5 through D5. You will use cell references in the formula as the operands and the + arithmetic operator to specify addition. A formula is entered in the cell where you want the calculated value to be displayed. As you enter the formula, to help you keep track of the cell references Excel identifies the referenced cell by adding a color to the cell border and using the same color for the cell reference in the formula.

① ● Move to E5.

● Type =b5+c5+d5.

● Press [Ctrl] + [←Enter] or click ☑.

Your screen should be similar to Figure 1.37

Figure 1.37

The number 43800 is displayed in cell E5 and the formula that calculates this value is displayed in the formula bar.

Copying Formulas

The formulas to calculate the total sales for rows 5 through 8 can be entered next. Just as you can with text and numeric entries, you can copy formulas from one cell to another.

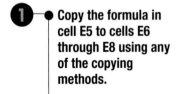

① ● Copy the formula in cell E5 to cells E6 through E8 using any of the copying methods.

● Move to E6.

Your screen should be similar to Figure 1.38

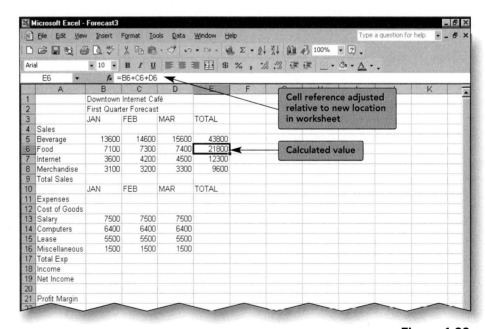

Figure 1.38

The calculated result, 21800 is displayed in the cell. The formula displayed in the formula bar is =B6+C6+D6. The formula to calculate the Food total sales is not an exact duplicate of the formula used to calculate the Beverage total sales (=B5+C5+D5). Instead, the cells referenced in the formula have been changed to reflect the new location of the formula in row 6. This is because the references in the formula are relative references.

concept 8

Relative Reference

8 A **relative reference** is a cell or range reference in a formula whose location is interpreted by Excel in relation to the position of the cell that contains the formula. When a formula is copied, the referenced cells in the formula automatically adjust to reflect the new worksheet location. The relative relationship between the referenced cell and the new location is maintained. Because relative references automatically adjust for the new location, the relative references in a copied formula refer to different cells than the references in the original formula. The relationship between cells in both the copied and pasted formula is the same although the cell references are different.

For example, in the figure here, cell A1 references the value in cell A4 (in this case, 10). If the formula in A1 is copied to B2, the reference for B2 is adjusted to the value in cell B5 (in this case, 20).

2 ● Move to cell E7 and then to cell E8.

Your screen should be similar to Figure 1.39

Additional Information
If you move cells containing formulas, the formulas are not adjusted relative to their new worksheet location.

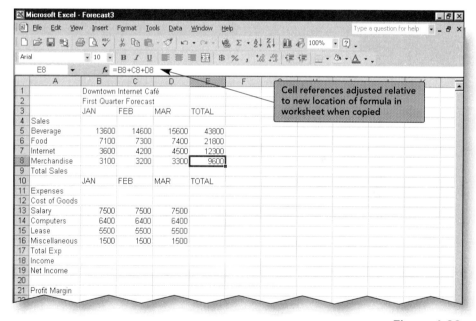

Figure 1.39

The formulas in these cells have also changed to reflect the new row location and to appropriately calculate the total based on the sales.

Entering Functions

Next you will calculate the monthly total sales. The formula to calculate the total sales for January needs to be entered in cell B9 and copied across the row. You could use a formula similar to the formula used to calculate the category sales in column E. The formula would be =B5+B6+B7+B8. However, it is faster and more accurate to use a function.

concept 9

Functions

1 **Functions** are prewritten formulas that perform certain types of calculations automatically. The **syntax** or rules of structure for entering all functions is:

=function name (argument1, argument2,...)

The function name identifies the type of calculation to be performed. Most functions require that you enter one or more arguments following the function name. An **argument** is the data the function uses to perform the calculation. The type of data the function requires depends upon the type of calculation being performed. Most commonly, the argument consists of numbers or references to cells that contain numbers. The argument is enclosed in parentheses, and commas separate multiple arguments. If a function starts the formula, enter an equal sign before the function name (=SUM(D5:F5)/25).

Additional Information

Use Help for detailed explanations of every function.

Excel includes several hundred functions divided into nine categories. Some common functions and the results they calculate are shown in the following table.

Category	Function	Calculates
Financial	PMT	Calculates the payment for a loan based on constant payments and a constant interest rate
	PV	Returns the present value of an investment; the total amount that a series of future payments is worth now
Time & Date	TODAY	Returns the serial number that represents today's date
	DATE	Returns the serial number of a particular date
	NOW	Returns the serial number of the current date and time
Math & Trig	SUM	Adds all the numbers in a range of cells
	ABS	Returns the absolute value of a number, a number without its sign
Statistical	AVERAGE	Returns the average (arithmetic mean) of its arguments
	MAX	Returns the largest value in a set of values; ignores logical values and text
Lookup & Reference	COLUMNS	Returns the number of columns in an array or reference
	CHOOSE	Chooses a value or action to perform from a list of values, based on an index number

Category	Function	Calculates
Database	DSUM	Adds the numbers in the field (column) or records in the database that match the conditions you specify
	DAVERAGE	Averages the values in a column in a list or database that match conditions you specify
Text	DOLLAR	Converts a number to text, using currency format
	UPPER	Converts text to uppercase
Logical	IF	Returns one value if a condition you specify evaluates to True and another value if it evaluates to False
	AND	Returns True if all its arguments are True; returns False if any arguments are False
Information	ISLOGICAL	Returns True if value is a logical value, either True or False
	ISREF	Returns True if value is a reference

You will use the SUM function to calculate the total sales for January. Because the SUM function is the most commonly used function, it has its own toolbar button.

● Move to **B9**.

● Click Σ **AutoSum**.

Another Method

Pressing Alt + = is the keyboard shortcut for AutoSum.

Your screen should be similar to Figure 1.40

Figure 1.40

Additional Information

The AutoSum button can also calculate a grand total if your worksheet contains subtotals. Select a cell below or to the right of a cell that contains a subtotal and then click Σ AutoSum.

Excel automatically proposes a range based upon the data above or to the left of the active cell. The name of the function followed by the range argument enclosed in parentheses is displayed in the formula bar. To accept the proposed range and enter the function,

2 ● Click ☑ Enter.

Your screen should be similar to Figure 1.41

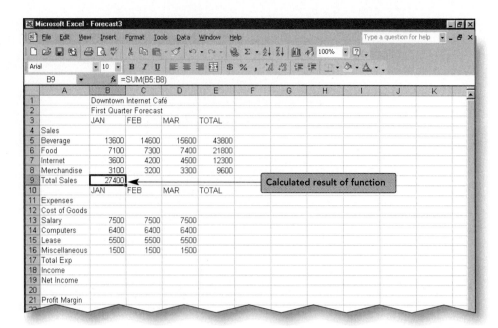

Figure 1.41

The result, 27400, calculated by the SUM function is displayed in cell B9. Next you need to calculate the total sales for February and March and the Total column.

3 ● Copy the function from cell B9 to cells C9 through E9.

● Move to C9.

Your screen should be similar to Figure 1.42

Figure 1.42

The result calculated by the function, 29300, is displayed in cell C9 and the copied function is displayed in the formula bar. The range reference in the function adjusted relative to its new cell location because it is a relative reference.

Using Pointing to Enter a Formula

Next you will enter the formula to calculate the cost of goods sold. These numbers are estimated by using a formula to calculate the number as a percent of sales. As a general rule, the Café calculates beverage expenses at 25 percent of beverage sales and food expenses at 50 percent of food sales.

Rather than typing in the cell references for the formula, you will enter them by selecting the worksheet cells. In addition, to make the process of entering and copying entries even easier, you can enter data into the first cell of a range and have it copied to all other cells in the range at the same time by using Ctrl + ←Enter to complete the entry. You will use this feature to enter the formulas to calculate the beverage expenses for January through March. This formula needs to first calculate the beverage cost of goods at 25 percent and add it to the food cost of goods calculated at 50 percent.

1 ● **Select B12:D12.**

● **Type =.**

● **Click cell B5.**

Additional Information
Even when a range is selected, you can still point to specify cells in the formula. You can also use the direction keys to move to the cell.

Your screen should be similar to Figure 1.43

Mode indicator

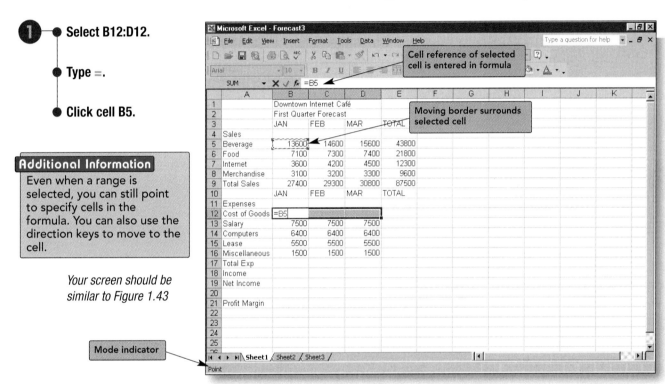

Figure 1.43

Notice that the status bar displays the current mode as Point. This tells you the program is allowing you to select cells by highlighting them. The cell reference, B5, is entered following the = sign. You will complete the formula by entering the percentage value to multiply by and adding the Food percentage to the formula.

2
- Type ***25%**.
- Type **+**.
- Click on **B6**.
- Type ***50%**.
- Press Ctrl + ←Enter.

Your screen should be similar to Figure 1.44

Figure 1.44

The formula to calculate the January cost of goods expense was entered in cell B12 and copied to all cells of the selected range. You can now calculate the total expenses in row 17 and column E. To do this quickly, you will pre-select the range and use the Σ AutoSum button. Then you will enter the formula to calculate the net income. Net income is calculated by subtracting total expenses from total sales.

Additional Information
The cells in the selected range can be adjacent or nonadjacent.

3
- Select **B12 through E17**.
- Click Σ **AutoSum**.
- In a similar manner, enter sum functions to calculate the expenses in column E.
- Select **B19 through E19**.
- Enter the formula **=B9–B17**.
- Press Ctrl + ←Enter.

Your screen should be similar to Figure 1.45

Figure 1.45

The formula is quickly entered into all cells of the range. The final formula you need enter is to calculate the profit margin.

4 ● **Select B21 through E21.**

● **Enter the formula =B19/B9.**

● **Press** Ctrl + ←Enter.

Your screen should be similar to Figure 1.46

Figure 1.46

The profit margins are calculated and displayed in cells B20 through E20.

Recalculating the Worksheet

Now that you have created the worksheet structure and entered some sample data for the forecasted sales for the first quarter, you want to test the formulas to verify they are operating correctly. A simple way to do this is to use a calculator to verify that the correct result is displayed. You can then further test the worksheet by changing values and verifying that all cells containing formulas that reference the value are appropriately recalculated.

After considering the sales estimates for the three months, you decide that the estimated Internet sales for January are too low and you want to increase this number from 3600 to 4000.

1 ● **Change the entry in cell B7 to 4000.**

Your screen should be similar to Figure 1.47

Figure 1.47

The Internet total in cell E7 has been automatically recalculated. The number displayed is now 12700. Likewise, the January total in cell B9 and the grand total in cell E9 have increased by 400 to reflect the change in cell B7.

concept 10

Recalculation

10 Whenever a number in a referenced cell in a formula changes, Excel automatically **recalculates** all formulas that are dependent on the changed value. Because only those formulas directly affected by a change in the data are recalculated, the time it takes to recalculate the workbook is reduced. Without this feature, in large worksheets it could take several minutes to recalculate all formulas each time a number is changed in the worksheet. Recalculation is one of the most powerful features of electronic worksheets.

The formulas in the worksheet are correctly calculating the desired result. The Sales portion of the worksheet is now complete.

Inserting Rows

Finally, you realize you forgot to include a row for the Advertising expenses. To add this data, you will insert a blank row below the Lease row. To indicate where you want to insert a single blank row, move the cell pointer to the row immediately below the row where you want the new row inserted. If you want to insert multiple rows, select a range of rows and Excel inserts the same number of rows you selected in the range.

Additional Information

To delete a row or column, move to it and choose **E**dit/**D**elete/Entire **R**ow or Entire **C**olumn.

1
● Move to A15.

● Choose **I**nsert/**R**ows.

● Enter the label **Advertising** in cell A15 and the value **1000** in cells B15 through D15.

● Copy the function from cell E14 to E15 to calculate the Total Advertising expense.

● Move to cell B18.

● Click 🖫 Save to save the worksheet using the same file name.

Your screen should be similar to Figure 1.48

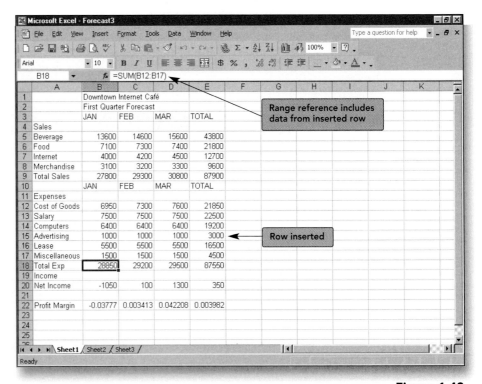

Figure 1.48

Formatting toolbar	Keyboard	Action
≣	Ctrl + L	Left align entry
≣	Ctrl + C	Center entry
≣	Ctrl + J	Right align entry

You can quickly align a range of cells by selecting the range and then using the command or button. A quick way to select a range of filled cells is to hold down ⇧Shift and double-click on the edge of the active cell in the direction in which you want the range expanded. For example, to select the range to the right of the active cell, you would double-click the right border. You will use this method to select and right-align the remaining column entries.

Additional Information

If you do not hold down ⇧Shift while double-clicking on a border, the cell selector moves to the last-used cell in the direction indicated.

3 ● **Move to cell C3.**

● **Hold down ⇧Shift and double-click the right cell border of cell C3.**

HAVING TROUBLE?

The mouse pointer must be ⇱ when you click the cell border.

● **Click ≣ Align Right.**

● **In a similar manner, right align the entries in row 10.**

Your screen should be similar to Figure 1.51

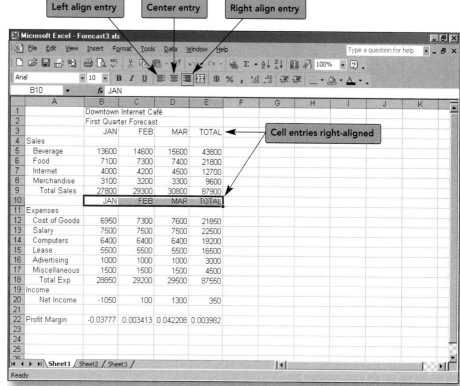

Figure 1.51

The entries in the selected range are right-aligned in their cell spaces.

Indenting Entries

Next you would like to indent the row headings in cells A5 through A8 and A12 through A17 from the left edge of the cell. You want to indent the headings in both ranges at the same time. To select nonadjacent cells or cell ranges, after selecting the first cell or range hold down Ctrl while selecting each additional cell or range. You will select the cells and indent their contents.

Additional Information

You can also select entire nonadjacent rows or columns by holding down Ctrl while selecting the rows or columns.

1 ● **Select A5 through A8.**

● **Hold down** Ctrl.

● **Select A12 through A17.**

● **Release** Ctrl.

● **Click** ⬚ **Increase Indent.**

Another Method

The menu equivalent is Format/Cells/Alignment/ Horizontal/Left(Indent)/1.

Your screen should be similar to Figure 1.52

Figure 1.52

Each entry in the selected range is indented two spaces from the left edge of the cell. You would also like to indent the Total Sales, Total Exp, and Net Income headings four spaces.

2 ● **Select A9, A18, and A20.**

● **Click** ⬚ **Increase Indent twice.**

Your screen should be similar to Figure 1.53

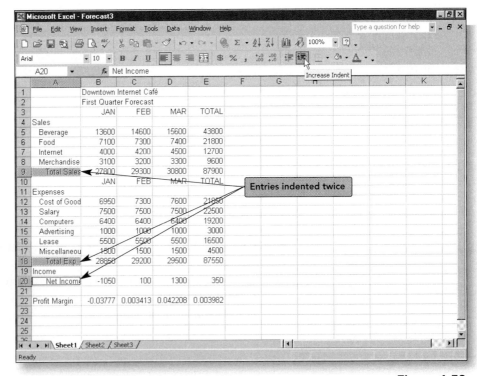

Figure 1.53

Centering across a Selection

Next you want to center the worksheet titles across columns A through E so they are centered over the worksheet data.

1 ● **Select A1 through E1.**

● **Click ☷ Merge and Center.**

Another Method

The menu equivalent is Format/Cells/Alignment/Horizontal/Center Across Selection/Merge cells.

Your screen should be similar to Figure 1.54

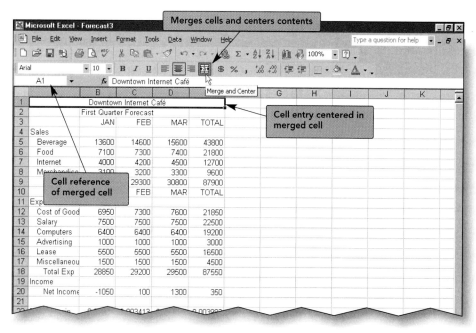

Figure 1.54

Another Method

You could also use Format/Cells/Alignment/Horizontal/Center Across Selection to center the contents across a range. The cells however, are not merged and the cell contents to be centered must be in the leftmost cell of the selected range.

The contents of the range are centered in the range. Additionally, the five cells in the selection have been combined into a single large **merged cell**. The cell reference for a merged cell is the upper-left cell in the original selected range, in this case A1. When creating a merged cell and centering the contents, only the contents of the upper-leftmost data in the selected range are centered. If other cells in the range contained data, it would be deleted.

2 ● **Center and merge the second title line.**

Your screen should be similar to Figure 1.55

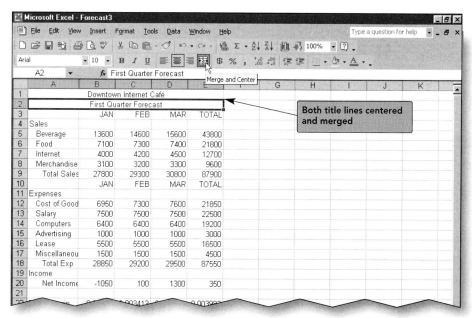

Figure 1.55

Once cells have been merged, you can split them back into their original cells by selecting the merged cell and clicking ☷ to unmerge the cells.

Changing Fonts and Font Styles

Finally, you want to improve the worksheet appearance by enhancing the appearance of the title. One way to do this is to change the font and font size used in the title.

concept 12

Fonts

12 A **font**, also commonly referred to as a **typeface**, is a set of characters with a specific design. The designs have names such as Times New Roman and Courier. Using fonts as a design element can add interest to your document and give readers visual cues to help them find information quickly.

There are two basic types of fonts, serif and sans serif. **Serif** fonts have a flair at the base of each letter that visually leads the reader to the next letter. Two common serif fonts are Roman and Times New Roman. Serif fonts generally are used in paragraphs. **Sans serif** fonts do not have a flair at the base of each letter. Arial and

Helvetica are two common sans serif fonts. Because sans serif fonts have a clean look, they are often used for headings in documents. It is good practice to use only two types of fonts in a document, one for text and one for headings. Too many styles can make your document look cluttered and unprofessional.

Each font has one or more sizes. **Size** is the height and width of the character and is commonly measured in **points**, abbreviated pt. One point equals about 1/72 inch, and text in most documents is 10 pt or 12 pt.

Here are several examples of the same text in various fonts and sizes.

Typeface	Font Size (12 pt/18 pt)
Arial (Sans Serif)	This is 12 pt. This is 18 pt.
Courier New (Serif)	This is 12 pt. This is 18 pt.
Times New Roman (Serif)	This is 12 pt. This is 18 pt.

1 ● **Select A1 and A2.**

● **Open the** [Times New Roman ▼] **Font drop-down list box.**

Another Method

The menu equivalent is Format/Cells/Font/Font.

Your screen should be similar to Figure 1.56

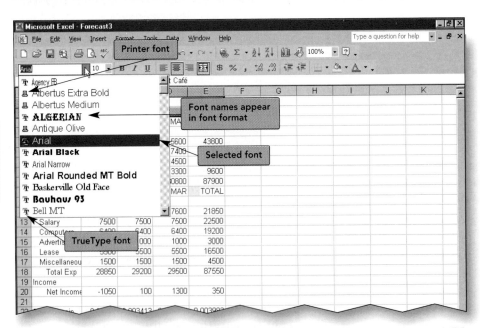

Figure 1.56

The Font drop-down menu displays examples of the available fonts on your system in alphabetical order. The default worksheet font, Arial, is highlighted. Notice the TT preceding the font name. This indicates the font is a TrueType font. TrueType fonts appear onscreen as they will appear when printed. They are installed when Windows is installed. Fonts that are preceded with a blank space or 🖺 are printer fonts. These fonts are supported by your printer and are displayed as closely as possible to how they will appear onscreen, but may not match exactly when printed.

2 ● **Scroll the list and select Times New Roman.**

Your screen should be similar to Figure 1.57

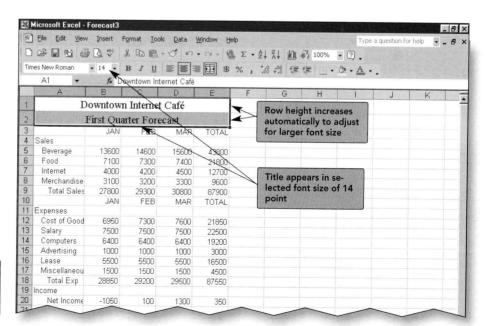

Figure 1.57

The title appears in the selected typeface and the Font button displays the name of the font in the active cell. Next you will increase the font size to 14.

3 ● **Open the [10 ▾] Font Size drop-down list box.**

● **Click 14.**

Another Method

The menu equivalent is Format/Cells/Font/Size.

Your screen should be similar to Figure 1.58

Figure 1.58

Notice that the height of the row has increased to accommodate the larger font size of the heading.

Applying Character Effects

In addition to changing font and font size, you can apply different **character effects** to enhance the appearance of text. The table below describes some of the effects and their uses.

Format	Example	Use
Bold	**Bold**	Adds emphasis
Italic	*Italic*	Adds emphasis
Underline	<u>Underline</u>	Adds emphasis
Strikethrough	~~Strikethrough~~	Indicates words to be deleted
Superscript	"To be or not to be."[1]	Used in footnotes and formulas
Subscript	H_2O	Used in formulas
Color	**Color Color** Color	Adds interest

You want to add bold, italic, and underlines to several worksheet entries. First you will bold the two title lines that are already selected.

1 — ● Click **Bold.**

Another Method

The menu equivalent is Format/Cells/Font/Font Style/Bold and the keyboard shortcut is Ctrl + B.

Your screen should be similar to Figure 1.59

Figure 1.59

Next you would like to bold, underline, and italicize some of the other entries in the worksheet.

2 ● Select B3 through E3.

● Click **B** Bold.

● Click **U** Underline.

● Bold and italicize the entries in cells A5 through A8.

Another Method

The menu equivalent for underline is F**o**rmat/C**e**lls/Font/**U**nderline/Single or Ctrl + U and for italic is F**o**rmat/C**e**lls/Font/F**o**nt Style/Italic or Ctrl + I.

Your screen should be similar to Figure 1.60

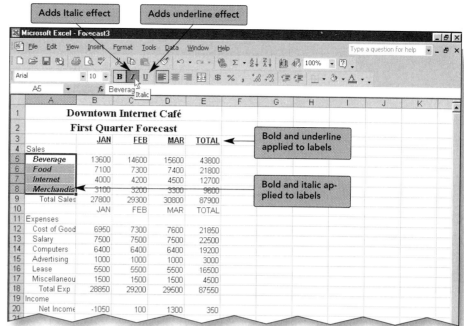

Figure 1.60

Using Undo

Sometimes formatting changes you make do not have the expected result. In this case, you feel that the sales category names would look better without the formatting. To quickly undo the last two actions you performed,

1 ● Open the 🔄 Undo drop-down list.

● Move the mouse pointer down the list to highlight the Italic and Bold actions.

Another Method

The menu equivalent is **E**dit/**U**ndo or Ctrl + Z. You can also click 🔄 repeatedly to undo the actions in the list one by one.

Your screen should be similar to Figure 1.61

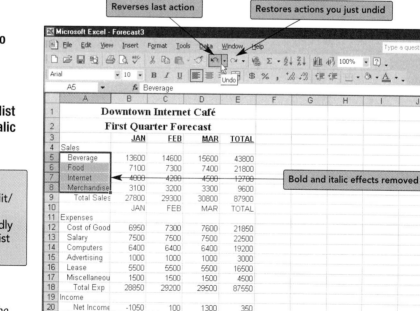

Figure 1.61

Additional Information

The menu equivalent is **E**dit/**R**edo or Ctrl + Y.

The two actions you selected are undone. Undo reverses the selected actions regardless of the current cell pointer location. If you change your mind after you Undo an action, the 🔄 Redo button is available so that you can restore the action you just undid.

Using Format Painter

You do think, however, that the Total Sales, Total Exp, and Net Income labels would look good in bold. You will bold the entry in cell A9 and then copy the format from A9 to the other cells using Format Painter. This feature applies the formats associated with the current selection to new selections. To turn on the feature, move the insertion point to the cell whose formats you want to copy and click the 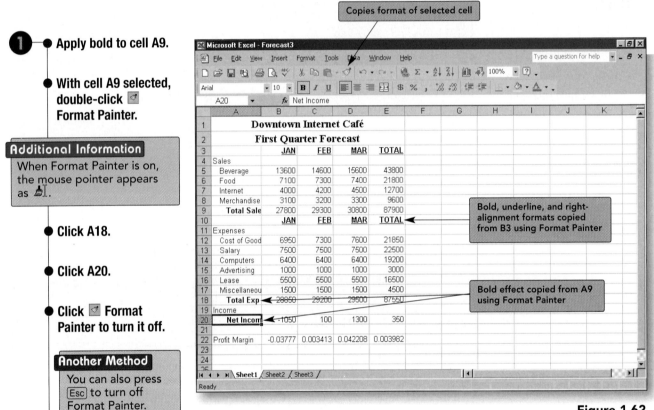 Format Painter button. Then you select the cell you want the formats applied to. The format is automatically applied to an entire cell contents simply by clicking on the cell. If you double-click the 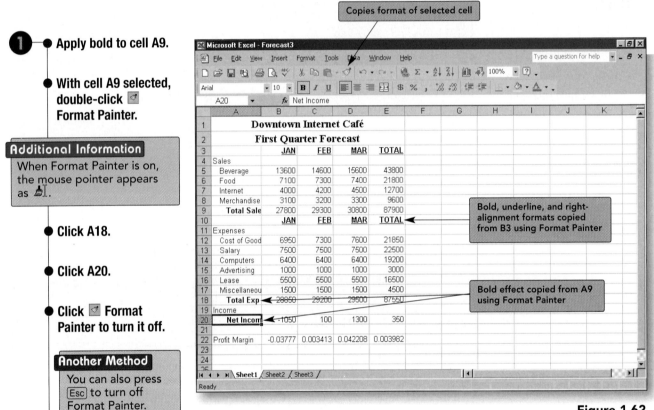 Format Painter button, you can apply the format multiple times. You will also format the labels in row 10.

① ● Apply bold to cell A9.

● With cell A9 selected, double-click ⬧ Format Painter.

Additional Information

When Format Painter is on, the mouse pointer appears as 🖌️.

● Click A18.

● Click A20.

● Click ⬧ Format Painter to turn it off.

Another Method

You can also press [Esc] to turn off Format Painter.

● Use Format Painter to copy the format from cell B3 to cells B10 through E10.

Your screen should be similar to Figure 1.62

Copies format of selected cell

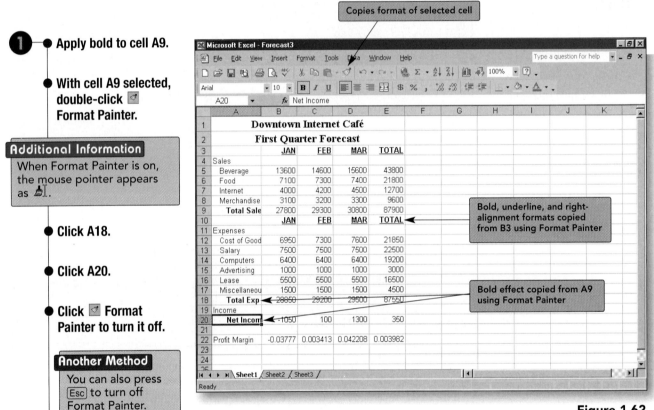

Figure 1.62

The formatting was quickly added to each cell as it was selected.

Formatting Numbers

You also want to improve the appearance of the numbers in the worksheet by changing their format.

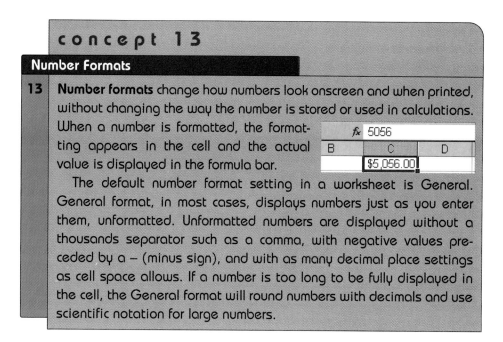

concept 13

Number Formats

13 **Number formats** change how numbers look onscreen and when printed, without changing the way the number is stored or used in calculations. When a number is formatted, the formatting appears in the cell and the actual value is displayed in the formula bar.

The default number format setting in a worksheet is General. General format, in most cases, displays numbers just as you enter them, unformatted. Unformatted numbers are displayed without a thousands separator such as a comma, with negative values preceded by a – (minus sign), and with as many decimal place settings as cell space allows. If a number is too long to be fully displayed in the cell, the General format will round numbers with decimals and use scientific notation for large numbers.

First you will change the number format of cells B5 through E8 to display dollar signs, commas, and decimal places.

1 ● **Select cells B5 through E9.**

● **Choose F*o*rmat/C*e*lls.**

> **Another Method**
> The keyboard shortcut is Ctrl + 1.

● **If necessary, open the Number tab.**

● **From the Category list box, select Currency.**

Your screen should be similar to Figure 1.63

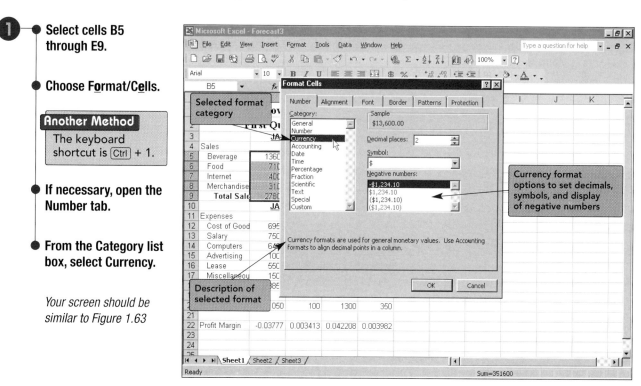

Figure 1.63

The Currency category includes options that allow you to specify the number of decimal places, how negative numbers will appear, and whether a currency symbol such as a dollar sign will be displayed.

2 Click [OK] to use the default Currency format settings.

Your screen should be similar to Figure 1.64

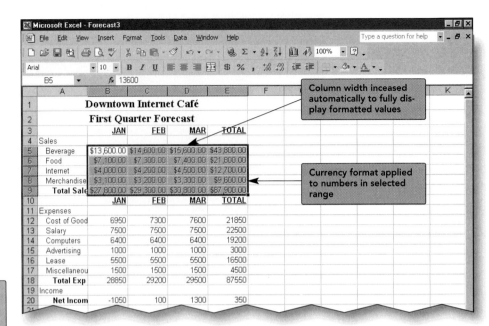

Figure 1.64

The number entries in the selected range appear with a currency symbol, comma, and two decimal places. The column widths increased automatically to fully display the formatted values.

A second format category that displays numbers as currency is Accounting. You will try this format next on the same range. Additionally, you will specify zero as the number of decimal places since all the values are whole values.

Additional Information

Excel will also automatically apply a format to a cell based on the symbols you use when entering the number. For example, entering 10,000 in a cell formats the cell to Comma format and entering $102.20 formats the cell to Currency with two decimal places.

3 Choose Format/Cells/Accounting.

● Reduce the decimal places to 0.

● Click [OK].

Your screen should be similar to Figure 1.65

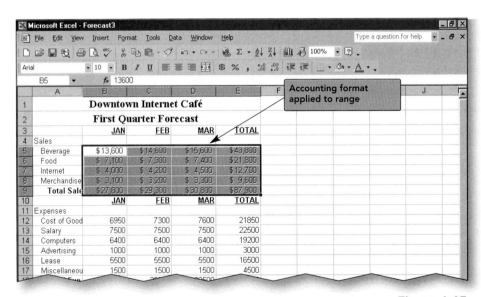

Figure 1.65

The numbers now appear in Accounting format. The primary difference between the Accounting and the Currency formats is that the Accounting format aligns numbers at the decimal place and places the dollar sign in a column at the left edge of the cell space. In addition, it does not allow you to select different ways of displaying negative numbers but displays them in black in parentheses. You decide the Accounting format will make it easier to read the numbers in a column.

Using Styles

You want to apply the same format to the expense range of cells. Another way to apply number formats is to select a predefined format style.

concept 14

Styles

14 A **style** consists of a combination of formats that have been named and that can be quickly applied to a selection. Excel includes six predefined styles, or you can create your own custom styles. Normal is the default style used in the Book template. It sets the number format to General and controls other format settings that are applied to all entries, including font type, font size, alignment, and indentation.

Examples of the six predefined styles are shown on the right. Notice the two Currency styles. They will display dollar signs, commas, and two or zero decimal places, just as if you had selected these formats from the Format Cells dialog box.

Style	Example
Normal	89522
Comma	89,522.00
Comma [0]	89,522
Currency	$ 89,522.00
Currency [0]	$ 89,522
Percent	89.52200%

1 ● **Drag to select the range B12 through E20.**

● **Choose Format/Style.**

Your screen should be similar to Figure 1.66

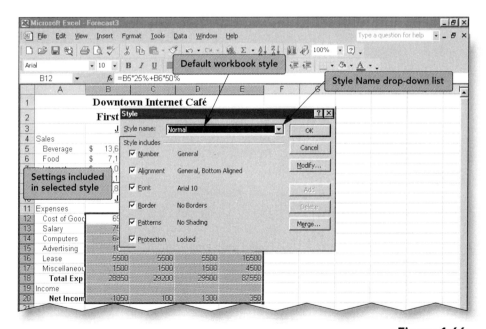

Figure 1.66

The Style dialog box displays the name of the default workbook style, Normal, in the Style Name list box. The check boxes in the Style Includes area of the dialog box show the options that are included in this style and a description or sample. You want to use the Currency $ style.

2 ● **Open the Style Name drop-down list box.**

● **Select Currency $.**

● **Click** OK .

Additional Information

Using $ Currency Style on the Formatting toolbar applies the Accounting number format with two decimal places.

Your screen should be similar to Figure 1.67

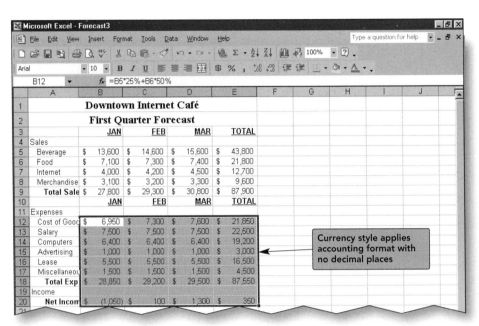

Currency style applies accounting format with no decimal places

Figure 1.67

The Currency $ style applies the Accounting number format with zero decimal places.

Finally, you want the Profit Margin values to be displayed as percentages with two decimal places.

3 ● **Select B22 through E22.**

● **Click % Percent Style.**

Another Method

The menu equivalent is Format/Style/Percent.

● **Click Increase decimal twice.**

Another Method

You could also use Format/Cells/Percentage/Decimal Places/2.

Your screen should be similar to Figure 1.68

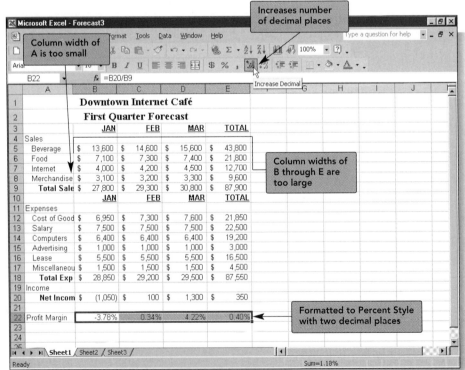

Increases number of decimal places

Column width of A is too small

Column widths of B through E are too large

Formatted to Percent Style with two decimal places

Figure 1.68

Now that the numbers are displayed as a percentage and the number of decimal places has been decreased, the column widths are larger than they need to be. Because Excel does not automatically reduce column widths, you need to make this change yourself. Additionally, you want column A to fully display the row headings. You will use the AutoFit feature to adjust the column widths for all cells in columns A through E.

4 ● Click the A column letter and drag to the right to expand the selection to include column E.

● Double-click any column border line in the selection to AutoFit the selection.

Additional Information

You could also press Ctrl + A or click the button at the intersection of the row numbers and column letters to select the entire worksheet and then double-click on any border line to AutoFit the column width of all columns containing entries.

Your screen should be similar to Figure 1.69

Figure 1.69

The width of columns B through E automatically decreased to the minimum column width needed to fully display the entries. The width of column A increased to accommodate the longest entry.

Adding Color

The last formatting change you would like to make to the worksheet is to add color to the text and to the background of selected cells. First you will change the color of the text.

1 Select A1 through A2.

● Open the Font Color palette.

● Select a color of your choice.

Your screen should be similar to Figure 1.70

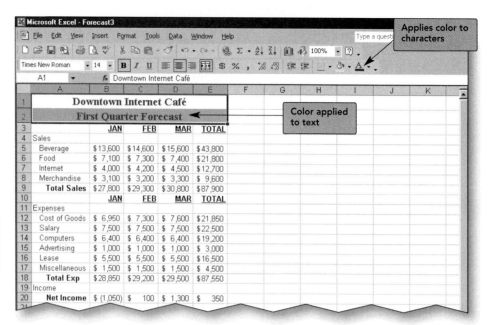

Figure 1.70

The selected color appears in the button and can be applied again simply by clicking the button. Next you will change the cell background color, also called the fill color.

2 Open the Fill Color palette.

● Select a color of your choice.

● Apply the same font color, fill color, and bold to cell A4.

● Use Format Painter to quickly copy the format from cell A4 to cells A11, A19, and A22.

● Apply the same fill color to B4 through E4, B11 through E11, B19 through E19, and B22 through E22.

Your screen should be similar to Figure 1.71

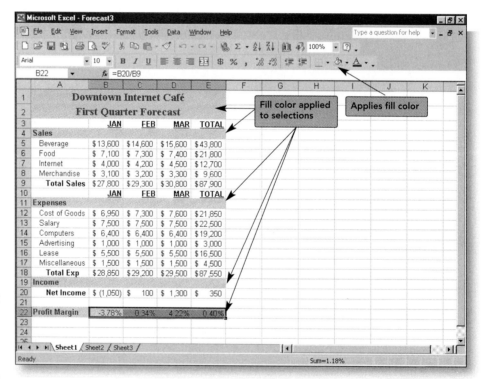

Figure 1.71

Working with Graphics

Finally you want to add a graphic to add interest. A ClipArt image is one of several different graphic objects that can be added to an Excel document.

concept 15

Graphics

15 A **graphic** is a non-text element or object, such as a drawing or picture that can be added to a workbook. An **object** is an item that can be sized, moved, and manipulated. A graphic can be a simple drawing object consisting of shapes such as lines and boxes that can be created using features on the Drawing toolbar. A **drawing object** is part of the Excel workbook. A **picture** is an illustration such as a scanned photograph. They are graphics that were created from another program. Pictures are inserted as embedded objects. An **embedded object** becomes part of the Excel workbook and can be opened and edited using the source program, the program in which it was created.

Inserting Graphics

You want to insert a graphic to the right of the data in the worksheet. Graphic files can be obtained from a variety of sources. Many simple drawings called **clip art** are available in the Clip Organizer that comes with Office XP. You can also create graphic files using a scanner to convert any printed document, including photographs, to an electronic format. Most images that are scanned are stored as Windows bitmap files (.bmp). All types of graphics, including clip art, photographs, and other types of images, can be found on the Internet. These files are commonly stored as .jpg or .pcx files. Keep in mind that any images you locate on the Internet may be copyrighted and should only be used with permission. You can also purchase CDs containing graphics for your use.

You decide to use the Clip Organizer to find a suitable graphic.

Move to F3.

Choose Insert/Picture/Clip Art.

Your screen should be similar to Figure 1.72

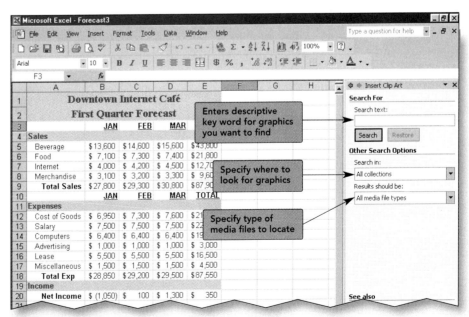

Figure 1.72

The Insert Clip Art task pane appears in which you can enter a key word, a word or phrase that is descriptive of the type of graphic you want to locate. The graphics in the Clip Organizer are organized by topic and are identified with several keywords that describe the graphic. You can also specify the locations to search and the type of media files, such as clip art, movies, photographs or sound, to display in the search results. You want to find clip art and photographs of computers.

2 ● In the Search Text box, type **computer**.

● Open the Results Should Be drop-down list.

● Select Photographs and Clip Art.

● Deselect all other options and click outside the drop-down list to close it.

HAVING TROUBLE?

Make sure all other options are deselected. If there is a checkmark next to an item, click the checkmark to deselect that item.

● Click [Search].

Your screen should be similar to Figure 1.73

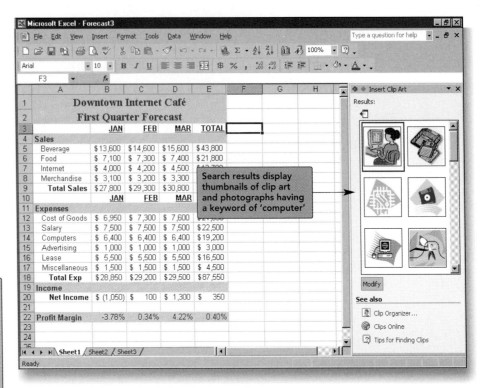

Search results display thumbnails of clip art and photographs having a keyword of 'computer'

Figure 1.73

The Clip Organizer displays **thumbnails**, miniature images, of all clip art and photographs that are identified with the keyword "computer." You want to use a graphic showing people and a computer.

3 ● Scroll the list and point to the thumbnail of the computer and two people (see Figure 1.74).

● Click on the thumbnail to insert it.

● Click ☒ in the task pane title bar to close it.

HAVING TROUBLE?
If this graphic is not available in the Clip Organizer, choose Insert/Picture/From File and select Internet.wmf from your data file location.

Another Method
You could also choose Insert from the graphics shortcut menu to insert it in the worksheet.

Your screen should be similar to Figure 1.74

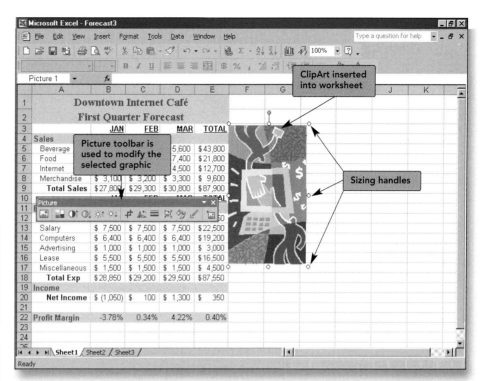

Figure 1.74

Sizing Graphics

The ClipArt image is inserted in the document at the current cell. Once a graphic object is inserted into the workbook, it can be manipulated in many ways. You can change its size, add borders or shading, or move it to another location including in the margin, in headers and footers, or on top of or below other objects. It cannot, however, be placed behind the worksheet data.

You want to reduce the size of the graphic and move it to the top row of the worksheet. The picture is surrounded by eight boxes, called **sizing handles**, indicating it is a selected object and can now be sized and moved anywhere in the document. The handles are used to size the object. A graphic object is moved by dragging it to the new location.

The Picture toolbar is also automatically displayed. Its buttons are used to modify the selected picture object. Your Picture toolbar may be floating or docked along an edge of the window, depending on where it was when last used.

Additional Information
A selected graphic object can be deleted by pressing Del.

HAVING TROUBLE?
If the Picture toolbar is not displayed, right-click on any toolbar to open the Shortcut menu and select Picture, or use View/Toolbars/Picture.

1 ● Point to the lower-right corner handle.

Additional Information
The mouse pointer changes to ↘ when you can drag to resize the graphic.

● Drag the mouse inward to reduce the size of the graphic until the bottom of the graphic is even with row 12.

Additional Information
Dragging a corner handle maintains the original proportions of the picture.

● Point to the graphic and drag upward to move the graphic to row 1 of columns F and G.

● Click outside the graphic to deselect it.

● Add the same background fill color as in the other areas of the worksheet to cells F1:G22.

Your screen should be similar to Figure 1.75

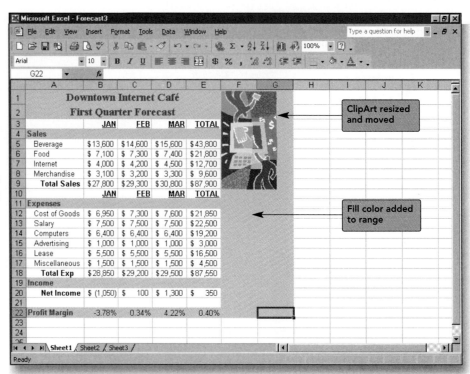

Figure 1.75

The three-month forecast is now complete.

Entering the Date

Now that the worksheet is complete, you want to include your name and the date in the worksheet as documentation.

1

- **Enter your first initial and last name in cell A24.**

- **Enter the current date in cell B24 in the format mm/dd/yy (for example, 10/10/02).**

- **Move to B24.**

- **Click ⊞ Save to save the worksheet changes.**

Another Method

You can quickly insert the current date using Ctrl + ;.

Your screen should be similar to Figure 1.76

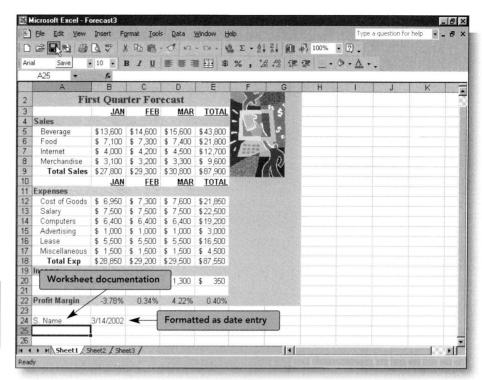

Figure 1.76

Additional Information

Dates, like other numeric entries, can be formatted to display in many different ways. Use Format/Cells/Number/**C**ategory/Date to change the date format.

Excel automatically recognized your entry as a date and formatted the entry using the short date format. If you had preceded the date entry with =, Excel would have interpreted it as a formula and a calculation of division would have been performed on the numbers.

Excel stores all dates as serial numbers with each day numbered from the beginning of the century; the date serial number 1 corresponds to the date January 1, 1900, and the integer 65380 is December 31, 2078. The integers are assigned consecutively beginning with 1 and ending with 65,380. They are called **date numbers**. Conversion of the date to a serial number allows dates to be used in calculations.

Previewing and Printing a Workbook

If you have printer capability, you can print a copy of the worksheet. To save time and unnecessary printing and paper waste, it is always a good idea to preview onscreen how the worksheet will appear when printed.

1 ● Click ⬛ **Print Preview.**

Another Method

The menu equivalent is File/Print Preview.

Your screen should be similar to Figure 1.77

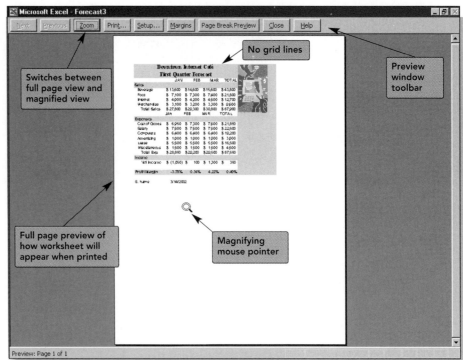

Figure 1.77

Additional Information

If you have a monochrome printer, the preview appears in shades of gray as it will appear when printed.

The print preview window displays the worksheet as it will appear on the printed page. Notice that the row and column lines are not displayed and will not print. The worksheet looks good and does not appear to need any further modifications immediately.

The preview window also includes its own toolbar. While previewing, you can change from full-page view to a magnified view using ⬛ Zoom or by clicking on the preview page.

2 ● Click the worksheet title.

Additional Information

The area you click on is the area that will display in the preview window.

Your screen should be similar to Figure 1.78

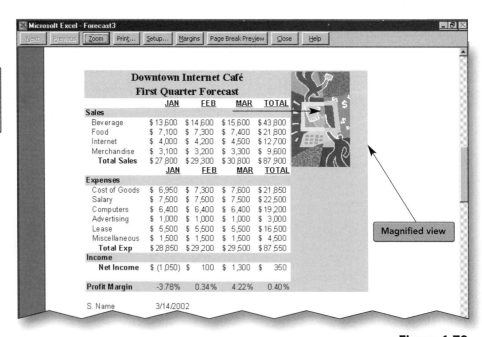

Figure 1.78

The worksheet is displayed in the actual size it will appear when printed. Now you are ready to print the worksheet.

3 ● **Click on the worksheet again to return to full-page view.**

● **Click** [Print...] **.**

Your screen should be similar to Figure 1.79

Another Method

You can also use File/Print or the keyboard shortcut Ctrl + P from the worksheet window. Clicking 🖨 Print on the Standard toolbar will send the workbook directly to the printer.

Figure 1.79

Note: Please consult your instructor for printing procedures that may differ from the following directions.

From the Print dialog box, you need to specify the printer you will be using and the document settings. The printer that is currently selected is displayed in the Name drop-down list box in the Printer section of the dialog box.

The Print Range area lets you specify how much of the worksheet you want printed. The range options are described in the following table:

Option	Action
All	Prints the entire worksheet
Pages	Prints pages you specify by typing page numbers in the text box
Selection	Prints selected range only
Active Sheet	Prints the active worksheet
Entire Workbook	Prints all worksheets in the workbook

The default settings of All and Active sheet are correct. In the Copies section, the default setting of one copy of the worksheet is acceptable.

4 ● If necessary, make sure your printer is on and ready to print.

● If you need to change the selected printer to another printer, open the Name drop-down list box and select the appropriate printer.

● Click [OK].

The printed copy should be similar to the document shown here.

Additional Information
If you do not have a color printer, the colors appear as shades of gray.

Downtown Internet Café								
First Quarter Forecast								
		JAN		**FEB**		**MAR**		**TOTAL**
Sales								
Beverage	$	13,600	$	14,600	$	15,600	$	43,800
Food	$	7,100	$	7,300	$	7,400	$	21,800
Internet	$	4,000	$	4,200	$	4,500	$	12,700
Merchandise	$	3,100	$	3,200	$	3,300	$	9,600
Total Sales	$	27,800	$	29,300	$	30,800	$	87,900
		JAN		FEB		MAR		TOTAL
Expenses								
Cost of Goods	$	6,950	$	7,300	$	7,600	$	21,850
Salary	$	7,500	$	7,500	$	7,500	$	22,500
Computers	$	6,400	$	6,400	$	6,400	$	19,200
Advertising	$	1,000	$	1,000	$	1,000	$	3,000
Lease	$	5,500	$	5,500	$	5,500	$	16,500
Miscellaneous	$	1,500	$	1,500	$	1,500	$	4,500
Total Exp	$	28,850	$	29,200	$	29,500	$	87,550
Income								
Net Income	$	(1,050)	$	100	$	1,300	$	350
Profit Margin		-3.78%		0.34%		4.22%		0.40%

S. Name   3/14/2002

Exiting Excel 2002

The Exit command in the File menu is used to quit the Excel program. Alternatively, you can click the ☒ Close button in the application window title bar. If you attempt to close the application without first saving the workbook, Excel displays a warning asking if you want to save your work. If you do not save your work and you exit the application, all changes you made from the last time you saved are lost.

1 ● **Move to cell A1.**

● **Click ☒ (in the application window title bar).**

● **Click** [Yes] **to resave the document.**

Additional Information
Excel saves the file with the cell selector in the same cell it is in when saved.

Template (EX1.12)

A template is a workbook file that includes predefined settings that can be used as a pattern to create many common types of workbooks.

Text and Numeric Entries (EX1.14)

The information or data you enter in a cell can be text, numbers, or formulas.

AutoCorrect (EX1.20)

The AutoCorrect feature makes some basic assumptions about the text you are typing and, based on these assumptions, automatically corrects the entry.

Column Width (EX1.24)

The size or width of a column controls how much information can be displayed in a cell.

Copy and Move (EX1.31)

The contents of worksheet cells can be duplicated (copied) or moved to other locations in the worksheet or between worksheets, saving you time by not having to retype the same information.

Range (EX1.34)

A selection consisting of two or more cells on a worksheet is a range.

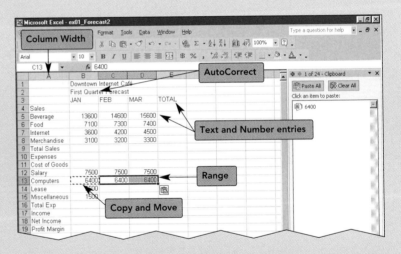

Formulas (EX1.39)

A formula is an equation that performs a calculation on data contained in a worksheet.

Relative Reference (EX1.41)

A relative reference is a cell or range reference in a formula whose location is interpreted by Excel in relation to the position of the cell that contains the formula.

Functions (EX1.42)

Functions are prewritten formulas that perform certain types of calculations automatically.

Recalculation (EX1.48)

Excel automatically recalculates formulas whenever a change occurs in a referenced cell.

Alignment (EX1.49)

Alignment settings allow you to change the horizontal and vertical placement and the orientation of an entry in a cell.

Fonts (EX1.54)

Fonts consist of typefaces, point sizes, and styles that can be applied to characters to improve their appearance.

Number Formats (EX1.59)

Number formats affect how numbers look onscreen and when printed.

Styles (EX1.61)

A style consists of a combination of formats that have been named and that can be quickly applied to a selection.

Graphics (EX1.65)

A graphic is a non-text element or object, such as a drawing or picture, that can be added to a document.

key terms

active cell   EX1.7

active sheet   EX1.8

adjacent range   EX1.34

alignment   EX1.17

argument   EX1.42

AutoCorrect   EX1.20

cell   EX1.7

cell selector   EX1.7

character effects   EX1.56

clip art   EX1.65

column   EX1.7

column letter   EX1.7

constant   EX1.14

copy area   EX1.31

date number   EX1.69

defaults   EX1.12

destination   EX1.31

drawing object   EX1.65

embedded object   EX1.65

fill handle   EX1.36

font   EX1.54

format   EX1.49

Formatting toolbar   EX1.5

formula   EX1.14

formula bar   EX1.5

functions   EX1.42

graphic   EX1.65

heading   EX1.15

merged cell   EX1.53

Name box   EX1.5

nonadjacent range   EX1.34

number   EX1.14

number formats   EX1.49

object   EX1.65

operand   EX1.39

operator   EX1.39

paste area   EX1.31

picture   EX1.65

point   EX1.54

range   EX1.34

reference   EX1.8

recalculate   EX1.48

relative reference   EX1.41

row   EX1.7

row number   EX1.7

sans serif   EX1.54

serif   EX1.54

sheet tab   EX1.8

size   EX1.54

sizing handle   EX1.67

source   EX1.31

spreadsheet   EX1.7

Standard toolbar   EX1.5

style   EX1.61

syntax   EX1.42

tab scroll button   EX1.8

task pane   EX1.5

template   EX1.12

text   EX1.14

thumbnail   EX1.66

typeface   EX1.54

variable   EX1.14

workbook   EX1.6

workbook window   EX1.6

worksheet   EX1.7

mous skills

The Microsoft Office User Specialist (MOUS) certification program is designed to measure your proficiency in performing basic tasks using the Office XP applications. Getting certified demonstrates that you have the skills and provides a valuable industry credential for employment. After completing this lab, you have learned the following Microsoft Office User Specialist skills:

Skill	Description	Page
Working with Cells and Cell Data	Insert, delete, and move cells	EX1.36,1.53
	Enter and edit cell data including text, numbers and formulas	EX1.15–1.23,1.39–1.44, 1.54
Managing Workbooks	Manage workbook files and folders	EX1.28
	Save workbooks using different names and file formats	EX1.26
Formatting and Printing Worksheets	Apply and modify cell formats	EX1.54
	Modify row and column formats	EX1.48
	Modify column and row settings	EX1.24
	Apply styles	EX1.61
	Preview and print worksheets and workbooks	EX1.69
Creating and Revising Formulas	Create and revise formulas	EX1.39
	Use statistical, date and time, financial, and logical functions	EX1.42
Creating and Modifying Graphics	Create, modify, and position graphics	EX1.65

command summary

Command	Shortcut Key	Button	Action
File/Open <file name>	Ctrl + O	🖿	Opens an existing workbook file
File/Close		✕	Closes open workbook file
File/Save <file name>	Ctrl + S	🖫	Saves current file on disk using same file name
File/Save As <file name>			Saves current file on disk using a new file name
File/Print Preview		🔍	Displays worksheet as it will appear when printed
File/Print	Ctrl + P	🖨	Prints a worksheet
File/Exit		✕	Exits Excel
Edit/Undo	Ctrl + Z	↺▾	Undoes last editing or formatting change
Edit/Redo	Ctrl + Y	↻▾	Restores changes after using Undo
Edit/Copy	Ctrl + C	📋	Copies selected data to Clipboard
Edit/Office Clipboard			Displays Office Clipboard task pane
Edit/Paste	Ctrl + V	📋	Pastes selections stored in Clipboard
Edit/Fill			Fills selected cells with contents of source cell
Edit/Clear/Contents	Delete		Clears cell contents
Edit/Delete/Entire Row			Deletes selected rows

command summary (continued)

Command	Shortcut Key	Button	Action
Edit/Delete/Entire column			Deletes selected columns
View/Toolbars			Displays or hides selected toolbar
Insert/Copied Cells			Inserts row and copies text from Clipboard
Insert/Rows			Inserts a blank row
Insert/Columns			Inserts a blank column
Insert/Picture/From File			Inserts picture at insertion point from disk
Format/Cells/Number/Currency			Applies Currency format to selection
Format/Cells/Number/Accounting		$	Applies Accounting format to selection
Format/Cells/Number/Date			Applies Date format to selection
Format/Cells/Number/Percent		%	Applies Percent format to selection
Format/Cells/Number/Decimal places		.00 / .00	Increases or decreases the number of decimal places associated with a number value
Format/Cells/Alignment/Horizontal/Left (Indent)			Left-aligns entry in cell space
Format/Cells/Alignment/Horizontal/Center			Center-aligns entry in cell space
Format/Cells/Alignment/Horizontal/Right			Right-aligns entry in cell space
Format/Cells/Alignment/Indent			Indents cell entry
Format/Cells/Alignment/Horizontal/Center Across Selection			Centers cell contents across selected cells
Format/Cells	Ctrl + 1		Changes font and attributes of cells
Format/Cells/Font/Font Style/Bold	Ctrl + B	B	Bolds selected text
Format/Cells/Font/Font Style/Italic	Ctrl + I	I	Italicizes selected text
Format/Cells/Font/Underline/Single	Ctrl + U	U	Underlines selected text
Format/Cells/Font/Color		A ·	Adds color to text
Format/Cells/Patterns/Color		·	Adds color to cell background
Format/Row/Height			Changes height of selected rows
Format/Column/Width			Changes width of columns
Format/Column/Autofit Selection			Changes column width to match widest cell entry
Format/Style			Applies selected style to selection

Terminology

screen identification

In the following worksheet, several items are identified by letters. Enter the correct term for each item in the space provided.

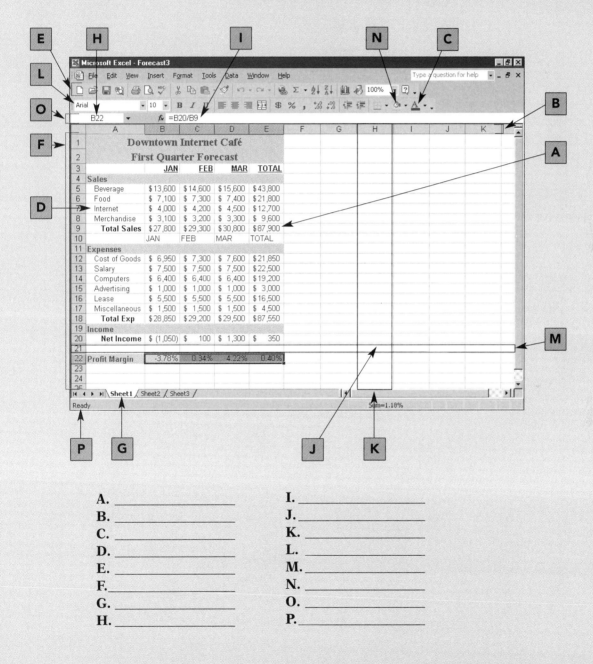

A. _____   I. _____

B. _____   J. _____

C. _____   K. _____

D. _____   L. _____

E. _____   M. _____

F._____   N. _____

G. _____   O. _____

H. _____   P._____

lab exercises

matching

Match the lettered item on the right with the numbered item on the left.

1. source _____ a. undoes last action
2. * _____ b. a set of characters with a specific design
3. ▣ _____ c. the cell you copy from
4. font _____ d. two or more worksheet cells
5. .xls _____ e. a cell reference
6. ↶▾ _____ f. enters a sum function
7. =C19+A21 _____ g. an arithmetic operator
8. range _____ h. merges cells and centers entry
9. D11 _____ i. a formula summing two cells
10. Σ _____ j. Excel workbook file name extension

multiple choice

Circle the correct response to the questions below.

1. Row and column _____ are entries that are used to create the structure of the worksheet and describe other worksheet entries.
   a. cells
   b. headings
   c. objects
   d. formats

2. _____ entries can contain any combination of letters, numbers, spaces, and any other special characters.
   a. Number
   b. Variable
   c. Constant
   d. Text

3. The _____ feature automatically corrects common typing errors as they are made.
   a. AutoFix
   b. Fixit
   c. AutoComplete
   d. AutoCorrect

4. The _____ is a small black square, located in the lower-right corner of the selection, used to create a series or copy to adjacent cells.
   a. scroll bar
   b. sheet tab
   c. sizing handle
   d. fill handle

5. The values on which a numeric formula performs a calculation are called:
   a. operators
   b. operands
   c. accounts
   d. data

6. Whenever a formula containing _____ references is copied, the referenced cells are automatically adjusted.
   a. relative
   b. automatic
   c. fixed
   d. variable

7. A(n)_____ is a box used to size a selected object.
   a. sizing handle
   b. cell selector
   c. operand
   d. fill handle

8. _____ can be applied to selections to add emphasis or interest to a document.
   a. Alignments
   b. Pictures
   c. Character effects
   d. Text formats

9. The currency number format can display:
   a. dollar signs
   b. commas
   c. decimal places
   d. all the above

10. The integers assigned to the days from January 1, 1900, through December 31, 2099, that allow dates to be used in calculations are called:
    a. date numbers
    b. syntax
    c. number formats
    d. reference

lab exercises

true/false

Circle the correct answer to the following questions.

1.	Formulas are used to create, edit, and position graphics.	True	False
2.	The default column width setting in Excel is 15.0.	True	False
3.	A nonadjacent range is two or more selected cells or ranges that are adjoining.	True	False
4.	A formula is an entry that performs a calculation.	True	False
5.	When a formula containing relative references is copied, the cell references in the copied formula refer to different cells than the references in the original formula.	True	False
6.	Formulas are prewritten statements that perform certain types of calculations automatically.	True	False
7.	Recalculation is one of the most powerful features of electronic worksheets.	True	False
8.	Font settings allow you to change the horizontal and vertical placement and the orientation of an entry in a cell.	True	False
9.	Number formats affect how numbers look onscreen and when printed.	True	False
10.	A drawing object is created using a special drawing program that is not included with Excel.	True	False

Concepts

fill-in

Complete the following statements by filling in the blanks with the correct terms.

1. The _____ controls how much information can be displayed in a cell.

2. _____ affect how numbers look onscreen and when printed.

3. _____ placement allows you to specify whether the cell contents are displayed at the top, centered, or at the bottom of the vertical cell space.

4. Pictures are inserted as _____ objects.

5. The _____ feature decreases the recalculation time by only recalculating dependent formulas.

6. By default, text entries are _____ -aligned and number entries are _____ -aligned.

7. A(n) _____ in a formula automatically adjusts for the new location when copied.

8. The values on which a numeric formula performs a calculation are called _____.

9. Without _____ recalculation, large worksheets would take several minutes to recalculate all formulas each time a number was changed.

10. A(n) _____ is the data the function uses to perform the calculation.

discussion questions

1. Discuss four steps in developing a workbook. Why is it important to follow these steps?

2. What types of entries are used in worksheets? Discuss the uses of each type of entry.

3. Discuss how formulas and functions are created. Why are they the power behind workbooks?

4. Discuss the formatting features presented in the lab. Why are they important to the look of the worksheet?

Hands-On Exercises

step-by-step

Park Improvement Bid Analysis

★ 1. Kelly Fitzgerald is an analyst for the city parks and recreation department. One of her responsibilities is to collect and analyze data on future improvements. She has compiled a list of the parks that are scheduled for improvements for the next year and the project bids for each. Follow the directions below to complete the worksheet shown here.

Park Improvement Bids
Calendar Year 2005

Park	Bid 1	Bid 2	Bid 3	Bid 4
West Avenue	$127,000	$154,200	$135,700	$142,800
Amigo	154,500	251,000	202,500	220,300
Canyon Creek	13,600	18,900	15,500	14,700
Mountain View	1,300	2,500	1,800	1,600
East Hill	129,100	154,300	128,500	133,400
Maple Grove	1,200	1,500	1,400	1,600
Thompson-West	10,300	14,200	11,500	10,200
Marshall Way	19,300	19,900	18,900	22,300
Green Mountain	10,200	11,500	12,600	12,500
Blue Bird Pass	29,100	32,500	25,700	28,900
Total	$495,600	$660,500	$554,100	$588,300

Student Name
Date

a. Open the workbook ex01_Improvements.

b. Modify the label in cell B2 so that the first letter of each word is capitalized. Increase the font size to 14 point. Center both title lines across columns A through E.

c. Bold and center the titles in row 5.

d. Adjust the column widths so that all the data is fully displayed.

e. In row 16, enter a function to total the Bid 1 and Bid 2 columns.

f. Format the numbers in rows 6 and 16 using the Currency style with zero decimal places and the numbers in rows 7 through 15 using the Comma style with zero decimal places.

g. Kelly has just received the last two bids. Enter the following data in the cells indicated.

Row	Col D	Col E
5	Bid 3	Bid 4
6	135700	142800
7	202500	220300
8	15500	14700
9	1800	1600
10	128500	133400
11	1400	1600
12	11500	10200
13	18900	22300
14	12600	12500
15	25700	28900

h. Format the data to match the style of the corresponding information in columns B and C.

i. Copy the total function to calculate the total for the new bids.

j. Insert a blank row above the Total row.

k. Add font and fill colors to the worksheet, as you like.

l. Insert a Clip Art graphic of your choice from the Clip Organizer. Size and position it appropriately to fit the worksheet.

m. Enter your name and the current date on separate rows just below the worksheet.

n. Move to cell A1. Save the workbook as Park Improvements. Preview and print the worksheet.

Job Trends Analysis Worksheet

★ **2.** Lisa Sutton is an employment analyst working for the state of New Jersey. One of her responsibilities is to collect and analyze data on future job opportunities in the state. Lisa has compiled a list of the jobs that are expected to offer the most new positions. Follow the directions below to complete the worksheet shown here.

a. Open the workbook ex01_New Positions.

b. Modify the label in cell B2 so that the first letter of each word is capitalized; move the label in cell B2 to A2; move the label in cell B3 to A3; center the titles across the columns A through D; and finally, increase the font size to 14 point.

Jobs With Most New Positions 1994 - 2005			
Title	N.J. Projected New Positions	Avg Pay Per Hour	Percent Above National Average
Systems Analysts/Programmers	27,000	$26.59	14.4%
Nursing Aides and Orderlies	15,400	$9.17	18.3%
Waiters and Waitresses	13,600	$6.09	8.4%
Home Health Aides	13,400	$7.97	1.8%
Marketing and Sales Supv.	12,900	$19.81	25.9%
Janitors and Cleaners	12,500	$8.79	11.3%
Salespersons, retail	11,300	$8.66	4.8%
Cashiers	11,300	$7.44	13.1%
Guards and watch guards	10,200	$8.21	2.8%
Nurse: Registered, Practitioner etc.	9,100	$22.46	15.9%

Student Name
Date

c. Format the numbers in column B as number with a comma to separate thousands and 0 decimal places. Format the numbers in column C as currency with dollar signs and two decimal places. Format the numbers in column D as percent with one decimal place.

d. Insert a new row below row 3 and a new row below row 6.

e. Bold the titles in rows 5 and 6. Underline the titles in row 6. Adjust the column widths so that all the data is fully displayed.

f. Add font and fill colors to the worksheet as you like.

g. Insert a Clip Art graphic of your choice from the Clip Organizer. Size and position it appropriately to fit the page.

h. Enter your name and the current date on separate rows just below the worksheet.

i. Move to cell A1. Save the workbook as Jobs. Preview and print the worksheet.

Comparative U.S. Families at Poverty Level

★ ★ **3.** Mark Ernster works for an agency that provides help to families in poverty. He has been doing some research on the percent of families that fall into this category. He has started a worksheet with data from the years 1990–1999. Follow the directions below to complete the worksheet shown here.

   a. Open the workbook ex01_Poverty Level.

   b. Edit the title in cell D2 so that the first letter of each word is upper-case except the words 'of' and 'or'. Center the title across columns A through J. Increase the font size to 14 and bold and apply a font color of your choice to the title.

   c. Center-align and underline the column headings in row 4. Left-align cells A5 through A14.

   d. Calculate the average for the Official percentage in cell B15 using the Average function (=Average(B5:B14)). Format the cell as a percentage with two decimal places. Copy the formula to cells C15 through J15.

   e. Next, you would like to calculate the percent of change from 1990 to 1999. Enter the label Percent Change in cell A16. Enter the formula =(B14-B5)/B15 in cell B16. Format the cell as a percentage with two decimal places. Copy the formula to cells C16 through J16.

   f. Format the data in cells B5 through J14 as a percentage with one decimal place. Best-fit columns B through J.

   g. Adjust the width of column A to fully display the labels.

   h. Insert a blank row between rows 14 and 15 and another between rows 16 and 17.

   i. Add fill colors to the worksheet as you like.

   j. Insert the picture ex01_family. Size and position it to fit on the left side of the title.

   k. Enter your name and the current date on separate rows just below the legend.

   l. Move to cell A1. Save and replace the workbook as Poverty Level. Preview and print the worksheet.

Percentage of Families At or Below Poverty Level

	Official	NAS	NAS-U	DES	DES-U	NGA	NGA-J	DCM	DCM-U
1990	13.5%	13.7%	16.1%	13.6%	16.7%	13.8%	16.6%	13.6%	16.4%
1991	14.2%	14.5%	16.9%	14.4%	17.6%	14.6%	17.3%	14.3%	17.3%
1992	14.8%	15.1%	17.6%	15.1%	18.3%	15.2%	18.2%	15.0%	18.0%
1993	15.1%	15.8%	18.3%	15.8%	19.0%	15.8%	18.6%	15.7%	18.8%
1994	14.6%	14.6%	17.0%	14.6%	17.5%	14.6%	17.3%	14.5%	17.5%
1995	13.8%	13.8%	16.3%	13.8%	16.9%	13.9%	16.6%	13.8%	16.8%
1996	13.7%	13.6%	16.0%	13.6%	16.7%	13.5%	16.2%	13.7%	16.6%
1997	13.3%	13.3%	15.4%	13.3%	16.0%	13.3%	15.8%	13.3%	15.9%
1998	12.7%	12.5%	14.4%	12.5%	15.1%	12.3%	14.6%	12.5%	15.0%
1999	11.8%	11.7%	13.8%	11.8%	14.3%	11.7%	14.0%	11.9%	14.4%
Average	13.75%	13.86%	16.18%	13.85%	16.81%	13.87%	16.52%	13.83%	16.67%
Percent Change	-12.59%	-14.60%	-14.29%	-13.24%	-14.37%	-15.22%	-15.66%	-12.50%	-12.20%

Legend
Official U.S. government
NAS   National Academy of Sciences methodology - standardized
NAS-U National Academy of Sciences methodology - unstandardized
DES   Different Equivalence Scale: uses three parameters to adjust thresholds by family size, presence of children and family structure (but otherwise similar to NAS) - standardized
DES-U Different Equivalence Scale: uses three parameters to adjust thresholds by family size, presence of children and family structure (but otherwise similar to NAS) - unstandardized
NGA   No Geographic Adjustment (but otherwise similar to NAS) - standardized
NGA-U No Geographic Adjustment (but otherwise similar to NAS) - unstandardized
DCM   Different Child Care Method: assigns fixed amounts of child care expenditures to families based on the number and ages of children present (but otherwise similar to NAS) - standardized
DCM-U Different Child Care Method: assigns fixed amounts of child care expenditures to families based on the number and ages of children present (but otherwise similar to NAS) - unstandardized

Student Name
Date

Information Technology Job and Salary Analysis

★ ★ **4.** Jake Bell is a writer for a local television station. The station is planning a series about information technology. In his research on this topic, he has found some interesting data on information technology jobs and salaries. He has entered this data into a worksheet but still needs to format the data and perform some analysis of the information. Follow the directions below to complete the worksheet shown here.

a. Open the workbook ex01_IT Salaries.

b. Adjust the width of column A to fully display the row labels.

c. Center the title in row 2 over the worksheet columns A through F. Format the title in row 2 to Tahoma 14 point. Apply a font color and fill color of your choice to row 2.

d. Bold and center the column labels in row 4.

e. Format the data in B6 through D15 using the Comma style and no decimal places.

Information Technology Median Salaries

Management Level	1995	1999	% Change 1995 - 1999	2000	% Change 1999 - 2000
CIO/Vice President	102,500	146,400	42.83%	158,000	7.92%
IS Director	76,650	106,500	38.94%	113,700	6.76%
Manager, Sys. Analysis & Prog.	69,950	91,100	30.24%	97,100	6.59%
Manager, Sys. Prog./Tech. Support	66,200	89,700	35.50%	95,800	6.80%
Network Manager LAN/WAN	56,300	85,200	51.33%	92,100	8.10%
Sys. Analyst/Prog./Proj. Leader	48,250	72,200	49.64%	77,900	7.89%
Database Admin. Manager	64,500	89,000	37.98%	96,500	8.43%
Manager Telecommunications	67,450	79,100	17.27%	84,800	7.21%
Data Center Manager	62,800	73,600	17.20%	77,400	5.16%
PC Work Station Manager	44,650	59,400	33.03%	63,100	6.23%

Student Name
Date

f. Insert a new column between C and D. Calculate the % of change from 1995 to 1999. Format the data as a percentage with two decimal places. (*Hint:* Subtract the 1995 value from the 1999 value and divide the result by the 1995 value.)

g. Calculate the % of change from 1999 to 2000 in column F. Format the data as a percentage with two decimal places.

h. Label the new columns in row 4 **% Change**. Enter **1995–1999** in cell D5 and **1999–2000** in cell F5. Format the headings appropriately. Best-fit the columns to display the labels. Change the widths of columns B, C, and E to the same width as columns D and F.

i. Insert a blank row above row 6.

j. Insert the Disks Clip Art graphic (located in the Computer category of the Clip Organizer or ex01_Disks from your data files) to the right and left of the title on the worksheet. Adjust the size and location of the pictures as necessary.

k. Apply a fill color of your choice behind all rows of the worksheet (except row 2, which already contains a fill color.)

l. Enter your name and the current date on separate rows below the worksheet.

m. Move to cell A1. Save and replace the workbook file as IT Salaries. Preview and print the worksheet.

Homeowners Association Projected Budget

★ ★ ★ **5.** Stuart Philips is president of the Garden Springs Homeowners Association. The Association is planning a large improvement project and wants to project how much there is likely to be in the cash budget after expenses. Using last year's final budget numbers, he wants to create a projected budget for 2004. Follow the directions below to complete the worksheet shown here.

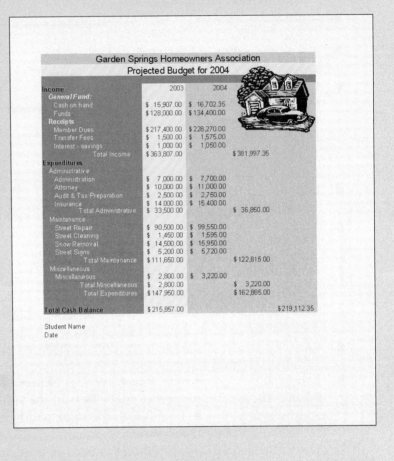

a. Open the workbook file ex01_Springs Budget. Adjust the width of column A to fully display the labels.

b. In column C, calculate a 5 percent increase for all the income numbers for the year 2004. Calculate a 10 percent increase in Administrative and Maintenance expenditures, and a 15 percent increase in Miscellaneous expenditures.

c. Format the data with the Accounting number format.

d. In column D, calculate the totals for Total Income, Total Administrative, Total Maintenance, and Total Expenditures for 2004. In column E, calculate the Total Cash Balance by subtracting the total income from the total expenditures for 2004.

e. Indent the row label subheads and further indent the items under each subhead. Right-align the total labels except for the Total Cash Balance.

f. Delete rows 13 and 14.

g. Change the font type, size, and color of the worksheet title lines to a format of your choice. Center the titles across columns A through E.

h. Apply character effects and color of your choice to the worksheet.

i. Insert a Clip Art image of your choice from the Clip Organizer. Position and size it to fit the worksheet.

j. Enter your name and the current date on separate rows just below the worksheet.

k. Move to cell A1. Save the workbook file as Springs Projected Budget. Preview and print the worksheet.

Tracking Your Grades

★ ★ **1.** A worksheet can be used to track your grades in a class or for each semester. Design and create a worksheet to record your grades in any class. The worksheet should include grades for at least four test scores showing the number of points you earned on each test and the number of possible points. Include an appropriate title, row and column headings, and formulas to calculate your total points earned and total possible points. Include a formula to calculate your percent. Format the worksheet appropriately using features presented in this lab. Enter real or sample data for the four tests. Include your name and date above the worksheet. Save the workbook as Class Grades and print the worksheet.

Creating a Personal Budget

★ ★ **2.** Create a personal three-month budget using a worksheet. Enter an appropriate title and use descriptive labels for your monthly expenses (food, rent, car payments, insurance, credit card payments, etc.). Enter your monthly expenses (or, if you prefer, any reasonable sample data). Use formulas to calculate total expenses for each month and to calculate the average monthly expenditures for each expense item. Enhance the worksheet using features you learned in this lab. Enter your name and the current date on separate rows just below the worksheet. Save the workbook as Personal Budget. Preview and print the worksheet.

Tracking Sales

★ ★ **3.** Trevor Grey is the new owner and manager of a small custom publishing company. He has four salespeople (Kevin, April, Karen, and Sam) and is planning an intense marketing campaign for the next month. Using the steps in the planning process, plan and create a worksheet for Trevor that can be used to record and analyze sales for that month.

Weekly sales data for each employee will be entered into the worksheet. Using that data, the worksheet will calculate the total monthly sales for each person. Additionally, it will calculate the total weekly sales for the company. Write a short paragraph describing how you used each of the planning steps. Enter sample data in the worksheet. Include your name and the current date on separate rows just below the worksheet. Save the workbook as Weekly Sales. Preview and print the worksheet.

Job Analysis

★ ★ ★ **4.** Use the library and/or the Web to locate information on employment opportunities and salary trends related to your area of study. Create a worksheet to display information relating to job titles, years of experience, and starting and top salaries for positions in your field. Calculate the median salary (the average of the starting and the top salary). Enhance the worksheet using features you learned in this lab. Enter your name and the current date on separate rows just below the worksheet. Save the workbook as Job Analysis. Preview and print the worksheet.

Membership Analysis

★★ 5. LifeStyle Fitness Club wants to analyze their membership growth for the past 3 years. Design and
★ create a worksheet to record the membership enrollment for three years in the three membership
categories: Single, Family, and Senior. Include an appropriate title, row and column headings, and
formulas to calculate total enrollment by category and by year. Include a formula to calculate the
percent growth over the three years. Format the worksheet appropriately using features presented
in this tutorial. Enter sample data for the three years. Include your name and date above the
worksheet. Save the workbook as Membership and print the worksheet.

on the web

Design, planning and testing are very important steps in the development of an accurate
worksheet. A poorly designed worksheet can lead to serious errors in the analysis of data. Use the
Web to find information about spreadsheet errors and spreadsheet design. Write a short paper
summarizing your findings. Include proper citations for your sources. If you are using a word
processor to write the report, save the document as Spreadsheet Design.

Charting Worksheet Data

LAB 2

objectives

After completing this lab, you will know how to:

1.	Select a chart data range.
2.	Change the type of chart.
3.	Move the chart location.
4.	Format chart elements.
5.	Add chart titles and move the legend.
6.	Create a combination chart.
7.	Change worksheet data.
8.	Add data labels, text boxes, and arrows.
9.	Create, explode, and rotate a pie chart.
10.	Apply patterns and color.
11.	Size and align a sheet on a page.
12.	Add predefined headers and footers.
13.	Document, preview, and print a workbook.

The chart Wizard makes it easy to create a chart from data in a worksheet.

Many different types of charts can be created and modified to visually represent worksheet data.

The addition of features such as data labels, text boxes, arrows, and color add emphasis to the chart.

Downtown Internet Café

After creating the first quarter forecast for the Downtown Internet Café, you contacted several other Internet cafes to inquire about their startup experiences. You heard many exciting success stories! Internet connections attract more customers and the typical customer stays longer at an Internet café than at a regular café. As a result, they end up spending more money.

You now believe that your initial sales estimates are too low. You too should be able to increase sales dramatically. In addition to sales of coffee and food items to customers, the Café also derives sales from charging for Internet connection time. In your discussions with other Internet café managers, you have found that Internet connection sales account for ap-

proximately 25 percent of their total sales. You would like to launch an aggressive advertising campaign to promote the new Internet aspect of the Downtown Internet Café. You believe that the campaign will lead to an increase in sales not only in Internet connection time but also in food and beverage sales.

To convince Evan, you need an effective way to illustrate the sales growth you are forecasting. In this lab, you will learn to use Excel 2002's chart-creating and formatting features to produce several different charts of your sales estimates, as shown on the preceding page.

The following concepts will be introduced in this lab:

1	**Chart** A chart is visual representation of data that is used to convey information in an easy-to-understand and attractive manner. Different types of charts are used to represent data in different ways.
2	**Chart Elements** Chart elements consist of a number of parts that are used to graphically display the worksheet data.
3	**Chart Objects** A chart object is a graphic object that is created using charting features included in Excel. A chart object can be inserted into a worksheet or into a special chart sheet.
4	**Group** Because it consists of many separate objects, a chart object is a group. A group is two or more objects that behave as a single object when it is moved or sized.
5	**Data Label** Data labels provide additional information about a data marker.
6	**Text Box** A text box is a rectangular object in which you type text. Text boxes can be added to a sheet or an embedded chart.
7	**Header and Footer** Lines of text displayed above the top margin or below the bottom margin of each page are called headers and footers.

Learning About Charts

Creating charts of the sales projections makes it easy to visually understand numeric data. Excel 2002 can create many types of charts from data in a worksheet.

You have decided to chart the sales forecast data for the Downtown Internet Café to better see the sales trends. The sales data is in a separate workbook file.

1 ● **Open the file** ex02_Cafe Sales.

Your screen should be similar to Figure 2.1

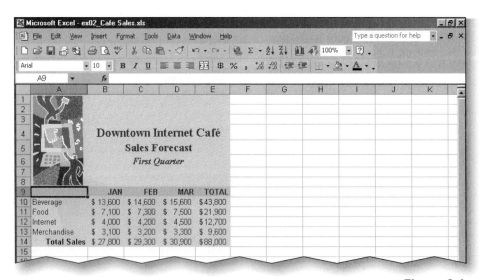

Figure 2.1

Although the worksheet shows the sales data for each category, it is hard to see how the different categories change over time. To make it easier to see the sales trends, you decide to create a chart of this data.

Charts

1 A **chart** is visual representation of data that is used to convey information in an easy-to-understand and attractive manner. Different types of charts are used to represent data in different ways. The type of chart you create depends on the type of data you are charting and the emphasis you want the chart to impart.

Excel 2002 can produce 14 standard types of graphs or charts, with many different sub-types for each standard type. In addition, Excel includes professionally designed built-in custom charts that include additional formatting and chart refinements. The basic chart types and how they represent data are described in the following table.

Type	Description	Type	Description
	Area charts show the magnitude of change over time by emphasizing the area under the curve created by each data series.		Radar charts display a line or area chart wrapped around a central point. Each axis represents a set of data points.
	Bar charts display data as evenly spaced bars. The categories are displayed along the Y axis and the values are displayed horizontally, placing more emphasis on comparisons and less on time.		XY (scatter) charts are used to show the relationship between two ranges of numeric data.
	Column charts display data as evenly spaced bars. They are similar to bar charts, except that categories are organized horizontally and values vertically to emphasize variation over time.		Surface charts display values as what appears to be a rubber sheet stretched over a 3-D column chart. These are useful for finding the best combination between sets of data.
	Line charts display data along a line. They are used to show changes in data over time, emphasizing time and rate of change rather than the amount of change.		Bubble charts compare sets of three values. It is like a scatter chart with the third value displayed as the size of bubble markers.
	Pie charts display data as slices of a circle or pie. They show the relationship of each value in a data series to the series as a whole. Each slice of the pie represents a single value in the series.		A stock chart is a high-low-close chart. It requires three series of values in this order.
			Cylinder charts display values with a cylindrical shape.
	Doughnut charts are similar to pie charts except that they can show more than one data series.		Cone charts display values with a conical shape.
			Pyramid charts display values with a pyramid shape.

Creating a Single Data Series Chart

All charts are drawn from data contained in a worksheet. To create a new chart, you select the worksheet range containing the data you want displayed as a chart plus any row or column headings you want used in the chart. Excel then translates the selected data into a chart based upon the shape and contents of the worksheet selection.

A chart consists of a number of parts that are important to understand so that you can identify the appropriate data to select in the worksheet.

c o n c e p t 2

Chart Elements

2 A chart consists of a number of parts or elements that are used to graphically display the worksheet data. In a two-dimensional chart, the selected worksheet data is visually displayed within the X- and Y-axis boundaries. The **X axis**, also called the **category axis**, is the bottom boundary line of the chart and is used to label the data being charted, such as a point in time or a category. The left boundary line of the chart is the **Y axis**, also called the **value axis**. This axis is a numbered scale whose numbers are determined by the data used in the chart. Typically the X-axis line is the horizontal line and the Y-axis line is the vertical line. In 3-D charts there can also be an additional axis, called the **Z axis**, which allows you to compare data within a series more easily. This axis is the vertical axis. The X and Y axes delineate the horizontal surface of the chart.

Other basic elements of a 2-dimensional chart are:

Element	Description
category names	Labels that correspond to the headings for the worksheet data that is plotted along the X axis.
plot area	The area within the X- and Y-axis boundaries where the chart appears
data series	Related data points that are distinguished by different colors or patterns
data marker	A bar, dot, or other symbol that represents one number from the worksheet.
chart gridlines	Lines extending from the axis line across the plot area that make it easier to read the chart data.
legend	A box that identifies the chart data series
chart title	A descriptive label displayed above the charted data that explains the contents of the chart.
category-axis title	A descriptive label displayed along the X axis
value-axis title	A descriptive label displayed along the Y axis

The basic parts of a two-dimensional chart are shown in the figure below.

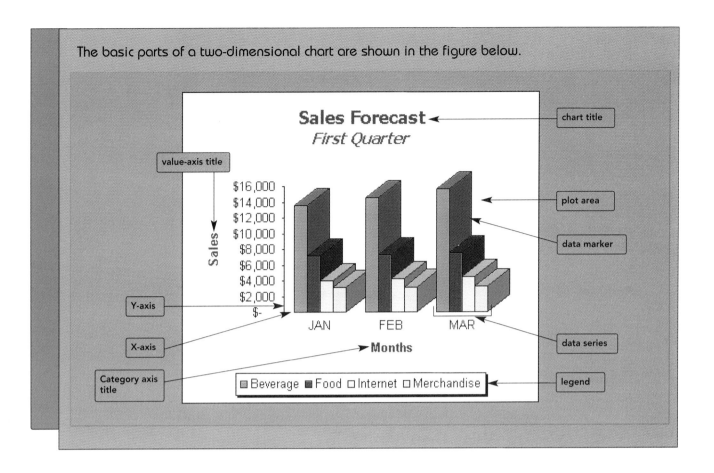

Selecting the Data to Chart

The first chart you want to create will show the total sales pattern over the three months. This chart will use the month labels in cells B9 through D9 to label the X-axis. The numbers to be charted are in cells B14 through D14. In addition, the label Total Sales in cell A14 will be used as the chart legend, making the entire range A14 through D14.

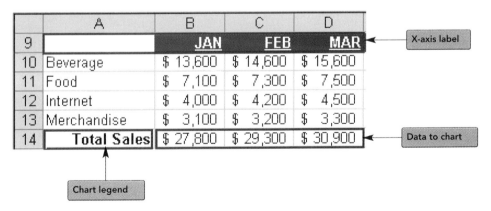

Notice that the two ranges, B9 through D9 and A14 through D14, are not adjacent and are not the same size. When plotting nonadjacent ranges in a chart, the selections must form a rectangular shape. To do this, the blank cell A9 will be included in the selection. You will specify the range and create the chart.

1
- Select A9 through D9.
- Hold down Ctrl.
- Select A14 through D14.

Your screen should be similar to Figure 2.2

Selected non-adjacent ranges

Starts the Chart Wizard

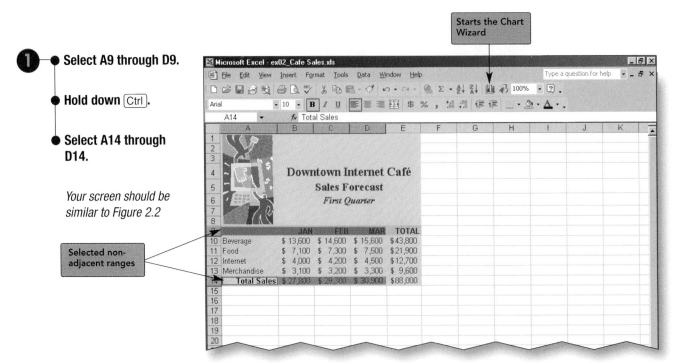

Figure 2.2

Additional Information
Office XP includes many different Wizards that provide step-by-step guidance to help you quickly perform many complicated tasks.

Using Chart Wizard

Next you will use the Chart Wizard to help you create the chart. Chart Wizard is an interactive program that guides you through the steps to create a chart by asking you questions and creating a chart based on your responses.

1
- Click Chart Wizard.

Another Method
The menu equivalent is Insert/Chart.

- Move the Chart Wizard dialog box to the right to see as much of the worksheet as possible.

HAVING TROUBLE?
Drag the title bar of the dialog box to move it.

Your screen should be similar to Figure 2.3

Selected default chart type

Selected sub-type

Selected chart ranges

Description of selected sub-type

Moves to next page

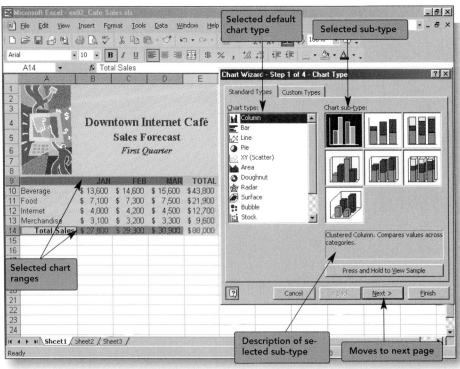

Figure 2.3

The first step is to select the chart type from the Chart Type list box. The default chart type is a column chart. Each type of chart includes many variations. The variations associated with the column chart type are displayed as buttons in the Chart Sub-type section of the dialog box. The default column sub-type is a clustered column. A description of the selected sub-type is displayed in the area below the sub-type buttons. You will use the default column chart type and move to the next step.

2 ● **Click** `Next >` .

Your screen should be similar to Figure 2.4

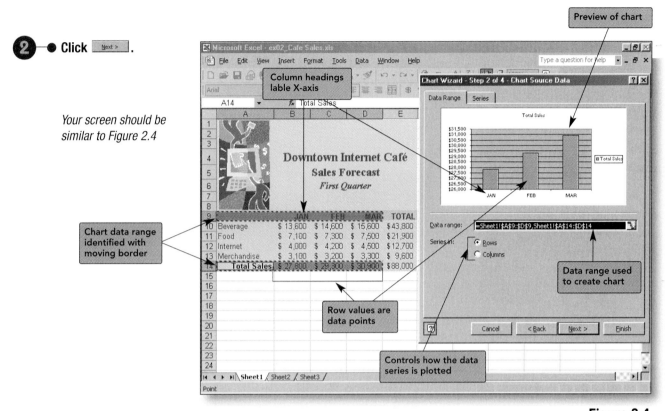

Figure 2.4

In the second Chart Wizard dialog box, you specify the data range on the worksheet you want to plot. Because you selected the data range before starting the Chart Wizard, the range is correctly displayed in the Data range text box. In addition, the data range is identified with a moving border in the worksheet. The dialog box also displays a preview of the chart that will be created using the specified data and selected chart type.

The two Series In options change how Excel plots the data series from the rows or columns in the selected data range. The orientation Excel uses by default varies depending upon the type of chart selected and the number of rows and columns defined in a series. The worksheet data range that has the greater number of rows or columns appears along the X-axis and the smaller number is charted as the data series. When the data series is an equal number of rows and columns, as it is in this case, the default is to plot the rows. The first row defines the X-axis category labels and the second row the plotted data. The content of the first cell in the second row is used as the legend text. To accept the default settings,

3 Click Next >.

If necessary, open the Titles tab.

Your screen should be similar to Figure 2.5

Row label used as default chart title and legend

Figure 2.5

In the step 3 dialog box, you can turn some standard options on and off and change the appearance of chart elements such as a legend and titles. To clarify the data in the chart, you will add a more descriptive chart title as well as titles along the X and Y axes. As you add the titles, the preview chart will update to display the new settings.

4 In the Chart Title text box, replace the default title with Downtown Internet Cafe Sales.

Press Tab.

In the Category (X) Axis text box, enter Months.

In the Value (Y) Axis text box, enter Total Sales.

Your screen should be similar to Figure 2.6

Titles clarify meaning of chart

Figure 2.6

The titles clearly describe the information displayed in the chart. Now, because there is only one data range, and the category title fully explains this data, you decide to clear the display of the legend.

5 ● **Open the Legend tab.**

● **Click Show Legend to clear the checkmark.**

Your screen should be similar to Figure 2.7

Figure 2.7

The legend is removed and the chart area resized to occupy the extra space.

6 ● Click **Next >** .

*Your screen should be
similar to Figure 2.8*

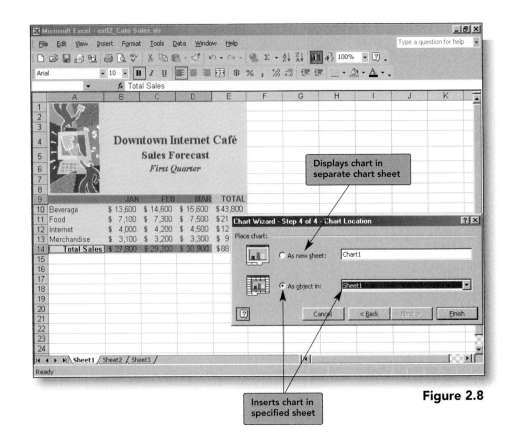

Figure 2.8

In the last step, you specify where you want the chart displayed in the worksheet. A chart can be displayed in a separate chart sheet or as an object in
an existing sheet.

concept 3

Chart Objects

3 A **chart object** is a graphic object that is created
using charting features included in Excel. A chart
object can be inserted into a worksheet or into a
special chart sheet.

Charts that are inserted into a worksheet are
embedded objects. An **embedded chart** becomes part of the sheet in which it is inserted
and is saved as part of the worksheet when you

save the workbook file. Like all graphic objects,
an embedded chart object can be sized and
moved in a worksheet. A worksheet can contain
multiple charts.

A chart that is inserted into a separate chart
sheet is also saved with the workbook file. Only
one chart can be added to a chart sheet and it
cannot be sized and moved.

You would like this chart displayed as an object in the Sales worksheet.
This is the default selection. You have provided all the information needed
by the Wizard to create the chart.

7 • Click [Finish].

• If necessary, move the Chart toolbar to the bottom right corner of the window.

HAVING TROUBLE?

If your chart toolbar is not automatically displayed, open it by selecting it from the toolbar shortcut menu. Move toolbars by dragging the title bar of the floating toolbar or the move handle ⫿ of a docked toolbar.

Your screen should be similar to Figure 2.9

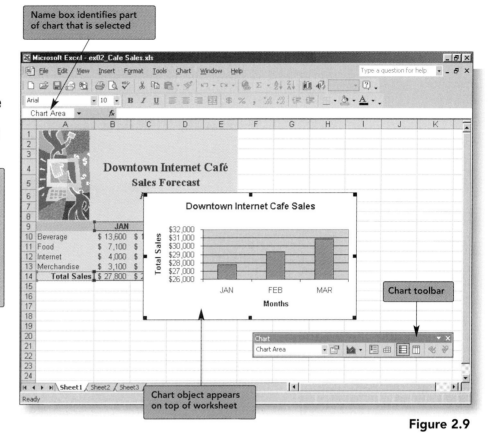

Figure 2.9

The chart with the settings you specified using the Chart Wizard is displayed on the worksheet. It covers some of the worksheet data because it is a separate chart object that can be moved and sized within the worksheet.

Notice that the Name box displays Chart Area. The Name box identifies the part of the chart that is selected, in this case the entire chart and all its contents.

Also notice that the Chart toolbar is automatically displayed whenever a chart is selected. The Chart toolbar contains buttons for the most frequently used chart editing and formatting features. These buttons are identified below.

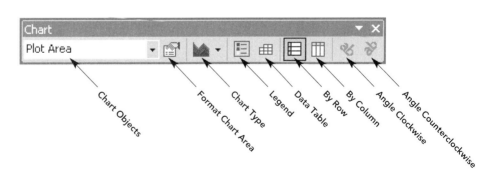

Moving and Sizing a Chart

You want to move the chart so that it is displayed to the right of the worksheet data. In addition, you want to increase the size of the chart. A selected chart object is moved by pointing to it and dragging it to a new location. When you move the mouse pointer into the selected chart object, it will display a chart tip to advise you of the chart element that will be affected by your action. When moving the entire chart, the chart tip must display Chart Area.

● Move the mouse pointer to different elements within the chart and note the different chart ScreenTips that appear.

● With the chart ScreenTip displaying Chart Area, drag the chart object so that the upper-left corner is in cell F4.

Additional Information

The mouse pointer changes to a ✛ while dragging to move an object.

Your screen should be similar to Figure 2.10

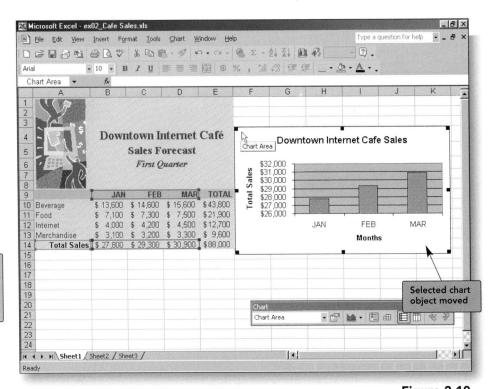

Figure 2.10

Next you will increase the size of the chart by dragging a sizing handle. This is the same as sizing a graphic object.

2 ● **Point to the lower-center sizing handle, hold down Alt, and drag the chart box down until it is displayed over cells F4 through K20.**

Your screen should be similar to Figure 2.11

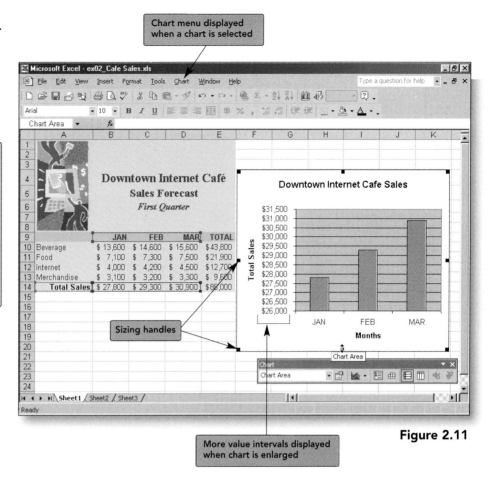

Figure 2.11

As you enlarge the chart, more value intervals are displayed along the Y axis, making the data in the chart easier to read. Additionally, the fonts in the chart scale proportionally as you resize the chart. The chart includes standard formats that are applied to the selected chart sub-type, such as a shaded background in the plot area and blue columns.

It is now easy to see how the worksheet data you selected is represented in the chart. Each column represents the total sales for that month in row 14. The month labels in row 9 have been used to label the X axis category labels. The range or scale of values along the Y axis is determined from the data in the worksheet. The upper limit is the maximum value in the worksheet rounded upward to the next highest interval.

Changing the Chart Location

Although this chart compares the total sales for the three months, you decide you are more interested in seeing a comparison for the sales categories. You could delete this chart simply by pressing Delete while the chart is selected. Instead, however, you will move it to a separate worksheet in case you want to refer to it again.

When a chart is selected, the Data menu changes to the Chart menu. In addition, many of the commands under the other menus change to commands that apply to charts only. The Chart menu contains commands that can be used to modify the chart.

1 ● **Choose Chart/Location**

● **Select As new sheet.**

● **Click** OK.

● **Save the workbook as**
Cafe Sales Charts.

*Your screen should be
similar to Figure 2.12*

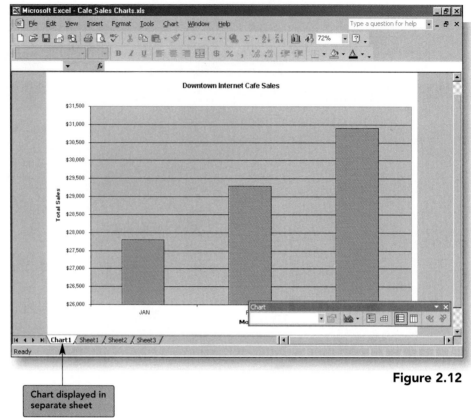

Figure 2.12

Chart displayed in
separate sheet

The column chart is now an object displayed in a separate chart sheet. Generally, you display a chart in a chart sheet when you want the chart displayed separately from the associated worksheet data. The chart is still automatically linked to the worksheet data from which it was created.

The new chart sheet named Chart1 was inserted to the left of the worksheet, Sheet1. The Chart sheet is the active sheet, or the sheet you are currently viewing and working in.

Creating a Multiple Data Series Chart

Now you are ready to continue your analysis of sales trends. You want to create a second chart to display the sales data for each category for the three months. You could create a separate chart for each category and then compare the charts; however, to make the comparisons between the categories easier, you will display all the categories on a single chart.

The data for the three months for the four categories is in cells B10 through D13. The month headings (X-axis data series) are in cells B9 through D9, and the legend text is in the range A10 through A13.

1 • **Click the Sheet1 tab.**

• **Select A9 through D13.**

• **Click** 📊 **Chart Wizard.**

• **Click** Next > .

Your screen should be similar to Figure 2.13

Selected data range

Legend displays names of months

Series plotted by columns

Figure 2.13

Additional Information
If you want to change the series orientation of an existing chart, you can use ▤ By Row or ▥ By Column in the Chart toolbar.

When plotting the data for this chart, the Chart Wizard selected Columns as the data series orientation because there are fewer columns than rows in the data range. This time, however, you want to change the data series to Rows so that the months are along the X axis.

2 • **Select Rows.**

Your screen should be similar to Figure 2.14

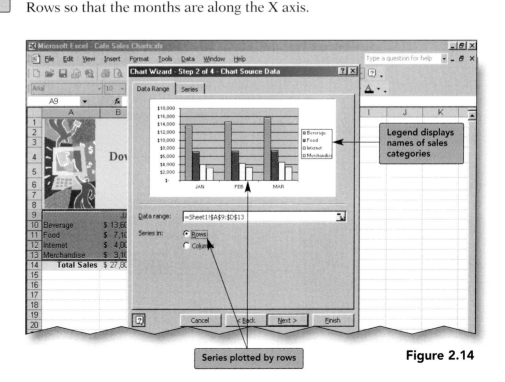

Legend displays names of sales categories

Series plotted by rows

Figure 2.14

Creating a Multiple Data Series Chart   **EX2.17**

Excel 2002

The sample chart is redrawn with the new orientation. The column chart now compares the sales by month rather than by category. The Legend displays the names of the sales categories. Next, you will specify the chart titles and finish the chart.

3 ● **Click** Next > .

● **Open the Titles tab. Enter the following titles:**

Title	Entry
Chart	Sales Forecast
Category	Months
Value	Sales

● **Click** Finish .

● **Move and size the chart until it covers cells F2 through K19.**

Your screen should be similar to Figure 2.15

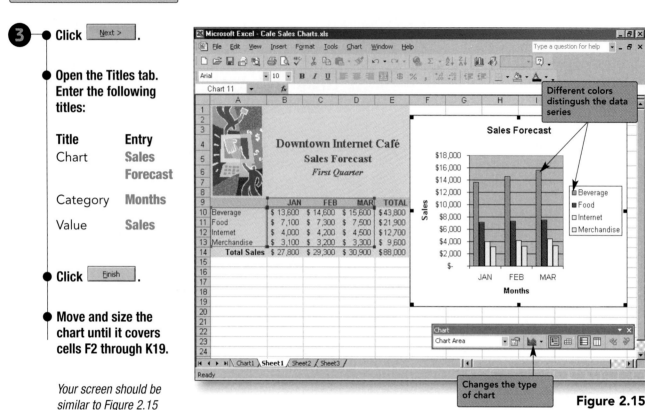

Figure 2.15

A different column color identifies each data series and the legend identifies the categories. The column chart shows that sales in all categories are increasing, with the greatest increase occurring in beverage sales.

Changing the Chart Type

Next you would like to see how the same data displayed in the column chart would look as a line chart. A line chart displays data as a line and is commonly used to show trends over time. This is easily done by changing the chart type using the ☒ Chart Type button on the Chart toolbar.

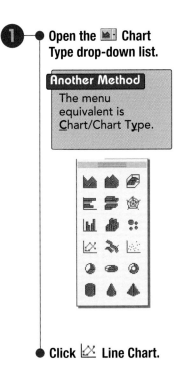

1 ● Open the 📊 Chart Type drop-down list.

Another Method

The menu equivalent is Chart/Chart Type.

● Click 📈 Line Chart.

Your screen should be similar to Figure 2.16

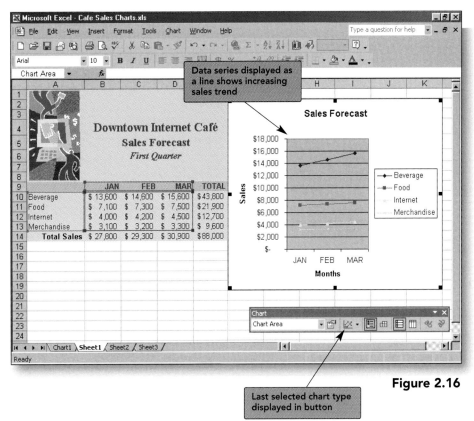

Data series displayed as a line shows increasing sales trend

Figure 2.16

Last selected chart type displayed in button

The line chart shows the increasing sales trend from month to month. Notice the 📈 Chart Type button displays a line chart, reflecting the last-selected chart type. You still don't find this chart very interesting so you will change it to a 3-D bar chart next.

2 ● Open the 📈 Chart Type drop-down list.

● Click 📊 3-D Bar Chart.

Your screen should be similar to Figure 2.17

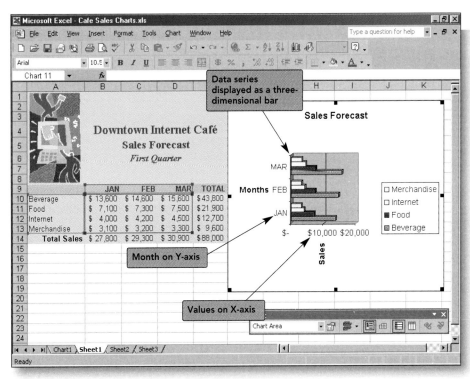

Data series displayed as a three-dimensional bar

Month on Y-axis

Values on X-axis

Figure 2.17

The 3-D bar chart reverses the X and Y axes and displays the data series as a three-dimensional bar.

As you can see, it is very easy to change the chart type and format once the data series are specified. The same data can be displayed in many different ways. Depending upon the emphasis you want the chart to make, a different chart style can be selected.

Although the 3-D bar chart shows the sales trends for the three months for the sales categories, again it does not look very interesting. You decide to look at several other chart types to see if you can improve the appearance.

First you would like to see the data represented as an area chart. An area chart represents data the same as a line chart but, in addition, it shades the area below each line to emphasize the degree of change.

3 ● **Open the** **Chart Type drop-down list.**

● **Click** 📈 **Area Chart.**

Your screen should be similar to Figure 2.18

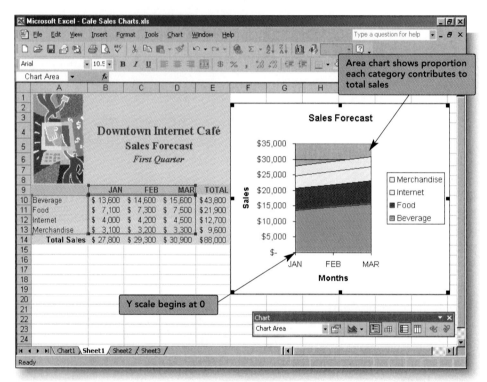

Figure 2.18

The Y-axis scale has changed to reflect the new range of data. The new Y-axis range is the sum of the four categories, or the same as the total number in the worksheet. Using this chart type, you can see the magnitude of change each category contributes to the total sales in each month.

Again you decide this is not the emphasis you want to show and will continue looking at other types of charts. Because not all chart types are available from the Chart Type drop-down list, you will use the Chart Type menu option in the Chart menu instead.

4 ● **Choose Chart/Chart Type.**

Your screen should be similar to Figure 2.19

Figure 2.19

The Chart Type dialog box contains the same options as the Chart Wizard— Step 1 dialog box. The current chart type, Area, is the selected option. You want to see how this data will look as a stacked column chart.

5 ● **Select** 📊 **Column.**

● **Select** 📊 **Stacked column with a 3-D visual effect.**

● **Click and hold**

Press and Hold to View Sample.

Your screen should be similar to Figure 2.20

Figure 2.20

The sample chart is redrawn showing the data as a stacked-column chart. This type of chart also shows the proportion of each sales category to the total sales. To see what other types of charts are available,

6 ● **Open the Custom Types tab.**

● **Click ⛰ Area Blocks.**

Your screen should be similar to Figure 2.21

Figure 2.21

The Sample area shows how the data you selected for the chart will appear in this style. Custom charts are based upon standard types that are enhanced with additional display settings and custom formatting. Although this is interesting, you feel the data is difficult to read.

7 ● **Select several other custom chart types to see how the data appears in the Sample area.**

● **Select � Columns with Depth.**

Your screen should be similar to Figure 2.22

Figure 2.22

This chart shows the sales for each category for each month with more interesting colors and three-dimensional depth.

8 Click .

Your screen should be similar to Figure 2.23

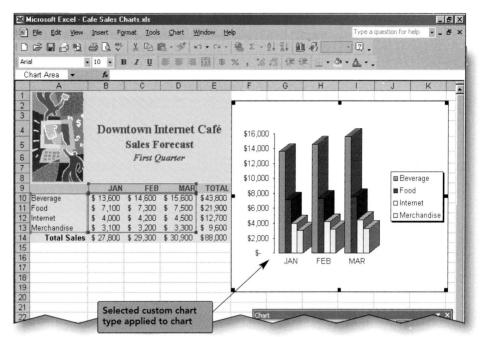

Selected custom chart type applied to chart

Figure 2.23

Adding Chart Titles

Unfortunately, when applying a custom chart type, the chart titles are deleted and you need to add them again.

1 Choose Chart/Chart Options.

● In the Titles tab, enter the following titles:

Title	Entry
Chart	**Sales Forecast**
Category	**Months**
Value	**Sales**

Your screen should be similar to Figure 2.24

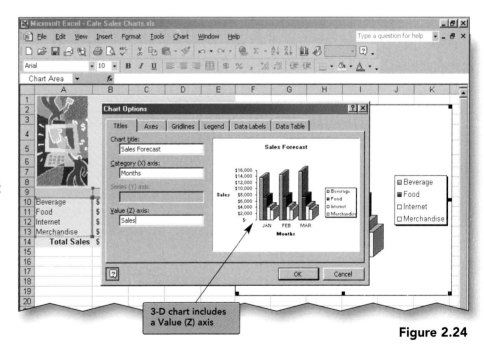

3-D chart includes a Value (Z) axis

Figure 2.24

Notice that this time instead of entering the Value axis data in the Y axis, you entered it in the Z axis. This is because the Y axis is used as a Series axis on a three-dimensional chart. This three-dimensional chart only has one series of data so the Y axis is not used.

Moving the Legend

While looking at the preview chart, you decide to move the legend below the X axis.

- Open the Legend tab.

- Select Botto**m**.

- Click [OK].

Your screen should be similar to Figure 2.25

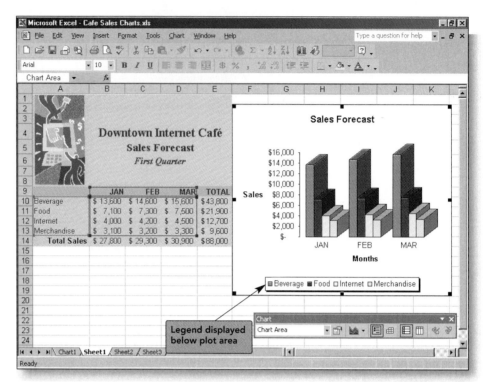

Figure 2.25

The legend is centered below the plot area of the chart and resized to fit the space.

Formatting Chart Elements

Next you want to improve the appearance of the chart by applying formatting to the different chart parts. All the different parts of a chart are separate objects. Because a chart consists of many separate objects, it is a group.

Groups

4 A **group** is two or more objects that behave as a single object when moved or sized. A chart consists of many separate objects. For example, the chart title is a single object within the chart object. Some of the objects in a chart are also groups that consist of other objects. For example, the legend is a group object consisting of separate items, each identifying a different data series.

Other objects in a chart are the axis lines, a data series, a data marker, the entire plot area, or the entire chart.

The first formatting change you want to make is to improve the appearance of the chart title. An entire group or each object in a group can be individually selected and then formatted or edited. By selecting the entire group, you can format all objects within the group at once. Alternatively, you can select an object within a group and format it individually.

① Click on the chart title to select it.

Your screen should be similar to Figure 2.26

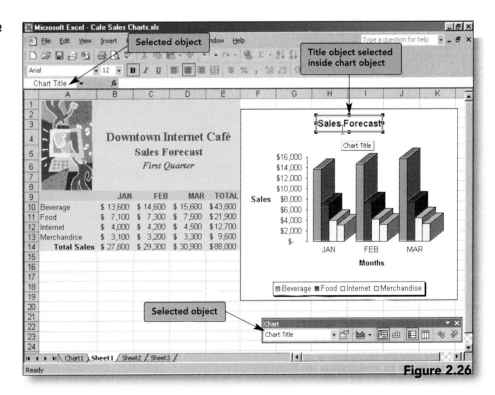

Figure 2.26

The title object is surrounded by a dotted border indicating it is a selected object and that the text inside it can be modified. In addition, the Name box and Chart Objects button display Chart Title as the selected chart object.

As different objects in the chart are selected, the commands on the Format menu change to commands that can be used on the selected object. In addition, the 🖃 Format Object button on the Chart toolbar can be used to format the selected object.

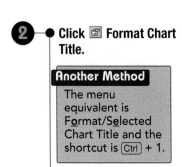

2 ● **Click 🗔 Format Chart Title.**

Another Method

The menu equivalent is **F**ormat/Selected Chart Title and the shortcut is Ctrl + 1.

● **Open the Font tab.**

Your screen should be similar to Figure 2.27

Formats selected object in chart

Figure 2.27

The Format Chart Title dialog box is used to change the patterns, font, and placement of the title.

3 ● **Scroll the Font list and select Tahoma.**

● **Scroll the Size list and select 14.**

● **Open the Color list and select Indigo (1st row, 7th column).**

● **Click [OK].**

Your screen should be similar to Figure 2.28

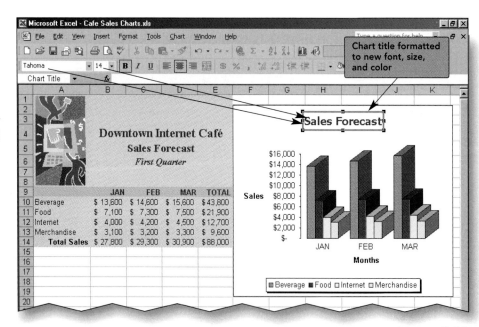

Chart title formatted to new font, size, and color

Figure 2.28

Next you want to change the color of the axis titles. A quicker way to make many formatting changes is to use the Formatting toolbar buttons.

④ ● Click the category-axis title **Months**.

● Open the 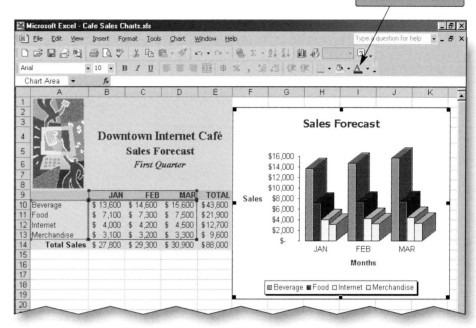 Font Color palette and change the color to Indigo.

● Change the color of the Sales title to Indigo in the same manner.

● Click outside the title to deselect it.

Your screen should be similar to Figure 2.29

Figure 2.29

Changing Orientation

You also want to change the orientation of the Sales title along the axis so that it is parallel with the axis line. To do this, you will rotate the label 90 degrees. You can quickly select a chart object and open the related Format dialog box by double-clicking the object.

① ● Double-click the Sales title to open the Format Axis Title dialog box.

● Open the Alignment tab.

● Drag the Orientation indicator line upward to rotate the text 90 degrees.

Additional Information

You can use Angle Text Downward or Angle Text Upward on the Chart toolbar to quickly change the angle of a label to 45 degrees.

Your screen should be similar to Figure 2.30

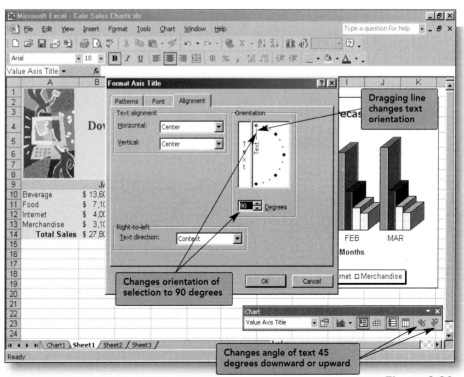

Figure 2.30

You could also enter a positive number in the Degrees box to rotate the selection from lower left to upper right or a negative number to rotate text in the opposite direction. Alternatively, you can use the Degrees scroll buttons to increase and decrease the degrees.

 Click OK .

Your screen should be similar to Figure 2.31

Figure 2.31

The Sales label is now displayed parallel with the Y-axis line.

Finally, you want to add a second line to the chart title. You want the subtitle to be in a smaller font size and italicized. You can select individual sections of text in an object and apply formatting to them just as you would format any other text entry.

3 • Select the chart title.

• Click at the end of the title to place the insertion point.

• Press `←Enter`.

• Type First Quarter.

• Drag to select the words First Quarter.

• Click *I* Italic.

• Choose 12 from the `14 ▾` Font Size drop-down list.

• Click in the title to deselect it.

• Save the workbook using the same file name.

Your screen should be similar to Figure 2.32

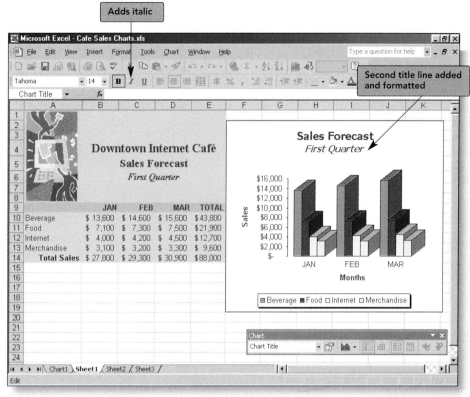

Figure 2.32

Creating a New Chart from an Existing Chart

Now you want to create another chart that will emphasize the sales trend for the Internet connection data series. This chart will use the same data series and titles as the current chart. Rather than recreate much of the same chart for the new chart, you will create a copy of the column chart and then modify it. The original chart remains in the workbook unchanged.

Copying a Chart

Copying a chart object is the same as copying any other Excel data or objects.

1 ● Select the entire chart.

HAVING TROUBLE?
When the chart ScreenTip displays Chart Area, click on the chart.

● Click 🖹 Copy.

● Move to A16.

● Click 🖹 Paste.

Another Method
You can also hold down Ctrl while clicking on the chart to create a copy.

Your screen should be similar to Figure 2.33

Copy of chart

Figure 2.33

2 ● Change the location of the new chart to a new chart sheet (Chart2).

HAVING TROUBLE?
Select the chart and choose Chart/Location.

● Move to Sheet1.

Creating a Combination Chart

To emphasize the Internet data, you want to display the data series as a line and all other data series as columns. This type of chart is called a **combination chart**. It uses two or more chart types to emphasize different information. Because you cannot mix a three-dimensional chart type with a one-dimensional chart type, you first need to change the chart type for the entire chart to a standard one-dimensional column chart. Then you can change the Internet data series to a line.

1. • Select the chart and change the chart type to Column Chart.

• Click on one of the yellow columns to select the Internet data series.

HAVING TROUBLE?

Sometimes when there are many objects close together, it is easier to select the object from the Chart Objects drop-down list.

• From the [📊▾] Chart Type drop-down menu, select [📈] Line.

Your screen should be similar to Figure 2.34

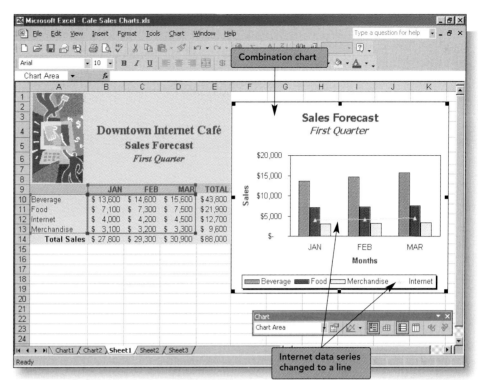

Figure 2.34

A combination chart makes it easy to see comparisons between groups of data or to show different types of data in a single chart. In this case, you can now easily pick out the Internet sales from the other sales categories.

Adding Data Labels

You would like to display data labels containing the actual numbers plotted for the Internet sales on the combination chart.

concept 5

Data Labels

5 **Data labels** provide additional information about a data marker. They can consist of the value of the marker, the name of the data series or category, a percent value, or a bubble size. The different types of data labels that are available depend on the type of chart and the data that is plotted.

Value data labels are helpful when the values are large and you want to know the exact value for one data series. Data labels that display a name are helpful when the size of the chart is large and it is hard to tell what value the data point is over. The percent data label is used when you want to display the percent of each series on charts that show parts of the whole. Bubble size is used on bubble charts to help the reader quickly see how the different bubbles vary in size.

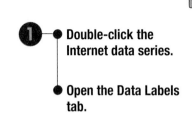

1 ● Double-click the Internet data series.

● Open the Data Labels tab.

Another Method

The menu equivalent is Format/Selected Data Series/Data Labels.

Your screen should be similar to Figure 2.35

Figure 2.35

Notice that the formula bar displays a **series formula**. This formula links the chart object to the source worksheet, Sheet1. The formula contains four arguments: a reference to the cell that includes the data series name (used in the legend), references to the cells that contain the categories (X-axis numbers), references to the numbers plotted, and an integer that specifies the number of data series plotted.

2 ● Select **V**alue.

● Click **OK** .

Your screen should be similar to Figure 2.36

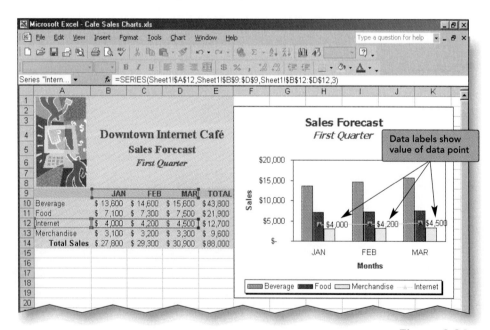

Figure 2.36

Data labels containing the actual values for Internet sales are displayed next to the data points on the line in the chart.

Changing Data Series Fill Colors

To enhance the appearance of a chart, you can change the format of the data series from the default colors to colors of your choice. As the yellow line is difficult to see on a white background, you want to change the color of the line to make it more visible.

1 ● **Double-click the Internet data series line to open the Format Data Series dialog box.**

● **Open the Patterns tab.**

Your screen should be similar to Figure 2.37

Figure 2.37

The current line and data marker settings are displayed in the Patterns tab. The Sample area shows how your selections will appear.

2 ● **Open the Line Color palette and change the color to blue.**

● **Open the Line Weight drop-down list and increase the line weight setting by one.**

● **Change the Foreground and Background marker color to blue.**

● **Click** OK **.**

Your screen should be similar to Figure 2.38

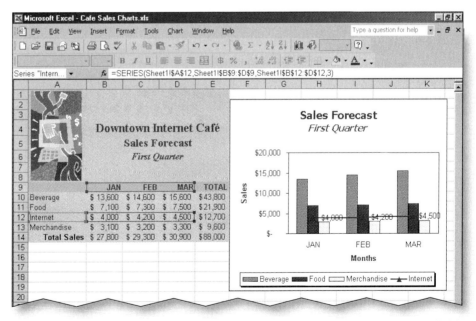

Figure 2.38

Changing Plot Area Colors

Although changing the line color increased its visibility, you think that changing the color of the plot area would also help. You could use the Format Plot Area dialog box to change the color or the Fill Color button on the Formatting toolbar.

1
● Select the plot area.

● Open the 🎨▾ Fill Color drop-down list.

● Choose tan.

Your screen should be similar to Figure 2.39

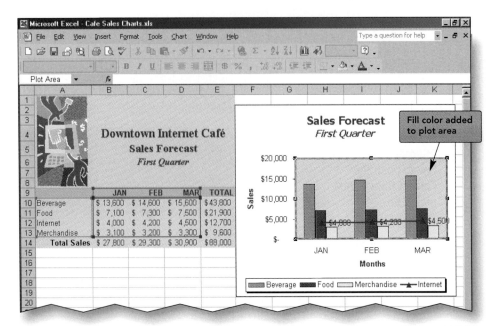

Figure 2.39

Changing Worksheet Data

After checking the worksheet and reconsidering the amounts you have budgeted for the different categories, you now feel that you have underestimated the increase in Internet sales. You are planning to heavily promote the Internet aspect of the Café and anticipate that Internet usage will increase dramatically in February and March and then level off in the following months. You want to change the worksheet to reflect this increase.

1
● Change the February Internet sales value to **6000**.

● Change the March Internet sales value to **12000**.

Your screen should be similar to Figure 2.40

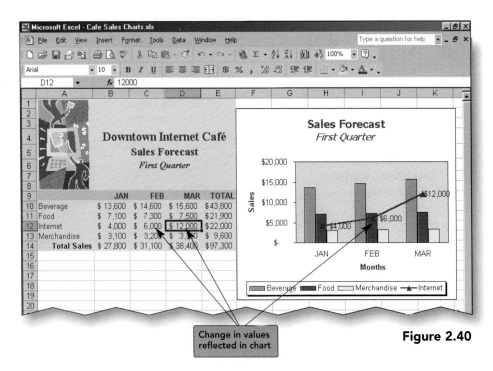

Figure 2.40

The worksheet has been recalculated and all charts that reference those worksheet cells have been redrawn to reflect the change in the data for the Internet sales. Since the chart document is linked to the source data, changes to the source data are automatically reflected in the chart.

2 ● **Look at the charts in the Chart1 and Chart2 sheets to see how they have changed to reflect the change in data.**

Your screen should be similar to Figure 2.41

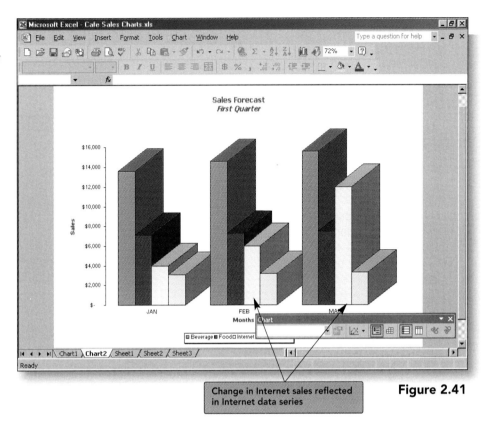

Change in Internet sales reflected in Internet data series

Figure 2.41

The Internet Sales column reflects the change in data in both charts.

Adding a Text Box

Sometimes the information you want to convey in a chart is complicated and may need clarification. In this case, although the chart reflects the Internet sales changes you made in the worksheet, it does not identify the reason for the increase. This information can be entered in a text box.

concept 6

Text Box

6 A **text box** is a rectangular object in which you type text. Text boxes can be added to a sheet or a chart object. To add it to a chart, the chart object must be selected first, otherwise the text box is added to the worksheet. A text box that is part of a chart object can only be sized and moved within the chart object. If you move the chart object, the text box moves with it because it is part of the group. If you do not add it to the chart, it will not move as part of the chart if you move the chart to another location.

Text that is entered in a text box wraps to fit within the boundaries of the text box. This feature is called **word wrap** and eliminates the need to press [Enter] to end a line. If you change the size and shape of the text box, the text automatically rewraps on the line to adjust to the new size.

You will add a text box containing the text Internet Promotion to draw attention to the increase in Internet sales. A text box is created using the Text Box button on the Drawing toolbar.

1 ● **Switch to Sheet1.**

● **Select the chart.**

● **Click** **Drawing (on the Standard toolbar).**

● **Click** **Text Box (on the Drawing toolbar).**

● **Move the mouse pointer to the space above the February columns of data and drag to create a text box that is approximately 1 1/2 inch by 1/2 inch (see Figure 2.42).**

Additional Information

The mouse pointer appears as ↓, indicating a text box will be created as you drag the mouse.

Your screen should be similar to Figure 2.42

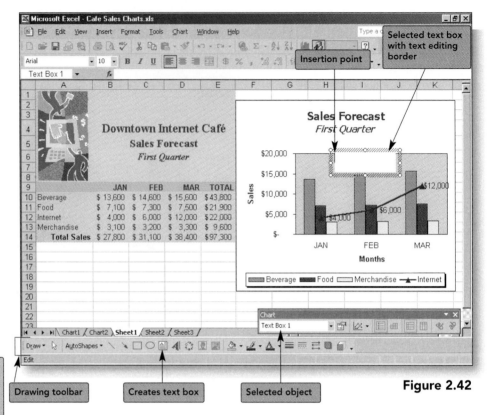

Figure 2.42

Additional Information

A dotted border around a selected object indicates that you can format the box itself. Clicking the hatched border changes it to dotted border.

The text box is a selected object and is surrounded with a hatched border that indicates you can enter, delete, select, and format the text inside the box. It also displays an insertion point indicating that it is waiting for you to enter the text. As you type the text in the text box, do not be concerned if all the text is not visible within the text box. You will resize the box if needed to display the entire entry.

2 ● **Type** Effects of Internet Promotion.

● **If necessary, adjust the size of the text box by dragging the sizing handles until it is just large enough to fully display the text on two lines.**

● **Click outside the text box to deselect it.**

Your screen should be similar to Figure 2.43

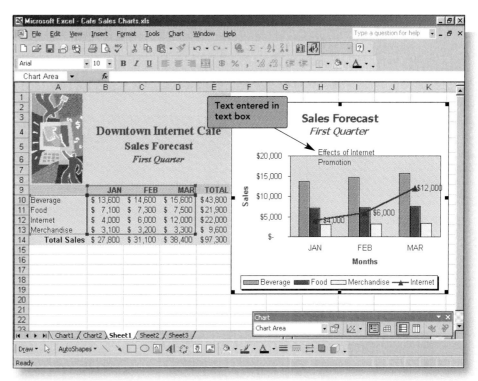

Figure 2.43

The text in the text box is difficult to read because it overlaps the plot area and the box does not include a border line or fill color. To make it stand out better, you will add a fill color to the text box.

3 ● **Select the text box.**

● **Click the hatched text box border to turn off text editing (the insertion point disappears).**

Additional Information

The text box border is dotted and the insertion point is not displayed, indicating you can edit the text box.

● **Open the** 🎨 **Fill Color drop-down list and select Indigo.**

Additional Information

You can use the 🎨 and 🅰 buttons on either the Formatting or Drawing toolbars.

● **From the** 🅰 **Font Color list, select White.**

● **Readjust the size of the text box and move it to the position displayed in Figure 2.44.**

Your screen should be similar to Figure 2.44

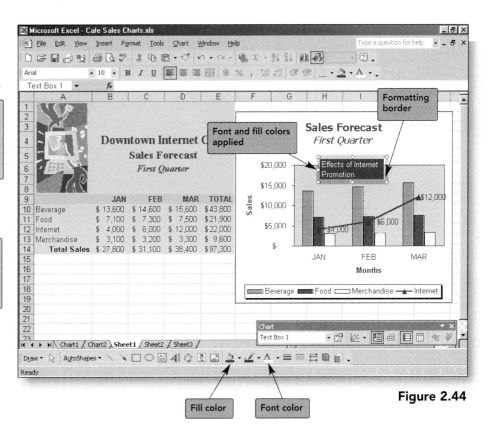

Figure 2.44

Adding Arrows

Next you want to draw an arrow from the text box to the Internet data series line. Like a text box, an arrow is a separate object that can be added to a worksheet or a chart.

1 ● Click Arrow (on the Drawing toolbar).

Additional Information

The mouse pointer appears as a ✛.

● To draw the arrow, click on the lower-right corner of the text box and drag to the Internet line. (See Figure 2.45)

Additional Information

If you hold down ⇧Shift while dragging, a straight horizontal line is drawn.

Your screen should be similar to Figure 2.45

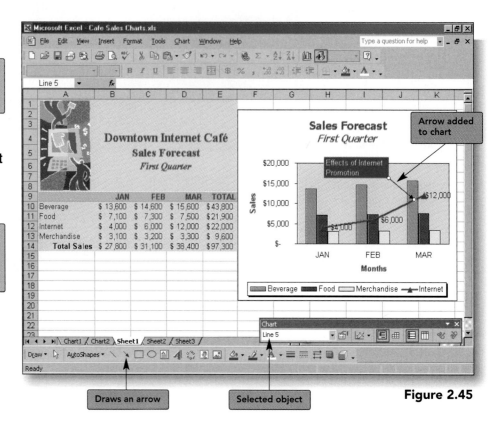

Figure 2.45

A line with an arrowhead at the end is displayed. The arrow is automatically a selected object. The handles at both ends of the arrow let you adjust its size and location. You can also change the color and weight of the line to make it stand out more.

② If necessary, move and size the arrow to adjust its position as in Figure 2.46.

● Click ![Line Color] Line Color and select Indigo.

● Click ![Line Style] Line Style and increase the line weight to 1 1/2 point.

● Deselect the arrow.

● Click ![Save] Save.

Your screen should be similar to Figure 2.46

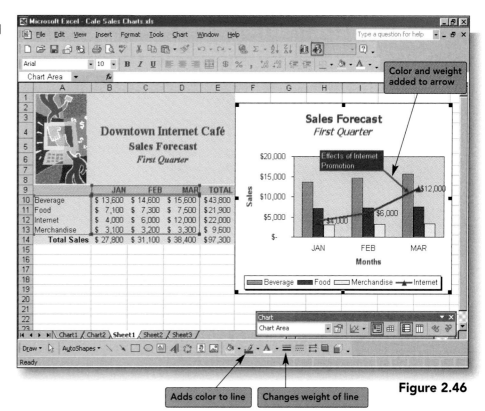

Figure 2.46

Adds color to line   Changes weight of line

Creating and Formatting a Pie Chart

The last chart you will make will use the Total worksheet data in column E. You want to see what proportion each type of sales are of all sales for the quarter. The best chart for this purpose is a pie chart.

A pie chart compares parts to the whole in a similar manner to a stacked-column chart. However, in pie charts, there are no axes. Instead, the worksheet data that is charted is displayed as slices in a circle or pie. Each slice is displayed as a percentage of the total.

Selecting the Pie Chart Data

The use of X (category) and data series settings in a pie chart is different from their use in a column or line chart. The X series labels the slices of the pie rather than the X axis. The data series is used to create the slices in the pie. Only one data series can be specified in a pie chart.

The row labels in column A will label the slices and the total values in column E will be used as the data series.

In addition to creating a chart using the Wizard, you can create a chart by selecting the chart type from the Chart Type toolbar button after the data series has been selected.

Additional Information
You can also create a chart using the default chart type (column) in a new chart sheet by selecting the data range and pressing F11.

1 ● Select A10 through
A13 and E10 through
E13.

HAVING TROUBLE?
Hold down Ctrl
while selecting
nonadjacent ranges.

● If necessary, display
the Chart toolbar.

● Open the [icon] Chart
Type drop-down menu
and choose [icon] 3-D
Pie Chart.

*Your screen should be
similar to Figure 2.47*

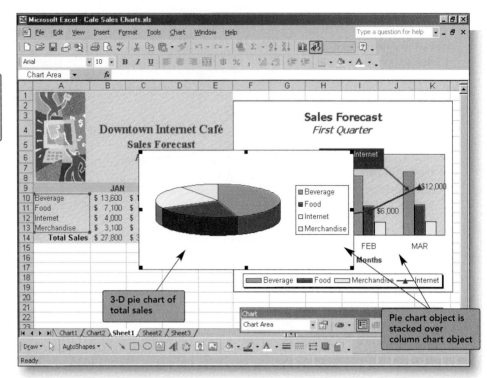

Figure 2.47

A three-dimensional pie chart is drawn in the worksheet. Each value in the data series is displayed as a slice of the pie chart. The size of the slice represents the proportion each sales category is of total sales.

As objects are added to the worksheet, they automatically **stack** in individual layers. The stacking order is apparent when objects overlap. Stacking allows you to create different effects by overlapping objects. Because you can rearrange the stacking order, you do not have to add or create the objects in the order in which you want them to appear.

2 ● Move the combination
chart to top-align with
cell A16 below the
worksheet data.

● Move and size the pie
chart to be displayed
over cells F1 through
K14.

Additional Information
Hold down Alt while moving
to snap the chart to the cells.

*Your screen should be
similar to Figure 2.48*

Figure 2.48

Formatting the Pie Chart

To clarify the meaning of the chart, you need to add a chart title. In addition, you want to turn off the legend and display data labels instead to label the slices of the pie.

1 ● Choose **C**hart/Chart Op**t**ions.

● Open the Titles tab.

● In the Chart Title text box, enter Total Sales by Category.

● Open the Legend tab and clear the Show Legend option.

Another Method

You can also click Legend to turn on/off the display of the legend.

● Open the Data Labels tab and select the Category name and **P**ercentage options.

● Click OK .

Your screen should be similar to Figure 2.49

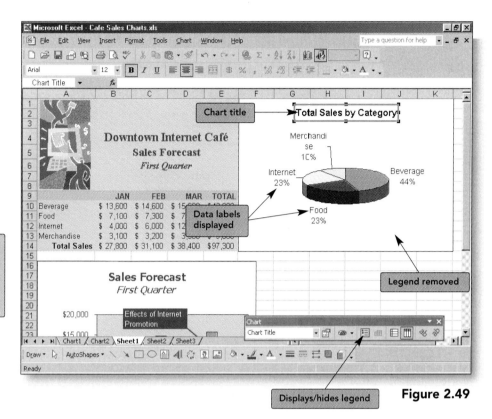

Figure 2.49

The pie chart is redrawn to show the data labels and percents. The data label text box size is based on the size of the chart and the text is appropriately sized to fit in the box. Because the default size of data labels is a little too large, the entire Merchandise label does not appear on one line. To fix this, you will change the font of the data label text. You also want to enhance the appearance of the data labels and title.

2 ● Change the title to Tahoma, 14 pt and Indigo.

● Select the data labels.

● Change the font to Arial Narrow.

● Change the font color to Indigo.

Your screen should be similar to Figure 2.50

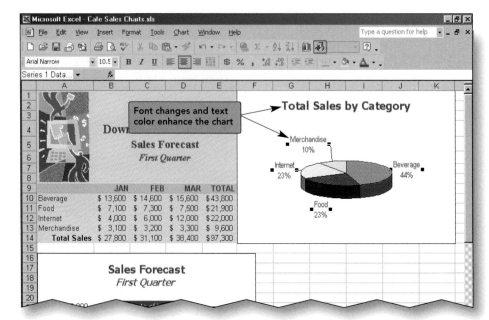

Figure 2.50

Exploding and Rotating the Pie

Next, you want to separate slightly or **explode** the Internet slice of the pie to emphasize the data in that category.

1 ● Select the Internet slice.

HAVING TROUBLE?
To select an object within a group, select the group first and then select the object within the group. Selection handles surround the selected object.

● Drag the selected slice away from the pie.

Additional Information
If all slices on the pie are selected, dragging one slice explodes all slices at the same time.

Your screen should be similar to Figure 2.51

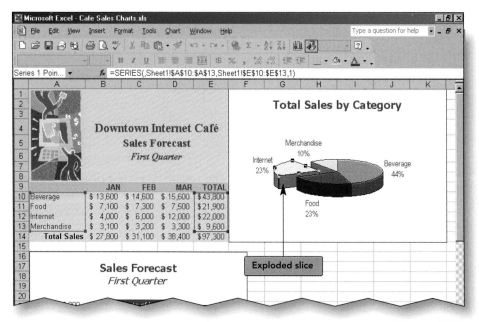

Figure 2.51

The slice is separated from the rest of the pie chart. You also want to change the position of the Internet slice so that it is toward the front of the pie. When a pie chart is created, the first data point is placed to the right of the middle at the top of the chart. The rest of the data points are placed in order to the right until the circle is complete. To change the order in which the slices are displayed, you can rotate the pie chart.

2
- **Double-click the Internet data series slice.**
- **Open the Options tab.**
- **Change the Angle of first slice setting to 180 degrees.**
- **Click** OK **.**

Your screen should be similar to Figure 2.52

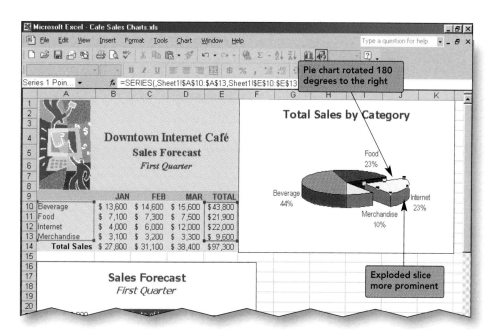

Figure 2.52

The entire pie chart has rotated 180 degrees to the right and now the Internet data slice appears toward the front of the chart.

Applying Patterns and Color

The last change you would like to make is to add patterns to the pie chart data points. As you have seen, when Excel creates a chart each data series (or data point in the case of a pie chart) is automatically displayed in a different color. Although the data series are easy to distinguish from one another onscreen, if you do not have a color printer the colors are printed as shades of gray and may be difficult to distinguish. To make the data series more distinguishable on a black-and-white printer, you can apply a different pattern to each data series object.

1
- **Double-click the Beverage data series slice.**
- **Open the Patterns tab.**

Your screen should be similar to Figure 2.53

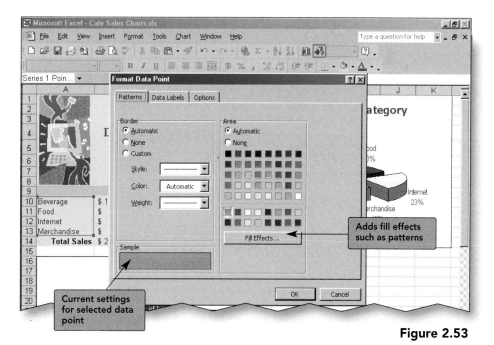

Figure 2.53

The options available in the Pattern tab vary depending upon the type of data point that is selected. In this case, because the selected data point is a pie slice, the options let you change the border and the background area. The current setting for the selected data point is displayed in the sample area. This consists of a black border with a fill color of periwinkle blue. You will add a pattern.

2 • Click [Fill Effects...] .

• Open the Pattern tab.

Your screen should be similar to Figure 2.54

Figure 2.54

From the Fill Effects dialog box, you can change options for gradients, textures, patterns, and pictures used in formatting the selected object. You will add a pattern to the existing fill.

3 • From the Pattern palette, select a pattern of your choice.

• Click [OK] (twice) to close both dialog boxes.

Your screen should be similar to Figure 2.55

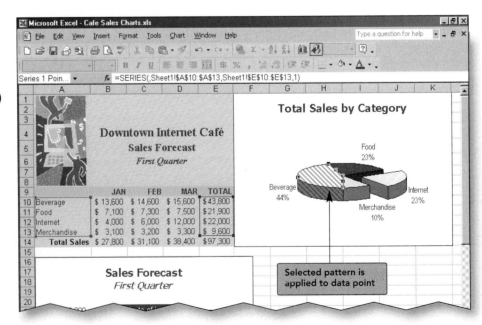

Figure 2.55

The pattern is applied to the selected data point. Next you will add a pattern to the Internet data series slice.

4 ● **Double-click the Internet data series slice.**

● **Click** Fill Effects... .

● **Open the Pattern tab.**

Your screen should be similar to Figure 2.56

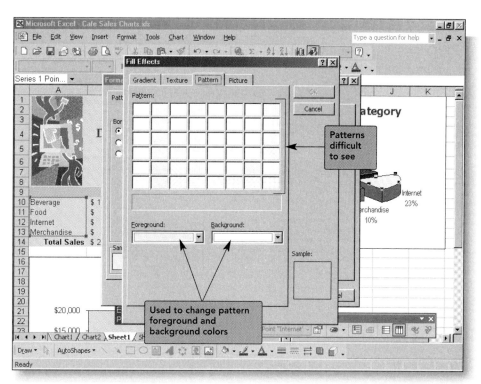

Figure 2.56

Because yellow is a light color, it is difficult to see the patterns in the Fill Effects dialog box. A pattern consists of a foreground color and a background color. The default foreground color is the same as the fill color and the background color is white. To increase the contrast, you can change the color selection of either.

5 ● **From the Foreground color drop-down list, select a darker color of your choice.**

● **Select a different pattern.**

● **Click** OK **(twice).**

Your screen should be similar to Figure 2.57

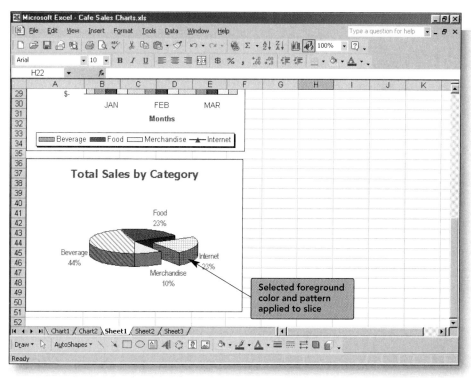

Figure 2.57

You will leave the other two data points without patterns. Finally you want to make the pie chart plot area larger.

6 ● Select the plot area.

● Drag the sizing handle outward to increase the pie chart size slightly as in Figure 2.58.

● Select the pie chart and move it below the combination chart to top-align with cell A36.

● Deselect the chart.

● Close the Chart toolbar.

● Save the workbook.

Your screen should be similar to Figure 2.58

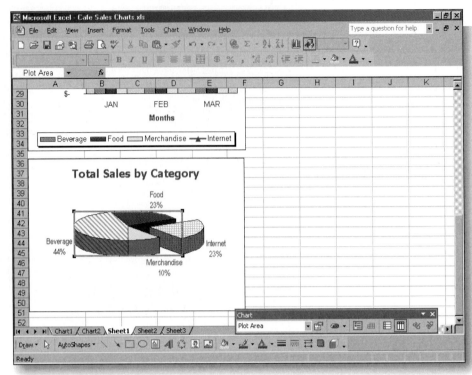

Figure 2.58

Documenting a Workbook

Now you are ready to preview and print the worksheet and charts. Before doing this, however, you will add documentation to the workbook. Each workbook includes summary information that is associated with the file.

1 ● Choose File/Properties.

● Select each tab in the Properties dialog box and look at the recorded information.

● Open the Summary tab.

Your screen should be similar to Figure 2.59

Figure 2.59

The Summary tab is used to specify information you want associated with the file such as a title, subject, author, keywords, and comments about the workbook file. Additionally, you can specify to save a picture of the first page of the file for previewing in the Open dialog box. This information helps you locate the workbook file you want to use as well as indicate the objectives and use of the workbook.

Additional Information

Saving a preview picture with your file increases the file size.

2 ● Enter the following information in the Summary tab.

Title	Downtown Internet Cafe
Subject	Sales Forecast
Author	your name

Additional Information

The Author text box may be blank or may show your school or some other name. Clear the existing contents first if necessary.

● Select the Save preview picture option.

● Click ___OK___ .

Your chart should be similar to Figure 2.60

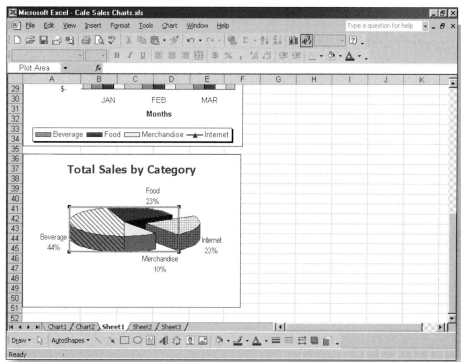

Figure 2.60

Preparing the Workbook for Printing

It is very important before printing charts to preview how they will appear when printed. Formats that look good onscreen may not produce good printed results.

Before printing, you can change the layout of the worksheet and charts to improve the appearance of the printed output. The size and alignment of the worksheet can be changed to make it more attractive on the paper. Additionally, you can include information in a header on each page.

Previewing the Workbook

Your workbook file includes two new chart sheets and a worksheet. You decide the worksheet would look better with more space between the data and charts. You will adjust the placement of the charts and then preview the entire workbook. To preview them all at once, you need to change the print setting to print the entire workbook first.

1 ● **Move the combination chart to top-align with cell A18.**

● **Move the pie chart to top-align with cell A40.**

Your screen should be similar to Figure 2.61

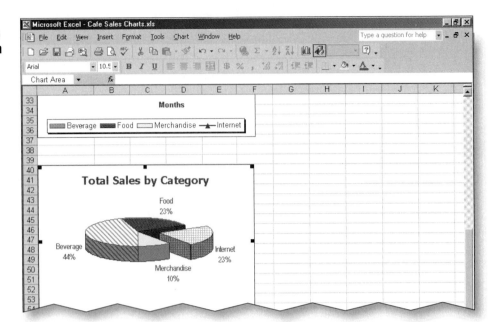

Figure 2.61

Changes settings associated with sheet you are previewing

2 ● **Deselect the chart object.**

● **Choose File/Print/Entire workbook.**

● **Click** `Preview`.

● **If necessary, reduce the zoom to see the full page.**

Your screen should be similar to Figure 2.62

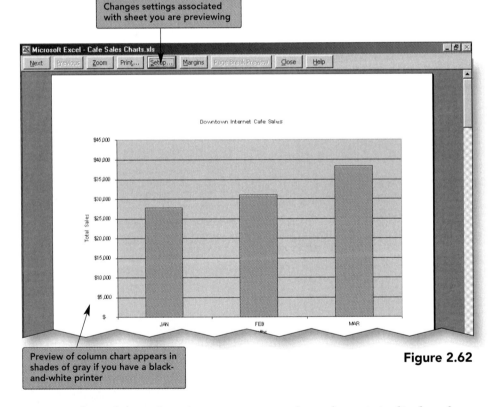

Preview of column chart appears in shades of gray if you have a black-and-white printer

Figure 2.62

Because the column chart is on a separate chart sheet, it is displayed on a page by itself. In addition, if you are not using a color printer, the preview displays the chart colors in shades of gray as it will appear when printed on a black-and-white printer. You will change the print setting associated with this chart sheet to fix this problem. The Print Preview toolbar buttons are used to access many print and page layout changes while you are previewing a document.

3 ● Click `Setup...`.

● Open the Chart tab.

*Your screen should be
similar to Figure 2.63*

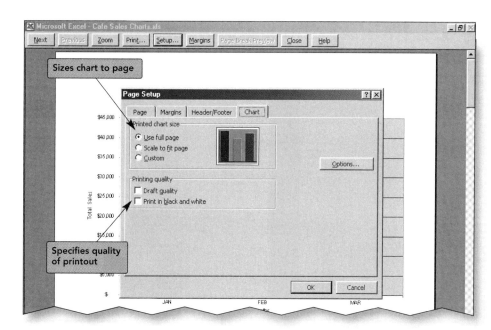

Sizes chart to page

Specifies quality
of printout

Figure 2.63

Additional Information

You can print an embedded
chart without the worksheet
by selecting it before using
the command to print.

Because chart sheets print only one chart on a page, the default setting is to
size the chart to fill the entire page. The Draft Quality setting suppresses the
printing of graphics and gridlines, thereby reducing printing time. The
black-and-white option applies patterns to data series in place of colors
while leaving other areas in shades of gray. If there is a single data series, it
is changed to solid black. On a color printer, all other areas are still printed
in color when this option is selected.

4 ● Select Print in black
and white.

● Click `OK`.

*Your screen should be
similar to Figure 2.64*

Another Method

The menu equivalent is
File/Page Setup/Chart/Print
in **b**lack and white.

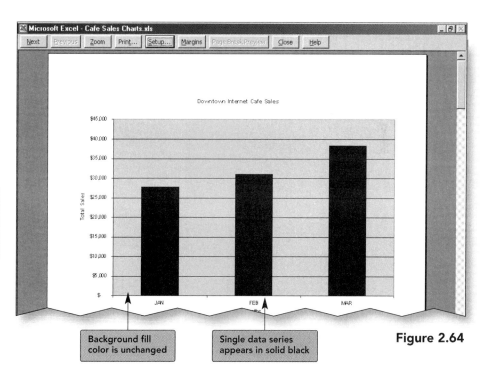

Background fill
color is unchanged

Single data series
appears in solid black

Figure 2.64

The data series changes to black and the background fill has not changed.

5 ● Click [Next] to see the chart in the next Chart sheet.

Your screen should be similar to Figure 2.65

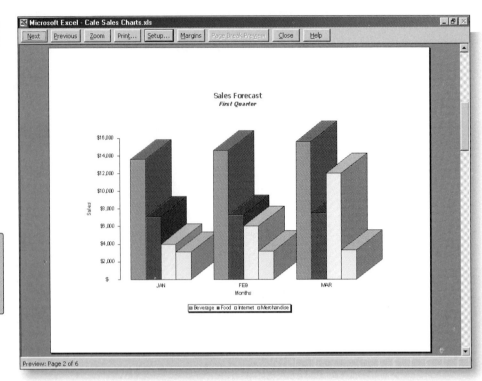

Figure 2.65

Chart 2 looks as if it will print satisfactorily using the default print settings.

6 ● Click [Next] to see the worksheet and charts in Sheet 1.

Your screen should be similar to Figure 2.66

Figure 2.66

HAVING TROUBLE?

Depending upon the printer, your chart may not exceed the margins. If this is the case, skip the next section.

You can now see that the bottom of the pie chart exceeds the page margins and will not print on the page. You can also see that the printout will not appear balanced between the page margins. You will make several changes to the layout of the page to correct these problems.

Sizing the Worksheet

First you will reduce the worksheet and chart sizes so that they will fit on one page. Although you could resize the charts in the worksheet, a quicker way is to use the scaling feature to reduce or enlarge the worksheet contents by a percentage or to fit it to a specific number of pages. You want to have the program scale the worksheet to fit on one page.

1 ● Click Setup... .

● If necessary, open the Page tab.

● Select **F**it to.

● Click OK .

Your screen should be similar to Figure 2.67

Another Method

The menu equivalent is File/Page Setup/Page/Fit to.

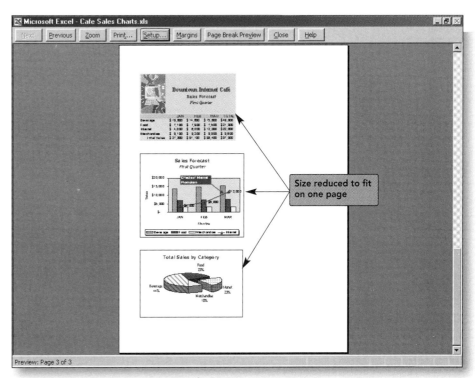

Size reduced to fit on one page

Preview: Page 3 of 3

Figure 2.67

The size of the worksheet and charts has been reduced and they now fit on a single page.

Aligning a Sheet on a Page

Additional Information

The margins can be changed individually by adjusting the size of the settings.

You would also like to center the worksheet horizontally on the page. The default worksheet margin settings include 1-inch top and bottom margins and .75-inch right and left margins. The **margins** are the blank space outside the printing area around the edges of the paper. The worksheet contents appear in the printable area inside the margins. You want to center the worksheet data horizontally within the existing margins.

1 • Click [Setup...] .

• Open the Margins tab.

• Select Hori**z**ontally.

Your screen should be similar to Figure 2.68

Another Method

The menu equivalent is **F**ile/Page Set**u**p/Margins/ Hori**z**ontally.

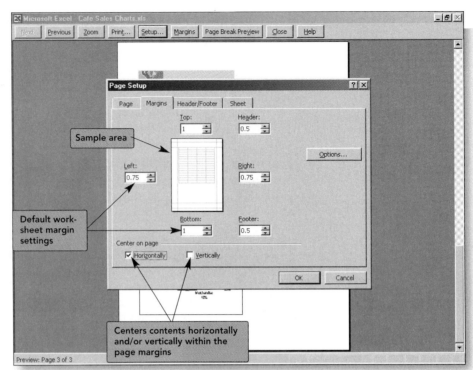

Figure 2.68

The sample area shows the effect of this change on the page layout.

Adding Predefined Headers and Footers

Finally, you want to include your name and the date in a header.

---

concept 7

Header and Footer

7 A **header** is a line or several lines of text that appears at the top of a page just above the top margin line. A **footer** is a line or several lines of text that appears at the bottom of a page just below the bottom margin line. Information that is commonly placed in a header or footer includes the date and page number.

You can select from predefined header and footer text or enter your own custom text. The information contained in the predefined header and footer text is obtained from the document properties associated with the workbook and from the program and system settings.

Header and footer text can be formatted like any other text. In addition, you can control the placement of the header and footer text by specifying where it should appear: left-aligned, centered, or right-aligned in the header or footer space.

You will add a predefined header to the worksheet that displays your name, the date and page number.

1 ● Open the
Header/Footer tab.

● Open the Header drop-
down list box and se-
lect the Prepared By
[your name] [date],
Page 3 option.

Another Method

The menu equivalent is File/
Page Setup/Header/Footer.

*Your screen should be
similar to Figure 2.69*

Additional Information

Predefined footers can be
added by selecting the
footer option from the
Footer drop-down list.

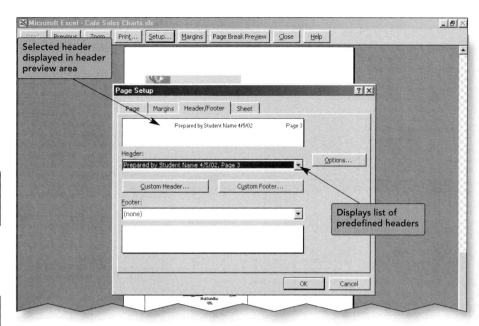

Figure 2.69

The selected header is displayed in the header area of the dialog box. It
could then be edited or formatted to meet your needs.

2 ● Click [OK].

*Your screen should be
similar to Figure 2.70*

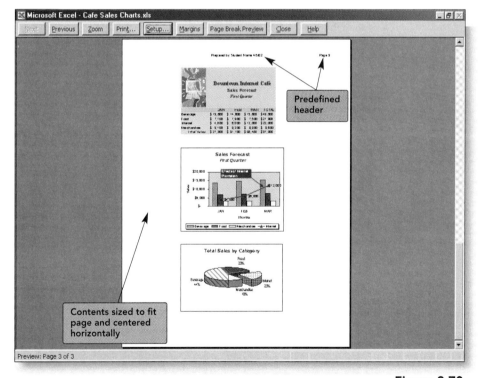

Figure 2.70

The preview window displays the worksheet centered horizontally between
the right and left margins. The header you selected is displayed above the
top margin line. It now appears the way you want it to look when printed.

3 ● Add a predefined footer to each of the chart sheets that displays your name, page number, and date.

HAVING TROUBLE?
Click Previous to display previous sheets.

Your screen should be similar to Figure 2.71

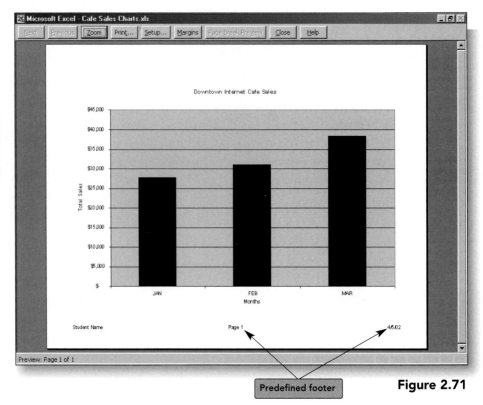

Predefined footer

Figure 2.71

Printing the Workbook

Printing a worksheet that includes charts requires a printer with graphics capability. However, the actual procedure to print is the same as printing a worksheet that does not include charts.

1 ● Click Print....

● Move to cell A9 of Sheet1.

● If necessary, close the Chart and Drawing toolbars.

● Exit Excel, saving the workbook again.

The workbook documentation and page layout settings you specified have been saved with the workbook file.

Your printed output should be similar to that shown here.

LAB 2
Organizing Your Work

Chart (EX2.5)

A **chart** is visual representation of data that is used to convey information in an easy-to-understand and attractive manner. Different types of charts are used to represent data in different ways.

Chart Elements (EX2.6)

Chart elements consist of a number of parts that are used to graphically display the worksheet data.

Chart Objects (EX2.12)

A **chart object** is a graphic object that is created using charting features included in Excel. A chart object can be inserted into a worksheet or into a special chart sheet.

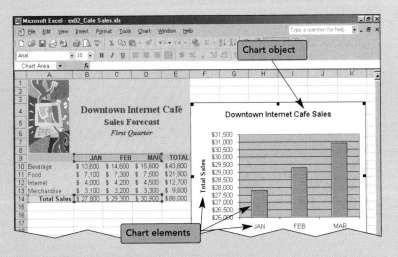

Group (EX2.25)

Because it consists of many separate objects, a chart object is a group. A **group** is two or more objects that behave as a single object when moved or sized.

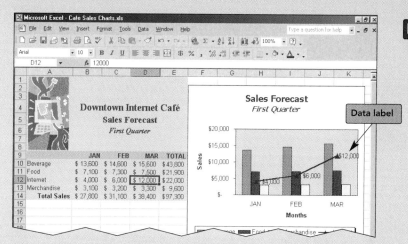

Data Label (EX2.31)

Data labels provide additional information about a data marker.

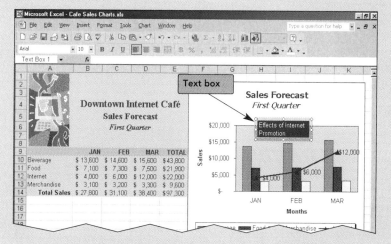

Text Box (EX2.35)

A **text box** is a rectangular object in which you type text. Text boxes can be added to a sheet or to a chart object.

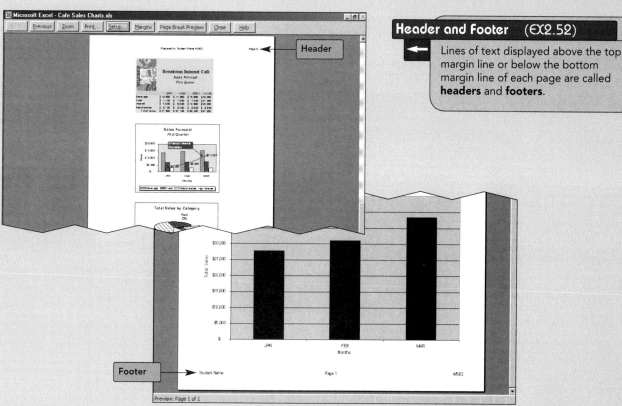

Header and Footer (EX2.52)

Lines of text displayed above the top margin line or below the bottom margin line of each page are called **headers** and **footers**.

key terms

category-axis EX2.6

category-axis title EX2.6

category name   EX2.6

chart   EX2.5

chart gridlines   EX2.6

chart object   EX2.12

chart title   EX2.6

combination chart   EX2.30

data label   EX2.31

data marker   EX2.6

data series   EX2.6

embedded chart   EX2.12

explode   EX2.42

footer   EX2.52

group   EX2.25

header   EX2.52

legend   EX2.6

margins   EX2.51

plot area   EX2.6

series formula   EX2.32

stack   EX2.40

text box   EX2.35

value axis   EX2.6

value-axis title   EX2.6

word wrap   EX2.35

X axis   EX2.6

Y axis   EX2.6

Z axis   EX2.6

mous skills

The Microsoft Office User Specialist (MOUS) certification program is designed to measure your proficiency in performing basic tasks using the Office XP applications. Getting certified demonstrates that you have the skills and provides a valuable industry credential for employment. After completing this lab, you have learned the following Microsoft Office User Specialist skills:

Skill	Description	Page
Formatting and Printing Worksheets	Modify Page Setup options for worksheets	EX2.51
Creating and Modifying Graphics	Create, modify, and position and print charts	EX2.49

command summary

Command	Shortcut Keys	Button	Action
File/Print/Entire Workbook			Prints all the sheets in a workbook
File/Properties/Summary			Specify information to document file
File/Page Setup/Header/Footer			Adds header and/or footer
File/Page Setup/Chart/ Print in black and white			Prints chart in black and white
File/Page Setup/Margins/ Horizontally			Horizontally centers contents between margins
File/Page Setup/Page/Fit to			Sizes print area to fit on a specified number of pages
Insert/Chart		📊	Starts the Chart Wizard
Format/Selected Data Series/ Data Labels			Adds data labels to data points
Format/Selected Legend	Ctrl + 1		Changes format of legend
Format/Selected Chart Title	Ctrl + 1	🔲	Changes format of selected chart title
Format/Selected Data Series	Ctrl + 1	🔲	Changes format of selected data series
Chart/Chart Type		📉▾	Changes type of chart
Chart/Chart Options/Legend/ Show Legend		📄	Displays/Hides legend
Chart/Location			Places chart in selected worksheet or chart sheet

Terminology

screen identification

In the following worksheet and chart, letters identify important elements. Enter the correct term for each screen element in the space provided.

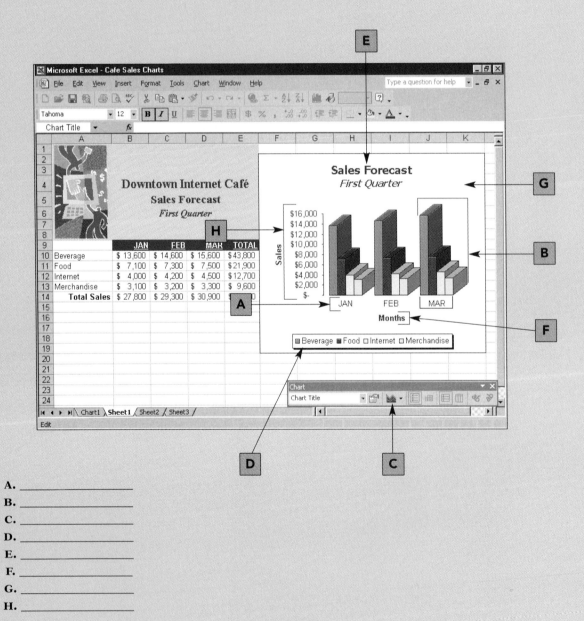

A. _____

B. _____

C. _____

D. _____

E. _____

F. _____

G. _____

H. _____

matching

Match the lettered item on the right with the numbered item on the left.

1. [icon] _____ **a.** numbered scale along left boundary line of the chart

2. data marker _____ **b.** bottom boundary line of the chart

3. [icon] _____ **c.** identifies each number represented in a data series

4. X-axis _____ **d.** area of chart bounded by X- and Y-axes

5. explode _____ **e.** changes the type of chart

6. plot area _____ **f.** identifies the chart data series names and data markers

7. column chart _____ **g.** a chart that displays data as vertical columns

8. Value axis _____ **h.** starts the Chart Wizard

9. legend _____ **i.** to separate wedge slightly from other wedges of pie

10. combination chart _____ **j.** includes mixed data markers

multiple choice

Circle the correct response to the questions below.

1. A(n) _____ links a chart object to the source worksheet.
   a. embedded chart
   b. stack
   c. series formula
   d. data marker

2. The _____ names displayed along the X-axis correspond to the headings for the worksheet data that is plotted along the X-axis.
   a. variable
   b. category
   c. value
   d. option

3. A _____ identifies the chart data series names and data markers that correspond to each data series.
   a. category
   b. value axis
   c. legend
   d. data label

4. Charts that are inserted into a worksheet are called:
   a. embedded objects
   b. attached objects
   c. inserted objects
   d. active objects

5. A(n) _____ represents data like a line chart and shades the area below each line to emphasize the degree of change.
   a. combination chart
   b. area chart
   c. surface chart
   d. doughnut chart

6. _____ can consist of the value of the marker, the name of the data series or category, a percent value, or a bubble size.
   a. legends
   b. X axis
   c. Y axis
   d. data labels

7. A(n) _____ is a rectangular object in which you type text.
   a. text box
   b. label
   c. input box
   d. embedded object

8. A _____ displays the data values as columns stacked upon each other.
   a. line chart
   b. bar chart
   c. stacked-column chart
   d. combination chart

9. Charts that display data as slices of a circle and show the relationship of each value in a data series to the series as a whole are called:
   a. area charts
   b. value charts
   c. pie charts
   d. bar charts

10. A chart that uses two or more chart types to emphasize different information is called a(n):
    a. area chart
    b. pie chart
    c. bar chart
    d. combination chart

true/false

Circle the correct answer to the following questions.

1.	The plot area is visually displayed within the X- and Y-axis boundaries.	True	False
2.	A bar chart displays data as a line and is commonly used to show trends over time.	True	False
3.	The Y-axis title line is called the category-axis title.	True	False
4.	An entire group or each object in a group can be individually selected and then formatted or edited.	True	False
5.	A series formula links the chart object to the source worksheet.	True	False
6.	Value data labels are helpful when the values are large and you want to know the exact value for one data series.	True	False
7.	Text that is entered in a text box wraps to fit within the boundaries of the text box.	True	False
8.	Separating slightly or exploding a slice of a pie chart emphasizes the data.	True	False
9.	Patterns can be added to slices of a pie chart to make it easier to read.	True	False
10.	A header is a line or several lines of text that appears at the bottom of each page just below the top margin.	True	False

Concepts

fill-in questions

Complete the following statements by filling in the blanks with the correct terms.

1. A visual representation of data in an easy-to-understand and attractive manner is called a(n) _____.

2. A(n) _____ describes the symbols used within the chart to identify different data series.

3. The bottom boundary of a chart is the _____ and the left boundary is the _____.

4. A chart that is inserted into a worksheet is a(n) _____ object.

5. A(n) _____ is a line or several lines of text that appears at the top of each page just below the top margin.

6. A(n) _____ is two or more objects that behave as a single object.

7. _____ provide additional information about a data marker.

8. A(n) _____ identifies the chart data series names and data markers that correspond to each data series.

9. The _____ is a numbered scale whose numbers are determined by the data used in the chart.

10. A chart that is inserted into a separate chart sheet is also saved with the _____ file.

discussion questions

1. Define each of the following terms and discuss how they are related to one another: chart type, chart element, and chart object.

2. Discuss how column and bar charts represent data. How do they differ from pie charts?

3. What type of information would best be represented by a line chart?

4. Describe how a 3-D column chart differs from a 2-D column chart.

Hands-on Exercises

step-by-step

Charting U.S. Home Values

★ **1.** Kevin Young works for a real estate company and has been collecting information on sales prices for existing homes across the country. Kevin wants to graph some of the data in the worksheet for his upcoming presentation on home prices in the Midwest. The completed worksheet with charts is shown here.

a. Open the workbook file ex02_Real Estate Prices.

b. Create a line chart on a separate sheet showing the housing prices for the four years for the Midwest only. Title the chart appropriately. Remove the legend.

c. Make the line heavier and change the line and data marker color. Change the fill of the plot area to a gradient effect with two colors of your choice.

d. Add data labels that display the values. Increase the size of the data labels and position them below the line.

e. Increase the size of the chart title and axis labels and add a text color of your choice. Save the workbook as Real Estate Charts.

f. Create a column chart in the worksheet showing housing prices for the four regions for the four years. The X axis will display the years and the regions will be the legend. Title the chart appropriately. Move the legend to the bottom of the chart.

g. Position the chart below the worksheet data and size it appropriately. Increase the size of the chart title and add color. Turn off the plot area fill color.

h. Document the workbook file by adding your name as author and include a preview picture.

i. Preview the workbook. Add a predefined header to the worksheet and chart sheet that displays your name, page number, and date. Center the worksheet horizontally on the page. Print the worksheet. Print the chart sheet

j. Save the workbook again.

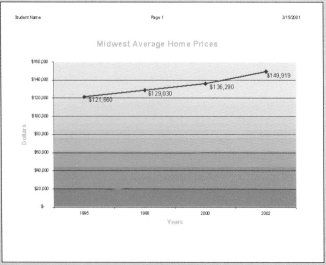

Bengal Tiger Populations

★★ **2.** Jennifer's environmental studies paper is on the endangered Bengal tiger. She has some data saved in a worksheet on the estimated number of tigers in 1997. She has asked you to help her chart the data and make the worksheet look more attractive. The completed worksheet with charts is shown here.

a. Open the workbook ex02_Tiger Data.

b. Use ChartWizard to create a stacked column with 3-D effect chart of the data in cells B6 through D11. Plot the data series from the rows. Enter the chart title Tiger Population Estimates. Enter the Value (Z) axis title of Number of Tigers. Embed the chart in the worksheet.

c. Size the chart over cells A13 through E30.

d. Rotate the Z-axis title 90 degrees. Change the chart and axis title color to green. Change the color for the China data series to green.

e. Save the workbook as Tiger Charts.

f. Create a 3-D pie chart in the worksheet showing the maximum tiger population estimates. Include the title Maximum Estimated Tiger Population and display the category name and percents as data labels. Do not include a legend.

g. Move the pie chart below the column chart and size it over cells A32 through E48.

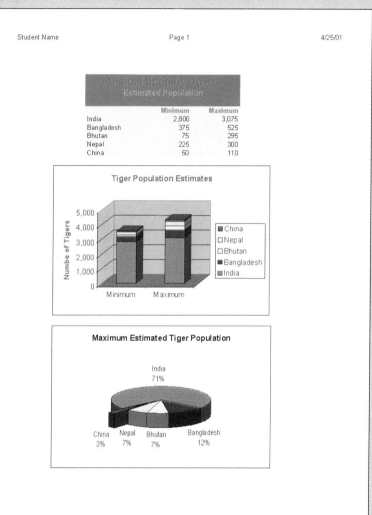

h. Change the data label font to Arial Narrow. Rotate the chart 230 degrees. Explode the China slice. Change the color of the China slice to green.

i. Change the maximum estimated tiger population for China to 110.

j. Document the workbook file by adding your name as author.

k. Preview the worksheet. Add a predefined header to the worksheet that displays your name, page number, and date. Center the worksheet horizontally on the page.

l. Print the worksheet on one page.

m. Save the workbook again.

Tracking Winter Bird Populations

★★ **3.** Richard Johnson volunteers for the Downtown City Park Bird Observation Society. He has compiled a worksheet of the number of bird observations in the park for the last year. He would like a chart that shows the society how the winter bird population differs by month and a chart that shows the total number of bird sightings this year. The completed worksheet with charts is shown here.

a. Open the file ex02_Birds.

b. Chart the monthly data for the 3 types of birds as a line chart. Set the series to be displayed in Rows.

c. Enter the Chart title **Bird Observations by Month**, and the Value (Y) axis as **Number of Birds**. Display the legend below the chart.

d. Position the chart over cells A11 through N27.

e. Add color and font refinements to the chart titles as you like. Change the plot area color to blue. Change the Fox Sparrow data series color to red.

f. Save the workbook as Bird Observations.

g. Create another chart of the data in columns A and N as a 3-D Pie Chart. Title the chart **Total Bird Observations**. Turn off the legend and use the category name and percentage to label the data labels.

h. Position the chart over cells A29 through N45. Add color and font refinements to the chart title as you like. Rotate the chart 120 degrees so the Pied-billed Grebe slice is at the front of the chart. Increase the size of the plot area. Change the data label point size to 12. Explode the Pied-billed Grebe slice.

i. Document the workbook file by adding your name as author. Save the workbook with a picture preview.

j. Preview the worksheet. Add a predefined header to the worksheet that displays your name, page number, and date. Center the worksheet horizontally on the page. Print the worksheet.

k. Save the workbook file again.

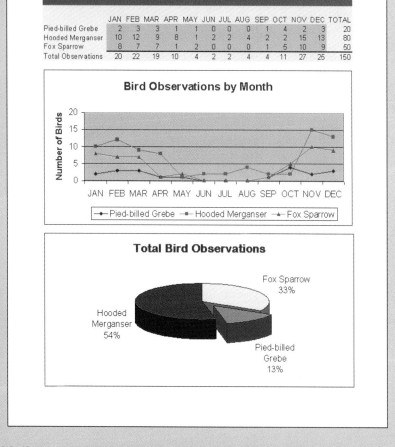

Student Name — Page 1 — 4/25/01

Bird Observations

	JAN	FEB	MAR	APR	MAY	JUN	JUL	AUG	SEP	OCT	NOV	DEC	TOTAL
Pied-billed Grebe	2	3	3	1	1	0	0	0	1	4	2	3	20
Hooded Merganser	10	12	9	8	1	2	2	4	2	2	15	13	80
Fox Sparrow	8	7	7	1	2	0	0	0	1	5	10	9	50
Total Observations	20	22	19	10	4	2	2	4	4	11	27	25	150

Children's Athletic Programs

★ ★ ★ **4.** Carol Hayes is the program coordinator for Fitness Lifestyles, a physical conditioning and health center. She is proposing to management that they increase their emphasis on child fitness. To reinforce the need for this type of investment, she has found some recent data about growth in the number of children (in millions) participating in sports. She wants to create several charts of this data to emphasize the demand.

a. Create a worksheet of the following data.

	1992	1995	2000
Baseball	3320	3421	3694
Basketball	6125	6200	7420
In-line Skating	1893	7110	8176
Running/Jogging	3510	3429	3257
Slow-pitch Softball	3652	3946	4261
Soccer	2585	2674	3510
Touch Football	4500	4040	4363
Volleyball	3620	3941	4295

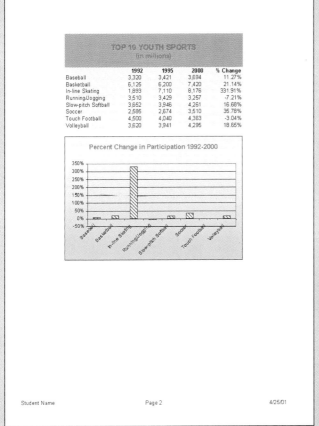

b. Add an appropriate title over the data and format the numbers to show commas with no decimal places. Calculate the percent change from 1992 to 2000 in column E (2000 value – 1992 value)/1992 value). Add a column heading. Enhance the worksheet as you like to improve its appearance. Save the workbook as Youth Sports Charts.

c. Create a clustered column chart of the worksheet data in columns A through D as a new sheet. Enter a chart title and Y axis title. Include a text box and arrow pointing to the increase in basketball and indicate that this would be an easy fit into the existing program. Enhance the chart using features presented in the lab.

d. Create an embedded column chart in the worksheet showing the Gain/Loss data for the sports. Include the title Percent Change in Participation 1992–2000. Remove the legend and format the Y-axis to a font size of 12 and no decimal places. Format the X-axis to a font size of 12 and display the labels at a 45-degree angle.

e. Move the chart below the worksheet and re-size.

f. Enhance the chart using features presented in the lab.

g. Document the workbook by adding your name as author. Save the workbook with a picture preview.

h. Preview the worksheet. Add a predefined footer to the worksheet that displays your name, page number, and date to both sheets. Center the worksheet horizontally on the page. Print the worksheet and the area chart.

i. Save the workbook again.

Salaries in Higher Education

★ ★ 5. Wendy Murray's class is studying career opportunities. Part of her class is interested in pursuing
★   careers in higher education. She has done some research and found data that she entered into a worksheet. She would like to chart the data to make an impression on her students.

a. Open the workbook ex02_Higher Education.

b. Format the worksheet using the features you have learned.

c. Create an embedded column chart for the six levels for the four school categories and Average. Move the legend to the bottom of the chart.

d. Display the chart below the worksheet. Change the Average data to a line. Display the average values as data labels. Format the chart to your liking.

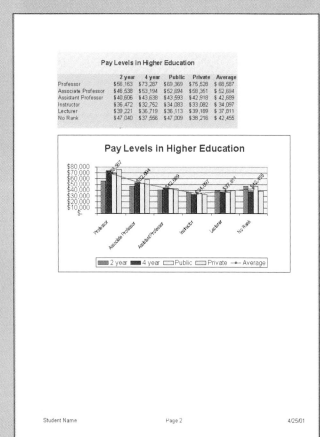

e. Create a bar chart of the Public and Private data as a new sheet. Display the values as data labels. Format the chart similar to your previous chart.

f. Document the workbook file by adding your name as author. Save the workbook with a preview picture.

g. Preview the worksheet. Add a predefined footer to the worksheet and chart sheets that displays your name, page number, and date. Center the worksheet horizontally on the page. Print the worksheet and the charts.

h. Save the workbook file as Higher Education Charts.

Market Seminar

★ **1.** Tom Duggan is preparing for an upcoming job market seminar he is presenting. He has collected data comparing the average hourly pay rate for several professional jobs in the state to the U.S. average rates. He thinks the information would be much more meaningful and have greater impact if it was presented in a chart. Using the data in the workbook ex02_ Job Market, create an appropriate chart of the data for Physicians and Surgeons, Podiatrists, Dentists, and Lawyers on a separate chart sheet. Include appropriate chart titles. Add a pattern to the data series and change the plot area fill color. Enhance the chart in other ways using different font sizes and font colors. Position the legend at the bottom of the chart. Document the workbook by adding your name as author. Add a predefined header to the chart sheet that displays your name, page number, and date. Save the workbook as Seminar and print the chart.

Grade Tracking

★ **2.** Create a worksheet that tracks your grades. It can be a record of the test scores you received this semester, or it can be a record of your GPA each semester. Create an embedded chart that best represents your grade trends. Use the formatting techniques you have learned to change the appearance of the worksheet and the chart. Save the workbook as Grades. Include a header or footer that displays your name and the current date in the worksheet. Print the worksheet with the chart.

Stock Market Workbook

★ ★ **3.** You are interested in the stock market. Use Help to learn more about the Stock chart type. Pick four related stocks and create an embedded stock chart of the data. Save the worksheet with the chart as Stocks. Include a header or footer that displays your name and the current date in the worksheet. Print the worksheet and the chart.

Win/Loss Data

★ ★ ★ **4.** Kevin Tillman has started a new job with Baseball Statistics, Inc. He would like some help creating a worksheet that contains team win/loss records for the last five years. He asks you to search the Web for records. Choose a MLB team of your choice and locate the win/loss record for the last five years. Enter the data into a worksheet. Enhance the worksheet using the features you have learned. Create an embedded chart that displays the information over the five years. Include a header or footer that displays your name and the current date in the worksheet. Save the workbook as Statistics. Print the worksheet with the chart.

Insurance Comparisons

★ ★ ★ **5.** Robert Sanchez is thinking about purchasing a new SUV. However, he is concerned about the insurance rates for the vehicles he is considering. Before purchasing, he wants to find out the insurance rates on the vehicles he is evaluating. Select three different comparable SUVs and use the Web or visit several insurance agents to get the insurance premium cost information for the same amount of coverage from two different insurance companies. Use your own personal information as the basis for the insurance quotes. Create a worksheet that contains the SUV models, purchase price, and insurance premium quotes for each vehicle. Create an embedded chart of the data that shows the models and premiums. Enhance the chart appropriately. Include a header or footer that displays your name and the current date in the worksheet. Save the workbook as Insurance. Print the worksheet and chart.

Managing and Analyzing a Workbook

LAB 3

objectives

After completing this lab, you will know how to:

1.	Spell-check a sheet.
2.	Use Paste Function.
3.	Use absolute references.
4.	Copy, move, and name sheets.
5.	Use Autofill.
6.	Reference multiple sheets.
7.	Zoom the worksheet.
8.	Split windows and freeze panes.
9.	Use What-If analysis and Goal Seek.
10.	Change page orientation.
11.	Add custom headers and footers.
12.	Print selected sheets.

Formula errors are identified and easily corrected using the error checking feature.

Multiple sheets in a workbook make it easy to edit several sheets simultaneously and to perform calculations based on data from multiple sheets.

Forecasting values using Goal Seek to help perform what-if analysis are powerful features of Excel

Downtown Internet Café

You present your new, more optimistic, first quarter forecast for the Downtown Internet Café to Evan, who has made several formatting and design changes. In addition, he asks you to include an Average calculation and to extend the forecast for the next three quarters. Moreover, he wants to hold back on your idea of an aggressive Internet sales promotion. The Café's funds are low due to the cost of the recent renovations. Evan feels, therefore, that you should stick with a more conservative forecast of income derived from Internet sales.

After discussing the situation, you agree that the Café will likely lose money during the first month of operations. Then the Café should show increasing profitability. Evan stresses that the monthly profit margin should reach 5 per cent in the second quarter.

As you develop the Café's financial forecast, the worksheet grows in size and complexity. You will learn about features of Excel 2002 that help you manage a large workbook efficiently. You will also learn how you can manipulate the data in a worksheet to reach a goal using the what-if analysis capabilities of Excel. The completed annual forecast is shown here.

1	**Spell Checking** The spell-checking feature locates misspelled words, duplicate words, and capitalization irregularities in the active worksheet and proposes the correct spelling.
2	**Absolute References** An absolute reference is a cell or range reference in a formula whose location does not change when the formula is copied.
3	**Sheet Names** Each sheet in a workbook can be assigned a descriptive name to identify the contents of the sheet.
4	**AutoFill** The AutoFill feature makes entering long or complicated headings easier by logically repeating and extending the series.
5	**Sheet and 3-D References** A formula containing sheet and 3-D references to cells in different worksheets in a workbook allows you to use data from other worksheets and to calculate new values based on this data.
6	**Split Windows** A sheet window can be split into sections called panes to make it easier to view different parts of the sheet at the same time.
7	**Freeze Panes** Freezing panes prevents the data in the panes from scrolling as you move to different areas in the worksheet.
8	**What-If Analysis** What-if analysis is a technique used to evaluate the effects of changing selected factors in a worksheet.
9	**Goal Seek** Goal Seek is a tool that is used to find the value needed in one cell to attain a result you want in another cell.

Correcting Worksheet Errors

Excel 2002 includes several tools to help you find and correct errors in both text and formula entries. Text errors, such as spelling and typing errors, can be located quickly and corrected using the spelling checker. Potential problems in formulas are identified and can be corrected using the formula error checking features.

Checking Spelling

After talking with Evan, the owner of the Café, about the first quarter forecast, you are ready to begin making the changes he suggested. Evan returned the workbook file to you containing the changes he made to the format of the worksheet. To see the workbook file with these changes,

1 Start Excel 2002.

● **Open the workbook** ex03_First Quarter Forecast.

Your screen should be similar to Figure 3.1

Misspelled row label

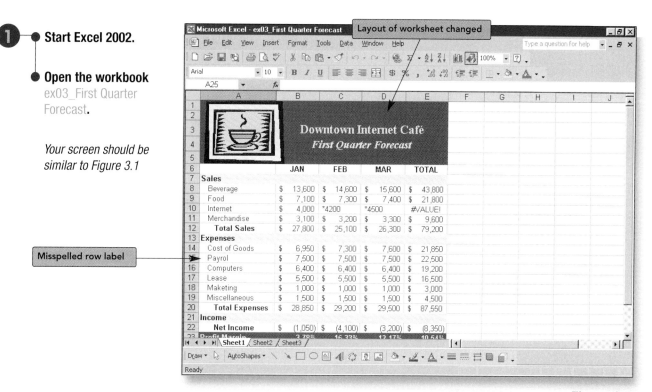

Figure 3.1

As you can see, Evan made several formatting changes to the worksheet. He found a new graphic and changed the fill and text colors to coordinate with the picture. Additionally, he made several changes to the row labels. For example, the Salary label has been replaced with Payroll. However, the new label is misspelled. Just to make sure there are no other spelling errors, you will check the spelling of all text entries in this worksheet.

concept 1

Spell Checking

1 The **spelling checker** locates all misspelled words, duplicate words, and capitalization irregularities in the active worksheet and proposes the correct spelling. This feature works by comparing each word to a dictionary of words. If the word does not appear in the **main dictionary** or in a custom dictionary, it is identified as misspelled. The main dictionary is supplied with the program; a **custom dictionary** is one you can create to hold words you commonly use but that are not included in the main dictionary.

When you check spelling, the entire active worksheet including cell values, text boxes, headers and footers, and text in embedded charts is checked. It does not check spelling in formulas or text that results from formulas. You can also restrict the area to be checked by first selecting a range. If the formula bar is active when you check spelling, only the contents of the formula bar are checked.

Excel begins checking all worksheet entries from the active cell forward. To check the spelling in the worksheet,

2 ● Click ✓ **Spelling.**

Your screen should be similar to Figure 3.2

Located misspelled word

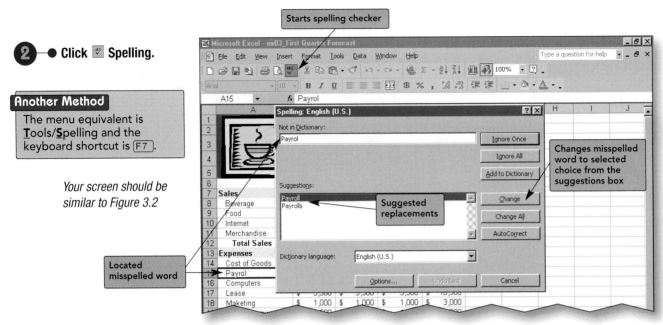

Figure 3.2

The spelling checker immediately begins checking the worksheet for words that it cannot locate in its main dictionary. The cell selector moves to the first cell containing a misspelled word, in this case Payrol, and the Spelling dialog box is displayed. The word it cannot locate in the dictionary is displayed in the Not in Dictionary text box. The Suggestions text box displays a list of possible replacements. If the selected replacement is not correct, you can select another choice from the suggestions list or type the correct word in the Not in Dictionary text box.

The option buttons shown in the table below have the following effects:

Option	Effect
Ignore Once	Leaves selected word unchanged
Ignore All	Leaves this word and all identical words in worksheet unchanged
Change	Changes selected word to word highlighted in Suggestions text box
Add to Dictionary	Adds selected word to a custom dictionary so Excel will not question this word during subsequent spell checks
Change All	Changes this word and all identical words in worksheet to word highlighted in Suggestions text box
AutoCorrect	Adds a word to the AutoCorrect list so the word will be corrected as you type

You want to accept the suggested replacement, Payroll.

3 ● Click [Change].

Your screen should be similar to Figure 3.3

Spelling error corrected

Next located spelling error

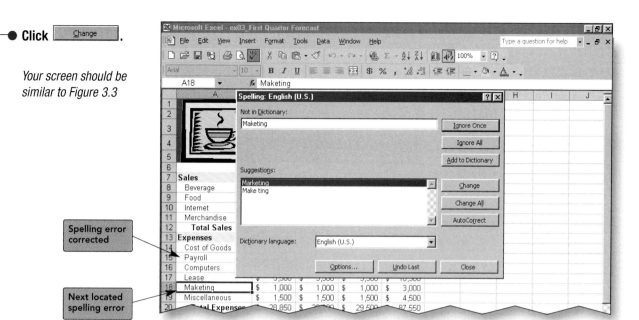

Figure 3.3

The correction is made in the worksheet, and the program continues checking the worksheet and locates another error, Maketing.

4 ● **Change this word to Marketing.**

Your screen should be similar to Figure 3.4

Spelling error corrected

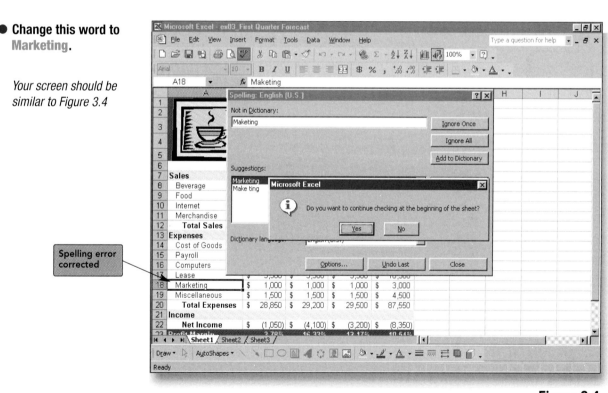

Figure 3.4

The program continues checking the worksheet. When it reaches the end of the sheet, because the cell selector was not at the beginning of the sheet when checking started, the program asks if you want to continue checking at the beginning of the sheet. When no other errors are located, a dialog box is displayed, informing you that the entire worksheet has been checked.

5 ● Click [Yes].

● Click [OK] to end spell checking.

Your screen should be similar to Figure 3.5

Figure 3.5

Correcting Formula Errors

As you continue to check over the worksheet, you notice a problem in cell E10. If a formula cannot properly calculate a result, an error value is displayed and a triangle appears in the top-left corner of the cell. Each type of error value has a different cause as described in the following table.

Error value	Cause
#####	Column not wide enough to display result or negative date or time is used
#VALUE!	Wrong type of argument or operand is used
#DIV/0!	Number is divided by zero
#NAME?	Text in formula not recognized
#N/A	Value not available
#REF!	Cell reference is not valid
#NUM!	Invalid number values
#NULL!	Intersection operator is not valid

You can correct each identified error individually or use the formula checker to check them all, one at a time. To correct them individually, select the cell and click ⊕ Error Options to display the menu of options that can be used to correct the problem. The formula checker is similar to the spelling checker in that it goes to each location in the worksheet containing a formula error, identifies the problem, and suggests corrections. You will use the formula checker to correct this error and check the entire worksheet for others.

1 Choose **T**ools/Error
Chec**k**ing.

If necessary, move the
dialog box to see the
located formula error.

*Your screen should be
similar to Figure 3.6*

Asterisks change
entry type to text

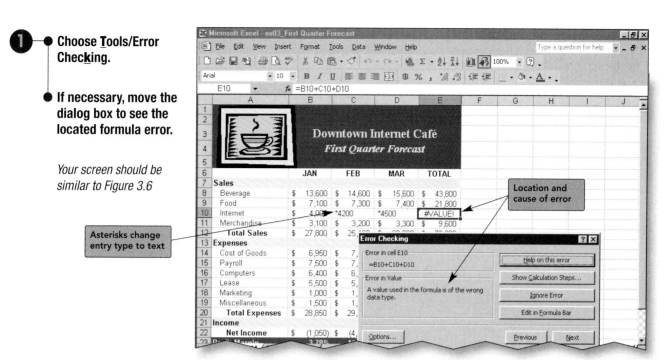

Figure 3.6

The Error Checking dialog box identifies the location and cause of the
error. In this case, when Evan changed the Internet sales values back to the
original estimates, he included an * in the cell entry to make sure you no-
ticed the change. Because Excel interprets this entry as a text entry, it cannot be used in this formula.. To correct the problem, you need to enter the
values correctly.

2 Move to cell C10 and
enter **4200**.

Enter **4500** in cell D10.

*Your screen should be
similar to Figure 3.7*

Entries are
value entries

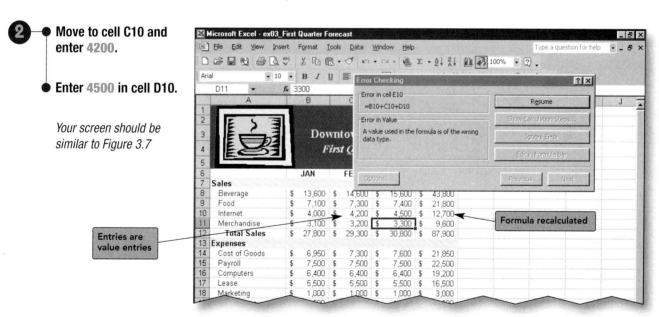

Figure 3.7

Cell E10 now displays the correctly calculated result. The two values you
entered will need to be formatted again to Accounting. You will continue
checking the worksheet for formula errors and, when error checking is
complete, you will reformat the values.

3 ● Click [Resume].

● Click [OK].

● **Apply the Accounting format to cells C10 and D10.**

Your screen should be similar to Figure 3.8

Figure 3.8

Now you are ready to make several of the changes requested by Evan. First you will add a column showing the average values for the first quarter.

4 ● **Enter the heading AVG in cell F6.**

● **Move to F8.**

Your screen should be similar to Figure 3.9

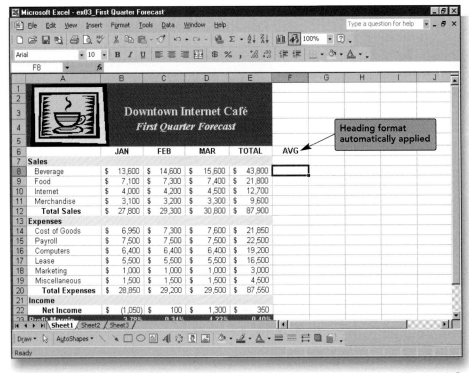

Heading format automatically applied

Figure 3.9

Notice the new heading is already appropriately formatted to bold and centered. This is because Excel automatically extends formats to new cells if the format of at least three of the last five preceding columns appears that way.

In addition to the SUM function, you can also use Σ AutoSum to enter several other commonly used functions. This includes functions to calculate an Average, Minimum, Maximum, and Count.

5 ● **Open the Σ AutoSum drop-down menu.**

● **Choose Average.**

Your screen should be similar to Figure 3.10

Figure 3.10

Excel identifies the range of cells B8 through E8 for the function argument. Because it incorrectly includes the total value in cell E8, you need to specify the correct range.

6 ● **Drag to select cells B8 through D8.**

● **Press ←Enter.**

Your screen should be similar to Figure 3.11

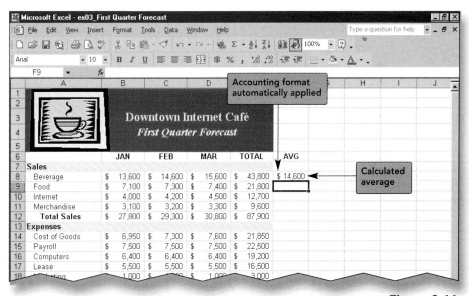

Figure 3.11

The average of the beverage sales for the quarter, 14,600, is calculated and displayed in cell F8. Notice that Excel again extended the format to the new cell, saving you the step of applying the Accounting format.

Next you need to copy the function down column F.

7 ● **Copy the function into cells F9 through F22.**

Your screen should be similar to Figure 3.12

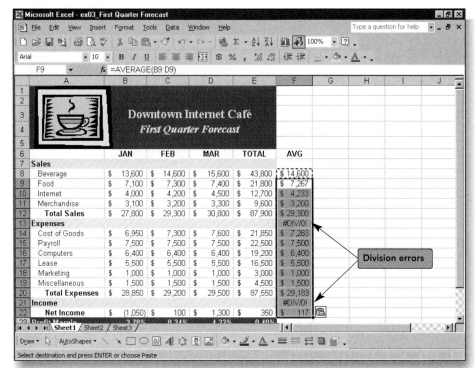

Figure 3.12

The average value has been correctly calculated for each row. Notice, however, that two cells display the error value #DIV/0! indicating the cells contains a formula error.

8 ● **Move to cell F13.**

● **Point to** ⬦ **Error Options.**

Your screen should be similar to Figure 3.13

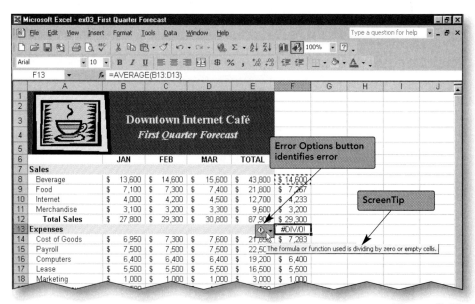

Figure 3.13

The Error Options button displays a ScreenTip identifying the cause of the error; in this case the formula is attempting to divide by zero or empty cells. This time you will individually correct the error.

9 ● Click ⓘ Error Options.

● Choose Edit in Formula Bar.

Your screen should be similar to Figure 3.14

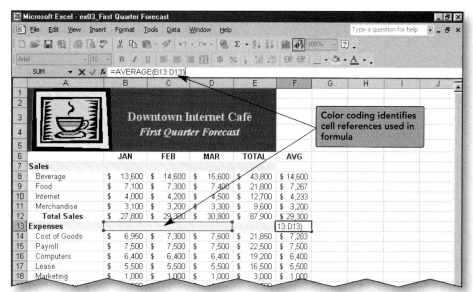

Figure 3.14

Notice that the cell references in the formula are color coded to match the borders Excel displays around the referenced worksheet cells. It is designed to provide visual cues to the relationships between the cells that provide values to the formulas or the cells that depend on the formulas. You can now easily see the error is caused by references to blank cells when the function was copied. Since you do not need this formula, you will delete it.

10 ● Press Esc.

● Press Delete.

Your screen should be similar to Figure 3.15

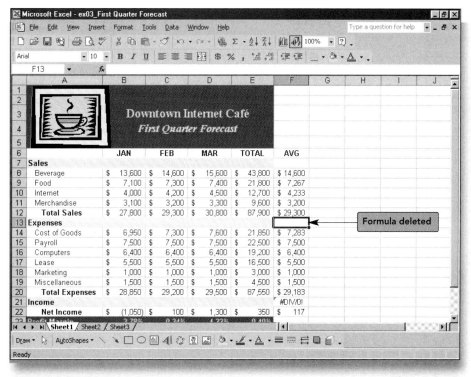

Figure 3.15

Likewise, you need to delete the function that was copied into cell F21. You will clear the entry in this cell using the fill handle.

Move to cell F21.

Point to the fill handle and when the mouse pointer changes to +, drag upward until the cell is gray.

Release the mouse button.

Your screen should be similar to Figure 3.16

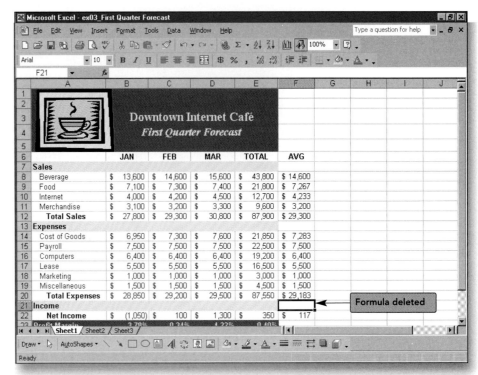

Figure 3.16

Using Absolute References

While looking at the sales data in the worksheet, you decide it may be interesting to find out what contribution each sales item makes to total sales. To find out, you will enter a formula to calculate the proportion of sales by each in column G. The formula to calculate the proportion for beverage sales is Total Beverage Sales/Total Sales.

Enter the heading Proportion in cell G6.

Enter the formula =E8/E12 in cell G8.

If necessary, move to G8.

Your screen should be similar to Figure 3.17

Figure 3.17

The value 0.498294 is displayed in cell G8. This shows that the beverage sales are approximately 50 percent of total sales.

Next, to calculate the proportion for Food Sales, you will copy the formula from G8 to G9. Another quick way to copy cell contents is to drag the cell border while holding down $\boxed{\text{Ctrl}}$. This method is most useful when the distance between cells is short and they are both visible in the window. It cannot be used if you are copying to a larger range than the source range.

2 ● **Point to the border of cell G8 and when the mouse pointer shape is $\stackrel{\mathbb{k}}{\rightarrow}$, hold down $\boxed{\text{Ctrl}}$ and drag the mouse pointer to cell G9.**

Your screen should be similar to Figure 3.18

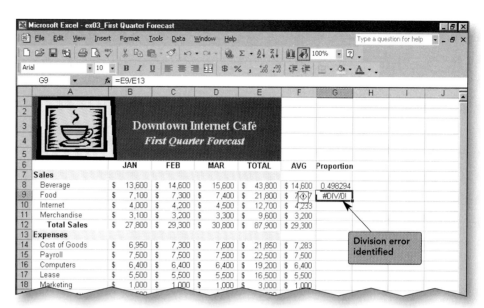

Figure 3.18

You see a #DIV/0! error value is displayed in cell G9 and want to check the formula in that cell.

3 ● **If necessary, move to cell G9.**

● **Choose Edit in Formula Bar from the $\boxed{\diamond}$ Error Options drop-down menu.**

Your screen should be similar to Figure 3.19

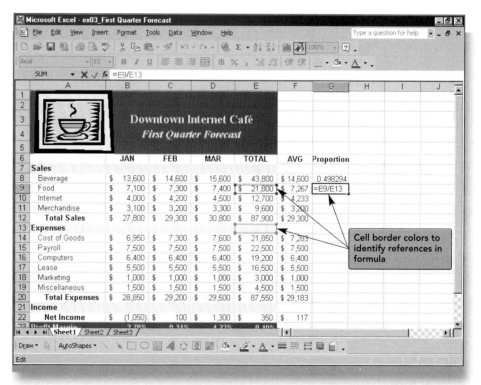

Figure 3.19

You can now see the error occurred because the relative reference to cell E12 adjusted correctly to the new location when the formula was copied and now references cell E13, a blank cell. The formula in G8 needs to be entered so that the reference to the Total Sales value in cell E12 does not change when the formula is copied. To do this, you need to make the cell reference absolute.

concept 2

Absolute References

2   An **absolute reference** is a cell or range reference in a formula whose location does not change when the formula is copied.

To stop the relative adjustment of cell references, enter a $ (dollar sign) character before the column letter and row number. This changes the cell reference to absolute. When a formula containing an absolute cell reference is copied to another row and column location in the worksheet, the cell reference does not change. It is an exact duplicate of the cell reference in the original formula.

A cell reference can also be a **mixed reference**. In this type of reference, either the column letter or the row number is preceded with the $. This makes only the row or column absolute. When a formula containing a mixed cell reference is copied to another location in the worksheet, only the part of the cell reference that is not absolute changes relative to its new location in the worksheet.

The table below shows examples of relative and absolute references and the results when a reference in cell G8 to cell E8 is copied to cell H9.

Cell Contents of G8	Copied to Cell H9	Type of Reference
E8	E8	Absolute reference
E$8	F$8	Mixed reference
$E8	$E9	Mixed reference
E8	F9	Relative reference

You will change the formula in cell G8 to include an absolute reference for cell E12. Then you will copy the formula to cells G9 through G11.

You can change a cell reference to absolute or mixed by typing in the dollar sign directly or by using the ABS (Absolute) key, [F4]. To use the ABS key, the program must be in the Edit mode and the cell reference that you want to change must be selected.

4 Move to G8.

Click on the reference to E12 in the formula bar to enter Edit mode and select the reference.

Press F4.

Your screen should be similar to Figure 3.20

Dollar sign symbols change reference to absolute

Figure 3.20

The cell reference now displays $ characters before the column letter and row number, making this cell reference absolute. If you continue to press F4, the cell reference will cycle through all possible combinations of cell reference types. Leaving the cell reference absolute, as it is now, will stop the relative adjustment of the cell reference when you copy it again.

5 Click ✓ Enter.

Copy the revised formula to cells G9 through G11.

Move to cell G9.

Your screen should be similar to Figure 3.21

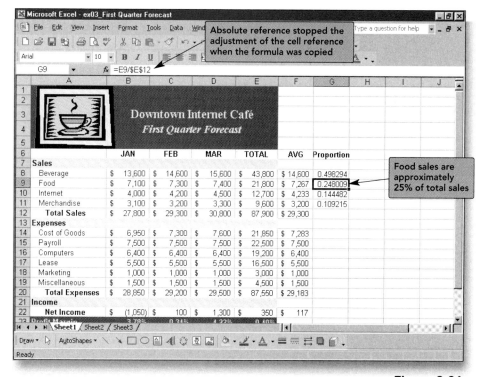

Absolute reference stopped the adjustment of the cell reference when the formula was copied

Food sales are approximately 25% of total sales

Figure 3.21

The formula when copied correctly adjusted the relative cell reference to Food sales in cell E9 and did not adjust the reference to E12 because it is an absolute reference.

The last change you need to make to the proportion data is to format it to the Percent style.

6 — **Select G8 through G11.**

● **Click** 📊 **Percent Style.**

● **Click** 📊 **Increase Decimal (twice).**

● **Size column G to fit the contents.**

● **Move to cell A6 and save the workbook as** Forecast4.

Your screen should be similar to Figure 3.22

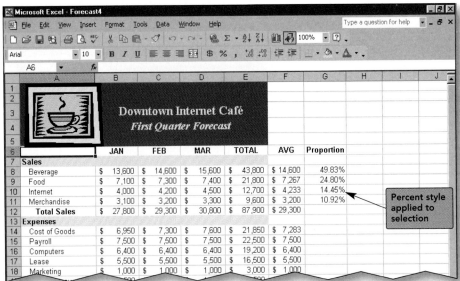

Figure 3.22

The calculated proportion shows the same values that a pie chart of this data would show.

Working with Sheets

Next you want to add the second quarter forecast to the workbook. You want this data in a separate sheet in the same workbook file. To make it easier to enter the forecast for the next quarter, you will copy the contents of the first quarter forecast in Sheet1 into another sheet in the workbook. Then you will change the month headings, the title, and the number data for the second quarter. Finally, you want to include a formula to calculate a year-to-date total for the six months.

Copying Between Sheets

You want to copy the worksheet data from Sheet1 to Sheet2. Copying between sheets is the same as copying within a sheet, except that you switch to the new sheet to specify the destination.

● Select the worksheet range A1 through G23.

● Click Copy.

● Click on the Sheet2 tab.

● Click ▣ Paste.

Your screen should be similar to Figure 3.23

Another Method
You can also use **E**dit/**M**ove or Copy Sheet to move or copy a sheet into a new sheet in the workbook.

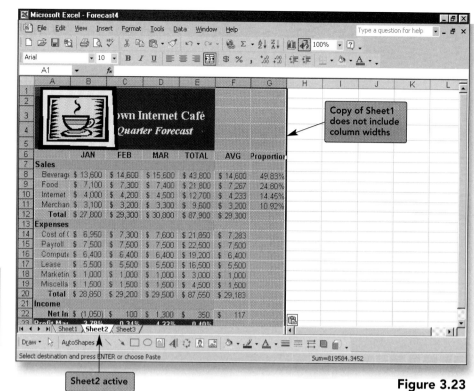

Figure 3.23

All the worksheet data and formatting, except for the column width settings, are copied into the existing Sheet2. You want to include the column width settings from the source.

● Click ▣ Paste Options.

● Choose Keep Source Column **W**idths.

Your screen should be similar to Figure 3.24

Additional Information
If you select and copy the entire source sheet, all formatting including column widths is copied into the destination sheet.

Another Method
You can also create a copy of the active sheet in a new sheet by holding down [Ctrl] while dragging the active sheet tab to where you want the new sheet inserted.

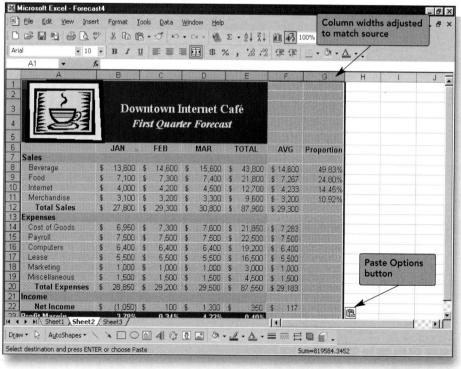

Figure 3.24

Sheet2 now contains a duplicate of the first quarter forecast in Sheet1.

Renaming Sheets and Coloring Sheet Tabs

As more sheets are added to a workbook, remembering what information is in each sheet becomes more difficult. To help clarify the contents of the sheets, you can rename the sheets.

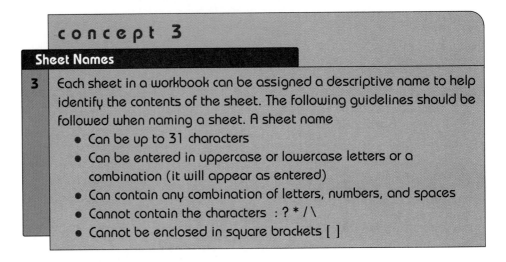

concept 3

Sheet Names

3 Each sheet in a workbook can be assigned a descriptive name to help identify the contents of the sheet. The following guidelines should be followed when naming a sheet. A sheet name

- Can be up to 31 characters
- Can be entered in uppercase or lowercase letters or a combination (it will appear as entered)
- Can contain any combination of letters, numbers, and spaces
- Cannot contain the characters : ? * / \
- Cannot be enclosed in square brackets [ ]

Double-clicking the sheet tab activates the tab and highlights the existing sheet name. The existing name is cleared as soon as you begin to type the new name. You will change the name of Sheet1 to First Quarter and Sheet2 to Second Quarter.

- **Double-click the Sheet1 tab.**

- **Type First Quarter.**

- **Press ←Enter.**

- **Change the name of the Sheet2 tab to Second Quarter.**

Another Method

The menu equivalent is Format/Sheet/Rename.

Your screen should be similar to Figure 3.25

Sheet tabs renamed

Figure 3.25

To further differentiate the sheets, you can add color to the sheet tabs.

2 ● Right-click on the First Quarter tab.

● Choose **T**ab Color from the shortcut menu.

● Select yellow from the color pallet.

● Click [OK].

● In the same manner, change the color of the Second Quarter sheet tab to green.

Another Method

The menu equivalent is Format/Sheet/Tab Color.

Your screen should be similar to Figure 3.26

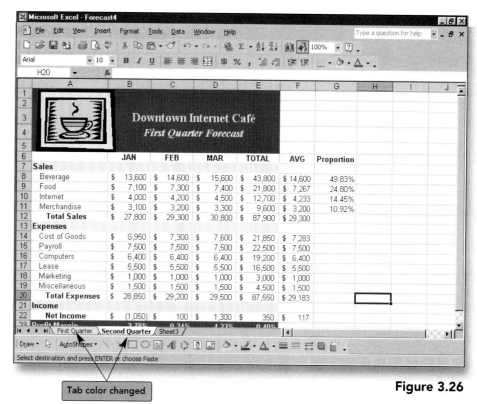

Tab color changed

Figure 3.26

Filling a Series

Now you can change the worksheet title and data in the second quarter sheet.

1 ● Change the title in cell B4 to Second Quarter Forecast.

● Change the month heading in cell B6 to APR.

Your screen should be similar to Figure 3.27

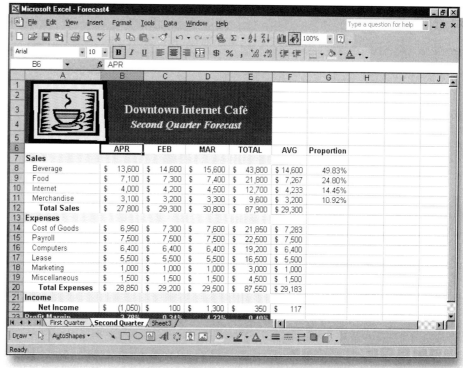

Figure 3.27

Now you need to change the remaining month headings to MAY and JUN. You will use the AutoFill feature to enter the month headings.

concept 4

AutoFill

4 The **AutoFill** feature makes entering a series of headings easier by logically repeating and extending the series. AutoFill recognizes trends and automatically extends data and alphanumeric headings as far as you specify.

Dragging the fill handle activates the AutoFill feature if Excel recognizes the entry in the cell as an entry that can be incremented. When AutoFill extends the entries, it uses the same style as the original entry. For example, if you enter the heading for July as JUL (abbreviated with all letters uppercase), all the extended entries in the series will be abbreviated and uppercase. Dragging down or right increments in increasing order, and up or left increments in decreasing order. A linear series increases or decreases values by a constant value, and a growth series multiplies values by a constant factor.

Initial Selection	Extended series
Qtr1	Qtr2, Qtr3, Qtr4
Mon	Tue Wed Thu
Jan, Apr	Jul, Oct, Jan

Additional Information

A starting value of a series may contain more than one item that can be incremented, such as JAN-02, in which both the month and year can increment. You can specify which value to increment by selecting the appropriate option from the AutoFill Options menu.

The entry in cell B6, APR, is the starting value of a series of months. You will drag the fill handle to the right to increment the months. The mouse pointer displays the entry that will appear in each cell as you drag.

2 ● **Drag the fill handle of cell B6 to extend the range from cell B6 through cell D6.**

Additional Information

If you do not want a series created when you drag the fill handle, hold down Ctrl as you drag and the entries will be copied, not incremented.

Your screen should be similar to Figure 3.28

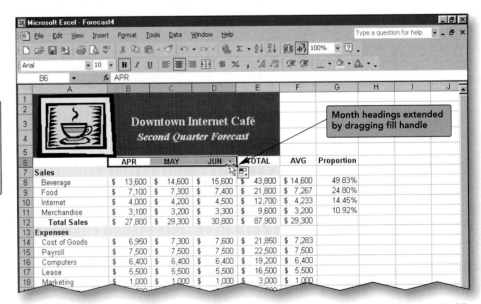

Figure 3.28

Referencing Multiple Sheets

Finally, you need to update the forecast for April through June beverage, food, Internet, and merchandise sales. Then you will enter a formula to calculate the year-to-date income total using data from both sheets.

1 ● **Enter the following values in the specified cells.**

Cell	Number
B8	15700
C8	15800
D8	15900
B9	7500
C9	7600
D9	7600
B10	4500
C10	4500
D10	4500
B11	3200
C11	3200
D11	3200

Your screen should be similar to Figure 3.29

Figure 3.29

The worksheet has been recalculated and now contains the data for the second quarter.

Now you can enter the formula to calculate a year-to-date income total. The formula to make this calculation will sum the total income numbers from the First Quarter sheet in cell E22 and the Second Quarter sheet in cell E22. To reference data in another sheet in the same workbook, you enter a formula that references cells in other worksheets.

concept 5

Sheet and 3-D References

5 A formula that contains references to cells in other sheets of a workbook allows you to use data from multiple sheets and to calculate new values based on this data. The formula contains a **sheet reference** consisting of the name of the sheet, followed by an exclamation point and the cell or range reference. If the sheet name contains non-alphabetic characters, such as a space, the sheet name (or path) must be enclosed in single quotation marks.

If you want to use the same cell or range of cells on multiple sheets, you can use a **3-D reference**. A 3-D reference consists of the names of the beginning and ending sheets enclosed in quotes and separated by a colon. This is followed by an exclamation point and the cell or range reference. The cell or range reference is the same on each sheet in the specified sheet range. If a sheet is inserted or deleted, the range is automatically updated. 3-D references make it easy to analyze data in the same cell or range of cells on multiple worksheets.

Reference	Description
=Sheet2!B17	Displays the entry in cell B17 of Sheet2 in the active cell of the current sheet
=Sheet1!A1+Sheet2!B2.	Sums the values in cell A1 of Sheet1 and B2 of Sheet2
=SUM(Sheet1:Sheet4!H6:K6)	Sums the values in cells H6 through K6 in Sheets 1, 2, 3, and 4
=SUM(Sheet1!H6:K6)	Sums the values in cells H6 through K6 in Sheet1
=SUM(Sheet1:Sheet4!H6)	Sums the values in cell H6 of Sheets 1, 2, 3, and 4

Just like a formula that references cells within a sheet, a formula that references cells in multiple sheets is automatically recalculated when data in a referenced cell changes.

You will enter a descriptive text entry in cell D24 and then use a 3-D reference in a SUM function to calculate the year-to-date total in cell E24.

The SUM function argument will consist of a 3-D reference to cell E22 in the First and Second Quarter sheets. Although a 3-D reference can be entered by typing it using the proper syntax, it is much easier to enter it by pointing to the cells on the sheets. To enter a 3-D reference, select the cell or range in the beginning sheet and then hold down ⇧Shift and click on the sheet tab of the last sheet in the range. This will include the indicated cell range on all sheets between and including the first and last sheet specified.

2
- In cell D24 enter and right-align the entry **Income Year-To-Date**.

- Move to E24.

- Click **Σ AutoSum**.

- Click cell E22.

- Hold down ⇧Shift and click the First Quarter tab.

- Release ⇧Shift.

- Press ←Enter.

- Move to E24.

Your screen should be similar to Figure 3.30

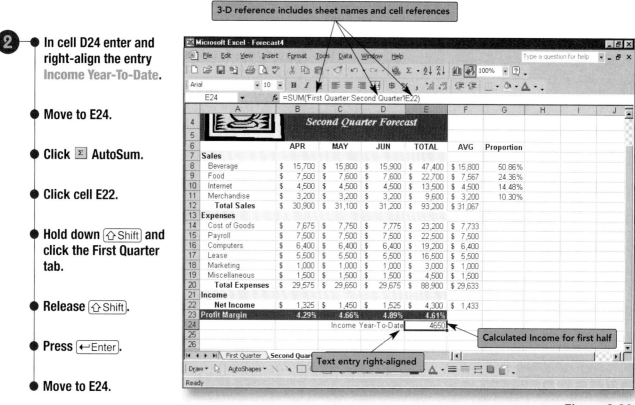

Figure 3.30

The calculated number 4650 appears in cell E24 and the function containing a 3-D reference appears in the formula bar.

You have now completed the forecast for the first half of the year.

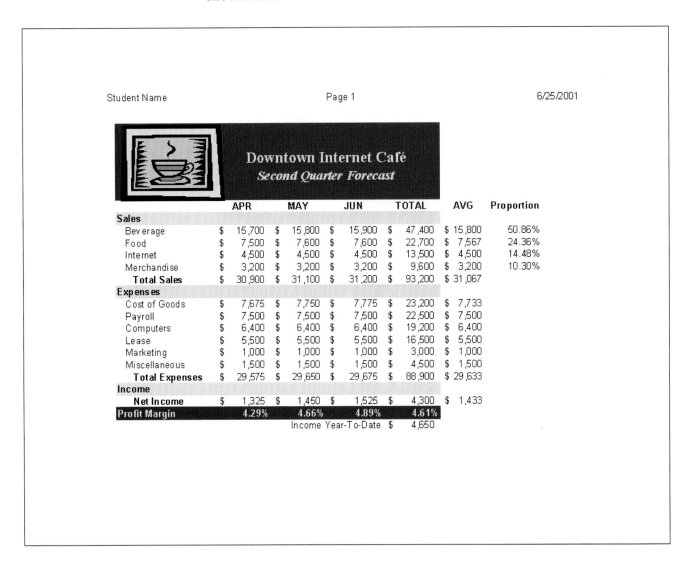

3 ● Change the format of cell E24 to Accounting with zero decimal places.

● Enter your name in the workbook file properties as the author.

● Add a predefined header containing your name, page number, and the date to both sheets.

● Preview the entire workbook. Print both worksheets.

● Close and save the workbook file.

Your printed output of the second quarter sheet should be similar to that shown here.

Student Name   Page 1   6/25/2001

Downtown Internet Café
Second Quarter Forecast

	APR	MAY	JUN	TOTAL	AVG	Proportion
Sales						
Beverage	$ 15,700	$ 15,800	$ 15,900	$ 47,400	$ 15,800	50.86%
Food	$ 7,500	$ 7,600	$ 7,600	$ 22,700	$ 7,567	24.36%
Internet	$ 4,500	$ 4,500	$ 4,500	$ 13,500	$ 4,500	14.48%
Merchandise	$ 3,200	$ 3,200	$ 3,200	$ 9,600	$ 3,200	10.30%
Total Sales	$ 30,900	$ 31,100	$ 31,200	$ 93,200	$ 31,067	
Expenses						
Cost of Goods	$ 7,675	$ 7,750	$ 7,775	$ 23,200	$ 7,733	
Payroll	$ 7,500	$ 7,500	$ 7,500	$ 22,500	$ 7,500	
Computers	$ 6,400	$ 6,400	$ 6,400	$ 19,200	$ 6,400	
Lease	$ 5,500	$ 5,500	$ 5,500	$ 16,500	$ 5,500	
Marketing	$ 1,000	$ 1,000	$ 1,000	$ 3,000	$ 1,000	
Miscellaneous	$ 1,500	$ 1,500	$ 1,500	$ 4,500	$ 1,500	
Total Expenses	$ 29,575	$ 29,650	$ 29,675	$ 88,900	$ 29,633	
Income						
Net Income	$ 1,325	$ 1,450	$ 1,525	$ 4,300	$ 1,433	
Profit Margin	4.29%	4.66%	4.89%	4.61%		
			Income Year-To-Date	$ 4,650		

Note: If you are running short on lab time, this is an appropriate place to end this session and begin again at a later time.

Deleting and Moving Sheets

You presented the completed first and second quarterly forecasts to Evan. He is very pleased with the results and now wants you to create worksheets for the third and fourth quarters and a combined annual forecast. Additionally, Evan has asked you to include a column chart of the data for each quarter. Finally, after looking at the forecast, Evan wants the forecast to show a profit margin of 5 percent for each month in the second quarter.

You have already made several of the changes requested and saved them as a workbook file. To see the revised and expanded forecast,

Open the workbook file ex03_Annual Forecast.

Your screen should be similar to Figure 3.31

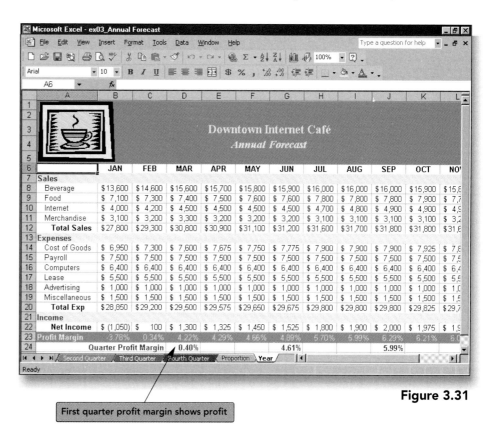

Figure 3.31

First quarter profit margin shows profit

The workbook file now contains six sheets: First Quarter, Second Quarter, Third Quarter, Fourth Quarter, Proportion, and Year. The Proportion sheet contains the proportion of sales values from the first and second quarters. The Year sheet contains the forecast data for the entire 12 months. Each quarter sheet also includes a chart of the profit margin for that quarter. As you can now easily see, the profit margin by the end of the first quarter is showing a profit.

2 ● **Click** on each of the Quarter sheet tabs to view the quarterly data and profit margin chart.

● **Display** the Proportion sheet.

Your screen should be similar to Figure 3.32

Figure 3.32

You decide this data, although interesting, is not needed in the forecast workbook and want to delete the entire sheet.

3 ● **Choose** Edit/Delete Sheet.

● **Click** [Delete] to confirm that you want to permanently remove the sheet.

Your screen should be similar to Figure 3.33

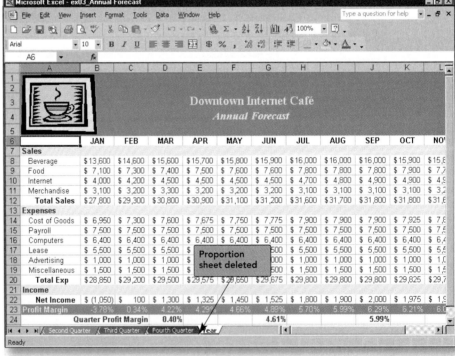

Figure 3.33

Additional Information
You can insert a blank new sheet using Insert/Worksheet. It is inserted to the left of the active sheet.

The entire sheet is deleted, and the Year sheet is now the active sheet. Next you want to move the Year sheet from the last position in the workbook to the first. You can quickly rearrange sheets in a workbook by dragging the sheet tab to the new location. The symbol ▼ indicates where the sheet will appear.

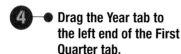

4 — ● Drag the Year tab to the left end of the First Quarter tab.

Another Method

You can also use Edit/Move or Copy Sheet to move a sheet to another location in the workbook.

Your screen should be similar to Figure 3.34

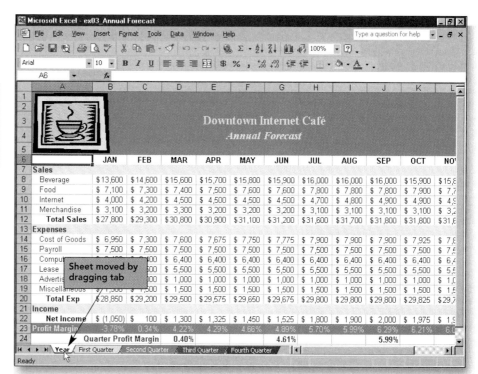

Figure 3.34

Managing Large Sheets

Now that the workbook is much larger you are finding that it takes a lot of time to scroll to different areas within and between sheets. To make managing large sheets easier, you can zoom a sheet, split the workbook window, and freeze panes.

Zooming the Worksheet

Additional Information

The Zoom feature is common in all Office XP programs.

The Year sheet displays all of the quarterly data. The entire sheet, however, is not visible in the window. You can change how much information is displayed in the window to make it easier to navigate, view, and select worksheet data by adjusting the zoom percentage. The default zoom setting is 100 percent. This setting displays data onscreen the same size that it will appear on the printed page. You can reduce or enlarge the amount of information displayed onscreen by changing the magnification from between 10 to 400 percent. You want to decrease the zoom percent to display more information in the window.

1 Open the `100%` Zoom drop-down menu.

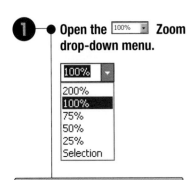

Additional Information

The Selection option adjusts the percentage to fit the selected range in the current window size.

● Choose 75%.

Another Method

The menu equivalent is View/Zoom.

Your screen should be similar to Figure 3.35

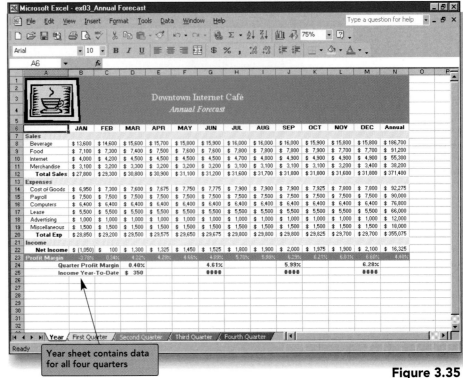

Figure 3.35

You can now see the entire worksheet.

2 Reduce the zoom percent to 50%.

Your screen should be similar to Figure 3.36

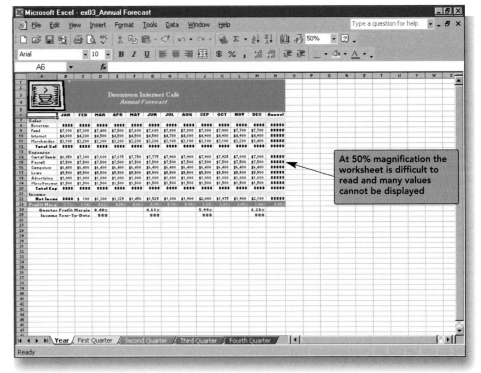

Figure 3.36

Additional Information

Pointing to the #### error value will display the cell value in a ScreenTip.

As you reduce the percentage, more worksheet area is visible in the window. However, it gets more difficult to read and many cells display the error value ##### because the column width is not wide enough to fully display the result.

Going to a Specific cell

Most of the monthly values in the Year sheet, such as cell B8, contain linking formulas that reference the appropriate cells in the appropriate quarter sheets. Others, such as the total formulas and the formula to calculate the income, do not reference cells outside the Year worksheet.

To see several of the formulas in cells that reference the quarter sheets,

1 ● **Return the zoom to 100%.**

● **Move to B8.**

● **Move to E12.**

● **Move to H16.**

Your screen should be similar to Figure 3.37

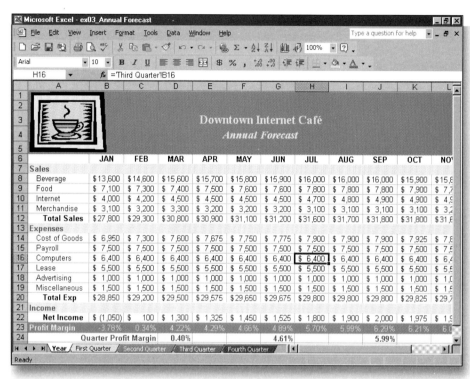

Figure 3.37

Each of these cells contained a formula that referenced a cell in the appropriate quarter sheet. To see the total formulas for the year in column N, you will move to cell N16 using the GoTo feature.

2 ● **Type N16 in the Name text box and press ←Enter.**

Another Method

The menu equivalent is Edit/GoTo and the keyboard shortcut is Ctrl + G or F5.

Your screen should be similar to Figure 3.38

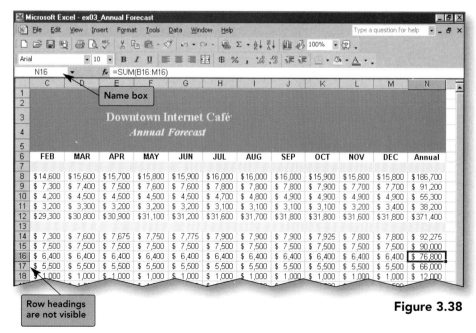

Figure 3.38

The cell selector jumps directly to cell N16 in the total column. The formula in this cell calculates the total of the values in row 16 and does not reference another sheet. However, it is difficult to know what the numbers represent in this row because the row headings are not visible. For example, is this number the total for the lease expenses, advertising expenses, or miscellaneous expenses? Without scrolling back to see the row headings, it is difficult to know.

Splitting Windows

Whenever you scroll a large worksheet, you will find that information you may need to view in one area scrolls out of view as you move to another area. Although you could reduce the zoom percent to view more of a worksheet in the window, you still may not be able to see the entire worksheet if it is very large. And as you saw, continuing to reduce the zoom makes the worksheet difficult to read and prevents some values from fully displaying. To view different areas of the same sheet at the same time, you can split the window.

concept 6

Split Windows

6   A sheet window can be split into sections called **panes** to make it easier to view different parts of the sheet at the same time. The panes can consist of any number of columns or rows along the top or left edge of the window. You can divide the sheet into two panes either horizontally or vertically, or into four panes if you split the window both vertically and horizontally.

Each pane can be scrolled independently to display different areas of the sheet. When split vertically, the panes scroll together when you scroll vertically, but scroll independently when you scroll horizontally. Horizontal panes scroll together when you scroll horizontally, but independently when you scroll vertically.

Panes are most useful for viewing a worksheet that consists of different areas or sections. Creating panes allows you to display the different sections of the worksheet in separate panes and then to quickly switch between panes to access the data in the different sections without having to repeatedly scroll to the areas.

two vertical panes   two horizontal panes   four panes

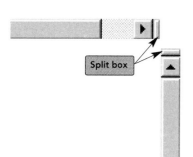

Split box

Dragging the split box at the top of the vertical scroll bar downward creates a horizontal split, and dragging the split box at the right end of the horizontal scroll bar leftward creates a vertical split.

You will split the window into two vertical panes. This will allow you to view the titles in column A at the same time as you are viewing data in column N.

1 ● **Point to the vertical split box in the horizontal scroll bar.**

Additional Information

The mouse pointer changes to a ✛║▸ to show you can drag to create a split.

● **Drag to the left and position the bar between columns D and E.**

Your screen should be similar to Figure 3.39

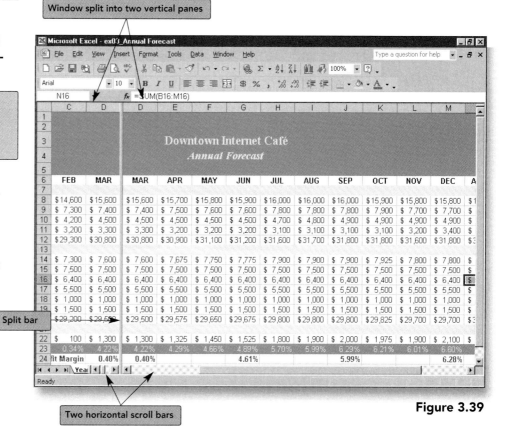

Window split into two vertical panes

Split bar

Two horizontal scroll bars

Figure 3.39

There are now two vertical panes with two separate horizontal scroll bars. The highlighted cell selector is visible in the right pane. The left pane also has a cell selector in cell N16, but it is not visible because that area of the worksheet is not displayed in the pane. When the same area of a worksheet is visible in multiple panes, the cell selector in the panes that are not active is highlighted whereas the cell selector in the active pane is clear. The active pane will be affected by your movement horizontally. The cell selector moves in both panes, but only the active pane scrolls.

Additional Information

The Window/Split command can be used to quickly create a four-way split at the active cell.

You will scroll the left pane horizontally to display the month headings in column A.

2 ● Click C16 in the left pane to display the active cell selector in the pane.

● Press ← twice.

Your screen should be similar to Figure 3.40

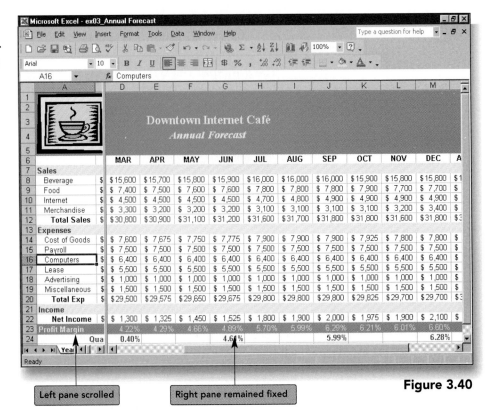

Left pane scrolled

Right pane remained fixed

Figure 3.40

The right pane did not scroll when you moved horizontally through the left pane to display the row headings. The cell selector in the right pane is in the same cell location as in the left pane (A16), although it is not visible. You want to change the location of the split so that you can view an entire quarter in the left pane in order to more easily compare quarters.

3 ● Drag the split bar to the right three columns.

● Click cell E16 in the right pane.

● Press End →.

● Press → (three times).

Your screen should be similar to Figure 3.41

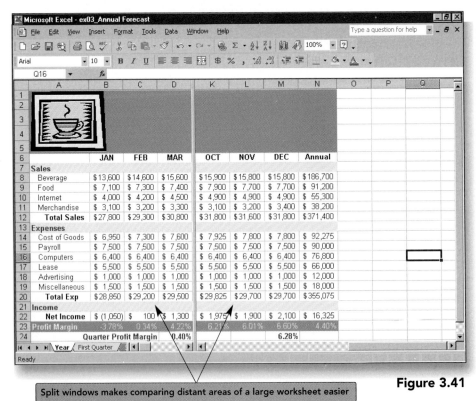

Split windows makes comparing distant areas of a large worksheet easier

Figure 3.41

Now you can easily compare the first quarter data to the last quarter data. As you can see, creating panes is helpful when you want to display and access distant areas of a worksheet quickly. After scrolling the data in the panes to display the appropriate worksheet area, you can then quickly switch between panes to make changes to the data that is visible in the pane. This saves you the time of scrolling to the area each time you want to view it or make changes to it. You will clear the horizontal split from the window.

4 ● **Double-click anywhere on the split bar.**

Another Method

The menu equivalent is **W**indow/Remove **S**plit.

Your screen should be similar to Figure 3.42

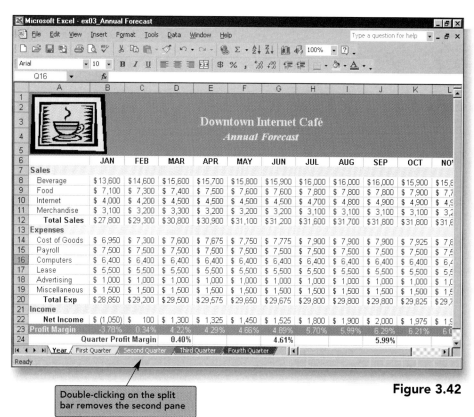

Double-clicking on the split bar removes the second pane

Figure 3.42

Freezing Panes

Another way to manage a large worksheet is to freeze panes.

concept 7

Freeze Panes

7 **Freezing panes** prevents the data in the pane from scrolling as you move to different areas in a worksheet. You can freeze the information in the top and left panes of a window only. This feature is most useful when your worksheet is organized using row and column headings. It allows you to keep the titles on the top and left edge of your worksheet in view as you scroll horizontally and vertically through the worksheet data.

You want to keep the month headings in row 6 and the row headings in column A visible in the window at all times while looking at the Income and Profit Margin data beginning in row 21. To do this, you will create four panes with the upper and left panes frozen.

When creating frozen panes, first position the worksheet in the window to display the information you want to appear in the top and left panes. This is because data in the frozen panes cannot be scrolled like data in regular panes. Then move to the location specified in the following table before using the Windows/Freeze Panes command to create and freeze panes.

To Create	Cell Selector Location	Example
Two horizontal panes with the top pane frozen	Move to the leftmost column in the window and to the row below where you want the split to appear.	**Top Pane Frozen**
		9 Food $ 7,100 $ 7,300
		10 Internet $ 4,000 $ 4,200
		11 Merchandise $ 3,100 $ 3,200
		12 Total Sales $27,800 $29,300
		20 Total Exp $28,850 $29,200
		21 Income
Two vertical panes with the left pane frozen	Move to the top row of the window and to the column to the right of where you want the split to appear.	**Left Pane Frozen**
		9 Food $ 7,600 $ 7,600
		10 Internet $ 4,500 $ 4,500
		11 Merchandise $ 3,200 $ 3,200
		12 Total Sales $31,100 $31,200
		13 Expenses
		14 Cost of Goods $ 7,750 $ 7,775
Four panes with the top and left panes frozen	Move to the cell below and to the right of where you want the split to appear.	**Top and Left Pane Frozen**
		6 MAY JUN
		7 Sales
		8 Beverage $15,800 $15,900
		9 Food $ 7,600 $ 7,600
		10 Internet $ 4,500 $ 4,500
		11 Merchandise $ 3,200 $ 3,200

You want to split the window into four panes with the month column headings at the top of the window and the row headings in column A at the left side of the window.

1 Scroll the window until row 6 is the top row in the window.

● Move to B7.

● Choose **W**indow/**F**reeze Panes.

Your screen should be similar to Figure 3.43

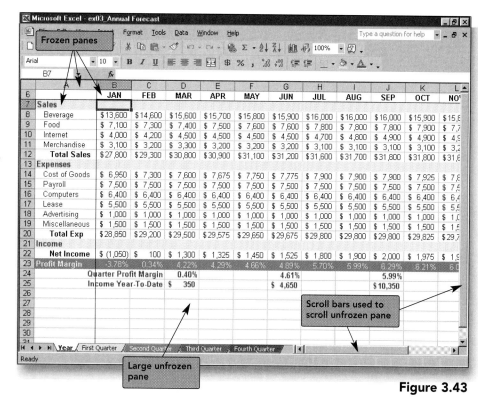

Figure 3.43

The window is divided into four panes at the cell selector location. Only one set of scroll bars is displayed because the only pane that can be scrolled is the larger lower-right pane. You can move the cell selector into a frozen pane, but the data in the frozen panes will not scroll. Also, there is only one cell selector that moves from one pane to another over the pane divider, making it unnecessary to click on the pane to make it active before moving the cell selector in it.

Because Evan has asked you to adjust the profit margin values, you want to view this area of the worksheet only.

2 Use the vertical scroll bar to scroll the window until row 21 is below row 6.

● Move to cell G24.

Your screen should be similar to Figure 3.44

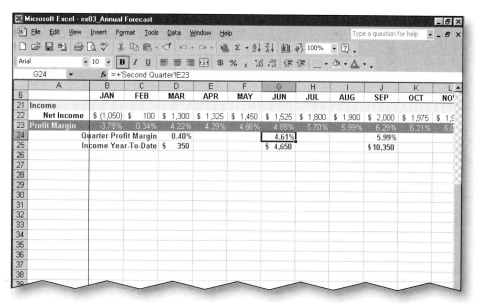

Figure 3.44

Now the Income and profit margin data is displayed immediately below the month headings in row six. The data in rows 7 through 20 is no longer visible, allowing you to concentrate on this area of the worksheet.

Watching Cells

While using a workbook with large worksheets and/or multiple sheets, you may want to keep an eye on how changes you make to values in one area effect cells in another. For example, if you change a value in one sheet that is referenced in a formula in another, you can view the effect on the calculated value using the Watch Window toolbar.

You will be changing values in the second quarter sheet next and want to be able to see the effect on the linked formulas in the Year sheet at the same time.

1 ● Select cells G24 and N23.

● Choose **T**ools/Formula A**u**diting/Show **W**atch Window.

● Click Add Watch... from the Watch window toolbar.

Another Method
You can also open the Watch Window toolbar from the toolbar shortcut menu.

Your screen should be similar to Figure 3.45

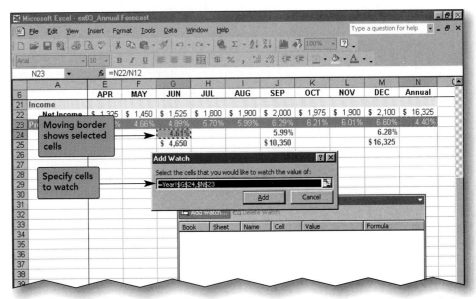

Figure 3.45

The Add Watch dialog box is used to specify the cells you want to see in the Watch Window toolbar. The currently selected cells are identified with a moving border. You will add these cells to the Watch Window.

2 ● Click Add .

● Size the Watch window toolbar just large enough to display the two cell values rows.

● Move the Watch window toolbar to the upper-right corner of the workbook window.

Your screen should be similar to Figure 3.46

Additional Information
You can also watch linked cells in other open workbooks.

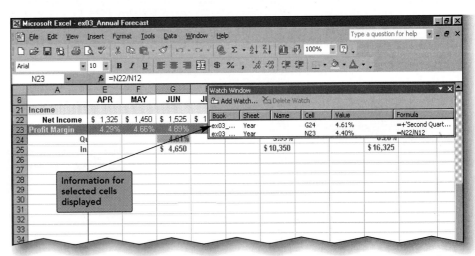

Figure 3.46

The values in the selected cells as well as the formula and location information are displayed in the Watch Window. The toolbar will remain open on top of the workbook as you move from one sheet to another.

Forecasting Values

Evan has asked you to adjust the forecast for the second quarter to show a profit margin of at least 5 percent for each month. After some consideration, you decide you can most easily reduce monthly payroll expenses by carefully scheduling employee work during these three months. Reducing the monthly expense will increase the profit margin for the quarter. You want to find out what the maximum payroll value you can spend during that period is for each month to accomplish this goal. The process of evaluating what effect changing the payroll expenses will have on the profit margin is called what-if analysis.

concept 8

What-If Analysis

8 **What-if analysis** is a technique used to evaluate the effects of changing selected factors in a worksheet. This technique is a common accounting function that has been made much easier with the introduction of spreadsheet programs. By substituting different values in cells that are referenced by formulas, you can quickly see the effect of the changes when the formulas are recalculated.

You can perform what-if analysis by manually substituting values or by using one of the what-if analysis tools included with Excel.

Performing What-If Analysis Manually

To do this, you will enter different payroll expense values for each month and see what the effect is on that month's profit margin. You will adjust the May payroll value first.

1 • Make the Second Quarter sheet active.

• Enter 7300 in cell C15.

Your screen should be similar to Figure 3.47

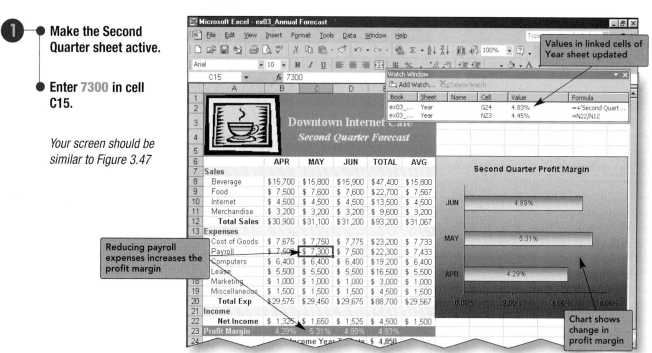

Figure 3.47

Now by looking in cell C23, you can see that decreasing the payroll expenses has increased the profit margin for the month to 5.31 percent. This is more than you need. Also notice the chart has changed to reflect the change in May's profit margin. The Watch Window shows that the values in the two linked cells in the Year sheet were updated accordingly.

You will continue to enter payroll values until the profit margin reaches the goal.

2 ● Enter **7400** in cell C15.

● Enter **7390** in cell C15.

● Enter **7395** in cell C15.

Your screen should be similar to Figure 3.48

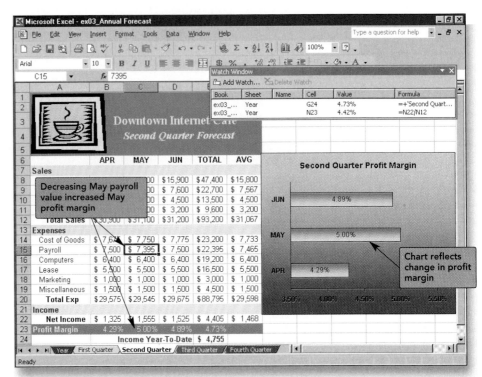

Figure 3.48

That's it! Reducing the payroll value from 7500 to 7395 will achieve the 5% profit margin goal for the month.

Using Goal Seek

It usually takes several tries to find the appropriate value when manually performing what-if analysis. A quicker way is to use the what-if analysis Goal Seek tool provided with Excel.

concept 9

Goal Seek

9 The **Goal Seek** tool is used to find the value needed in one cell to attain a result you want in another cell. Goal Seek varies the value in the cell you specify until a formula that is dependent on that cell returns the desired result. The value of only one cell can be changed.

You will use this method to find the payroll value for April that will produce a 5 percent profit margin for that month. The current profit margin value is 4.29 percent in cell B23.

1 ● Move to B23.

● Choose **T**ools/**G**oal Seek.

Your screen should be similar to Figure 3.49

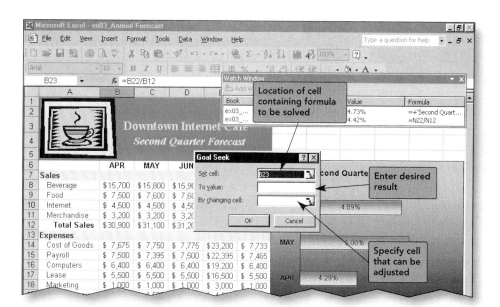

Figure 3.49

In the Goal Seek dialog box, you need to specify the location of the cell containing the formula to be solved, the desired calculated value, and the cell containing the number that can be adjusted to achieve the result. You want the formula in cell B23 to calculate a result of 5 percent by changing the payroll number in cell B15. The Set Cell text box correctly displays the current cell as the location of the formula to be solved. You will enter the information needed in the Goal Seek dialog box.

2 ● Click in the To **V**alue text box and enter the value 5.00%.

● Click in the By **C**hanging Cell text box and then click on cell B15 in the worksheet to enter the cell reference.

● Click OK .

Your screen should be similar to Figure 3.50

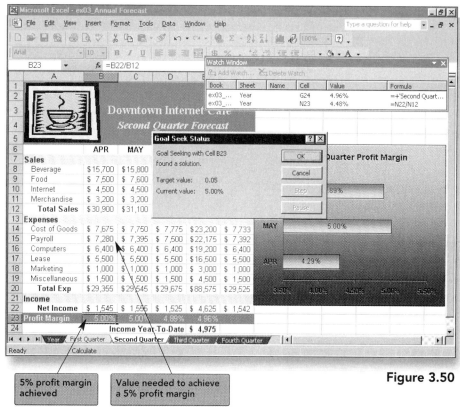

Figure 3.50

The Goal Seek Status dialog box tells you it found a solution that will achieve the 5 percent profit margin. The payroll value of 7280 that will achieve the desired result has been temporarily entered in the worksheet. You can reject the solution and restore the original value by choosing Cancel. In this case, however, you want to accept the solution.

3 ● Click OK .

Your screen should be similar to Figure 3.51

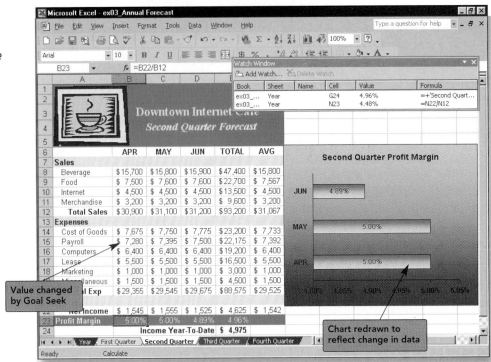

Figure 3.51

The payroll value is permanently updated and the chart redrawn to reflect the change in profit margin for April.

Changing Values Using a Chart

Finally, you need to adjust the June payroll value. This time you will find the value by dragging the June chart data marker to the 5% position on the chart. As you drag the data marker, a dotted bar line will show the new bar length and a ChartTip will display the new profit margin value. An indicator on the X axis also marks your location. Releasing the mouse button with the bar at the new position specifies the new value and opens the Goal Seek dialog box.

1 ● Click on the June data series bar twice (slowly) to select the individual bar.

Additional Information
The bar is surrounded by eight selection handles.

● Drag the middle selection handle on the right end of the bar to increase the length of the bar. When the bar ChartTip value is 0.05 or as close as you can get, release the mouse button.

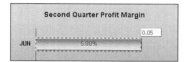

Your screen should be similar to Figure 3.52

Figure 3.52

Dragging the data marker specifies the value you want to change to and the location of the cell containing the formula. The Goal Seek dialog box is displayed. The Set Cell location and value to attain are entered. Depending on the value you were able to attain by dragging the data marker, you may still need to adjust the value to the exact value of 0.05. You also need to specify the cell location of the value to change.

2 ● If necessary, edit the To **V**alue contents to 0.05.

● Enter cell D15 in the By changing cell text box.

● Click [OK].

● Click [OK] to accept the solution.

Your screen should be similar to Figure 3.53

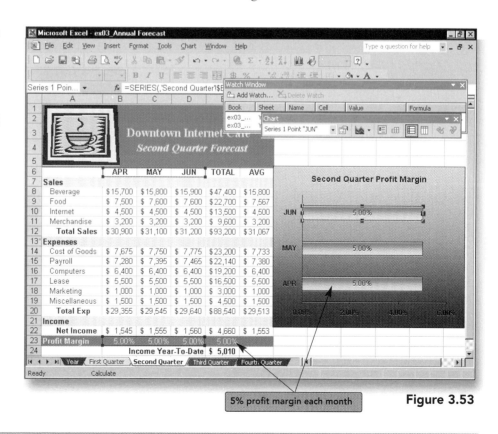

5% profit margin each month

Figure 3.53

The second quarter values are now at the 5 percent profit margin objective. The Watch Window also reflects te change in cell G24.

3 ● Click ☒ Close to close the Watch Window toolbar.

● Make the Year sheet active to further verify that the profit margin values for the second quarter were updated.

● Choose Window/Unfreeze Panes.

● Update the workbook properties by entering your name as author.

● Save the revised forecast as Annual Forecast Revised.

Customizing Print Settings

Now you are ready to print the workbook. Because your worksheet looks great on your screen, this does not mean it will look good when printed. Many times you will want to change the print and layout settings to improve the appearance of the output. Customizing the print settings by changing the orientation of the page, centering the worksheet on the page, hiding gridlines, and adding custom header and footer information are just a few of the ways you can make your printed output look more professional.

Changing Page Orientation

First you want to preview all the sheets in the workbook.

1 ● Right-click a sheet tab and choose Select All Sheets from the shortcut menu.

> **Additional Information**
> The tabs of all sheets appear white indicating they are selected; the active sheet tab name is bold.

● Click 🔍 Print Preview.

Your screen should be similar to Figure 3.54

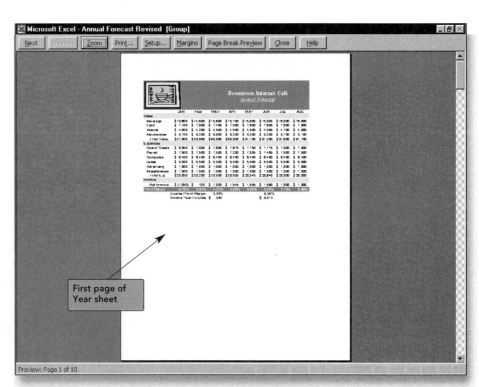

First page of Year sheet

Figure 3.54

The first page of the Year worksheet is displayed in the Preview window. Notice that the entire sheet does not fit across the width of the page. To see the second page,

 Click **Next** .

Your screen should be similar to Figure 3.55

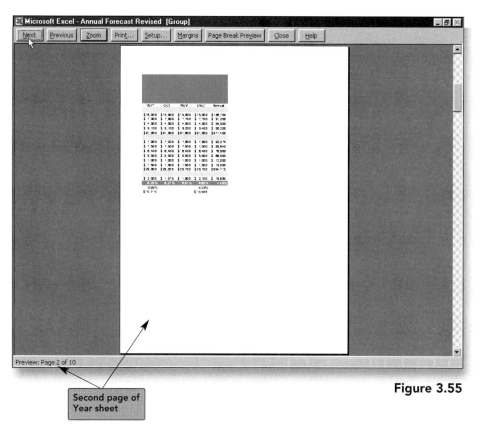

Second page of Year sheet

Figure 3.55

The last five columns of data appear on the second page. Although you could use the Fit To feature to compress the worksheet to a single page, this would make the data small and difficult to read. Instead you can change the orientation or the direction the output is printed on a page. The default orientation is **portrait**. This setting prints across the width of the page. You will change the orientation to **landscape** so that the worksheet prints across the length of the paper. Then you will use the Fit To feature to make sure it fits on one page with the new orientation.

In addition, notice that the total number of pages to be printed is 10. This is because each quarter sheet also requires two pages to print in portrait orientation. You will also change the orientation of these sheets to landscape.

3
- Click **Previous**.

- Click **Setup...**.

- If necessary, open the Page tab.

- Select **Landscape**.

- Select **Fit to**.

- Click **OK**.

Your screen should be similar to Figure 3.56

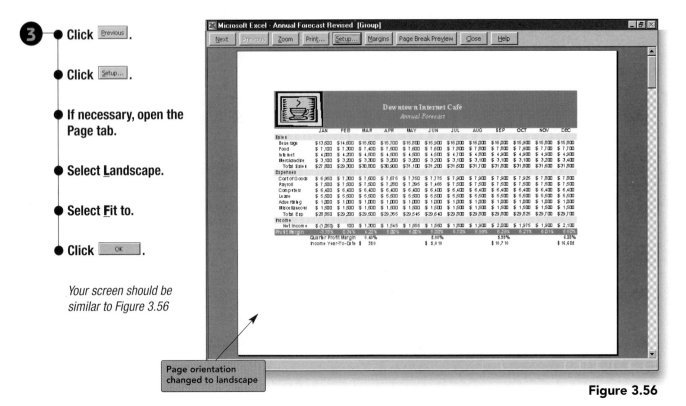

Page orientation changed to landscape

Figure 3.56

Displaying Gridlines and Centering on Page

The entire worksheet now easily fits across the length of the page. Because the worksheet is large, you also feel the worksheet may be easier to read if the row and column gridlines were printed. In addition, you want the worksheet to be centered horizontally on the page.

1
- Click **Setup...**.

- From the Sheet tab, select **Gridlines**.

- From the Margins tab, select **Horizontally**.

- Click **OK**.

Your screen should be similar to Figure 3.57

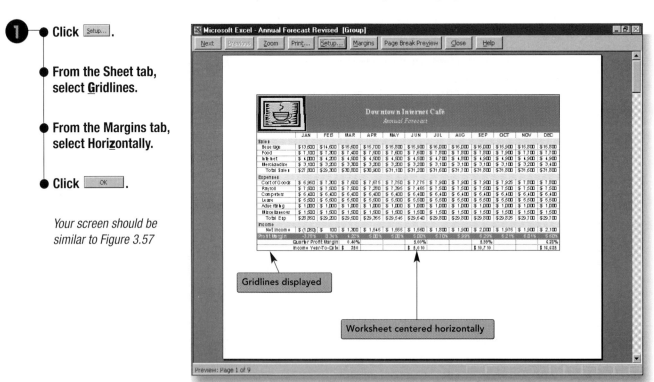

Gridlines displayed

Worksheet centered horizontally

Figure 3.57

The Preview screen is recreated showing how the sheet will appear centered horizontally and with gridlines.

Next, you want to change the orientation to landscape for the four quarterly sheets and to center them both horizontally and vertically on the page. Rather than change each sheet individually in the Preview window, you can make this change to the four sheets at the same time in the worksheet window.

<table>
<tr><td>2</td><td>● Click Next.</td></tr>
</table>

● Click Close.

● Hold down Ctrl and click the Year tab to deselect the sheet.

● Choose File/Page Setup.

● From the Page tab select Landscape.

● From the Margins tab select Horizontally and Vertically.

● Click Print Preview.

Your screen should be similar to Figure 3.58

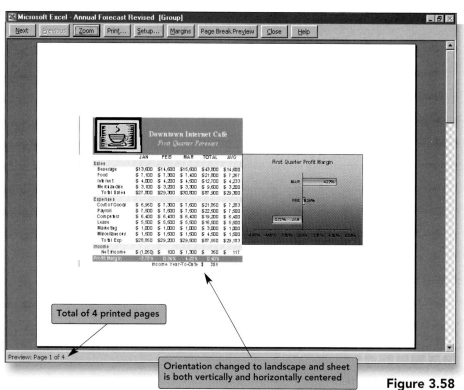

Total of 4 printed pages

Orientation changed to landscape and sheet is both vertically and horizontally centered

Figure 3.58

The worksheet is displayed in landscape orientation and centered both horizontally and vertically on the page. You can also see from the total number of pages to print (four) that the same changes have been made to the four selected sheets.

Adding Custom Headers and Footers

Additional Information
Be careful when making changes to multiple sheets as these changes may replace data on other sheets.

You would also like to add a custom footer to all the sheets. It is faster to add the footer to all sheets at the same time. If you make changes to the active sheet when multiple sheets are selected, the changes are made to all other selected sheets.

1 ● Click ☐Close☐.

● Hold down [Ctrl] and click the Year sheet tab to add it to the selection.

● Choose **F**ile/**P**age Set**u**p.

● Open the Header/Footer tab.

● Click [Custom Footer...].

Your screen should be similar to Figure 3.59

All sheets are selected

Figure 3.59

The Left Section text box will display the footer text you entered aligned with the left margin, the Center Section will center the text, and the Right Section will right-align the text. The insertion point is currently positioned in the Left Section text box. You want to enter your name, class, and the date in this box. You will enter your name and class by typing it directly in the box. Instead of typing the date, however, you will enter a code that will automatically insert the current date whenever the worksheet is printed.

The buttons above the section boxes (identified below) are used to enter the codes for common header and footer information.

2 • **Type** Created by [your name].

• **Press** Tab ⇥.

• **Enter the** name of your class **and the** section or time.

• **Press** Tab ⇥.

• **Click** 🗓 **Date.**

Your screen should be similar to Figure 3.60

Figure 3.60

You want to make one final check to see how the footer will look before printing the workbook.

3 ● Click [OK].

● Click [Print Preview].

● Look at the other sheets to confirm that the footer was added to them as well.

● Display the Year sheet again.

Your screen should be similar to Figure 3.61

Custom footer

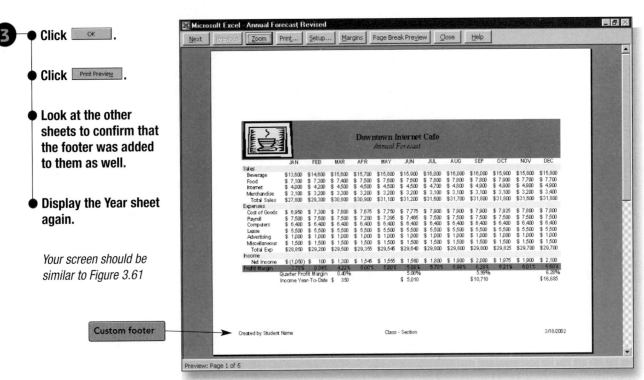

Figure 3.61

The footer as you entered it appears on all selected worksheets.

Printing Selected Sheets

You want to print the Year and Second Quarter worksheets only.

1 ● Best fit the Year sheet and display grid lines again.

● Close the Preview window.

● Right-click on a sheet tab and choose Ungroup Sheets.

● If necessary, make the Year sheet active.

● Save the file again.

● Hold down [Ctrl] and click the Second Quarter Sheet tab to add it to the selection of sheets to print.

● Click 🖨 Print.

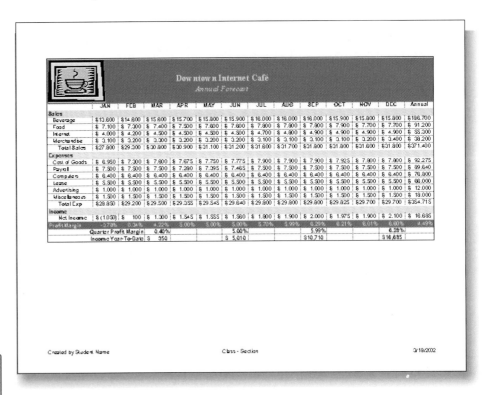

HAVING TROUBLE?
If you need to specify print settings that are different from the default settings on your system, use File/Print to print the worksheet.

Your printed output should look like that shown here and on the next page.

2 Close the workbook and exit Excel.

concept summary

Spell Checking (EX3.5)

The spell-checking feature locates all misspelled words, duplicate words, and capitalization irregularities in the active worksheet and proposes the correct spelling.

Absolute References (EX3.16)

An absolute reference is a cell or range reference in a formula whose location does not change when the formula is copied.

Sheet Names (EX3.20)

Each sheet in a workbook can be assigned a descriptive name to identify the contents of the sheet.

AutoFill (EX3.22)

The AutoFill feature makes entering long or complicated headings easier by logically repeating and extending the series.

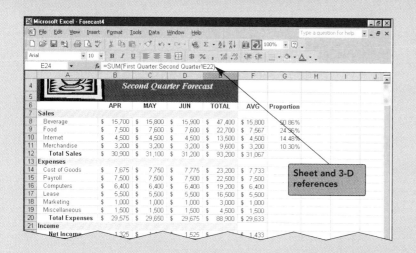

Sheet and 3-D References (EX3.24)

A formula containing sheet and 3-D references to cells in different worksheets in a workbook allows you to use data from other worksheets and to calculate new values based on this data.

Split Windows (EX3.32)

A sheet window can be split into sections called panes to make it easier to view different parts of the sheet at the same time.

Freeze Panes (EX3.35)

Freezing panes prevents the data in the panes from scrolling as you move to different areas in the worksheet.

What-If Analysis (EX3.39)

What-if analysis is a technique used to evaluate the effects of changing selected factors in a worksheet.

Goal Seek (EX3.40)

Goal Seek is a tool that is used to find the value needed in one cell to attain a result you want in another cell.

lab review

LAB 2
Managing and Analyzing a Workbook

key terms

mous skills

After completing this lab, you have learned the following Microsoft Office User Specialist skills:

Skill	Description	Page
Working with Cells and Cell Data	Check spelling	EX3.4
Formatting and Printing Worksheets	Modify row and column settings	EX3.5
	Modify Page Setup options for worksheets	EX3.44
	Preview and print worksheets and workbooks	EX3.44
Modifying Workbooks	Insert and delete worksheets	EX3.27
	Modify worksheet names and positions	EX3.25
	Use 3-D references	EX3.24
Creating and Revising Formulas	Create and revise formulas	EX3.11
	Use statitical, date and time, financial, and logical functions in formulas	EX3.11

command summary

Command	Shortcut Keys	Button	Action
<u>E</u>dit/<u>M</u>ove or Copy Sheet			Moves or copies selected sheet
<u>F</u>ile/Page Set<u>u</u>p/Page/<u>L</u>andscape			Changes orientation to landscape
Insert/<u>F</u>unction	⇧Shift + F3	*f*x	Inserts a function
F<u>o</u>rmat/S<u>h</u>eet/<u>R</u>ename			Renames sheet
F<u>o</u>rmat/<u>S</u>tyle/<u>S</u>tyle name/Currency			Applies currency style to selection
F<u>o</u>rmat/<u>S</u>tyle/<u>S</u>tyle name/Percent		%	Changes cell style to display percentage
<u>T</u>ools/<u>S</u>pelling	F7	ABC✓	Spell-checks worksheet
<u>T</u>ools/<u>G</u>oal Seek			Adjusts value in specified cell until a formula dependent on that cell reaches specified result
<u>T</u>ools/Formula A<u>u</u>diting/Show <u>W</u>atch Window			Opens the Watch Window toolbar
<u>V</u>iew/<u>Z</u>oom		100% ▾	Changes magnification of window
<u>W</u>indow/Un<u>f</u>reeze			Unfreezes window panes
<u>W</u>indow/<u>F</u>reeze Panes			Freezes top and/or leftmost panes
<u>W</u>indow/<u>S</u>plit			Divides window into four panes at active cell
<u>W</u>indow/Remove <u>S</u>plit			Removes split bar from active worksheet

lab exercises

Terminology

screen identification

In the following worksheet and chart, several items are identified by letters. Enter the correct term for each item in the space provided.

F **E** **D** **C**

Microsoft Excel - ex03_Annual Forecast

File Edit View Insert Format Tools Data Window Help

Type a question for help

Arial   10   B I U

Q16

B

	A	B	C	D	K	L	M	N	O	P	Q
6		JAN	FEB	MAR	OCT	NOV	DEC	Annual			
7	**Sales**										
8	Beverage	$13,600	$14,600	$15,600	$15,900	$15,800	$15,800	$186,700			
9	Food	$ 7,100	$ 7,300	$ 7,400	$ 7,900	$ 7,700	$ 7,700	$ 91,200			
10	Internet	$ 4,000	$ 4,200	$ 4,500	$ 4,900	$ 4,900	$ 4,900	$ 55,300			
11	Merchandise	$ 3,100	$ 3,200	$ 3,300	$ 3,100	$ 3,200	$ 3,400	$ 38,200			
12	**Total Sales**	$27,800	$29,300	$30,800	$31,800	$31,600	$31,800	$371,400			
13	**Expenses**										
14	Cost of Goods	$ 6,950	$ 7,300	$ 7,600	$ 7,925	$ 7,800	$ 7,800	$ 92,275			
15	Payroll	$ 7,500	$ 7,500	$ 7,500	$ 7,500	$ 7,500	$ 7,500	$ 90,000			
16	Computers	$ 6,400	$ 6,400	$ 6,400	$ 6,400	$ 6,400	$ 6,400	$ 76,800			
17	Lease	$ 5,500	$ 5,500	$ 5,500	$ 5,500	$ 5,500	$ 5,500	$ 66,000			
18	Advertising	$ 1,000	$ 1,000	$ 1,000	$ 1,000	$ 1,000	$ 1,000	$ 12,000			
19	Miscellaneous	$ 1,500	$ 1,500	$ 1,500	$ 1,500	$ 1,500	$ 1,500	$ 18,000			
20	**Total Exp**	$28,850	$29,200	$29,500	$29,825	$29,700	$29,700	$355,075			
21	**Income**										
22	**Net Income**	$ (1,050)	$ 100	$ 1,300	$ 1,975	$ 1,900	$ 2,100	$ 16,325			
23	Profit Margin	-3.78%	0.34%	4.22%	6.21%	6.01%	6.60%	4.40%			
24	Quarter Profit Margin			0.40%			6.28%				

Year First Quarter

Ready

G **A**

A. _____

B. _____

C. _____

D. _____

E. _____

F. _____

G. _____

Match the lettered item on the right with the numbered item on the left.

1. 'Second Quarter!'A13 _____   a. default page orientation

2. pane _____   b. spell-checks worksheet

3. portrait _____   c. pane that contains the cell selector

4. [F7] _____   d. the sections of a divided window

5. Sheet1:Sheet3!H3:K5 _____   e. sheet reference

6. #DIV/0! _____   f. mixed cell reference

7. landscape _____   g. 3-D reference

8. M34 _____   h. indicates division by zero error

9. active pane _____   i. prints across the length of the paper

10. $B12 _____   j. absolute cell reference

multiple choice

Circle the correct response to the questions below.

1. _____ styles display dollar signs, commas, and two or zero decimal places.
   a. currency
   b. comma
   c. normal
   d. percent

2. The cell reference to adjust row 4 without adjusting column C is:
   a. C4
   b. C4
   c. $C4
   d. C$4

3. The number 32534 displayed with the Currency[0] style would appear as _____ in a cell.
   a. 32,534
   b. $32534
   c. $32,534
   d. $32,534.00

4. Each sheet in a workbook can be assigned a descriptive name called a:
   a. sheet name
   b. reference name
   c. content name
   d. label name

5. A(n) _____ holds words you commonly use but that are not included in the dictionary supplied with the program.
   a. AutoFill
   b. custom dictionary
   c. spell checker
   d. main dictionary

6. A _____ reference is a reference to the same cell or range on multiple sheets in the same workbook.
   a. copied
   b. 3-D
   c. sheet
   d. workbook

7. A division of the worksheet window that allows different areas of the worksheet to be viewed at the same time is called a:
   a. window
   b. part
   c. pane
   d. section

8. The information in the worksheet can be _____ in the top and left panes of a window only.
   a. frozen
   b. fixed
   c. aligned
   d. adjusted

9. A common accounting function that helps evaluate data by allowing the user to adjust values to see the effect is called:
   a. auto calculate
   b. what-if analysis
   c. AutoFill
   d. value analysis

10. A cell address that is part absolute and part relative is called:
    a. absolute reference
    b. frozen
    c. adjusted
    d. mixed reference

true/false

Circle the correct answer to the following questions.

1. =SUM(Sheet15:Sheet50!H6) sums the values in cell H6 of sheets 15 and 50.	True	False
2. An absolute reference is a cell or range reference in a formula whose location does not change when the formula is copied.	True	False
3. G8 is an absolute reference.	True	False
4. If you hold down [Ctrl] while you drag the fill handle the entries will be incremented.	True	False
5. You can freeze the information in the top and left panes of a window only.	True	False
6. The sheet reference consists of the name of the sheet separated from the cell reference by an exclamation point.	True	False
7. The Window/Split command can be used to quickly create a four-way split at the active cell.	True	False

8. To create two horizontal panes with the left pane frozen, move the cell selector in the top row of the window and select the column to the left of where you want the split to appear.   True   False

9. Dragging the fill handle activates the AutoFill feature and recognizes the cell entry as one that can be incremented.   True   False

10. Goal Seek varies the value in the cell you specify until a formula that is dependent on that cell returns the desired result.   True   False

Concepts

fill-in

Complete the following statements by filling in the blanks with the correct terms.

1. Excel checks spelling by comparing text entries to words in a(n) _____.

2. A(n) _____ is used to identify the contents of a sheet.

3. Changing the page orientation to _____ prints across the length of the page.

4. A(n) _____ reference is a cell or range reference in a formula whose location does not change when the formula is copied.

5. _____ is used to evaluate the effects of changing selected factors in a worksheet.

6. _____ panes prevents the data in the pane from scrolling as you move to different areas in a worksheet.

7. A(n) _____ allows you to use data from other worksheets and to calculate values based on this data.

8. When a window is _____, each pane can be scrolled independently.

9. Use _____ to make entering long or complicated headings easier by logically repeating and extending the series.

10. Use _____ to find the value in a single cell to achieve the result you want in another cell.

discussion questions

1. Define, compare, and contrast relative references, sheet references, and 3-D references. Provide a brief example of each.

2. Discuss how absolute and mixed cell references can be used in a worksheet. What is an advantage of using these types of references over a relative cell reference?

3. Discuss the differences between splitting a window and freezing a window. When would it be appropriate to split a window? When would it be appropriate to freeze a window?

4. Discuss the differences between what-if analysis and Goal Seek. Under what conditions would it be more appropriate to use what-if analysis. When would it be more appropriate to use Goal Seek?

Hands-On Exercises

step-by-step

Sandwich Shop Sales Forecast

★ **1.** Nick Walsh owns seven Sandwich Shop franchises. He has created a worksheet to record each store's first quarter sales. Nick would like you to extend this first quarter sales worksheet to another worksheet that provides a sales forecast for the second quarter. The completed worksheets are shown here.

a. Open the workbook ex03_Sandwich Shop. Spell-check the worksheet and correct any misspelled words. Insert a copy of Sheet1 before Sheet2. Rename the Sheet1 tab to **1st Quarter Sales** and then rename Sheet1(2) tab to **2nd Quarter Sales**. Add color to the tabs.

b. In the 2nd Quarter Sales sheet, change the monthly labels to **Apr, May**, and **June** using AutoFill.

c. Enter the following projected April sales figures:

Type	Number
8th Avenue	19000
Price-Guadalupe	14250
Mountain Avenue	13000
Sunland Drive	7800
E. Thomas Road	9500
99th Street	3500
W. Monroe Street	5250

d. A new advertising campaign for May and June is expected to increase monthly sales. May sales for each location is expected to be 10 percent more than April sales and June sales are expected to be 15 percent more than May. Enter formulas to calculate May and June sales for the 8th Avenue location and then copy these formulas into the other appropriate cells.

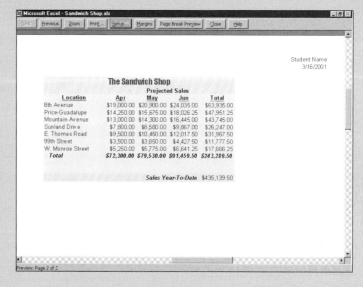

e. Enter and bold the heading **Projected Sales** in cell C2. Center the heading over columns C and D.

f. Enter, bold, italicize, and right-align the heading **Sales Year-To-Date**: in cell D14. In cell E14, enter a formula to calculate the total sales for the first six months by summing cells E11 on both sheets. Format the value to currency with two decimal places.

g. Make the following changes in both sheets:
  - Format the numbers to currency with two decimal places.
  - Format the column headings to centered, bold, and underlined.
  - Format the worksheet title to 14 pt, center it across columns A through E, and add a color and font of your choice.
  - Indent, bold, and italicize the Total row heading.
  - Bold and italicize the Total row values.
  - Add a custom header that contains your name and the date right-aligned to both work sheets.

h. Preview the workbook. Save the workbook as Sandwich Shop2. Print the workbook.

Forecasting Sales

★ **2.** West's Bed and Bath is a small privately owned retail store. Their accountant, Jeremy, has just completed the budgeted income statement for the first quarter. You are going to use this statement to test the sensitivity of Sales to Net Income. The completed worksheet is shown here.

a. Open the workbook ex03_West Income Statement. Examine the contents of the cells under Jan. You will notice that Sales and Fixed Costs are values while the other entries are formulas. This is also the case for the cells for Feb through Jun.

b. Jeremy has been told there may be a rent increase beginning in February that will increase fixed costs to 1755. Update the fixed expense values to see the effect of this increase.

c. Next Jeremy would like to know what level of sales would be necessary to generate a February Net Income of $5000, March of $5100, and $5500 for April through June. Use Goal Seek to answer these questions and update the sales figures.

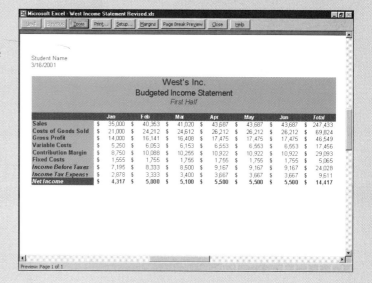

d. Add a custom header that contains your name and the date left-aligned. Change the print orientation to landscape. Save the workbook as West Income Statement2. Print the workbook.

Tracking Hours Worked

★★ **3.** Parker Brent works for United Can Corp. He is paid $8.50 per hour plus time and a half for overtime. For example, this past Monday Parker worked 10 hours. He earned $68 (8 hours times $8.50 per hour) for regular time plus $25.50 (2 hours times $8.50 per hour times 1.5) for overtime for a total of $93.50. He has started to create a worksheet to keep track of weekly hours. You are going to complete this worksheet and create another that Parker will use to schedule next week's hours. The completed worksheets are shown here.

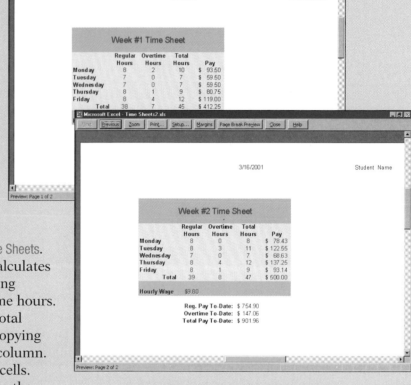

a. Open the workbook ex03_Time Sheets. Enter a formula in E8 that calculates Monday's total hours by adding Monday's regular and overtime hours. Enter formulas to calculate total hours for the other days by copying the formula in E8 down the column. Center the total hours in the cells.

b. Using an absolute reference to the Hourly Wage in cell C15, enter a formula in cell F8 to calculate Monday's pay. Be sure to include regular and overtime pay in the formula. Enter formulas to calculate pay for the other days by copying the formula in cell F8 down the column. Calculate the total Pay. Format the Pay column using the Accounting format with two decimal places.

c. Parker has received his work schedule for next week and would like to record those times by extending the current worksheet to a second week. Insert a copy of Sheet1 before Sheet2. Rename the Sheet1 tab to **First Week** and then rename Sheet1(2) tab to **Second Week**. Add color to the tabs.

d. In the Second Week sheet, change the title in cell B4 to **Week #2 Time Sheet** and enter the following work hours.

	Regular Hours	Overtime Hours
Monday	8	0
Tuesday	8	3
Wednesday	7	0
Thursday	8	4
Friday	8	1

e. Enter, bold, and right-align the following labels:

Reg. Pay To-Date: in cell D17

Overtime To-Date: in cell D18

Total Pay To-Date: in cell D19

f. Enter a formula in cell E17 to calculate the regular pay to date by summing cells C13 on both sheets and multiplying by the hourly wage. Enter a similar formula in cell E18 for overtime pay to date. Calculate the total pay to date in cell E19. Format these values using the Accounting format with two decimal places.

Parker is thinking about asking for a raise from $8.50 to $9.00 to be effective next week. To evaluate the impact of the raise, change the hourly rate in the Week 2 sheet.

g. Use Goal Seek to determine the hourly rate required to achieve a weekly total pay of $500 for Week 2.

h. Add a custom header to both sheets that contains the date centered and your name right-aligned. Preview the workbook. Save the workbook as Time Sheets2. Print the workbook.

Calculating Total Points and GPA

★ ★ **4.** Amy Marino is a college student who has just completed the first two years of her undergraduate program as a business major. In this exercise, you will calculate semester and cumulative totals and GPA for each semester. The completed worksheet for Spring 2002 is shown here.

a. Open the workbook ex03_Grade Report. Look at the four sheets. Rename the sheet tabs Fall 2000, Spring 2001, Fall 2001, and Spring 2002. Add color to the tabs.

b. You need to enter the formulas to calculate the Total Points and GPA for the four semesters. You will do this for all four sheets at the same time. Select the four sheets. In the Fall 2000 sheet, multiply the Grade by the Credits Earned to calculate Total Points for Intro to Business. Copy that formula down the column. Sum the Credits Attempted, Credits Earned, and Total Points columns and display the results in the Semester Total row.

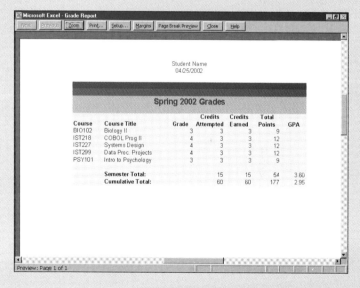

c. In cell G13, divide the Semester Total's Total Points by the Semester Total's Credits Earned to calculate the GPA for the semester. Use what-if analysis to see what Amy's GPA would be if she had earned a 3 instead of a 2 in Western Civ. Change the grade back to a 2.

d. Look at each sheet to see that the formulas were entered and the calculations performed.

e. Go to cell D14 in the Fall 2000 sheet. Enter the reference formula =D13 to copy the Semester Total Credits Attempted number to the Cumulative Total row. Copy the formula to cells E14 and F14 to calculate Credits Earned and Total Points.

f. Go to the Spring 2001 sheet and calculate a Cumulative Total for Credits Attempted by summing the Spring 2001 Semester Total and the Fall 2000 Cumulative Total. (*Hint:* You can use pointing to enter the Cumulative Totals formula.)

g. Copy that formula to the adjacent cells to calculate Cumulative Totals for Credits Earned and Total Points. Repeat this procedure on the Fall 2001 and Spring 2002 sheets.

h. Go to the Fall 2000 sheet. Select all four sheets. In cell G14, calculate the GPA for the Cumulative Total. Format the Semester Total GPA and the Cumulative Total GPA to display two decimals. Look at each sheet to see the cumulative GPA for each semester. (*Hint:* Amy's cumulative GPA at the end of the Spring 2002 semester is 2.95.) Display the Sheet tab shortcut menu and ungroup the sheets.

i. Go to the Fall 2000 sheet and preview the workbook. Add a custom header that contains your name and the date center-aligned to the sheets. Save the workbook file as Grade Report2. Print the Spring 2002 sheet centered horizontally on the page.

Preparing the Homeowners Association Budget

★★ **5.** Stuart Philips is president of the Garden Springs Homeowners Association. He has nearly
★   completed a six-month budget for the association. Stuart wants to complete the six-month budget, and extend it for the next six months; The completed second half budget is shown here.

a. Open the workbook ex03_Springs Forecast. Spell-check and correct any errors in the workbook.

b. Enter the function to calculate the Average in cell I6. Copy the function down the column. Clear any cells that contain division by zero errors.

c. Insert a copy of Sheet1 before Sheet2. Rename the Sheet1 tab to First Half and rename Sheet2 to Second Half. Add color to the tabs.

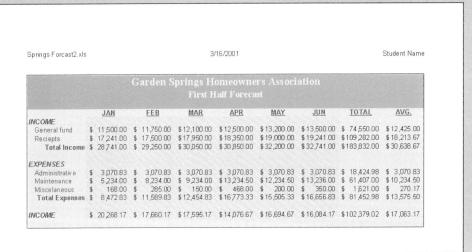

d. Use the AutoFill feature to replace the months JAN through JUN with JUL through DEC on the Second Half sheet. Update the title of the Second Half sheet to Second Half Forecast.

e. Stuart expects Receipts for July to increase by 2 percent over June and then to increase 1 percent per month beginning August until the end of the year. Create a formula to calculate the receipts for July by taking the receipts figure from June in the First Half sheet and multiplying it by 1.02. Create a formula to calculate August's receipts by taking the receipts in July and multiplying it by 1.01. Copy this formula down and across to calculate the remaining receipts.

f. The maintenance and miscellaneous expenses for July through December are difficult to determine. At this point Stuart would like to plug in values that average the expenses for the first half of the year. Enter 10200 for Maintenance expense and 270 for Miscellaneous expense for July. Copy the values to August through December.

g. Add a custom header that contains the file name left-aligned, the date centered, and your name right-aligned. Preview the workbook. Save the workbook as Springs Forecast2. Print the Second Half worksheet using landscape orientation.

African Safari Cost Analysis

★★★ **6.** Alice, a travel analyst for Adventure Travel Tours, is evaluating the profitability of a planned African Safari package. She has researched competing tours and has determined that a price of $4,900 is appropriate. Alice has determined the following costs for the package.

Item	Cost
Air transport	$1,800 per person
Ground transportation	$360 per person
Lodging	$775 per person
Food	$750 per person
Tour Guides	$3,000
Administrative	$1,200
Miscellaneous	$4,000

Alice has started a worksheet to evaluate the revenues and costs for the African Safari. She wants to know how many travelers are needed to break even (revenues equal costs), how many are needed to make $5,000, and how many are needed to make $10,000. The three worksheets of the completed analysis are shown here and on the next page.

a. Open the workbook ex03_African Safari. Notice that Alice has already entered the tour price and an estimated number of travelers.

b. Spell-check and correct any errors in the workbook.

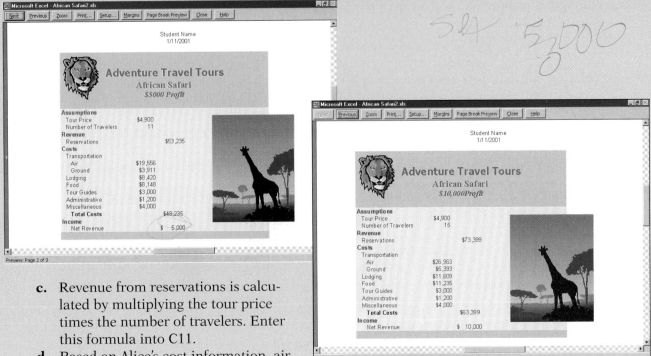

c. Revenue from reservations is calculated by multiplying the tour price times the number of travelers. Enter this formula into C11.

d. Based on Alice's cost information, air transportation is $1800 times the number of travelers. Enter this formula into B14. Enter formulas into B15, B16, and B17 for the other expenses (see table above) related to the number of travelers.

e. Enter the remaining expenses into cells B18, B19, and B20.

f. Calculate total costs in cell C21. Net revenue is the difference between revenue from reservations and total costs. Enter this formula into cell C23.

g. Format the currency values in the worksheet to Currency with no decimal places.

h. Use Goal Seek to determine the number of travelers required to just break even (net revenue equals zero).

i. Rename the sheet tab to Break Even. Insert a copy of the Break Even sheet before Sheet2 and rename the tab of the copy $5000. Add color to the tabs.

j. In the $5000 sheet, change the title in B5 to $5,000 Profit. Use Goal Seek to determine the number of travelers needed to produce a net revenue of $5,000.

k. Insert a copy of the $5000 sheet before Sheet2 and rename the tab of the copy to $10,000. Change the title in B5 to $10,000 Profit. Use Goal Seek to determine the number of travelers needed to produce a net revenue of $10,000.

l. Preview the workbook. Add a custom header that contains your name and the date center-aligned to the three sheets. Center the worksheet horizontally. Save the workbook file as African Safari2. Print the workbook.

lab exercises

on your own

Expanding Budget Projections

★ 1. In On Your Own exercise 2 of Lab 1, Personal Budget, you created a workbook for a three-month budget. Extend this workbook by adding two additional sheets. One sheet is to contain a budget for the next six months. The final sheet is to present a full year's summary using 3-D references to the values in the appropriate sheets.

Consider making a special purchase, such as a car, a new computer, or perhaps taking a trip. On a separate line below the total balance in the summary sheet, enter the amount you would need. Subtract this value from the total balance. If this value is negative, reevaluate your expenses and adjust them appropriately. Format the sheets using the features you have learned in the first three labs. Add a custom header on all sheets that includes your name. Preview, print, and save the workbook as Personal Budget2.

Program Expense Comparisons

★★ 2. Obtain yearly income and expense data for three major art programs at your college or university. In a workbook, record each program's data in a separate sheet. In a fourth sheet, calculate the total income, total expenses, and net income for each program. Also in this sheet, calculate the overall totals for income, expense, and net income. Format the sheets using the features you have learned in the first three labs. Add a custom header on all sheets that includes your name. Preview, print, and save the workbook as Art Expenses.

Stock Data Analysis

★★★ 3. Select three stocks listed on the New York Stock Exchange. Using the Internet or the library, determine each stock's month-ending price for the past year. In a workbook containing four sheets, record each stock's prices in separate worksheets. In a fourth sheet, calculate the average, standard deviation, and maximum and minimum for each of the three stocks. Also, in the final sheet, chart the average data for the three stocks. Format the sheets using the features you have learned in the first three labs. Add a custom header on all sheets that includes your name. Preview, print, and save the workbook as Stock Analysis.

on the web

★★★ Owning and managing a small business is a dream of many college students. Do some research on the Web and choose a business that interests you. Create a projected worksheet for four quarters in separate worksheets. In a fifth sheet, show the total for the year. Include a year-to-date value in each quarterly sheet. In the last quarter sheet, select one expense and determine what value the expense would have to have been so that the net income for that quarter would have been 10 percent higher than the current level. Format the sheets using the features you have learned in the first three labs. Add a custom header on all sheets that includes your name. Preview, print, and save the workbook as My Business.

Working Together: Linking, Embedding, and E-mailing

Evan, the Café owner, is particularly concerned about the first quarter forecast. Your analysis of the sales data for the first quarter shows a steady increase in total sales. However, as you suggested, if a strong sales promotion is mounted, Internet sales will increase sharply. Evan has asked you to send him a memo containing the worksheet data showing the expected sales without a strong sales promotion and the chart showing the projected Internet sales with a sales promotion.

Additionally, Evan wants a copy of the second quarter forecast showing the 5 percent profit margins for each month. He also wants a copy of the workbook file so that he can play with the sales values to see how they would affect the profit margin.

You will learn how to share information between applications while you create these memos. Additionally, you will learn how to send the workbook via e-mail. Your completed document will look like that shown below.

Note: This lab assumes that you already know how to use Word and that you have completed Labs 2 and 3 of Excel. You will need the file Café Sales Charts you created in Lab 2 and Annual Forecast Revised from Lab 3.

Copying between Applications

The memo to the manager about the analysis of the sales data has already been created using Word. However, you still need to add the Excel worksheet data and charts to the memo. All Microsoft Office applications have a common user interface such as similar commands and menu structures. In addition to these obvious features, they have been designed to work together, making it easy to share and exchange information between applications.

You will begin by copying the worksheet from Excel into a Word document. You can also use the same commands and procedure to copy information from Word or other Office XP applications into Excel.

Copying a Worksheet to a Word Document

1 ● **Start Word and open the document** exwt1_Sales Forecast Memo.

● **In the memo header, replace Professor's Name with your instructor's name and Student Name with your name.**

Your screen should be similar to Figure 1

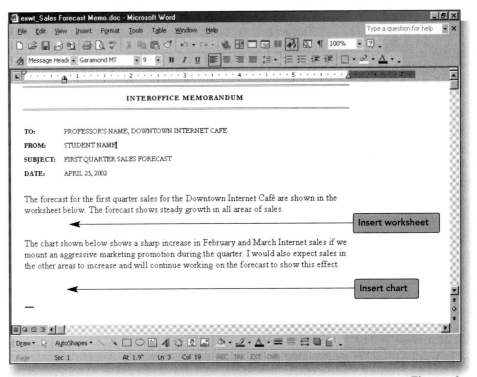

Figure 1

You will insert the worksheet data of the first quarter sales forecast below the first paragraph. Below the second paragraph, you will display the combination chart of sales by category. To insert the information from the Excel workbook file into the Word memo, you need to open the workbook.

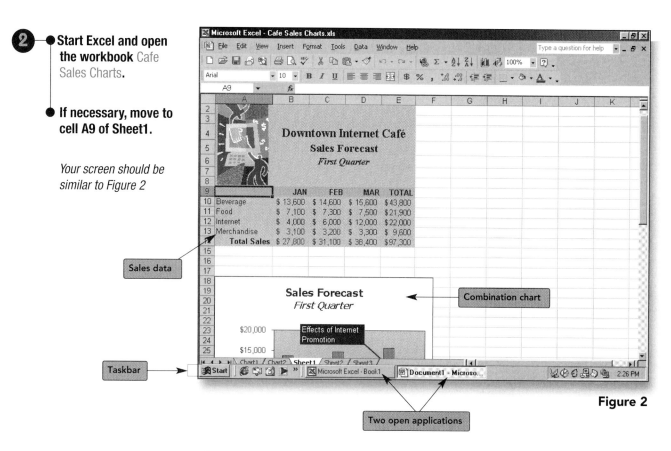

2 **Start Excel and open the workbook** Cafe Sales Charts.

● **If necessary, move to cell A9 of Sheet1.**

Your screen should be similar to Figure 2

Sales data

Combination chart

Taskbar

Two open applications

Figure 2

There are now two open applications, Word and Excel. Word is open in a window behind the Excel application window. Both application buttons are displayed in the taskbar. There are also two open files, Cafe Sales Charts in Excel and exwt1_Sales Forecast Memo in Word. Excel is the active application and Cafe Sales Charts is the active file.

First you will copy the worksheet data into the Word memo. While using the Excel application, you have learned how to use cut, copy, and paste to move or copy information within the same document. You can also perform these operations between documents in the same application and between documents in different applications. For example, you can copy information from a Word document and paste it into an Excel worksheet. The information is pasted in a format that the application can edit, if possible.

You want to copy the worksheet data in cells A9 through E14 into the memo.

3 • Select cells A9 through E14.

• Click 📋 Copy.

• Click in the taskbar.

• Move to the second blank line below the first paragraph of the memo.

• Click 📋 Paste to copy the contents of the Clipboard into the memo.

Your screen should be similar to Figure 3

Excel worksheet data inserted into Word document as a table

Figure 3

The worksheet data has been copied into the Word document as a table that can be edited and manipulated within Word. Much of the formatting associated with the copied information is also pasted into the document. You need to adjust the column widths of the table to display the data correctly. Then you will center the table between the margins.

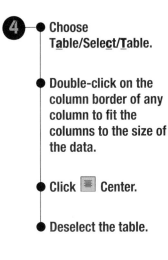

4 • Choose Table/Select/Table.

• Double-click on the column border of any column to fit the columns to the size of the data.

• Click 🔲 Center.

• Deselect the table.

Your screen should be similar to Figure 4

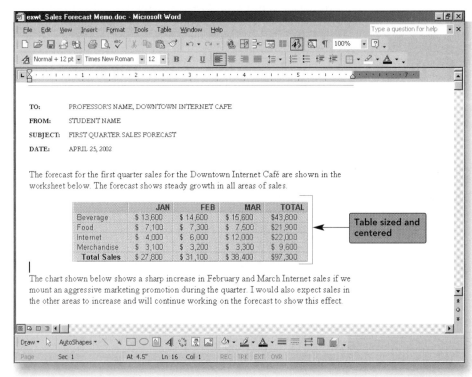

Table sized and centered

Figure 4

Next you want to return the Internet sales data in the table to the original forecasted values assuming an aggressive marketing campaign is not mounted.

5 ● **Change the value in C4 to 4,200, in D4 to 4,500 and E4 to 12,700.**

Your screen should be similar to Figure 5

Figure 5

6 ● **Switch to Excel.**

Your screen should be similar to Figure 6

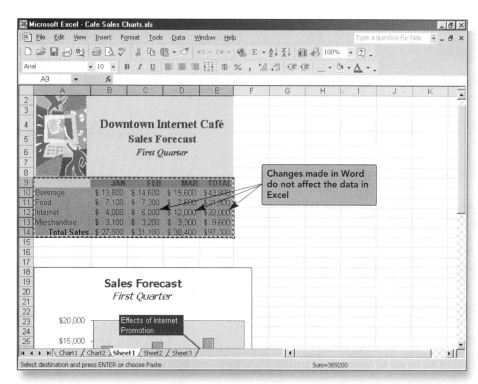

Figure 6

The change in data made in the Word table does not affect the data in the worksheet. This is because the Word table is simply a copy of the Excel worksheet.

Linking between Applications

Next you want to display the combination chart showing the sales trends for Internet sales if an aggressive marketing campaign is mounted below the second paragraph in the memo. You will insert the chart object into the memo as a **linked object**. Information created in one application can also be inserted as a linked object into a document created by another application. When an object is linked, the data is stored in the **source file** (the document it was created in). A graphic representation or picture of the data is displayed in the **destination file** (the document in which the object is inserted). A connection between the information in the destination file to the source file is established by the creation of a link. The link contains references to the location of the source file and the selection within the document that is linked to the destination file.

When changes are made in the source file that affect the linked object, the changes are automatically reflected in the destination file when it is opened. This is called a **live link**. When you create linked objects, the date and time on your machine should be accurate. This is because the program refers to the date of the source file to determine whether updates are needed when you open the destination file.

Linking a Chart Object to a Word Document

You will insert the chart as a linked object. By making the chart a linked object, it will be automatically updated if the source file is edited.

1
- Select the combination chart.

- Click ▣ Copy to copy the selected chart object to the Clipboard.

- Switch to the Word application and move to the second blank line below the second paragraph of the memo.

- Choose **E**dit/Paste **S**pecial.

- Select Paste **l**ink.

Your screen should be similar to Figure 7

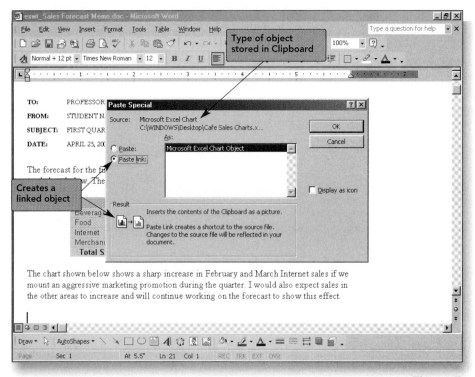

Figure 7

The Paste Special dialog box displays the type of object contained in the Clipboard and its location in the Source area. From the As list box you select the type of format in which you want the object inserted into the destination file. The only available option for this object is as a Microsoft Excel Chart Object. The Result area describes the effect of your selections. In this case, the object will be inserted as a picture and a link will be created to the chart in the source file. Selecting the Display as Icon option changes the display of the object from a picture to an icon. Double-clicking the icon displays the object picture. The default selections are appropriate.

- Click **OK**.

- Set the Zoom to 75%.

- Position the window so you can see both the worksheet and the chart on the page.

- Center the chart object on the page.

Your screen should be similar to Figure 8

Figure 8

Updating a Linked Object

While reading the memo and looking at the chart, you decide to change the chart type from a combination chart to a line chart. You feel a line chart will show the sales trends for all sales items more clearly. You also decide to lower your sales expectation for Internet sales from 12,000 to 10,000 for March.

To make these changes, you need to switch back to Excel.

1 ● Double-click the chart object.

Another Method
The menu equivalent is Edit/Linked Worksheet Object/Edit Link.

● If necessary, select the chart.

● Click Chart Type.

● Click 📈 Line chart.

● Change the value in cell D12 to 10000.

● Scroll the window to see both the chart and worksheet data.

Your screen should be similar to Figure 9

Figure 9

The chart type has changed to a line chart and the chart data series has been updated to reflect the change in data. Now you will look at the memo to see what changes were made to the worksheet and chart.

2 ● Switch to the Word document.

Your screen should be similar to Figure 10

Figure 10

The chart in the memo reflects the change in both chart type and the change in data for the Internet sales. This is because any changes you make in the chart in Excel will be automatically reflected in the linked chart in the Word document. However, because the worksheet data is a word table and not a linked object, it does not reflect the change in data made in Excel.

Editing Links

Whenever a document is opened that contains links, the application looks for the source file and automatically updates the linked objects. If there are many links, updating can take a lot of time. Additionally, if you move the source file to another location or perform other operations that may interfere with the link, your link will not work. To help with situations like these, you can edit the settings associated with links. To see how you do this,

1 ● **If necessary, select the chart object.**

● **Choose Edit/Links.**

Your screen should be similar to Figure 11

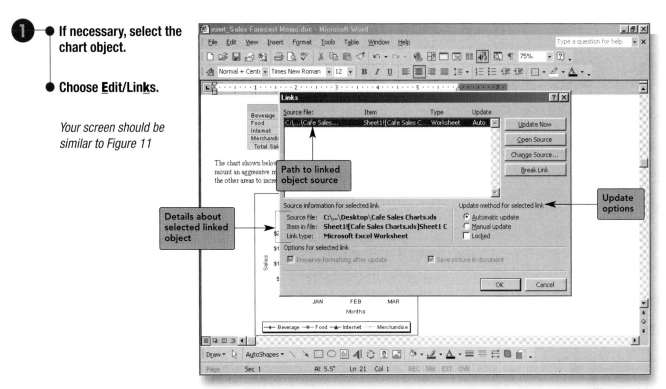

Figure 11

The Links dialog box displays the object path for all links in the document in the list box. The field code specifies the path and name of the source file, the range of linked cells or object name, the type of file, and the update status. Below the list box, the details for the selected link are displayed. The other options in this dialog box are described in the table below.

Option	Effect
Automatic	Updates the linked object whenever the destination document is opened or the source file changes. This is the default.
Manual	The destination document is not automatically updated and you must use the Update Now command button to update the link.
Locked	Prevents a linked object from being updated.
Open Source	Opens the source document for the selected link.
Change Source	Used to modify the path to the source document.
Break Link	Breaks the connection between the source document and the active document.

2 ● Click .

● **Deselect the chart and save the Word document as** Sales Forecast Memo Linked**.**

● **Preview, print, then close the document.**

● **Save the Excel workbook as** Cafe Sales Charts Linked **and close the file.**

Embedding an Object in Another Application

The last thing you need to send Evan is a memo that describes and shows the second quarter forecast. To do this, you'll open the memo already created for you in Word and **embed** the sections from the Annual Forecast Revised workbook that Evan wants in the appropriate locations. An object that is embedded is stored in the destination file and becomes part of that document. The entire file, not just the selection that is displayed in the destination file, becomes part of the document. This means that you can modify it without affecting the source document where the original object resides.

Embedding a Worksheet in a Word Document

1 ● **Open the Word document** exwt1_Forecast Memo**.**

● **In the memo header, replace the Student Name with your name.**

● **Move to the second blank line below the first paragraph of the memo.**

Your screen should be similar to Figure 12

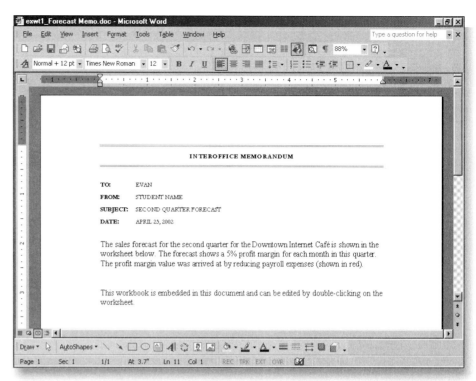

Figure 12

You will embed the first quarter 2002 forecast worksheet in the Word document.

2 ● **Switch to Excel and open the workbook file** Annual Forecast Revised**.**

● **Make the Second Quarter sheet active.**

● **Copy the range A1 through F24.**

● **Switch to Word.**

● **Choose Edit/Paste Special.**

Additional Information

To embed an entire file, use Insert/Object.

The dialog box on your screen should be similar to Figure 13

Figure 13

The Paste option inserts or embeds the Clipboard contents in the format you specify from the As list box. To embed the contents of the Clipboard into a document so it can be edited using the server application, select the option that displays the server name, in this case Excel.

3 ● **Select Microsoft Excel Worksheet Object.**

● **Click** OK .

Your screen should be similar to Figure 14

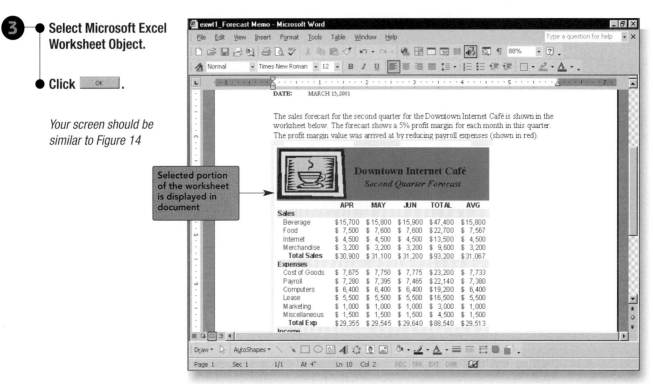

Figure 14

The selected portion of the worksheet is displayed in the memo at the location of the insertion point. As you can see, the object is a bit large.

4 ● **Decrease the size of the worksheet object slightly and center it between the margins.**

Your screen should be similar to Figure 15

Figure 15

Updating an Embedded Object

You want to add color to the payroll range of cells you adjusted to arrive at the 5% profit margin. Because the worksheet is embedded, you can do this from within the Word document. To demonstrate how an embedded object works, you will close the Excel source file and application and edit the worksheet from within the Word document.

1 ● **Switch to Excel.**

● **Close the workbook without saving changes and exit Excel.**

The server application is used to edit data in an embedded object. To open the server application and edit the worksheet, you double-click the embedded object.

2 ● **Double-click the work-sheet object.**

Your screen should be similar to Figure 16

HAVING TROUBLE?
If the worksheet does not fully display the numbers, click outside the worksheet to return to the document, make the worksheet object larger, and then open the server application again.

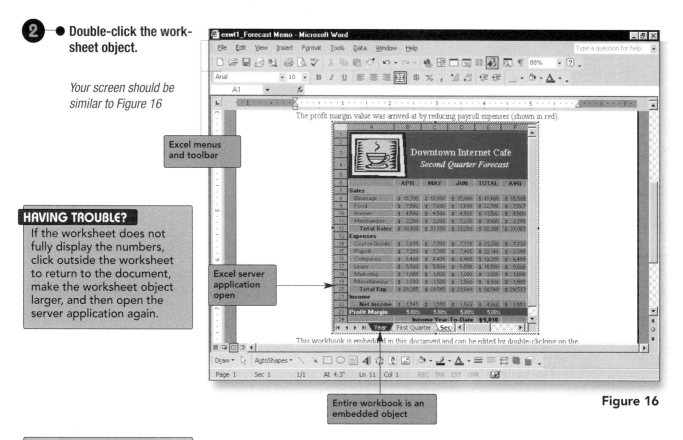

Figure 16

Additional Information
The user must have the server application on his or her system to be able to open and edit the embedded object.

The server application, in this case Excel, is opened. The Excel menus and toolbars replace the menus and toolbars in the Word application window. The selected portion of the embedded object is displayed in an editing worksheet window. Now you can use the server commands to edit the object.

3 ● Change the font color of cells B15 through D15 to red.

● Close the server application by clicking anywhere outside the object.

Your screen should be similar to Figure 17

Figure 17

The embedded object in the memo is updated to reflect the changes you made.

E-Mailing the Memo

Finally, you want to e-mail the memo to Evan.

1 ● Click 📧 E-mail.

HAVING TROUBLE?
If you do not have an e-mail program installed, the 📧 button is not displayed and you will need to skip this section.

Another Method
The menu equivalent is **File/Send to/Mail Recipient**.

Additional Information
The process to e-mail is the same in Excel.

Your screen should look similar to Figure 18

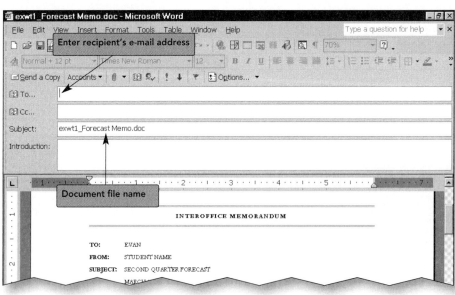

Figure 18

An e-mail message box is displayed at the top of the document. You use the message box to specify the recipient's e-mail address, the e-mail address of anyone you want to send a copy of this message to (cc:), and the subject of the message. You can also use the toolbar buttons to select recipient names from your e-mail address book, attach a file to the message, set the message priority (high, normal, or low priority), include a follow-up message flag, and set other e-mail options. The name of the document appears in the Subject box by default. And finally, you can use the Introduction box to include a brief note along with the copy of the memo.

2 ● Enter the e-mail address of the person you want to send the message to in the To: box.

HAVING TROUBLE?

Ask your instructor what e-mail address to use. For example, if you have a personal e-mail address, your instructor may want you to use it for this exercise.

● In place of the information displayed in the Subject box, enter **Second Quarter Forecast**.

Your screen should look similar to Figure 19

Figure 19

That is all the information that is required to send the e-mail message. You are now ready to send your e-mail message.

3 ● Click .

HAVING TROUBLE?

If you do not have an Internet connection established, you will not be able to send this message. Click Cancel to cancel the connection message.

Your message is sent and the e-mail message box is removed from the screen.

4 ● Save the memo as Second Quarter Forecast.

● Preview and print the memo.

● Exit Word.

Deciding When to Link or Embed Objects

Linking documents is a very handy feature, particularly in documents whose information is updated frequently. If you include a linked object in a document that you are giving to another person, make sure the user has access to the source file and application. Otherwise the links will not operate correctly.

Keep the following in mind when deciding whether to link or embed objects.

Use linking when:	Use embedding when:
File size is important	File size is not important
Users have access to the source file and application	Users have access to the application but not to the source file
The information is updated frequently	The data changes infrequently

Working Together: Linking, Embedding, and E-Mailing

key terms

destination file   EXWT1.6

embed   EXWT1.10

linked object   EXWT1.6

live link   EXWT1.6

source file   EXWT1.6

command summary

Command	Button	Action
File/Send to/Mail Recipient		Sends the active document to the e-mail recipient
Edit/Paste Special		Inserts the object as an embedded object
Edit/Paste Special/Paste Link		Creates a link to the source document
Edit/Links		Modifies selected link
Edit/Linked Object/Edit Link		Modifies selected linked object

Hands-On Exercises

step- by-step

Rescue Foundation Income Memo

★★ 1. The Animal Rescue Foundation's agency director has asked you to provide her with information about income for 2002. You want to create a memo to her and include a copy of the worksheet analysis of this data in the memo. The completed memo is shown below.

    a. Start Word and open the document exwt1_Rescue Memo.

    b. In the header, replace the From placeholder with your name.

    c. Start Excel and open the workbook exwt1_Contributions.

    d. Insert both worksheets as links below the first paragraph in the Word memo. Size and center the worksheets below the paragraph.

    e. Enter the income of $2,650 for May raffle ticket sales.

    f. Save the Excel workbook as Contributions2. Exit Excel.

    g. If necessary, adjust the size and placement of the worksheets in the memo. Save the Word document as Rescue Memo Linked. Preview and print the document.

    h. E-mail the memo to your instructor and carbon copy yourself. Include appropriate information in the subject.

Memo

To: Barbara Wood

From: Student Name

CC: Mark Wilson

Date: 04/25/2001

Re: Income

Below is the completed analysis of income for 2002. As you can see, the income for both periods is very close, with Fall/Winter slightly higher.

Animal Rescue Foundation

	March	April	May	June	July	August	Total
Annual Memberships	$4,000	$4,583	$9,395	$2,834	$5,384	$5,481	$30,677
Phone Solicitation	1200			2000			3200
Corporate Donations			12000			8000	20000
Raffle Tickets			2650				2650
Pet Shows		7000					7000
Other	2000	2000	2000	2000	2000	2000	12000
Total	$7,200	$13,583	$25,045	$6,834	$7,384	$15,481	$75,527

Animal Rescue Foundation

	September	October	November	December	January	February	Total
Annual Memberships	$6,540	$4,523	$4,395	$1,834	$1,384	$5,481	$24,157
Phone Solicitation	1,200					2,000	3,200
Corporate Donations		15,000				10,000	25,000
Raffle Tickets			2,894				2,894
Pet Shows		9,000					9,000
Other	2,000	2,000	2,000	2,000	2,000	2,000	12,000
Total	$9,740	$30,523	$9,289	$3,834	$3,384	$19,481	$76,251

I would like to set up a meeting for next week to brainstorm about ways we can increase income for next year. Please let me know what your schedules are like so I can set a date and time.

1

Tour Status Memo

★★ **2.** Adventure Travel Tours travel agency sends a monthly status report to all subsidiary offices showing the bookings for the specialty tours offered by the company. Previously the worksheet data was printed separately from the memo. Now you want to include the worksheet in the same document as the memo.

a. Start Word and open the exwt1_Tour Status Report document. Replace Student Name with your name on the From line in the heading.

b. Start Excel and open the exwt1_Adventure Travel Monthly workbook.

c. Copy the worksheet as a linked object into the memo below the paragraph.

d. Enter the following data for the March bookings in the worksheet.

Tour	March Data
Tuolumne Clavey Falls	20
Costa Rica Rainforest	4
Kilimanjaro	4
Machu Picchu	3
Himalayas	6
Tanzania Safari	6

e. Save the workbook as Adventure Travel Monthly2. Exit Excel.

f. Center the worksheet object in the word document.

g. Save the Word document as March Status Report. Print the memo.

h. E-mail the memo to your instructor and carbon copy yourself. Include appropriate information in the subject.

INTEROFFICE MEMORANDUM

TO: ADVENTURE TRAVEL EMPLOYEES
FROM: STUDENT NAME
SUBJECT: TOUR STATUS REPORT
DATE: 3/20/01

The bookings to date for our upcoming specialty tours are displayed in the following table. As you can see the new white water rafting tour to below the Tuolumne Clavey Falls in California is almost full to capacity and we are considering offering a second week. Because several others are also close to capacity you may want to advise any clients who are considering one of these tours to make reservations as soon as possible.

Adventure Travel Tours
Speciality Tours Status Report

Tour	Jan	Feb	Mar	Total	Tour Capacity
Tuolumne Clavey Falls	8	14	20	42	46
Costa Rica Rainforests	5	9	4	18	36
Kilimanjaro	2	2	4	8	15
Machu Picchu	4	8	3	15	30
Himalayas	0	0	6	6	18
Tanzania Safari	4	3	6	13	21

Hotel Occupancy Memo

★★ **3.** Karen works for a large hotel chain in the marketing department. She has recently researched hotel occupancy rates for the Phoenix area and has created a worksheet and stacked-column chart of the data. Now Karen wants to send a memo containing the chart to her supervisor.

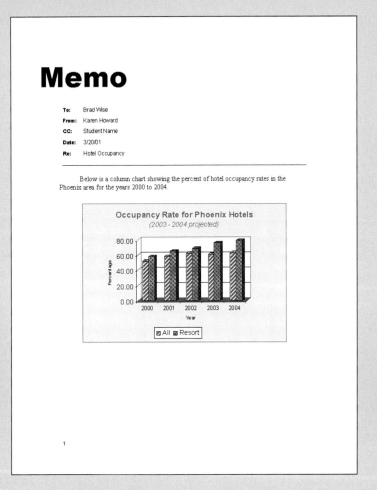

a. Start Word and open the document exwt1_Hotel Memo.

b. In the header, replace the placeholder information in brackets with the following:

> TO: Brad Wise
> FROM: Karen Howard
> CC: [your name]
> RE: Hotel Occupancy

c. Start Excel and open the workbook exwt1_Hotel Data. Embed the column chart below the paragraph in the Word memo. Center the chart in the memo. Exit Excel.

d. You decide you need to clarify that the data for 2003 and 2004 is projected. Add a second title line (2003 – 2004 projected) to the embedded chart in 12 point, italic, no bold.

e. Save the Word document as Hotel Memo2. Preview and print the document.

f. E-mail the memo to your instructor and carbon copy yourself. Include appropriate information in the subject.

Using Solver, Creating Templates, and Evaluating Scenarios

Objectives

After completing this lab, you will know how to:

1. Use Solver.
2. Create and use workbook templates.
3. Protect a worksheet.
4. Open and use multiple workbooks.
5. Link workbooks.
6. Create and use Scenarios.
7. Create a Scenario Summary.
8. Create and modify 3-D shapes.
9. Display the current date and time.

Using solver, you can quickly determine the effect of changing values in two or more cells on another cell.

Creating links between workbooks allows changes you make on one file to be automatically reflected in the other file.

Using Scenario Manager, you can analyze various possible outcomes to help plan for the future.

Downtown Internet Café

After further discussion with Evan, the owner of the Downtown Internet Café, you continued to refine the forecast analysis. You suggested several formatting changes to the worksheet and revised some values. You continued to use Goal Seek to determine the monthly payroll expense needed to achieve monthly profit margins of 6 percent for the third quarter.

Evan wants you to further determine a fixed payroll expense for the fourth quarter that will achieve a quarterly profit margin of 6.5 percent. You will use the Solver tool to determine the values.

Once the annual forecast for 2002 is complete, Evan wants you to use the same procedure to create the forecast for 2003. You will use the 2002 annual forecast worksheet to create a template for the next year's forecast, and then you will use the template to create the first-quarter forecast for that year.

Additionally, you have been asked to create three different scenarios that will show the best, worst, and most likely scenarios for the 2003 first-quarter forecast.

© Corbis

Concept Overview

The following concepts will be introduced in this lab:

1   **Solver**   Solver is a tool used to perform what-if analyses to determine the effect of changing values in two or more cells on another cell.

2   **Workbook Template**   A workbook template is a workbook file that contains predesigned worksheets that can be used as a pattern for creating similar worksheets in new workbooks.

3   **Worksheet Protection**   Worksheet protection prevents users from changing a worksheet's contents by protecting the entire worksheet or specified areas of it.

4   **Arrange Windows**   The Arrange Windows feature displays all open workbook files in separate windows on the screen, in a tiled, horizontal, vertical, or cascade arrangement.

5   **Link Workbooks**   A link creates a connection between files that automatically updates the data in one file whenever the data in the other file changes.

6   **Scenario**   A scenario is a named set of input values that you can substitute in a worksheet to see the effects of a possible alternative course of action. Scenarios are designed to help forecast the outcome of various possible actions.

Analyzing the Worksheet

After seeing how the payroll values changed each month to achieve higher second- and third-quarter profit margins, Evan would like you to do a similar analysis on the fourth quarter. First you want to look at the current profit margin value for the fourth quarter.

1 ● **Open the workbook file** ex04_Revised Annual Forecast.

● **Make the Fourth Quarter sheet active.**

● **Select cell E23.**

Your screen should be similar to Figure 4.1

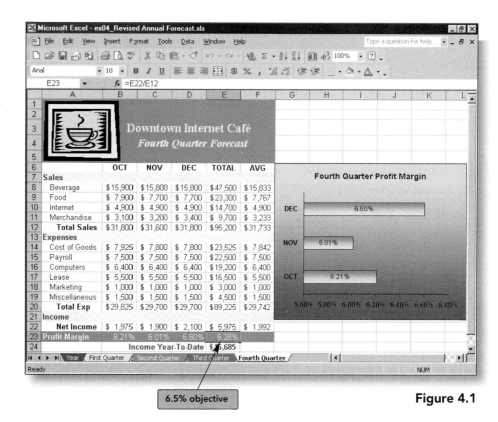

6.5% objective

Figure 4.1

The current profit margin for the fourth quarter is 6.28 percent. This time, Evan would like to keep the payroll expenses constant for the quarter while achieving a 6.5 percent quarterly profit margin.

While you are making changes to the quarterly worksheet, you will display the Watch Window to see how the changes affect the Annual Profit Margin.

2 ● **Move to the Year sheet.**

● **Select cell N23.**

● **Open the Watch Window.**

● **Set it to watch cell N23.**

● **Size and position the Watch Window as in Figure 4.2.**

HAVING TROUBLE?
To open the Watch Window, use Tools/Formula Auditing/Show Watch Window.

Your screen should be similar to Figure 4.2

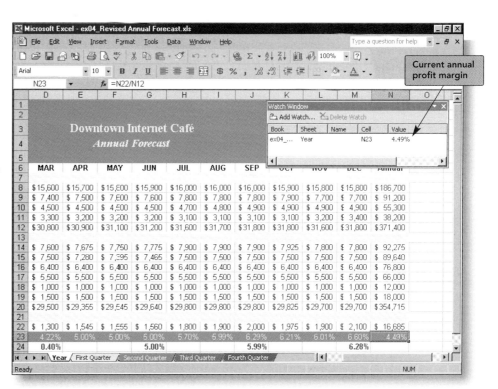

Figure 4.2

Using Solver

Although you could manually perform What-If analysis or use the Goal Seek feature to determine the desired profit margin value, it would be much quicker to use the Solver tool.

concept 1

Solver

1. **Solver** is a tool used to perform what-if analyses to determine the effect of changing values in two or more cells, called the **adjustable cells**, on another cell, called the **target cell**. Solver calculates a formula to achieve a given value by changing one of the variables that affect the formula. To do this, Solver works backward from the result of a formula to find the numbers. The cells you select must be related through formulas on the worksheet. If they are not related, changing one will not change the other.

   Solver can also produce three types of reports about the solution: Answer, Sensitivity, and Limits. In an Answer report, the original and final values of the target cell and adjustable cells are listed along with any constraints and information about the constraints. Information about how sensitive the solution is to small changes in the target cell formula or in the constraints is provided in a Sensitivity report. A Limits report includes the original and target values of the target cell and adjustable cells. It also lists the lower limit, the smallest value that the adjustable cell can take while holding all other adjustable cells fixed and still satisfying the constraints and upper or greatest value.

---

1 ● Display the Fourth Quarter sheet.

● Choose **T**ools/Sol**v**er.

● Move the Solver Parameters dialog box to the lower right corner of the screen.

Your screen should be similar to Figure 4.3

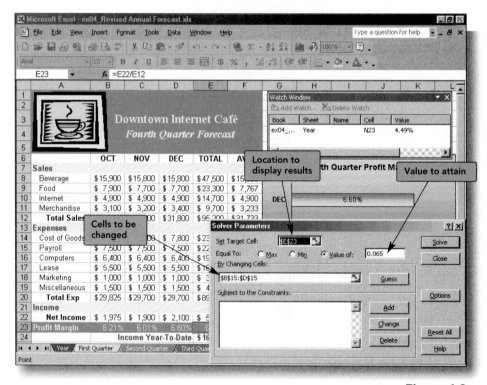

Figure 4.3

In the Solver Parameters dialog box, you need to supply three items of information: the target cell where the result will appear, the desired result value, and the cell or cells that will be changed to achieve the result.

The cell reference of the cell containing the formula you want to solve is entered in the Set Target Cell text box. The cell reference of the active cell, E23, is already correctly entered in this box.

The number you want as the result of the formula is entered in the Equal To text box. You can set the number to be a maximum, minimum, or an exact number. The maximum option sets the target cell to the highest possible number, while the minimum option sets the target cell for the lowest possible number.

The final information needed is the cell or cell range whose contents can be changed when the formula is computed. This range is entered in the By Changing Cells text box. In the fourth quarter, you are looking for a value of 6.5 percent by changing the values in the range of cells B15 through D15.

2 ● Select **V**alue of.

● Type **.065** in the Value Of text box.

● Specify the range B15 through D15 in the **By** Changing Cells text box.

HAVING TROUBLE?
You can minimize the dialog box using the ▣ button and select the range by highlighting it in the worksheet.

Your screen should be similar to Figure 4.4

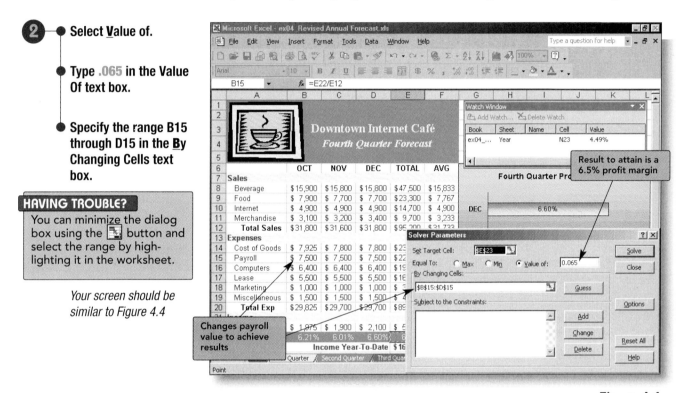

Figure 4.4

Now you are ready to have Solver find the values to meet the parameters you specified:

3 → • **Click** [Solve] .

Your screen should be similar to Figure 4.5

Callouts in figure:
- Anual profit margin increased
- Three types of reports can be created of solution results
- Solver solution changes payroll values to 7,429 to achieve the 6.5% profit margin

Figure 4.5

The Solver Results dialog box tells you that Solver found a solution. The new payroll numbers are entered in the worksheet range and the worksheet is automatically recalculated. By setting the payroll expense to $7,429, the monthly profit margins vary and the quarterly or total profit margin is 6.5 percent. As you can see in the Watch Window, the effect of changing the payroll expenses for the fourth quarter has affected the annual profit margin. The profit margin for the year increased from 4.49 to 4.55 percent due to the reduction of payroll expenses in the fourth quarter.

Creating an Answer Report

From the Solver Results dialog box, you can choose whether to keep the solution or restore the original values. In addition, you can have Solver create Answer, Sensitivity, and Limits Reports. You decide to keep the solution and create an Answer Report.

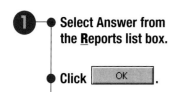

① ● Select Answer from the **R**eports list box.

● Click [OK].

● Make the Answer Report 1 sheet active.

Your screen should be similar to Figure 4.6

Figure 4.6

The Answer Report 1 sheet displays the Answer report that was generated. The target cell section of the report shows the original profit margin value of 6.28 percent and the final value of 6.50 percent. The Adjustable Cells area shows the original and final values for each cell that was changed to achieve the profit margin of 6.50 percent. The final value entered in each adjustable cell will be the same number even if the original values were different in each cell.

The forecast for 2002 is now complete.

② ● Close the Watch Window.

● Make the Year sheet active.

● Move to cell A6 and save the current workbook file as 2002 Forecast.

Creating a Custom Template

After seeing the effects of your analyses on the Year sheet, Evan has found Solver to be a valuable tool for planning and managing operations. He has asked you to create a new workbook containing a forecast for the following year. You could create this new forecast workbook by starting all over again, specifying the formats and formulas. However, as the current workbook already contains this information, you decide to use it as a model or template for future forecasts.

concept 2

Workbook Template

2 A workbook **template** is a workbook file that contains predesigned worksheets that can be used as a pattern for creating similar sheets in new workbooks. Templates can contain text, graphics, formats, page layouts, headers and footers, functions and formulas, and macros.

Templates are useful in any application where input and output are required using the same format. By not having to redesign the worksheet form each time the report is needed, you save time and increase accuracy. You can go back to the original design repeatedly by saving the workbook containing the data under a different file name than the one you used to save the workbook template.

Excel saves a workbook template using a special file format with the file extension .xlt. Workbook templates are also stored in a special Templates folder. To use a workbook template, you select the template file name from the General tab of the New File dialog box. When you save the workbook after entering data in the template, Excel automatically displays the Save As dialog box so that you can specify the new file name. It also changes the file type to an Excel workbook (.xls). This ensures that you do not unintentionally save over the template file.

Designing the Template

A well-designed template allows you to enter information into the appropriate locations while protecting formulas and basic formats. Since the basic workbook design you want to use for your template is already in place, you will modify the worksheets in the workbook to create the template. The first steps are to eliminate the Answer Report 1 sheet and to change the values in the quarter sheets to zeros.

1 ● Delete the Answer Report 1 sheet.

● Select the First Quarter through Fourth Quarter sheets.

HAVING TROUBLE?
Hold down ⇧Shift to extend the sheet selection.

● Enter **0** in cells B8 through D11 and cells B15 through D19 in the First Quarter sheet.

● Move to cell A23.

Your screen should look like Figure 4.7

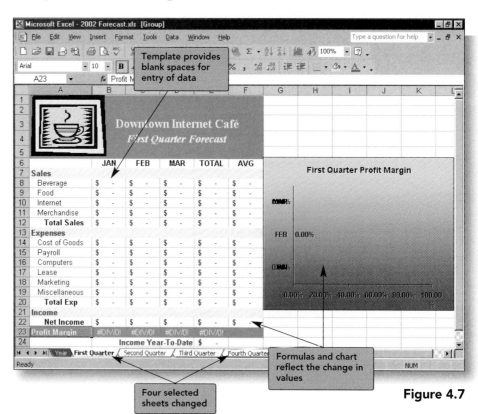

Four selected sheets changed

Figure 4.7

By replacing the values with 0, the underlying formulas remain intact. The selected cell format displays cells containing zero values with a dash symbol. All other worksheet cells containing formulas as well as the chart reflect the change in the values.

2 ● **Look at each of the three other quarter sheets to verify that the values have been replaced.**

● **Make the Year sheet active.**

Your screen should look like Figure 4.8

Values in Year sheet are zero because the cells contain links to the quarter sheets

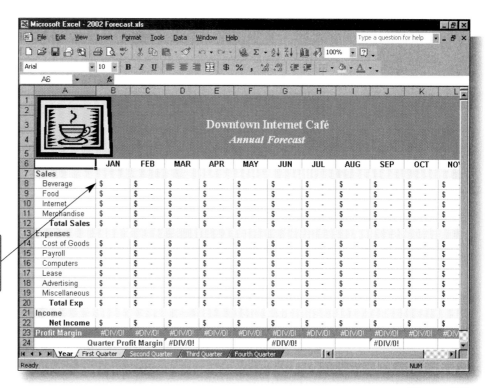

Figure 4.8

Because the Year sheet contains formulas that link to the values in the quarter sheets, this sheet also displays zero values. Now, whenever you are creating another annual forecast, you will simply enter the new values in place of the blanks in the quarter sheets and the annual sheet will automatically be completed.

Protecting the Worksheet

Now that all the values have been removed and the template is ready to use, you want to prevent unwanted changes to the worksheets that would cause headings and formulas to be altered or cleared. To do this, you can protect the worksheet.

concept 3

Protection

3 Excel includes two levels of **protection** that control what information can be changed in a workbook. Worksheet protection prevents users from changing a worksheet's contents by protecting the entire worksheet or specified areas of it. When a worksheet is protected, all cells and graphic objects on it are locked. The contents of a locked cell cannot be changed. If you want to leave some cells unlocked for editing, such as in a worksheet that you use as an entry form, you can lock cells containing labels and formulas but unlock the entry fields so that other users can fill them in. This type of protection prevents you from entering or changing an entry in any locked cells.

Workbook-level protection prevents changes to an entire workbook in two ways. First, you can protect the structure of a workbook so that sheets cannot be moved or deleted or new sheets inserted. Second, you can protect a workbook's windows. This prevents changes to the size and position of windows and ensures that they appear the same way each time the workbook is opened.

In addition, you can include a **password** that prevents any unauthorized person from either viewing or saving changes to the workbook. Two separate passwords can be used: one to open and view the file and another to edit and save the file. If you use a password, you must remember the password in order to turn protection off in the future.

Initially all cells in a worksheet are locked. However, you can enter data in the cells because the worksheet protection feature is not on. When protection is turned on, all locked cells are protected. Therefore, before protecting this sheet, you need to unlock the areas in the worksheet where you want to allow users to make changes to information.

The only area of the Year sheet that needs to be unprotected is the subtitle where the year will be entered when the template is used. You will unlock the cell containing the subtitle and add protection to the rest of the worksheet.

- Move to cell D4.

- Choose F**o**rmat/C**e**lls.

- Open the Protection tab.

- Clear the **L**ocked option.

Your screen should be similar to Figure 4.9

Figure 4.9

Lab 4: Using Solver, Creating Templates, and Evaluating Scenarios

www.mhhe.com/oleary

2 ● Click [OK].

● **Display the Protection toolbar.**

● **Click** **Protect Sheet.**

Another Method

The menu equivalent is Tools/Protection/Protect Sheet.

Your screen should be similar to Figure 4.10

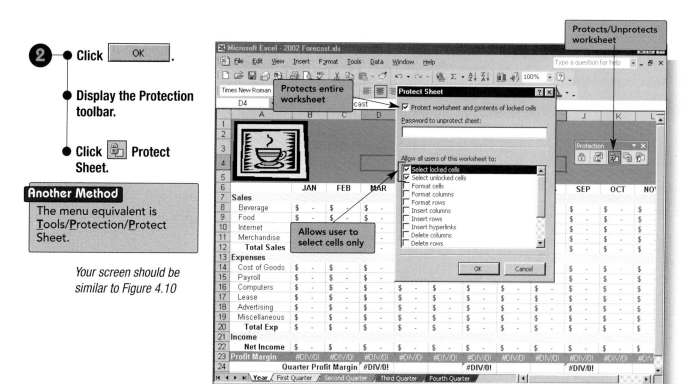

Figure 4.10

In the Protect Sheet dialog box, you select the options that you want to enable for all users of the template. The Select locked cells and Select unlocked cells options are enabled by default. Leaving these selected and the others unselected provides complete protection for the worksheet.

3 ● Click [OK].

Next, you need to unlock the data entry areas of the quarter sheets before you turn on protection for those sheets.

4 • Select the First Quarter through Fourth Quarter sheets.

• Select cells B8 through D11 and B15 through D19.

HAVING TROUBLE?
Hold down Ctrl to select non-adjacent ranges.

• Choose F**o**rmat/C**e**lls.

• Clear the L**o**cked option in the Protection tab.

• Click OK .

Your screen should be similar to Figure 4.11

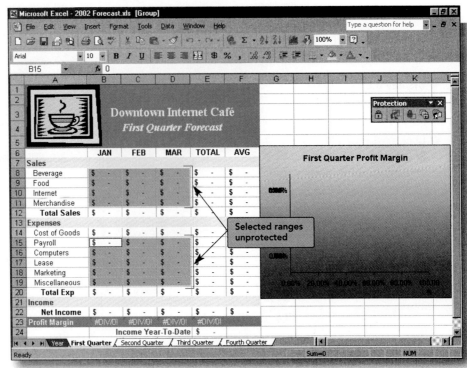

Figure 4.11

When protecting worksheets, you must protect each sheet individually. You will ungroup the sheets and protect each sheet.

5 • Select U**n**group sheets from the sheet tab shortcut menu.

Another Method
You can also hold down ⇧Shift while clicking a sheet tab to ungroup sheets.

• If necessary, make the First Quarter sheet active.

• Click 🔒 Protect Sheet.

• Click OK .

• In a similar manner protect the other three quarter sheets.

Your screen should be similar to Figure 4.12

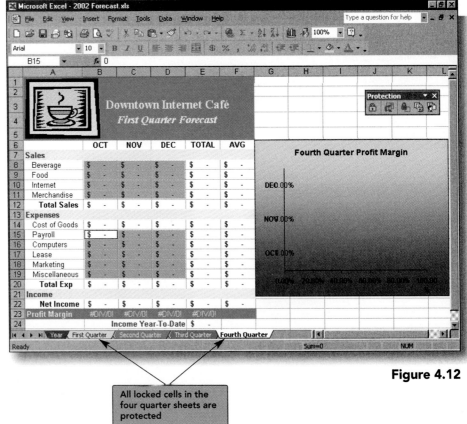

Figure 4.12

Now all locked cells in the four quarter sheets are protected. Only those cells you unlocked prior to turning on protection can be changed. To test this out, you will try to make an entry in a protected cell.

6 ● **Type** any character **in cell B6.**

Your screen should be similar to Figure 4.13

Locked cell is protected and cannot be changed

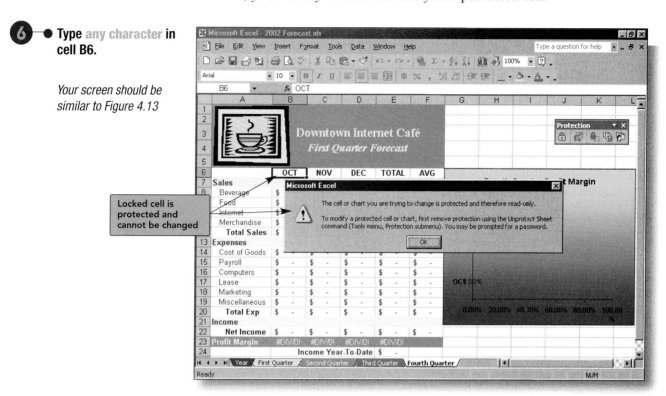

Figure 4.13

The warning dialog box informs you that you cannot change entries in locked cells. Next, you will enter a value in an unlocked cell.

7 ● **Click** OK **to clear the message.**

● **Type** 1250 **in cell B8 and press** ←Enter**.**

Your screen should be similar to Figure 4.14

Entry in un-locked cell is accepted

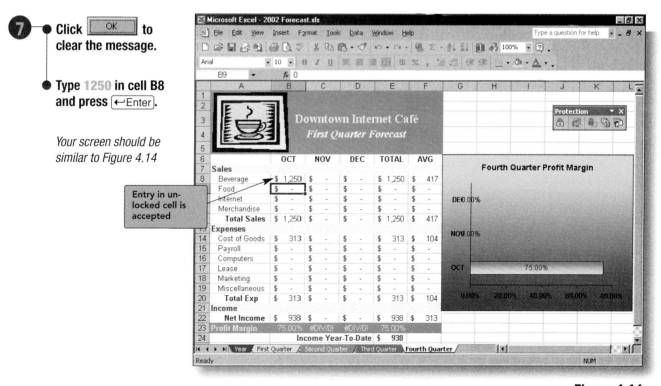

Figure 4.14

The entry is accepted because the cell was unlocked before protection was applied to the sheet.

Saving the Template

Now that the sheets are protected, you will save this workbook as a template file. First, you will clear the test entry and move the cell pointer to the location in the worksheet where you want it to appear when opened.

1 ● Click Undo to remove the test entry.

● Move to cell B8 in each of the other quarter sheets.

● Move to cell D4 in the Year sheet.

● Close the Protection toolbar.

● Choose **F**ile/Save **A**s.

● Enter the new name, **Forecast Template**, in the File **N**ame text box.

● From the Save As **T**ype list box, select Template (*.xlt).

Figure 4.15

Additional Information
You cannot save a workbook as a template by typing the file extension .xlt in a file name. You must select the Template (.xlt) file type from the Save As Type list box.

Your screen should be similar to Figure 4.15

Templates are saved by default to the Templates folder on your system. You can also save templates to other locations just like any other workbook file.

2 ● Click [**S**ave].

● Close the Forecast Template **file.**

HAVING TROUBLE?
If a file already exists with this name, click [Yes] to replace it.

The Forecast Template workbook is now ready to use.

Using the Template

Now you will use the Forecast Template file to create a new 2003 forecast workbook for the Downtown Internet Café.

● Choose **File/New**.

● Click **General Templates...** on the New Workbook task pane.

Your screen should be similar to Figure 4.16

Additional Information
Only templates saved to the Template folder will be listed.

Additional Information
Your General tab may display additional icons depending on how many and what kind of templates have been created and saved in Excel.

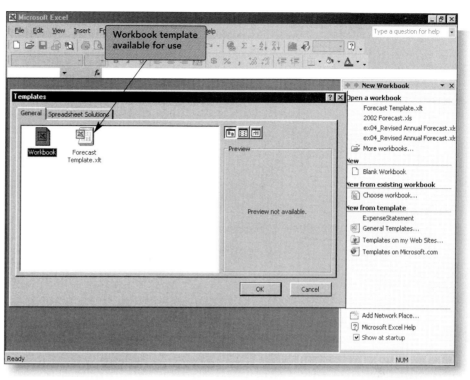

Figure 4.16

The Forecast Template file name appears in the General tab of the Templates dialog box. You will open the template and change the subtitle in the Year sheet to display the year 2003.

● **Select** Forecast Template.xlt.

● Click **OK**.

● Change the subtitle in cell D4 of the Year sheet to **2003 Annual Forecast**.

Your screen should be similar to Figure 4.17

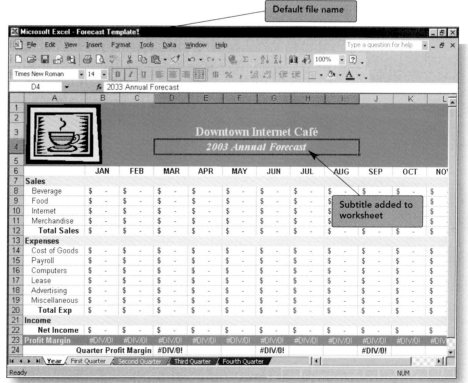

Figure 4.17

Before continuing, you want to save the revised template file as a new workbook file for use in entering the 2003 forecast data. Notice the file name in the title bar is Forecast Template1. Excel automatically adds a number to the file name when the template is opened to prevent you from accidentally overwriting the template when saving. Additionally, when using a template to create a new workbook file, even if you use the Save command, Excel automatically displays the Save As dialog box so that you can specify a new file name.

3 ● Click 🖫 Save.

● Enter the new name, **2003 Forecast**, in the File **N**ame text box.

Additional Information

To ensure that you don't unintentionally save over the template file, Excel automatically assigns the .xls workbook extension as the file type.

● Change the Save **i**n location to the appropriate location to save your files.

● Click   Save .

Your screen should be similar to Figure 4.18

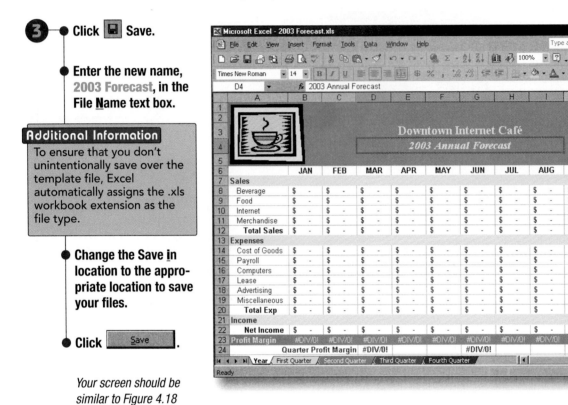

Figure 4.18

Working with Multiple Workbooks

Additional Information

Use the **N**ew Window command on the **W**indow menu to display a second window for the active workbook.

Evan wants you to focus on the 2003 first-quarter forecast. Because he expects all sales and expenses to remain the same as the December 2002 values, you can obtain this data from the 2002 Forecast workbook. To do this, you want to copy the data from one workbook to the other. In Excel, you can open multiple workbook files at the same time. Each workbook is opened in its own window. You can also open additional separate windows to display different parts of the active workbook. The open windows can be arranged so that you can see them simultaneously to make it easy to work with data in multiple workbooks at the same time.

Opening a Second Workbook File

You will open the workbook file containing the 2002 forecast data you saved earlier.

1 • **Open the** 2002 Forecast **workbook file.**

Your screen should be similar to Figure 4.19

Active workbook contains cell selector

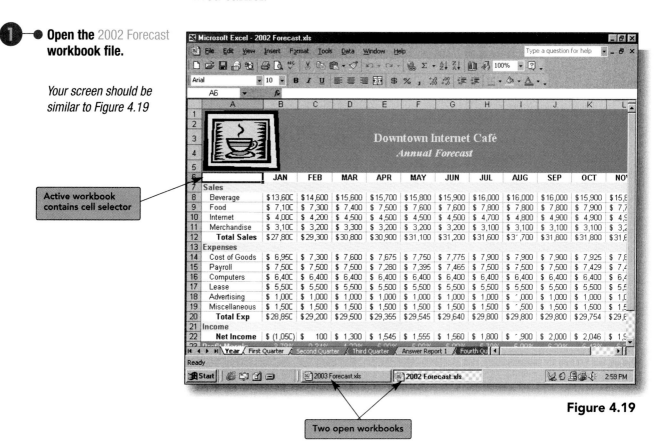

Two open workbooks

Figure 4.19

Now there are two active workbook files and the taskbar displays a button for each open window. The 2002 Forecast workbook file window is open on top of the 2003 Forecast workbook file window. The newly opened file is the **active workbook** file. It is the file that will be affected by changes and the file that contains the cell selector.

Arranging Windows

The way the workbooks are currently displayed makes it difficult to work with both files simultaneously. To make it easier to work with both files at the same time, you can change the arrangement of the windows.

You decide that the easiest way to work with the two files is to tile them.

1 • Choose **W**indow/**A**rrange.

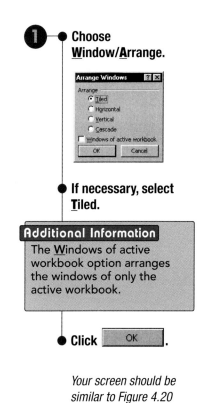

• If necessary, select **T**iled.

• Click [OK].

Your screen should be similar to Figure 4.20

Figure 4.20

The two workbook windows appear next to each other. The title bar of the active workbook file is highlighted. You want to see the December values in the Fourth Quarter sheet of the 2002 forecast and the First Quarter sheet from the 2003 forecast.

2 • Display the Fourth Quarter sheet in the 2002 Forecast workbook.

• Click in the 2003 Forecast workbook window to make it active.

• Display the First Quarter sheet.

Your screen should be similar to Figure 4.21

Figure 4.21

Linking Workbooks

You want to use the December data from the 2002 forecast workbook in the first quarter of the 2003 forecast workbook. Additionally, you want the data in the 2003 forecast to update automatically if the data in the 2002 forecast changes. To do this, you will create a link between the two workbook files.

concept 5

Link Workbooks

5 A **link** creates a connection between files that automatically updates the linked data in one file whenever the data in the other file changes. The link between the workbook files is formed by entering an **external reference** formula in one workbook that refers to a cell in another workbook. When data in a linked cell changes, the workbook that is affected by this change is automatically updated when it is opened.

The formula is entered in the workbook that receives the data. This workbook file is called the **dependent workbook**. The workbook that supplies the data is called the **source workbook**. The cell containing the external reference formula (the **dependent cell**) refers to the cell (the **source cell**) in the source file that contains the data to be copied.

An external reference formula uses the following format:

= [workbook file reference]sheet reference!cell reference

The file reference consists of the file name of the source file followed by the name of the worksheet. The cell reference of the cell or range of cells containing the number to be copied into the dependent workbook follows the file reference. The two parts of the formula are separated by an exclamation point.

You will create a link between the two workbook files by entering external reference formulas in the 2003 First Quarter worksheet that reference the cells containing the values in the Fourth Quarter sheet of the 2002 Forecast workbook. The 2002 Forecast workbook is the source workbook, and the 2003 Forecast workbook is the dependent workbook.

The first external reference formula you will enter will link the beverage sales numbers. To create an external reference formula, you copy the contents of the source cell to the Clipboard, switch to the dependent workbook, and then use the Edit/Paste Special command to create the external reference formula link in the specified cell of the dependent workbook.

The source cell is cell D8 of the Fourth Quarter sheet in the 2002 Forecast workbook. You will copy this source cell and paste it into the dependent cell.

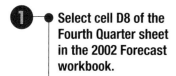

1 ● Select cell D8 of the Fourth Quarter sheet in the 2002 Forecast workbook.

● Click Copy.

● Select cell B8 in the First Quarter sheet of the 2003 Forecast workbook.

● Choose **E**dit/Paste **S**pecial.

Your screen should be similar to Figure 4.22

Creates a link between workbook cells

Figure 4.22

From the Paste Special dialog box, you specify how much of the cell contents you want pasted. You can paste either the entire cell contents (including formatting), or selected attributes associated with the cell, such as only the formula, value, format, comments, validation, or column width of the cell. You can also perform an addition, subtraction, multiplication, or division operation on the pasted cell. You can also create a link to the source cell contents so that when the source cell is changed, the linked cell is automatically changed as well.

2 ● Click .

Additional Information

The Paste Options button also includes the **L**ink Cells option.

Your screen should be similar to Figure 4.23

External reference formula

Absolute cell reference

Value from D8 of the 2002 workbook pasted as a link

Figure 4.23

The link has been established and an external reference formula has been entered into the selected cell of the dependent workbook. The formula is displayed in the formula bar, and the number in cell D8 of the source workbook is entered into the dependent workbook and displayed in cell B8. Notice that Excel uses absolute references in the external reference formula.

Next, you want to create a link between the other December values in the source workbook. To do this quickly, you can copy the external reference formula down the column and across the rows. However, you must first change the cell reference D8 in the external reference formula to a mixed reference of ($D8) so that it will adjust appropriately as the formula is copied.

3 ● **In cell B8 of the 2003 Forecast workbook edit the absolute reference (D8) in the formula to $D8.**

● **Copy the external reference formula in cell B8 to cells C8 and D8 and cells B9 through D11.**

● **Copy the external reference formula in cell B8 to the range B15 through D19.**

● **Click cell D19 to deselect the range.**

Your screen should be similar to Figure 4.24

Figure 4.24

The First Quarter data for 2003 is now complete. It is the same as the December 2002 data. Because the data in the worksheets is linked, a change in the December 2002 worksheet values will automatically be reflected in the First Quarter 2003 worksheet.

Lab 4: Using Solver, Creating Templates, and
Evaluating Scenarios

Updating Linked Data

Evan advises you that the lease for the café will increase to $6,000 a month beginning in October of 2002. You want to enter this new amount and see the effect of this change.

1 ● Enter 6,000 into cells B17, C17, and D17 in the Fourth Quarter sheet of the 2002 Forecast workbook.

Your screen should be similar to Figure 4.25

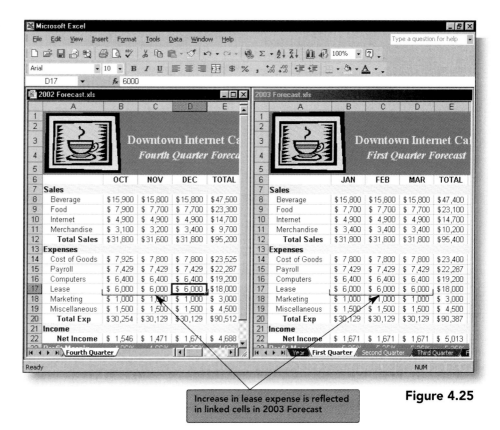

Increase in lease expense is reflected in linked cells in 2003 Forecast

Figure 4.25

All affected formulas are recalculated. Because the workbooks are linked, the change in the 2002 Forecast is automatically reflected in the 2003 Forecast. Once an external reference formula is entered in a worksheet, whenever the data in the cell referenced in the source file changes, the dependent file is automatically updated if it is open. However, if the dependent file is not open, it is not updated. To ensure that a dependent file gets updated when you open the source file, Excel displays an alert message asking if you want to update references to unopened documents. If you respond Yes, Excel checks the source documents and updates all references to them so that you will have the latest values from the source worksheet.

You do not need to obtain any further data from the 2002 Forecast workbook at this time. You can close it and enlarge the 2003 Forecast window to make it easier to work with.

2 ● Save the 2002
Forecast and close the
workbook.

● Maximize the 2003
Forecast window.

*Your screen should be
similar to Figure 4.26*

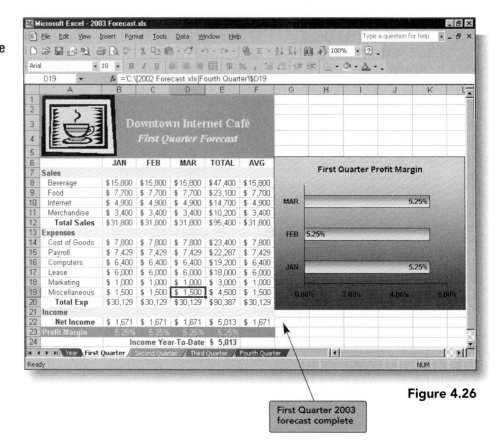

Figure 4.26

First Quarter 2003
forecast complete

Evaluating Scenarios

Evan has reviewed the First Quarter Forecast and is comfortable with it.
While he realizes that sales and costs may be higher or lower than those
presented, Evan believes the most likely scenario, or set of values, is reflected in the First Quarter worksheet. He has asked you to evaluate a best-
case scenario and a worst-case scenario.

concept 6

Scenario

6 A **scenario** is a named set of input values that you can substitute in a worksheet to see the effects
of a possible alternative course of action. Scenarios are designed to help forecast the outcome of
various possible actions. You can create and save different groups of scenario values on a worksheet and then switch to any of these scenarios to view the results.

For example, if you want to create a budget forecast based on various revenue values, you could
define the potential values and then switch between the scenarios to perform what-if analyses.
You can also create reports in separate sheets that summarize the scenarios you create.

The current workbook reflects the most likely scenario. Evan has identified the best-case scenario as one where sales from Internet use increase 25 percent above the current estimate of $4,900 in February and March and all other values remain unchanged. His worst-case scenario is if Internet sales decrease 10 percent below the current estimate for the entire quarter and the lease in March increases from $6,000 to $6,200.

Adding Scenarios

You are going to use the Scenario tool to evaluate the alternative scenarios by changing the values for Internet Sales for January (cell B10), February (cell C10), and March (cell D10), and for March Lease Expense (cell D17). You could create separate worksheets to evaluate each scenario. However, using the Scenario Manager tool, you can create different scenarios and insert these scenarios directly into the workbook to see how each affects the worksheet.

1 ● **Move to cell B10.**

● **Choose Tools/Scenarios.**

● **Move the Scenario Manager dialog box to the right of column F.**

Your screen should be similar to Figure 4.27

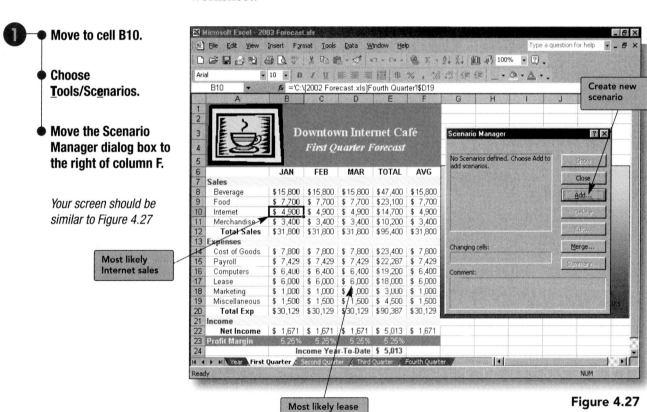

Most likely Internet sales

Most likely lease expense

Figure 4.27

The Scenario Manager dialog box is used to add, delete, and edit scenarios. There are no scenarios named yet. First, you will define the most likely scenario.

2 • Click [Add...].

Your screen should be similar to Figure 4.28

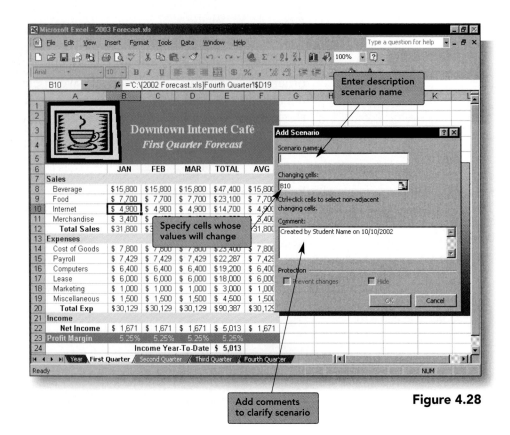

Figure 4.28

In the Add Scenario dialog box you enter a name for the first scenario and the range of cells that will contain the changing values in the Changing Cells text box.

3 • **Type Most Likely in the Scenario Name text box.**

• **Specify the range B10 through D10 and cell D17 as the changing cells in the Changing Cell text box.**

Additional Information

Click [⊞] to reduce the dialog box and select the range from the worksheet. Hold down Ctrl while selecting nonadjacent cells.

Your screen should be similar to Figure 4.29

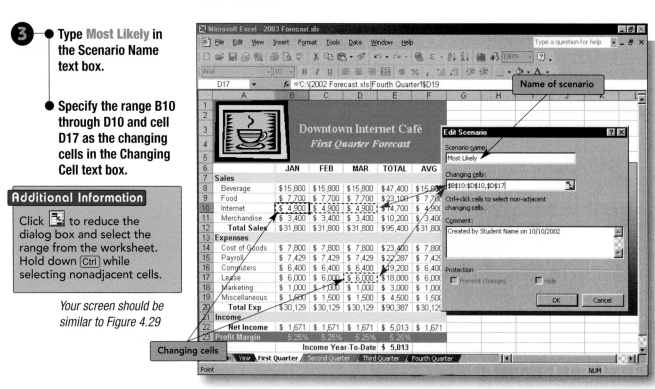

Figure 4.29

It is often helpful to add a comment to clarify the data included in the scenario. The default comment in the Comment text box displays the text "Created by [name] on [date]." You will include additional information to clarify the meaning of the scenario.

4 ● **Click in the Comment text box.**

● **If necessary, replace the name with your name. Add the following text after the date:** First quarter sales and expenses are the same as December 2002.

● **Click** [OK].

● **Click** [OK] **to accept that formulas will be replaced by values.**

Your screen should be similar to Figure 4.30

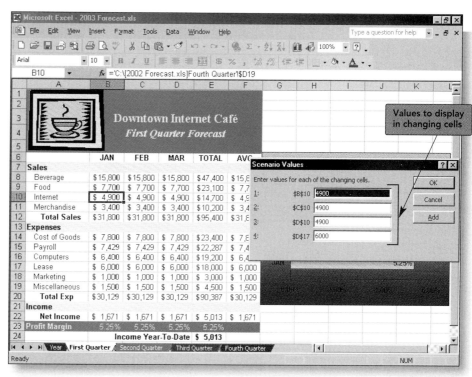

Figure 4.30

The Scenario Values dialog box is used to enter the values to be varied for the different scenarios. The current worksheet values are displayed. These are the values you want to use for the Most Likely scenario.

5 ● Click [OK] .

*Your screen should be
similar to Figure 4.31*

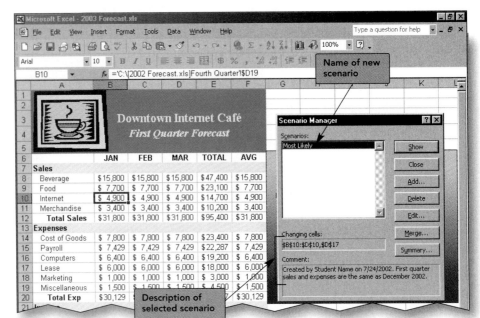

Figure 4.31

You are returned to the Scenario Manager dialog box and the name of the
new scenario is displayed in the Scenarios list box.

Next, you will create the worst-case scenario. You already calculated that
a 10 percent decrease in Internet Sales for the three months would be 4410.
Additionally the lease expense would increase to 6200.

6 ● Click [Add...] .

● In the Scenario Name
text box, type **Worst
Case.**

● In the Comment text
box, change the name
if necessary and enter
the following: **Internet
Sales are 10% less
than the most likely
values for February
and March and March
Lease increases to
$6,200.**

● Click [OK]
twice.

● Enter **4410** in the
B10, C10, and
D10 changing cells
text boxes.

● Enter **6200** in the
D17 changing cells
text box.

*Your screen should be
similar to Figure 4.32*

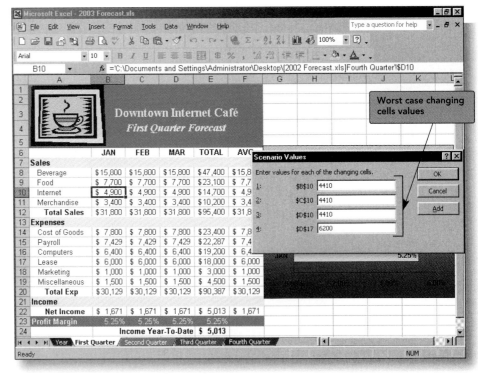

Figure 4.32

Lab 4: Using Solver, Creating Templates, and
Evaluating Scenarios

Next, you will create the best-case scenario. In this scenario, Evan antici-pates that Internet Sales will increase 25 percent for February and March above the most likely values and the March lease expense will remain the same. You could create the scenario in the same way by entering the new values in the changing cells. Another way, however, is to use Solver to cal-culate the expected values for you and then create the scenario from the Solver result. Because you will be changing values in the worksheet, you will need to unprotect the sheet first.

- Click **OK** .

- Click **Close** .

- Click **Tools/Protection/ Unprotect Sheet.**

- Choose **Tools/Solver.**

- Set the target cell as E10, the value equal to **17100**, and the chang-ing cells as C10:D10.

Additional Information

The value is an estimate of a 25 percent increase.

- Click **Solve** .

Your screen should be similar to Figure 4.33

Figure 4.33

The Solver solution increases the February and March Internet sales to 6100. You will create the scenario from these results. You will also not keep the Solver solution, as you want the original values maintained in the worksheet.

8 ● Click [Save Scenario...].

● Enter the scenario name of **Best Case**.

● Click [OK].

● Select Restore **O**riginal Values.

● Click [OK].

Your screen should be similar to Figure 4.34

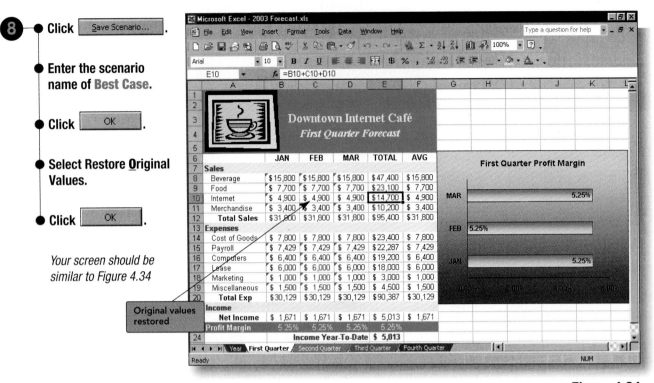

Figure 4.34

The original values are displayed in the worksheet again and the Solver results have been stored as a scenario.

Using Scenarios

There are now three different scenarios in the worksheet. You want to see the effect of the worst-case and best-case scenarios.

1 ● Choose **T**ools/**S**cenarios.

● From the Scenario Manager dialog box, select Worst Case.

● Click [Show].

● Move the Scenario Manager dialog box down so that you can see the chart.

Your screen should be similar to Figure 4.35

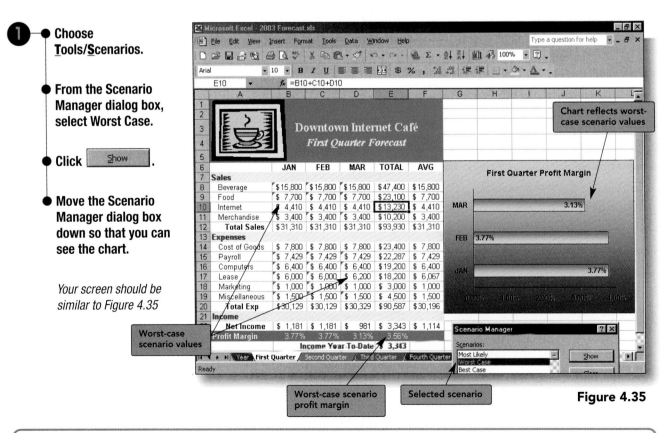

Figure 4.35

The worksheet displays the worst-case values. These values result in a total profit margin of 3.56 percent and the chart reflects the change in monthly profit margins.

2 — In a similar manner, display the Best Case scenario.

Your screen should be similar to Figure 4.36

Best-case scenario values

Best-case total profit margin

Selected scenario

Figure 4.36

Thc best-case values are displayed in the worksheet. The total profit margin is now 6.91 percent. You now only need to edit the scenario to add a comment.

3 ● Click [Edit...].

● **In the Comment text box, if necessary change the name and enter the following:** Internet Sales increase 25% for February and March above the most likely values and March lease expense remains the same.

● Click [OK] twice.

● **Move the Scenario Manager dialog box up to row 5.**

Your screen should be similar to Figure 4.37

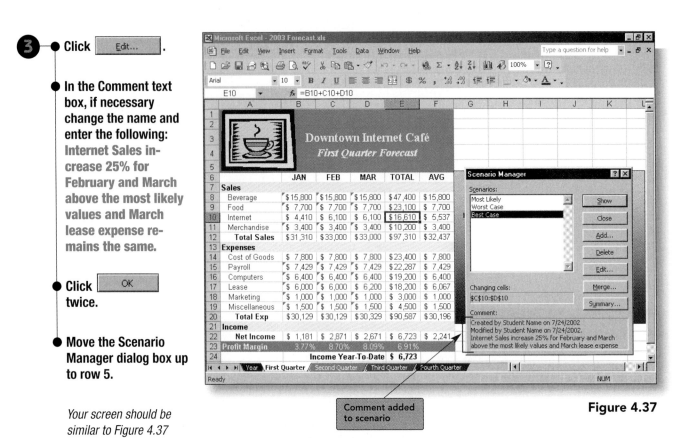

Comment added to scenario

Figure 4.37

Creating a Scenario Report

Another way to evaluate the scenarios is to create a summary report that will display the effect on the profit margins for each scenario.

1 ● Click [Summary...].

● **Specify the range B23 through E23 (containing the profit margin values) as the range of cells whose results you want summarized.**

● Click [OK].

Your screen should be similar to Figure 4.38

Scenario summary displayed in its own sheet

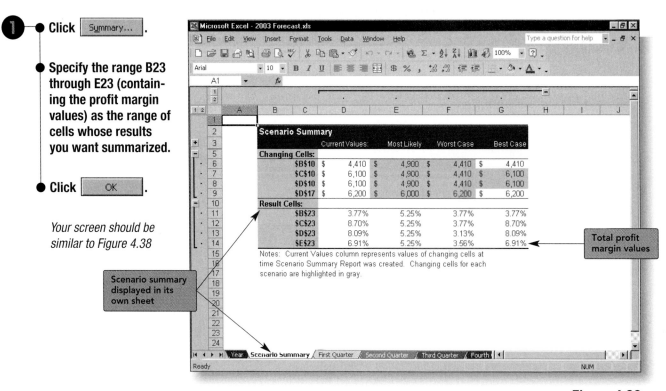

Total profit margin values

Figure 4.38

Lab 4: Using Solver, Creating Templates, and Evaluating Scenarios

www.mhhe.com/oleary

The Scenario Summary report is created and displayed in a separate sheet. It displays the values for the three scenarios and the results on the profit margin for each scenario. As you can see from the summary, the most likely scenario yields a constant 5.25 percent profit margin. The best-case scenario yields higher profit margins, with a total profit margin of 6.91 percent for the quarter. The worst-case scenario yields lower profit margins, with a total profit margin of 3.56 percent.

The report however, is hard to understand because it uses cell references as the labels. To clarify the meaning of the report, you will edit the row labels.

2 ● **Enter the labels in the following cells:**

C6	Internet JAN	**C11**	Profit Margin JAN
C7	Internet FEB	**C12**	Profit Margin FEB
C8	Internet MAR	**C13**	Profit Margin MAR
C9	Lease MAR	**C14**	Profit Margin TOTAL

● **Best Fit column C.**

● **Save the workbook.**

Your screen should be similar to Figure 4.39

Labels clarify meaning of report

Figure 4.39

You have now completed best- and worst-case scenarios for the year 2003, as Evan requested. However, before printing the Scenario Summary worksheet and giving it to Evan, you want to add some 3-D graphics to the worksheet to emphasize the best-case profit margin scenario.

Enhancing the Report

To emphasize the impact of Internet sales, you want to add a three-dimensional (3-D) shape to the Scenario Summary report to draw attention to the rising profits. A **3-D shape** is a line, AutoShape, or free-form drawing object that has a three-dimensional effect applied to it.

Creating a 3-D Effect

The first object you want to create is a text box that identifies the Internet promotion as the focus of the high-sales scenario.

1
- **If necessary, click [icon] Drawing to display the Drawing toolbar.**

- **Click** `AutoShapes ▾` **and from the Block Arrows shapes choose Up Arrow.**

- **Click anywhere in the blank area under the Notes text.**

- **Insert the text Profits from high Internet sales.**

HAVING TROUBLE?
Choose Add text from the arrow's Shortcut menu.

- **Change the font orientation to horizontal and horizontal alignment to center and text orientation to horizontal.**

- **Expand the width of the arrow to display each word on a line.**

HAVING TROUBLE?
Use Format/AutoShape/Alignment to change the text alignment and orientation.

Your screen should be similar to Figure 4.40

Block arrow AutoShape with text

Figure 4.40

Now you want to apply a 3-D effect to the text box. Excel includes many 3-D options you can use to change the depth (the extrusion) of the object and its color, rotation, angle, direction of lighting, and surface texture. When you change the color of a 3-D effect, only the 3-D effect of the object is changed, not the object itself.

2 ● Click 3-D Style on the Drawing toolbar.

[3-D style palette showing: No 3-D, multiple 3-D shape options, 3-D Settings...]

Additional Information

Pointing to the shapes displays the name of the 3-D shape in a ScreenTip.

● Choose 3-D Style 11 (3rd row, 3rd column).

Your screen should be similar to Figure 4.41

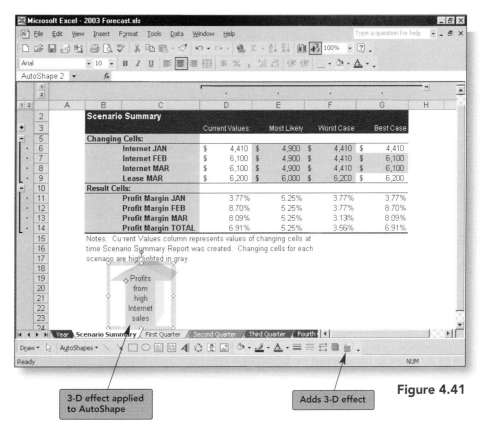

3-D effect applied to AutoShape

Adds 3-D effect

Figure 4.41

Enhancing a 3-D Object

Next, you want to change the fill color.

1 ● Open the 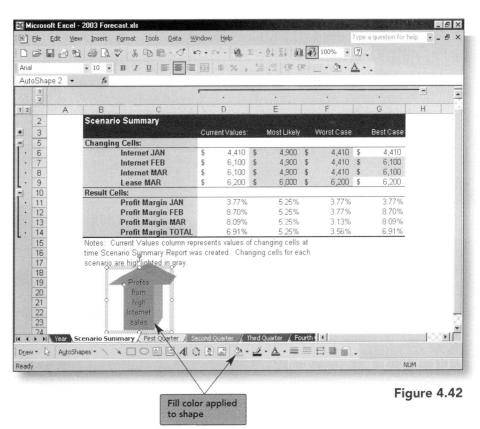 Fill Color drop-down menu and select Pale Blue.

Your screen should look like Figure 4.42

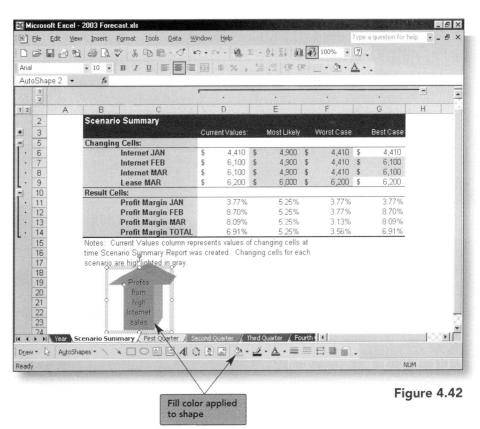

Fill color applied to shape

Figure 4.42

You would also like to see how the 3-D effect would look with different settings applied to it, such as a different lighting effect and a different box color.

2 ● Click 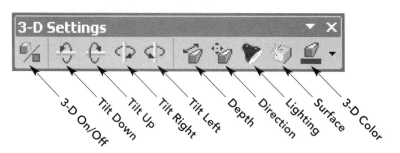 3-D Style and select 3-D Settings.

The 3-D Settings toolbar buttons (identified below) are used to modify the depth (the extrusion) of the 3-D effect and its color, rotation, angle, direction of lighting, and surface texture.

3 ● Click 🔦 Lighting and select a lighting option you like.

● From the 🖌 3-D Color menu select a color you like.

● Close the 3-D Settings toolbar.

Your screen should be similar to Figure 4.43

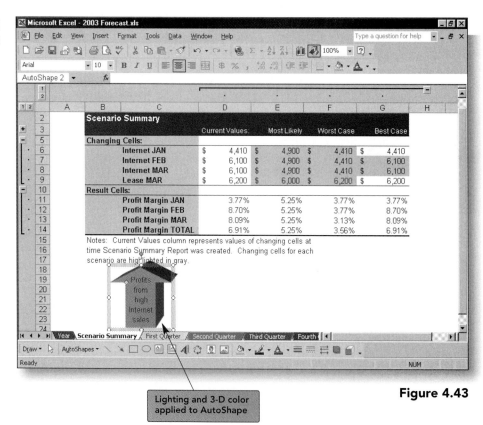

Lighting and 3-D color applied to AutoShape

Figure 4.43

Finally, you want to move the 3-D text box so that it points to the best-case result cells.

4 ● Drag the arrow to point to the bottom-center of the best-case result column.

Your screen should be similar to Figure 4.44

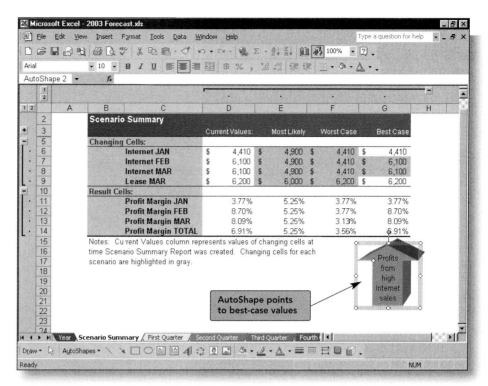

Figure 4.44

Displaying the Current Date and Time

You would also like to include a date and time stamp on the Scenario Summary worksheet to identify when the values were entered and the scenarios applied. You could just enter the current date and time on the worksheet, but you want to ensure that it reflects exactly when the most recent changes and analyses are done. To have the date and time automatically update whenever a worksheet is recalculated, the NOW date function is used.

Using the Insert function feature

You will enter the function in cell B3. You could enter the function directly by typing it. However, another way is to use the Insert Function feature. This feature simplifies entering functions by prompting you to select a function from a list and then helps you enter the arguments correctly.

1 ● Move to cell B3 on the Scenario worksheet.

● Click f_x Insert Function.

Another Method

The menu equivalent is Insert/Function and the keyboard shortcut is ⇧Shift + F3.

Your screen should be similar to Figure 4.45

Figure 4.45

The NOW function may not be displayed in the most recently used category. Any function you want to use can be found by typing a description of what you want to do in the Search text box or by selecting a category.

2 ● From the Or select a category drop down list, select Date & Time.

● Scroll the Select a Function list and select NOW.

● Click OK.

Your screen should be similar to Figure 4.46

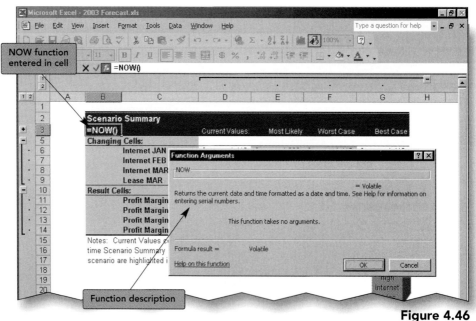

Figure 4.46

The Function Arguments dialog box displays a message telling you that this function displays the current date and time, and requires no arguments. To complete the function,

3 ● Click [OK].

Your screen should be similar to Figure 4.47

NOW function results displayed

Figure 4.47

Additional Information

You can also shift cells down the worksheet when inserting new cells.

The current date and time are displayed in cell B3. A final change you want to make is to move the Note at the bottom of the Scenario Summary to the right. Rather than cutting and pasting the cell contents, you will insert blank cells before the cells and shift the existing cells to the right.

4 ● Select cells A15:A17.

● Choose **I**nsert/C**e**lls/ Shift Cells R**i**ght/ [OK].

Your screen should be similar to Figure 4.48.

Inserted cells

Figure 4.48

Additional Information

You can also delete cells using **E**dit/**D**elete Cells and shift them to the left or up in the worksheet.

Three new cells have been inserted and the existing cells have shifted to the right. Now you are ready to print the worksheet.

5 ● Preview then print the worksheet centered horizontally in landscape orientation. Include your name and the worksheet name in a custom header.

● Save the worksheet and exit Excel.

LAB 4

Using Solver, Creating Templates, and Evaluating Scenarios

Solver   (EX4.6)

Solver is a tool used to perform what-if analyses to determine the effect of changing values in two or more cells on another cell.

Workbook Template   (EX4.10)

A workbook template is a workbook file that contains predesigned worksheets that can be used as patterns for creating similar worksheets in new workbooks.

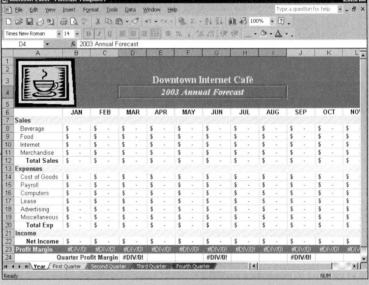

Worksheet Protection   (EX4.12)

Worksheet protection prevents users from changing a worksheet's contents by protecting the entire worksheet or specified areas of it.

Arrange Windows (EX4.20)

The Arrange Windows feature displays all open workbook files in separate windows on the screen in a tiled, horizontal, vertical, or cascade arrangement.

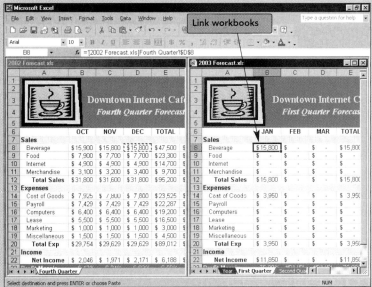

Link Workbooks (EX4.22)

A link creates a connection between files that automatically updates the data in one file whenever the data in the other file changes.

Scenario (EX4.26)

A scenario is a named set of input values that you can substitute in a worksheet to see the effects of a possible alternative course of action. Scenarios are designed to help forecast the outcome of various possible actions.

Using Solver, Creating Templates, and Evaluating Scenarios

key terms

3-D shape   EX4.36

active workbook   EX4.19

adjustable cell   EX4.6

arrange windows   EX4.20

cascade   EX4.20

dependent cell   EX4.22

dependent workbook   EX4.22

external reference formula   EX4.22

horizontal   EX4.20

link   EX4.22

password   EX4.12

protection   EX4.12

scenario   EX4.26

Solver   EX4.6

source cell   EX4.22

source workbook   EX4.22

target cell   EX4.6

template   EX4.

tiled   EX4.20

vertical   EX4.20

mous skills

The Microsoft Office User Specialist (MOUS) certification program is designed to measure your proficiency in performing basic tasks using the Office XP applications. Getting certified demonstrates that you have the skills and provides a valuable industry credential for employment. After completing this lab, you have learned the following Microsoft Office User Specialist skills:

Skill	Description	Page
Managing Workbooks	Manage workbook files and folders	EX4.16
	Create workbooks using templates	EX4.9
	Save workbooks using different names and file formats	EX4.16
Creating and Revising Formulas	Use statistical, date and time, financial, and logical functions in formulas	EX4.39

command summary

Command	Shortcut Keys	Button	Action
Edit/**D**elete/Shift Cells **L**eft			Deletes selected cells and shifts remaining cells to the left
Edit/**D**elete/Shift Cells **U**p			Deletes selected cells and shifts remaining cells up
Edit/**D**elete Sheet			Deletes selected worksheets from a workbook
Insert/**C**ells/Shift Cells Ri**g**ht			Moves existing cells to the right when new cells are inserted
Insert/**C**ells/Shift Cells **D**own			Moves existing cells down when new cells are inserted
Tools/**P**rotection/**P**rotect Sheet		🔒	Prevents unauthorized users from changing a worksheet's contents
Tools/Sc**e**narios			Creates and saves sets of data used to perform what-if analyses
Tools/Sol**v**er			Calculates a formula to achieve a given value by changing one of the variables that affects formulas
Window/**A**rrange			Arranges open windows side-by-side, vertically, horizontally, or tiled

Terminology

screen identification

In the following worksheet, several items are identified by letters. Enter the correct term for each item in the spaces provided.

A. _____ D. _____

B. _____ E. _____

C. _____ F. _____

matching

Match the lettered item on the right with the numbered list on the left.

1. Solver   _____ **a.** creates a connection between files that automatically updates the data in one file when a change is made in another file

2. source workbook   _____ **b.** determines the effects of changed values in adjustable cells

3. scenario   _____ **c.** cell containing the external reference formula

4. cascade   _____ **d.** forecasts the outcome of various possible actions

5. target cell   _____ **e.** object that has a three-dimensional effect applied to it

6. template   _____ **f.** cell containing value you want to solve for

7. 3-D shape   _____ **g.** prevents unauthorized users from viewing or changing a workbook

8. password   _____ **h.** supplies the data in a linked workbook

9. dependent cell   _____ **i.** used as a pattern for creating new workbooks

10. link   _____ **j.** windows displayed one on top of another

multiple choice

Circle the correct response to the questions below.

1. A(n)_____ is a named set of input values that you can substitute in a worksheet.
   a. scenario
   b. Solver
   c. adjustable cell
   d. template

2. In the external reference formula [Forecast.xls]Year$N$8, the name in brackets is
   _____.
   a. the source file
   b. the destination file
   c. the active file
   d. the current worksheet

3. The workbook that supplies that data is called the _____.
   a. source workbook
   b. dependent workbook
   c. link
   d. dependent cell

4. A(n)_____ creates a connection between files that automatically updates the linked data in one file when a change is made in another file.
   a. password
   b. source file
   c. link
   d. external reference

5. _____ calculate(s) a formula to achieve a given value.
   a. Target Cells
   b. Formulas
   c. Solver
   d. Source Cells

6. The _____ tool lets you view varying values applied to a worksheet:
   a. Scenario
   b. Solver
   c. What-If
   d. Goal-Seek

7. The _____ command permanently deletes a selected worksheet.
   a. Clear Sheet
   b. Remove Sheet
   c. Delete Sheet
   d. Clear Contents

8. _____ prevents user from changing the contents of a worksheet.
   a. Locking cells
   b. Protecting a worksheet
   c. Unlocking cells
   d. A password

9. The _____ tool is used to find the value needed in one cell by changing the values in one or more other cells in the worksheet.
   a. Query
   b. Solver
   c. Value Analysis
   d. Look Up

10. The workbook file that receives linked data is called the _____.
    a. source workbook
    b. reference workbook
    c. dependent workbook
    d. external workbook

true/false

Circle the correct answer to the following questions.

1. A Scenario Summary shows the results of all scenarios created for a worksheet.	True	False
2. Templates cannot contain graphics.	True	False
3. Cells you select as variables in Solver must be related through formulas on a worksheet.	True	False
4. You can save a workbook as a template by adding the .xlt extension to the file name.	True	False
5. Solver can produce six types of reports about a solution.	True	False
6. When the worksheet is protected, the contents of locked cells cannot be changed.	True	False

7. A password prevents unauthorized users from viewing or saving changes to a workbook.   True   False

8. The horizontal window arrangement displays windows side by side.   True   False

9. Whenever data containing an external reference formula are changed in the dependent workbook, data in the linked cell in the source workbook are automatically changed as well.   True   False

10. You cannot save different scenarios.   True   False

Concepts

Fill-In questions

Complete the following statements by filling in the blanks with the correct terms.

a. Use _____ to change the settings of a 3-D shape.

b. You can create and save different groups of _____ values.

c. Before protecting a worksheet, _____ those cells whose contents you want to change.

d. The _____ function automatically updates the date and time whenever a worksheet is recalculated.

e. The cell containing a formula you want to solve is called the _____.

f. The command for the Excel workbook template file extension is _____.

g. You cannot save a workbook as a _____ by typing the file extension .xlt.

h. Once a(n)_____ formula is entered in a worksheet the _____file is automatically updated if it is open.

i. The _____ dialog box is used to add, delete, and edit scenarios.

j. A _____ prevents unauthorized users from opening a workbook.

Discussion Questions

1. Discuss how templates can be used to make workbook creation easier. What types of templates do you think would be most helpful, and what should these templates contain?

2. Discuss what happens to formulas that are linked to another workbook when the original workbook is updated. When would it be appropriate to link data between workbooks?

3. Discuss how Solver and scenarios are used in a worksheet. How can they help with the analysis of data?

Hands-On Exercises

Step by Step

Nursery Revenue Analysis

★ **1.** The West Side Plant Nursery has a six-month income worksheet that it uses to track the amount of income from different sources. The company would like to create a template that they can use each year to track the information. Your completed worksheet will be similar to the one shown here.

   a. Open the file ex04_West Side Income.

   b. Make a copy of Sheet1. Rename sheet1 First Six Months and Sheet 1(2) Second Six Months. Add tab colors.

   c. Delete the other blank sheets from the workbook.

   d. Modify the month column labels in the Second Six Months sheet to reflect the last six months of the year.

   e. Add the column label Annual Total in cell I4. Best Fit the column. Change the font color of the new label to light orange. Enter formulas in the Anual total column to calculate the totals for the year.

   f. Extend the worksheet formatting to the new column. Re-center the worksheet titles. Fix the border lines appropriately.

   g. Select both sheets. Select cells A3 and B5 through G11 and unlock the cells. Deselect the selection. Protect both worksheets.

   h. Ungroup the worksheets. Move to cell B5 of the First Six Month sheet.

   i. Save the workbook as a template with the name West Side Income.xlt. Close the workbook. Open the workbook template and enter sample data in both worksheets. Enter the current year in cell A3.

j. Enter your name and the current date using the NOW function in cells A15 and A16, respectively, of both sheets.

k. Preview the workbook. Center the worksheets horizontally. Print the worksheets in landscape orientation, each on a single page.

l. Save the workbook as West Side Income1.xls.

Adventure Travel Tours Revenue Analysis

★★ **2.** Adventure Travel Tours has begun a new marketing program that emphasizes their tour packages. They expect this campaign to increase the annual income earned in this division by as much as 15 percent over last year's earnings. You have been asked to create a Scenario Summary that analyzes quarterly profits in three scenarios. The company would also like to create a template to allow easy analysis of next year's performance. Your completed worksheets and scenario summary should be similar to those shown here.

a. Open the file ex04_Travel Analysis.

b. Make a copy of Sheet1. Rename sheet1 Yearly Income and Sheet1(2) Projected Income. Add color to the sheet tabs.

c. Delete the other blank sheets from the workbook.

d. Change the subtitle of the Projected Income Sheet to Projected Annual Sources of Income.

e. The company expects to see a total profit margin increase to $6,300,000 (approximately 10 percent of last year's earnings) in the Tour Package category. They have determined that Worst Case increases would be $6,020,000 (5 percent). The Best Case scenario puts the profits at $6,600,000 (15 percent). Use Solver to calculate the quarterly profits needed to achieve these goals. Create a scenario for each case with the appropriate title and comments. Remember to save the original data in the worksheet.

Student Name   8/27/02

ADVENTURE TRAVEL
Annual Sources of Income

	1st Qtr	2nd Qtr	3rd Qtr	4th Qtr	Total
Car Rentals	$ 114,650	$ 114,875	$ 116,500	$ 119,145	$ 465,170
Airlines	$ 215,000	$ 218,750	$ 219,995	$ 225,390	$ 879,135
Tour Packages	$ 1,125,530	$ 1,350,655	$ 1,500,675	$ 1,755,850	$ 5,732,710
Hotels	$ 650,000	$ 650,545	$ 695,655	$ 705,115	$ 2,701,315
Total	$ 2,105,180	$ 2,334,825	$ 2,532,825	$ 2,805,500	$ 9,778,330

Student Name   8/27/02

TOUR PACKAGES SCENARIOS
Scenario Summary

Changing Cells:	Current Values:	Expected	Worst Case	Best Case
First Qtr	$ 1,125,530	$ 1,267,353	$ 1,125,530	$ 1,342,353
Second Qtr	$ 1,350,655	$ 1,492,478	$ 1,350,655	$ 1,567,478
Third Qtr	$ 1,500,675	$ 1,642,498	$ 1,500,675	$ 1,717,498
Fourth Qtr	$ 1,755,850	$ 1,897,673	$ 1,755,850	$ 1,972,673
Result Cells:				
Total	$ 5,732,710	$ 6,300,000	$ 5,732,710	$ 6,600,000

f. Create a Scenario Summary for the total tour packages. Delete the notes below the summary table. Delete the cell references and replace them with the names of the quarters (B7=First Quarter).

g. Add the worksheet title Tour Packages Scenarios centered over the Summary table. Change the formatting of the summary to match the other sheets. Print the summary.

h. Move the Summary worksheet to the third tab position. Include your name and the date in a custom header on all sheets. Save the workbook as ATT Revenue Analysis. Print the workbook with the best case values showing centered horizontally in landscape orientation.

i. Because this format will be useful in making projections for next year you want to save it as a template. Delete the data from both worksheets. Delete the Scenario Summary worksheet. Unlock cell B2 and the data entry areas in both sheets. Protect both sheets.

j. Save the workbook as a template with the name ATT Analysis Template. Close the workbook.

k. Open a new workbook using the template. Add the current year to the subtitle line. Copy the best case scenario projected income data from the ATT Revenue Analysis workbook into the yearly Income sheet of the new workbook. Best Fit column F and restore protection.

l. Print the Yearly Income sheet. Save the workbook as ATT Revenue Analysis2.

Personal Budget Analysis

★ ★ **3.** You have just graduated from college, started your first professional job, and purchased a new car and house. With all the new financial obligations you have, you decide to create an annual budget to help you meet your obligations as well as save to purchase new furniture for your home. You estimate your furniture will cost around $4200. You have already started a worksheet containing the labels and the monthly expenses. Your complete budget will be similar to the one shown here.

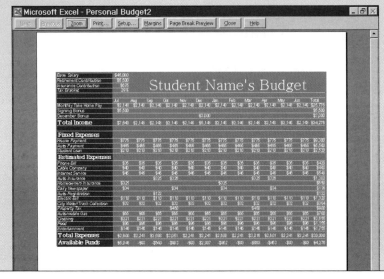

a. Open the file ex04_Personal Budget.

b. Add your name followed by Budget as the title at the top of the worksheet. Center and merge the title over the worksheet. Increase the font size to 14.

c. Calculate and enter the monthly take-home pay in cell B10. Use the formula =(B4-B5-B6-(B4*B7))/12. Copy this value into all the cells of row 10. Your yearly income will be calculated in N10.

d. Calculate the total expenses and available funds for rows 31 and 32.

e. After doing all the calculations, you realize that you are going to be short of funds for this year. Using Solver, reduce the clothing, food, and entertainment expenses to achieve a target value (cell N31) equal to your income. Keep the Solver solution in the worksheet. Looking over the solution, you realize that the values for these three categories are inappropriate and you would never be able to stay on budget. However, you know that, as part of your employment negotiations, you are going to receive a $5,500 signing bonus and a December bonus of $3,000.

f. Insert three rows below the Monthly Take Home Pay row. Label the new rows Signing Bonus, December Bonus, and Total Income. Enter 5,500 in July for the signing bonus and 3,000 in December. Total the income rows.

g. Adjust the formula in row 35 to calculate the new available funds.

h. Use Solver again to calculate the amount you can spend to equal your income. The solution gives you more than enough each month to meet your expenses. However, you would like to calculate a more realistic value for these cells. To do this, restore the original values and solve for $30,000. Keep the Solver solution.

i. Apply fill colors, font colors, and other features of your choice to enhance the worksheet.

j. Save the workbook as Personal Budget2. Print the worksheet in landscape orientation on one page.

University GPA Analysis

★ ★ **4.** You are working in the university's
★ graduation office. As part of your job, you have been asked to create a worksheet comparing college GPA's for the past four years. The school is concerned about inflated GPA's and would like to know what the trend is by major and overall. Additionally, you will create a base and two scenarios for increases in GPA's. Your completed worksheet will be similar to the one shown here.

a. Open the file ex04_School GPA.

b. Move to cell B4 in the Average GPA's worksheet. Enter the formula
=(Business!B4+Education!B4+'Fine Arts'!B4+Engineering!B4)/4
to calculate the total freshman class GPA's for the four colleges for 2001.

c. Copy the formula to cells C4 through E4. Then copy the formulas from B4 through E4 to B7 through E7.

d. Enter a formula in cell B8 that calculates the average of cells B4 through B7. Copy the formula through cell E8. Enter a formula that calculates the average of cells B4 through E4 in cell F4. Copy the formula through cell F8.

e. Next, you want to calculate the percent change for each class over the four years. Copy the worksheet from cells A1 through F8 to cells A11 through A18. Change the title to **Percent Increase** in cell A11. Delete the 2001 data in B14 through B18.

f. Enter the formula **=(C4-B4)/C4** in cell C14 to calculate the percent change from 2001 to 2002 for the freshman class. Copy the formula to calculate the percentages for the rest of the data.

g. Enter the formula **=(E4-B4)/E4** in cell F14 to calculate the total percent change over the four years. Copy the formula down the column through row 18. Format B14:F18 to display as percents.

h. In cell G2, enter the title **Projected** and, in cell G3, enter **2005**.

i. To calculate a base for your scenario, enter the formula **=E4+(E4*F14)** in cell G4. Copy the formula to cells G5 through G7. Format the column to two decimal places. Calculate the average in G8. Complete the border and color formatting as needed.

j. Create a scenario for the base values. Label this the **Base** scenario and use cells G4 through G7 as your changing cells. Add the comment **Projected GPA based on average for the previous years**. (Choose [OK] when the message to convert formula to fixed values appears.)

k. Create a scenario for a .05 increase and another for a .07 increase. Label and insert comments to the scenarios appropriately. Use the data in the following table for changing the cell values.

.05 Increase	.07 Increase
3.83	3.85
3.225	3.245
3.275	3.295
3.775	3.795

l. Create a Scenario Summary report using cell G8 as the result cell. Delete the note below the report. Add and format a title. Replace the cell references with appropriate labels. Change the text and fill colors to match the other sheets.

m. Add your name and the current date to a header in the Average GPA's worksheet and the Scenario Summary worksheet.

n. Save the workbook as **GPA Analysis**. Print the Average GPA worksheet showing the scenario values for a .07 percent increase centered horizontally. Print the Scenario Summary worksheet.

Animal Rescue Foundation Contribution Projections

★ ★ 5. The Animal Rescue Foundation, a nonprofit animal rescue agency, relies on donations to cover all
★   its expenses. You would like to do some analysis on the data and project the amount that will be
needed for next year based on scenarios that the committee feels are likely. Your completed
income analysis will be similar to the one shown here.

a. Open the file ex04_ARF Contributions to see last year's income.

b. Copy the Fall-Winter
sheet to a new sheet
and rename the tab
for the new sheet
Analysis. Delete col-
umn H.

c. Merge cells A3
through G3 when you
center the new title
Analysis and
Projections.

d. Enter the labels 2001
Income, 5% Increase,
10% Increase, 10%
Decrease, 5%
Decrease, and
Current Scenario in
cells B5 through
G5. Adjust the size
of the columns to
fully display the
labels.

e. Enter the reference
formula =Spring-
Summer!H6+Fall-
Winter!H6 in cell B6.
Copy the formula
down the column
to cell B11.

f. Use the number in
cell B6 to calculate
the values for cells
C6 through F6.
Copy the formulas down the columns to row 11.

g. Copy and paste just the values from column B to column G.

Student Name
8/27/02

Animal Rescue Foundation
Analysis and Projections

	2001 Income	5% Increase	10% Increase	10% Decrease	5% Decrease	Current Scenario
Annual Memberships	$54,834	$57,576	$60,317	$49,351	$52,092	$60,317
Phone Solicitation	$6,400	$6,720	$7,040	$5,760	$6,080	6,400
Corporate Donations	$45,000	$47,250	$49,500	$40,500	$42,750	42,750
Raffle Tickets	$2,894	$3,039	$3,183	$2,605	$2,749	2,894
Pet Shows	$16,000	$16,800	$17,600	$14,400	$15,200	16,000
Other	$24,000	$25,200	$26,400	$21,600	$22,800	24,000
Total	$149,128	$156,584	$164,041	$134,215	$141,672	$152,361

Student Name
8/27/2002

Projected Donations

Scenario Summary

	Current Values:	Most Likely	Least Likely	Ideal
Changing Cells:				
Annual Memberships	$54,834	$80,317	$49,351	$80,317
Phone Solicitation	6,400	6,400	6,400	7,040
Corporate Donations	45,000	42,750	40,500	49,500
Raffle Tickets	2,894	2,894	2,894	3,183
Pet Shows	16,000	16,000	16,000	17,600
Other	24,000	24,000	21,600	26,400
Result Cells:				
Total	$149,128	$152,361	$136,745	$164,040

IDEAL

h. Create the following scenarios using cells G6 through G11 as the changing cells and the following calculated values in the worksheet:

Most Likely

Annual Memberships	10% increase
Phone Solicitation	Current
Corporate Donations	5% decrease
Raffle Tickets	Current
Pet Shows	Current
Other	Current

Least Likely

Annual Memberships	10% decrease
Phone Solicitation	Current
Corporate Donations	10% decrease
Raffle Tickets	Current
Pet Shows	Current
Other	10% decrease

Ideal

Annual Memberships	10% increase
Phone Solicitation	10% increase
Corporate Donations	10% increase
Raffle Tickets	10% increase
Pet Shows	10% increase
Other	10% increase

i. Create a Scenario Summary displaying the results for cell G12. Delete the note below the summary report. Change the cell references to appropriate labels.

j. Create a 3-D object that highlights the Ideal scenario in the Scenario Summary worksheet. Add and format a worksheet title.

k. Enter your name and the current date in a header of the Analysis and Scenario Summary worksheets.

l. Print the Analysis worksheet centered horizontally in landscape orientation on one page with the Most Likely scenario displayed. Print the Scenario Summary worksheet centered horizontally in landscape orientation.

m. Save the workbook as ARF Analysis.

Fitness Club Revenue Tracking

★ 1. As the accounting manager of the Lifestyle Fitness Club, you have decided to create a workbook template to track the revenues from memberships, classes, equipment and clothing sales, and special events for each quarter. Create a worksheet for the first quarter with row labels that reflect revenue sources. Include a title and column labels for the months in the first quarter. Calculate totals where appropriate. Copy the worksheet to three other sheets to be used for the next three quarters, and appropriately adjust the column labels and title. Unlock the cells that will be used for value inputs. Enter your name and the current date as a footer for each sheet. Add worksheet protection and save as a template. Use the template to enter sample data in the First Quarter sheet. Save the file as LFC Revenue Analysis and print the worksheet.

LocalNet Growth Projections

★ ★ 2. You have been hired as a consultant by a local internet service provider (ISP) LocalNet, to help the ISP project expected growth over the next five years based on its research. Assume that the company currently has 15 percent of the local market. The current number of customers is 3,500 and available research estimates an increase of 2 percent in year 2; 4 percent in year 3; 7 percent in year 4; and 12 percent in year 5. Create a worksheet that shows the current customer figure and the projected increases for the next five years. Use these numbers to create revenue figures based on a yearly profit of $75 per customer. Create scenarios with the calculated values as the baseline, a 2 percent decrease in customers and revenue per year as the worst case, and an additional 4 percent increase per year as the best case. Create a Scenario Summary report. Create a 3-D object that highlights the best case scenario in the Scenario Summary worksheet. Enter your name and the current date in all the worksheets. Save the file as LocalNet Projections. Print the worksheets.

Spring Break Scenarios

★ ★ 3. Now that your personal budget is complete, you have decided to do some analysis to determine whether a trip during spring semester break is possible. Use the budget you created in Lab 3, On Your Own, exercise 1, and evaluate your yearly budget to determine whether you will have enough money to pay for a spring break trip next year. Use Solver to determine the number of hours you need to work to earn enough money for the trip in addition to the rest of your expenses. Create three scenarios: one showing the current values, a second showing a 5 percent decrease in entertainment expenses, and a third showing a decrease in one of your other expenses. Create a Scenario Summary. Enter your name and the current date in a header for all the worksheets. Save the file as Spring Break Analysis. Print the worksheets.

Art Department Expense Projections

★ ★ **4.** The College of Fine Arts would like you to use the data you collected in Lab 3, On Your Own,
★   exercise 2, to do some analysis for the coming year. They would like to refurbish one lab and
         purchase new equipment for one department. Use the information you collected in the previous
         exercise and create three scenarios: one showing the current values, a second showing a 5 percent
         decrease in expenses, and a third showing a decrease in another expense category. Create a
         Scenario Summary. Enter your name and the current date in a header for all the worksheets. Save
         the file as Art Equipment Analysis. Print the worksheets.

Small Business Expansion Projections

★ ★ **5.** You believe the small business you created in Lab 3, On Your Own, exercise 4, could see greater
★   profits with an additional location. Use the information you gathered in the previous workbook
         and the Solver to determine what variables would increase profits by 25 percent. Create three
         scenarios to determine the effects of a 5 percent, 10 percent, and 15 percent increase in profits in
         each quarter on the total yearly profits. Create a Scenario Summary. Add 3-D shapes and use the
         NOW function in the summary. Save your file as Expansion Projections. Print the summary.

On the Web

Stock Portfolio Analysis

You have been studying the stock market in your economics class and would like to evaluate a
portfolio of four different stocks. Using the Web or other news source, choose four stocks listed
on the New York Stock Exchange and enter the following information about each stock in
separate sheets of a workbook: stock exchange number, cost per share, brokerage fee, total cost
per share, price/earnings ratio, dividend return percentage, and week-ending price. Track your
stocks (or use historical values) for a month. Create scenarios of good, bad, and expected market
changes in the current month-ending price over the next month. Enter your name and the current
date in headers in the worksheets. Save the file as Stock Analysis. Print the workbook.

Using Data Tables, Creating Macros, and Designing Onscreen Forms

Objectives

After completing this lab, you will know how to:

1.	Use the PMT function.
2.	Use a data table.
3.	Add controls.
4.	Create a macro with the Visual Basic Editor.
5.	Create a macro with the Macro Recorder.
6.	Name a range.
7.	Use the IF function.
8.	Create a form.
9.	Add cell comments.
10.	Document a file.

Using a data table is another way to perform what-if analysis.

Macros automate repetitive tasks, saving both time and effort.

Using an IF function allows different calculations to be performed if certain conditions are met.

Downtown Internet Café

Evan, the owner of the Downtown Internet Café, has been impressed with your use of Excel to forecast the café's future through 2002. He has two more projects for you. First, he is considering the purchase of a new espresso/cappuccino machine to replace the current one, which is leased. Evan plans to finance the purchase and would like you to evaluate several different loan options. You will create a loan analysis spreadsheet that incorporates Excel's PMT function, macros, and Data Table feature.

Next, Evan would like you to develop a spreadsheet to calculate and record customer Bonus Dollars. Bonus Dollars are awarded to customers based on their monthly Internet connection-time usage and can be redeemed for more connection time or other merchandise at the café. They are an incentive for customers to extend their stay at the café and, of course, spend more money while they're there. You will create an onscreen form to calculate and record customer Bonus Dollars. The completed loan analysis and Bonus Dollars form are shown on the opposite page.

The following concepts will be introduced in this lab:

1	**Data Table**	A data table is a range of cells that is used to quickly calculate multiple what-if versions in one operation and to show the results of all variations together in the worksheet.
2	**Macro**	A macro is a stored series of keystrokes and commands that are executed automatically when the macro is run.
3	**Controls**	Controls are graphic objects that are designed to help the user interact with the worksheet.
4	**Visual Basic Editor**	The Visual Basic Editor is a tool used to write and edit macros attached to Excel workbooks.
5	**Macro Recorder**	The Macro Recorder automatically creates a macro by recording a series of actions as macro commands.
6	**Form**	A form is a formatted worksheet with blank spaces that can be filled in online or on paper.
7	**IF Function**	The IF function checks to see if certain conditions are met and then takes action based on the results of the check.
8	**Comments**	Comments are notes attached to cells that can be used to clarify the meaning of the cell contents, provide documentation, or ask a question.

Calculating a Loan Payment

Evan has researched different kinds of commercial espresso/cappuccino machines and would like to see an analysis of what the monthly loan payments would be for different down payments, interest rates, and repayment periods for each kind. You have already started to create the analysis by entering some descriptive labels and formats in a worksheet. You will open the workbook file and continue to work on the loan analysis.

1 ● **Start Excel and open the workbook file** ex05_Loan Analysis.

● **If necessary, maximize the application and worksheet windows.**

Your screen should be similar to Figure 5.1

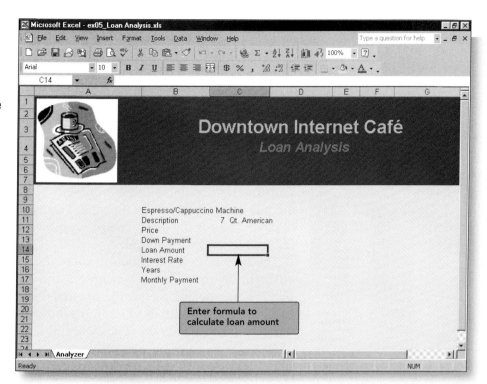

Figure 5.1

Much of the structure and formatting for the worksheet has already been completed. To continue to create the worksheet, you need to enter a formula to calculate the loan amount. The amount of the loan is the price of the item minus the down payment. Then you will enter the data for the first espresso/cappuccino machine Evan is considering.

2 ● **In cell C14 enter the formula** =C12-C13.

● **In cell C12 enter** 4,275.50.

● **In cell C13 enter** 1,000.

● **In cell C15 enter** .08.

● **In cell C16 enter** 1.

Your screen should be similar to Figure 5.2

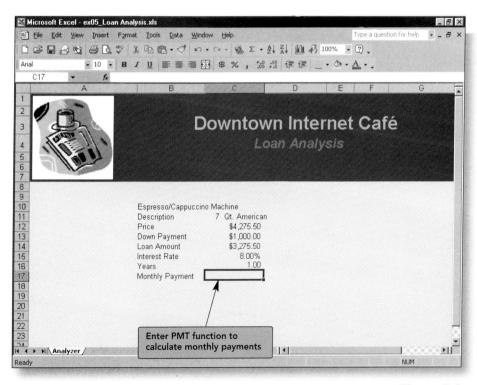

Figure 5.2

Using the PMT Function

The next thing that needs to be entered is the monthly payment. To calculate this value, you use the PMT function. The PMT function calculates a periodic payment on a loan. The value returned includes the loan amount and interest but no taxes, reserve payments, or fees sometimes associated with loans. The PMT function uses the following syntax:

PMT(rate, nper, pv)

Additional Information

When using the PMT function, it is important to use consistent units for specifying rate and nper.

This function contains three arguments: rate, nper, and pv. The **rate** argument is the interest rate of the loan. The **nper** argument is the total number of payments for the loan. The **pv** argument is the amount of the loan, also referred to as the **principal**.

The rate in the PMT function you will use to calculate the monthly loan payment for the espresso machine is the yearly interest rate (C15) divided by 12. This converts the yearly rate to a monthly rate. The nper argument is the length of the loan in years (C16) multiplied by 12 to calculate the number of monthly payments. The pv argument is the loan amount in cell C14.

1 ● In cell C17 enter the function =PMT(C15/12, C16*12,C14).

HAVING TROUBLE?

You can use the Insert Function feature to help enter this function.

Your screen should be similar to Figure 5.3

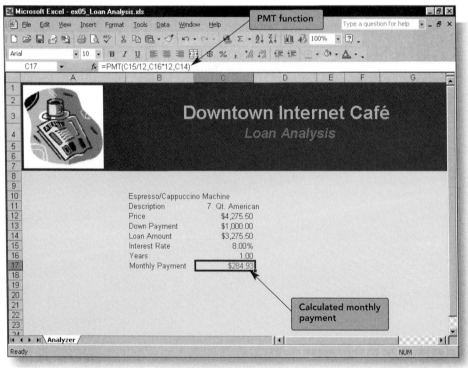

Figure 5.3

Excel calculates the monthly payment and displays it in cell C17.

Using a Data Table

You used an 8 percent interest rate to calculate the loan payments for the espresso/cappuccino machine, but you are aware that interest rates will vary, depending on which loan institution finances the purchase and when the loan is obtained. Therefore, you want to set up a data table that shows the effect of different interest rates on the monthly loan payment amount.

concept 1

Data Table

1 A **data table** is a range of cells that is used to quickly calculate multiple what-if versions in one operation and to show the results of all variations together in the worksheet. Data tables perform a type of what-if analysis in which one or more variables are changed to see the effect on the formulas that include these variables.

Espresso/Cappuccino Machine Description	
Price	$4,275.50
Down Payment	$1,000.00
Loan Amount	$3,275.50
Interest Rate	8.00%
Years	1.00
Monthly Payment	$284.93

One-variable Table Varying Interest Rates Only	
	$284.93
7.50%	$284.17
7.75%	$284.55
8.00%	$284.93
8.25%	$285.31
8.50%	$285.69
8.75%	$286.07
9.00%	$286.45
9.25%	$286.83
9.50%	$287.21

Two-variable Table Varying Interest Rates and Length of Loan			
$284.93	1.50	3.00	4.00
7.50%	$192.97	$101.89	$79.20
7.75%	$193.34	$102.26	$79.58
8.00%	$193.71	$102.64	$79.96
8.25%	$194.09	$103.02	$80.35
8.50%	$194.46	$103.40	$80.74
8.75%	$194.84	$103.78	$81.12
9.00%	$195.21	$104.16	$81.51
9.25%	$195.59	$104.54	$81.90
9.50%	$195.96	$104.92	$82.29

A **one-variable data table** can contain one or more formulas, and each formula refers to one input cell. An **input cell** is a cell in which a list of values is substituted to see the resulting effect on the related formulas. Input values can be listed down a column (**column-oriented**) or across a row (**row-oriented**).

A **two-variable data table** uses only one formula that refers to two different input cells, one column-oriented and one row-oriented. The purpose of this table is to show the resulting effect on the formula when the values in both of these cells are changed.

Creating a One-Variable Data Table

Since you are interested in seeing the effects of changing the interest rate only, you will create a one-variable data table. When designing a one-way data table, the input values and formulas must be in contiguous rows or columns. First, you need to set up the data table in an unused portion of the worksheet by entering a title and column headings and a series of interest rate percentages.

1 ● **In cell E10 enter the title Interest Rates.**

● **In cell E11 enter the column heading Rate and in cell F11 enter Payment.**

● **In cell E13 enter 7.5% and in cell E14 enter 7.75%.**

● **Select the range E13 through E14 and drag the fill handle through cell E21.**

Your screen should be similar to Figure 5.4

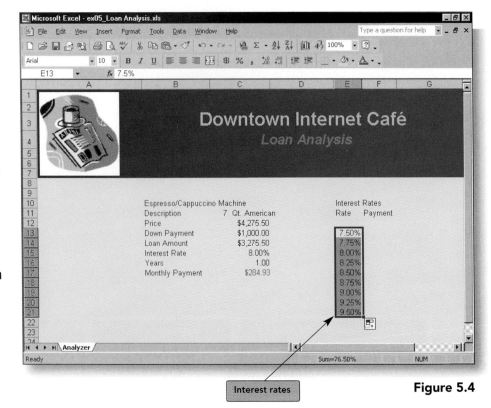

Interest rates

Figure 5.4

Dragging the fill handle filled column E with interest rates that range from 7.5 percent to 9.5 percent in 0.25 percent increments.

Next, you enter the monthly payment formula to be used in calculating the various payments in cell F12. The formula is always entered in the row above the first input value and one cell to the right of the column of values. Rather than just copying this formula from the monthly payment cell in the loan analysis section of the worksheet, you will define the new formula as equal to that cell. This way, the data table formula will be automatically updated if the original formula (the one in the loan analysis section of the worksheet) is changed.

Additional Information

If the input values are listed across the row, the formula is entered in the column to the left of the first value and one cell below the row of values.

2 ● In cell F12 enter =C17.

*Your screen should be
similar to Figure 5.5*

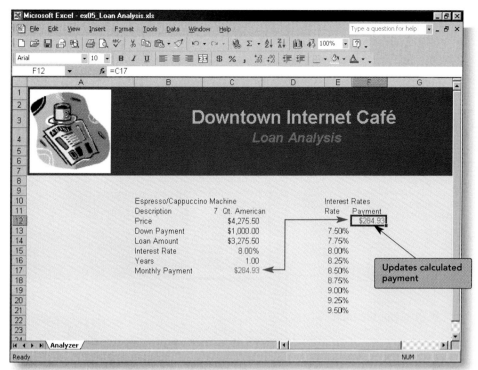

Figure 5.5

Finally, you need to define the range of cells that comprise the data table. In this case, the data table range consists of all cells except the ones containing the title and headings.

3 ● Select the range E12
through F21.

● Choose **D**ata/**T**able.

*Your screen should be
similar to Figure 5.6*

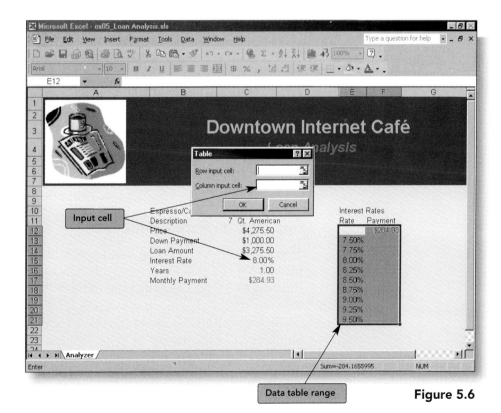

Figure 5.6

You use the Table dialog box to define the input cell in which values from the data table are substituted. Because the values in the data table are listed down a column, the input cell is entered as a Column Input Cell. In this case, the input cell is cell C15, the Interest Rate cell from the loan analysis section of the worksheet.

4 ● Enter **C15** in the **C**olumn Input Cell text box.

Another Method

You can also define the input cell by reducing the dialog box and selecting the input cell in the worksheet.

● Click [OK].

● Deselect the table.

Your screen should be similar to Figure 5.7

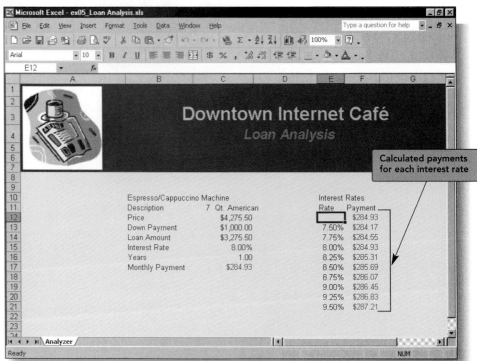

Figure 5.7

The data table shows the calculated monthly payments for each interest rate.

Automatically Formatting Worksheet Data

To quickly improve the appearance of the worksheet, you will apply an auto-format to the worksheet data and data table. An **autoformat** is a built-in combination of formats that can be applied to a range of cells. The autoformats consist of a combination of number formats, fonts and attributes, colors, patterns, borders, frames, and alignment settings.

Applying an Autoformat

To use an autoformat, you first specify the range you want affected by the formatting. In this case, you want to apply an autoformat to cells B10 through C17. You can select the range or you can let Excel select the range for you. To have Excel automatically select the range, the cell selector must be on any cell in the range. Excel determines that the range you want to autoformat is the range of cells that includes the active cell and is surrounded by blank cells.

1 ● Move to any cell in the worksheet data.

● Choose **F**ormat/**A**utoFormat

Your screen should be similar to Figure 5.8

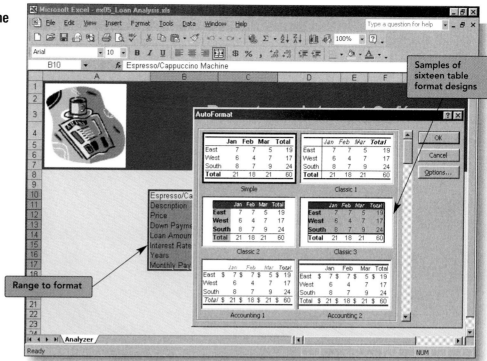

Figure 5.8

Additional Information

Use the None table format (located at the bottom of the list) to remove an existing AutoFormat.

The range B10 through C17 is correctly selected as the range to format. The AutoFormat dialog box displays samples of the sixteen different table format designs with the names assigned to the design below the sample.

You decide the Colorful 1 table format would be appropriate for the data.

2 ● Scroll the list and select Colorful 1.

● Click [OK].

Your screen should be similar to Figure 5.9

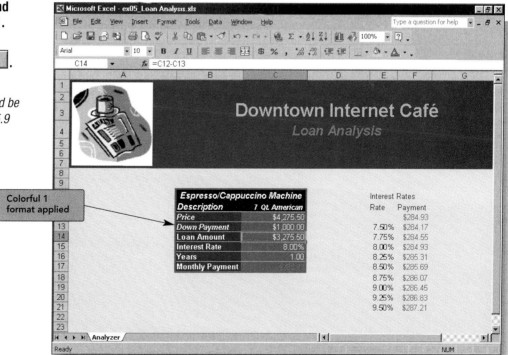

Figure 5.9

The Colorful 1 AutoFormat has been applied to the worksheet range. This format includes borderlines, fill and font colors, and adjustment of column widths to fit the entries in the selected range.

3 ● **Format the data table in cells E10 through F21 to the Classic 3 AutoFormat.**

● **Save the workbook as Loan Analysis.**

Your screen should be similar to Figure 5.10

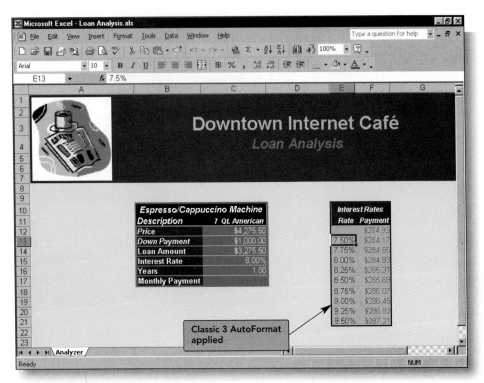

Figure 5.10

Automating Tasks with Macros

You now have the analysis worksheet for the espresso/cappuccino machine that Evan requested with a data table that calculates different interest rates for the loan. After showing the worksheet to Evan, he says he would like to see the same loan analysis applied to other espresso/cappuccino machines he is currently considering. He also wants to use it for other purchases he is considering.

Rather than enter the loan information for each item in the worksheet, you decide to create a macro that will automate the data entry process.

Lab 5: Using Data Tables, Creating Macros, and Designing Onscreen Forms

www.mhhe.com/oleary

Macro

2 A **macro** is a stored series of keystrokes and commands. When the macro is executed, or **run**, the stored actions are performed automatically. Macros are very useful for replacing a series of commands that are performed repeatedly. Instead of performing the same actions every time you need to perform a task, you use the macro, which performs the task automatically for you.

Some macros are very simple and are merely a duplicate of a series of keystrokes. For exam-

ple, a macro can be written that selects a range of cells. A more complex macro may perform a command, such as copying data from one cell to another or changing column widths. Even more complex macros can be written that let you create customized functions that combine math expressions, Excel functions, and programming code to perform special calculations. Other macros can be used to create your own customized menus and dialog boxes.

A macro for your loan analysis worksheet will not only help you enter the information, but will also come in handy if someone else needs to use this worksheet to enter loan information, especially if that person does not know what cells to select in order to obtain the necessary data.

Changing the Macro Security Level

When a workbook contains macros, a macro virus warning may be displayed when the file is opened advising you that macros are detected and asking you to confirm that you want them enabled. This is because macros can contain viruses that may adversely affect your system. As a protection, Excel includes three security levels—high, medium and low.

1 ● Choose **T**ools/**M**acro/ **S**ecurity

Your screen should be similar to Figure 5.11

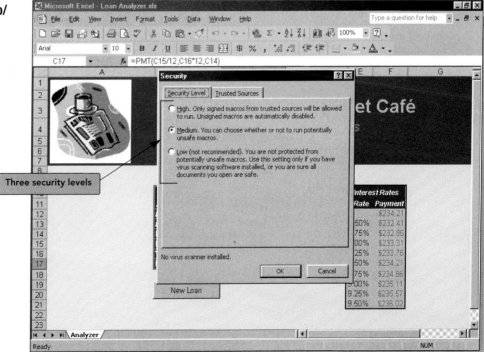

Figure 5.11

Initially, the security level is set to medium. Changing the setting to High provides the greatest amount of protection. This setting automatically disables macros if they are not digitally signed. A **digital signature** is an electronic encryption-based stamp of authentication that confirms the macro or document originated from the signer and has not been changed. The current security level, Medium, allows the user to decide to enable or disable unsigned macros. This is an appropriate level for this workbook.

 ● If necessary, change the security level to <u>M</u>edium.

● Click .

Creating a Command Button

One of the most common ways to run a macro is to create a command button in the worksheet that, when clicked, runs the macro instructions. You will create the command button before creating the macro so that the macro instructions can be assigned to the button. A command button is one of many different controls that can be added to a worksheet.

concept 3

Controls

3   **Controls** are graphic objects that are designed to help the user interact with the worksheet. They can be used to display or enter data, perform an action, or make the sheet easier to read. Controls include property settings that affect how they behave and work. The properties associated with many controls can be changed to customize the control for your own use. Examples of controls are check boxes, list boxes, option buttons, and command buttons.

Excel includes two ways to add controls to a worksheet: the Forms toolbar or the Control Toolbox toolbar. The controls on the Forms toolbar are for use with existing Excel macros and work best on worksheets that will be used only in Excel. The Control Toolbox controls are ActiveX controls that allow you to make the controls "active" by writing a macro using Microsoft Visual Basic or scripts in Microsoft Script Editor that customize the behavior of the control. The Control Toolbox controls are for when the worksheet will be used in interaction with other Office programs or on an Internet location.

You decide to create the command button using the Control Toolbox.

1 • Display the Control Toolbox toolbar and move it into column A.

• Click ☐ Command Button.

• Click on cell B19 to create the button.

• Move and size the command button to cover cells B19 and B20.

Your screen should be similar to Figure 5.12

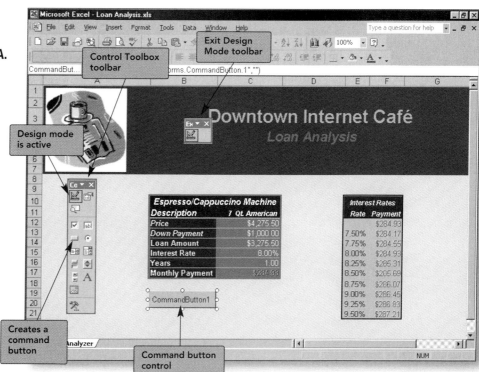

Figure 5.12

Additional Information

The 🖾 button appears recessed when design mode is active.

When you first create a control, Excel automatically changes to design mode so that you can modify the control. The Exit Design mode toolbar is automatically displayed. The first thing you need to do is change the default button name to a more descriptive name.

2 • Right-click the command button to open the shortcut menu.

• Choose CommandButton **O**bject/**E**dit.

• Select the default button name and replace it with New Loan.

• Click outside the button object to deselect it.

Additional Information

You can also change a command button's font attributes by selecting Properties from the button's shortcut menu and selecting font and color settings.

Your screen should be similar to Figure 5.13

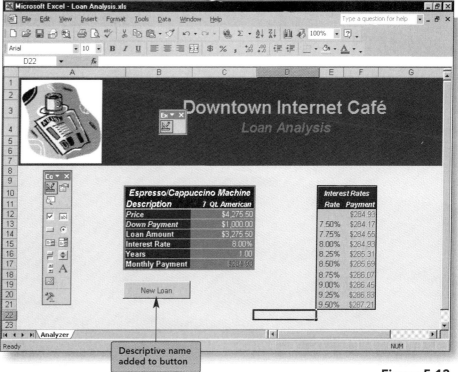

Figure 5.13

Create a Macro Using the Visual Basic Editor

After creating the command button, you use the Visual Basic Editor to create the macro instructions to automate the process of entering the new loan data.

concept 4

Visual Basic Editor

4 The **Visual Basic Editor** is an application used to write and edit macros attached to Excel workbooks. Although Visual Basic is a programming language, you can enter information into the Visual Basic Editor just as you would in a word processor—by typing to enter text, pressing [←Enter] to end a line, using the arrow keys to move around the screen, and pressing [Delete] and [Backspace] to remove and correct text.

The types of information you enter into the Visual Basic Editor are called **statements**. A statement is a complete instruction that tells Excel to execute a specific task. A series of statements is a **Sub procedure**. A Sub procedure begins with a statement that starts the macro (when the command button is pressed) and ends with one that closes the macro (an End Sub statement). Sub procedures can also include remarks about the macro (such as its name and purpose) and functions (such as returning values to the procedure).

The **syntax**, or rules of grammar of a Sub procedure statement, is as follows:

Object ("x").Property

The **object** is the item that the statement will affect (such as a cell, cell range, worksheet, or workbook). The object is enclosed in parentheses and surrounded by quotes.

The **property** is the action you want to perform on the object. The property consists of reserved words that have special meaning and direct Excel to perform the specified action. The object is separated from the property by a period. For example, the statement to tell Excel to select the range C2 through C10 is:

Range("C2:C10").Select

It is very important to plan a macro before creating it to ensure that the Visual Basic statements are in the exact order in which you want them to be executed. It is often helpful to write out the macro steps and then try them out manually in Excel before entering them in the Visual Basic Editor. You want this macro to perform the following actions:

1. Make the Analyzer sheet active.

2. Clear the cell ranges C11 through C15.

3. Display an input box that describes the information to be entered in cells C11, C12, C13, C15, and C16.

4. Move to cell C17.

Now you are ready to start the Visual Basic Editor and create the command button macro.

1 • Double-click the New Loan command button.

• If necessary, close the Project Explorer window along the left side of the Visual Basic window and maximize the Code window on the right.

Your screen should be similar to Figure 5.14

Figure 5.14

Additional Information
"Sub" is an abbreviation for "Sub procedure."

The Code window is used to write, display and edit the macro statements or code. It already contains the Sub and End Sub statements for the command button macro. You will enter the macro statements between the Sub statements. First, however, you want to include several **remark statements** that describe the macro and include overall procedural documentation. Remark statements always begin with an apostrophe, which tells Excel to ignore the information on that line.

2 • Enter a blank line above the Private Sub line in the window.

• Type **'New Loan Button Macro** on the newly inserted blank line.

• Press ⏎Enter.

HAVING TROUBLE?
If you forgot to enter the apostrophe, a Compile error message is displayed. Click OK to clear the message and edit the line.

Your screen should be similar to Figure 5.15

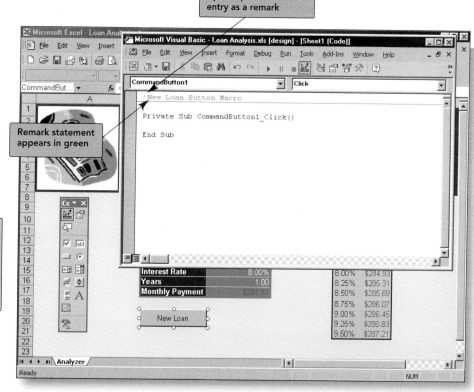

Figure 5.15

Remark lines generally appear in green type to distinguish them from the procedure statements.

3 ● In the same manner, enter the following three additional remarks:

'Date Created: today's date

'Run From: Loan Analysis worksheet by clicking the New Loan button.

'Purpose: To enter new loan data and calculate the monthly payment.

HAVING TROUBLE?
Remember to begin each remark statement with an apostrophe and press ←Enter to move to the next line.

Your screen should be similar to Figure 5.16

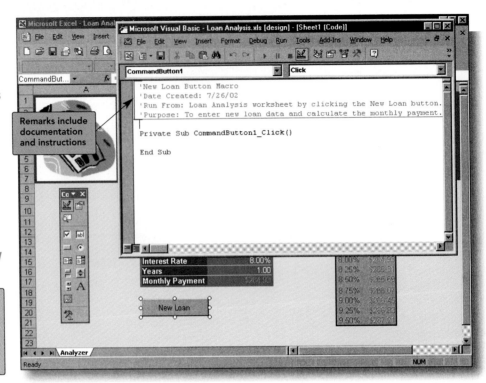

Remarks include documentation and instructions

Figure 5.16

Next, you will enter the Sub procedure statements. To differentiate the Sub statements from the rest of the code, you should indent them using Tab⇥. Once you indent the first Sub statement line, the subsequent lines are automatically indented the same number of spaces. As you are typing, the Visual Basic Editor displays a list of acceptable statement properties. You can select the property you want from the list or continue typing it yourself. Additionally, the first letter of reserved words that are not inside parentheses will be automatically capitalized.

4 ● **Move the insertion point to the blank line between the Private Sub and End Sub statements.**

● **Press** `Tab ⇥`.

● **Type Sheets("Analyzer"). Select.**

● **Press** `←Enter`.

HAVING TROUBLE?

If a Visual Basic statement is not entered using the correct syntax, an error message box is displayed and the error is identified in red. You must correct the error before you can move to the next line.

Your screen should be similar to Figure 5.17

Sub statement to select Analyzer sheet

Figure 5.17

You will continue entering the Visual Basic statements. The reserved word "InputBox" instructs Excel to display a box containing instructions on how to enter the data. The text in parentheses following InputBox is the text that will appear when the InputBox is displayed. You will also include an "Enter" statement that allows the user to Press `←Enter` as an alternative to clicking **OK**. To save time, you can copy the statements and then edit them. You can also type cell references and reserved words in lowercase. Reserved words are automatically capitalized and extra spaces are removed.

5 ● In the same manner, enter the following Sub statements each on separate lines:

Range("C11:C13").Select

Selection.ClearContents

Range("C15:C16").Select

Selection.ClearContents

Range("C11").Value = InputBox("Enter the type of machine.", "Enter")

Range("C12").Value = InputBox("Enter the price.", "Enter")

Range("C13").Value = InputBox("Enter the down payment.", "Enter")

Range("C15").Value = InputBox("Enter the interest rate.", "Enter")

Range("C16").Value = InputBox("Enter the number of years to repay the loan.", "Enter")

Range("C17").Select

Your screen should be similar to Figure 5.18

Figure 5.18

You are finished creating the command button macro. You will close the Visual Basic window and return to the worksheet to try out the command button. Before testing a new macro, it is a good idea to save the workbook file first in case the macro performs some unexpected actions.

6 • Click ☒ Close (in the title bar of the Visual Basic window).

Another Method

The menu equivalent is File/Close and Return to Microsoft Excel. The keyboard shortcut is Alt + Q.

• If necessary, maximize the Excel window.

• Click 🖳 Exit Design Mode on the Control Toolbox toolbar.

• Close the Control Toolbox toolbar.

• Save the workbook as Loan Analyzer.

Your screen should be similar to Figure 5.19

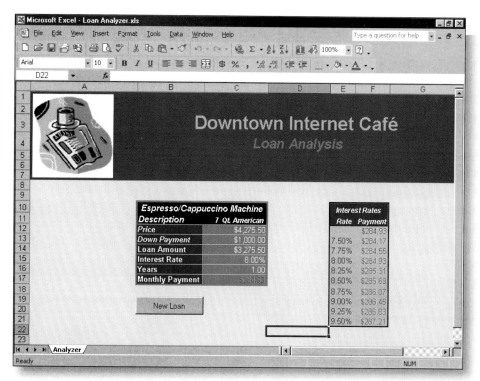

Figure 5.19

Running the Macro

The next step is to test the macro by clicking on the command button to run it. You will enter new loan information for another coffee machine that Evan is considering. The machine is 12 Qt. American that costs $5,445. Evan plans to make a down payment of $1,500 and to borrow the rest at 8.5 percent for 1.5 years.

1 • Click the New Loan command button.

• Type 12 Qt. American in the input box.

Additional Information

You can interrupt the execution of a macro at any time by pressing Esc.

Your screen should be similar to Figure 5.20

Figure 5.20

You can complete the entry by pressing ⏎Enter or clicking [OK]. Since your hands are already on the keyboard, it is quicker to press ⏎Enter. As you complete the entry, it is displayed in the appropriate worksheet cell. You will continue entering the remaining information in the input boxes.

2 ● **Press** ⏎Enter.

● **Using the following information, enter the remaining requested information in the input boxes.**

Price:	5445
Down Payment:	1500
Interest Rate:	8.5%
Loan Length:	1.5

HAVING TROUBLE?
Enter the interest rate as 8.5% or .085.

HAVING TROUBLE?
If your macro did not run correctly, you will need to correct or debug any statement errors.

Your screen should be similar to Figure 5.21

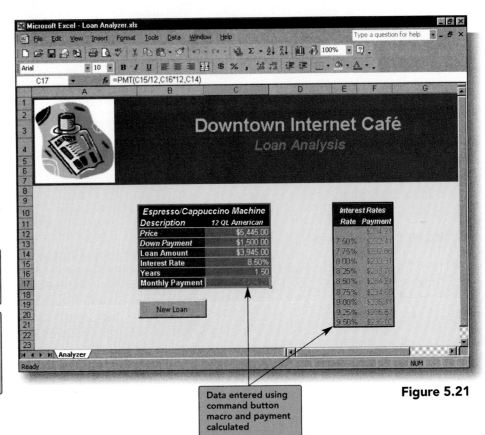

Data entered using command button macro and payment calculated

Figure 5.21

The worksheet now shows the loan analysis for the new set of information. Notice that the data table has also been recalculated based on the new monthly payment.

Using the Macro Recorder

Next, you want to create a macro that will print the worksheet. Instead of entering the Visual Basic instructions manually, you will use the Macro Recorder.

concept 5

Macro Recorder

5 The **Macro Recorder** automatically creates a macro by recording a series of actions as macro commands. When the recorder is on, Excel automatically records every action you perform and stores it as a Visual Basic statement. You can then easily select the recorded macro by name and play it back, or execute it, as often as you like.

The Macro Recorder method of creating macros is much easier than the Visual Basic Editor method, and both types of macros can be viewed and changed via the editor. However, it is recommended that the Macro Recorder method be used for short procedures only (such as basic worksheet functions like formatting and printing), because it can be difficult to decipher and troubleshoot complex Visual Basic statements after they have been recorded.

Additional Information

The worksheet will print when you are finished recording the macro, so make any needed printer setup preparations before you begin.

You will use Macro Recorder to create a separate macro that prints the worksheet in landscape orientation.

1 ● **Choose Tools/Macro/Record New Macro.**

Your screen should be similar to Figure 5.22

Figure 5.22

You use the Record Macro dialog box to name the macro, assign a shortcut key that will start the macro, select a location where it will be stored if other than in the active workbook, enter a description of the macro, and start the recording. You decide to name your macro PrintAnalysis and assign a shortcut key of Ctrl + ⇧Shift + P to it. You will leave the rest of the selections as they are.

2 ● Type **PrintAnalysis** in the Macro name box.

● Click in the Shortcut Key text box.

● Hold down ⇧Shift and type **P**.

● Click OK .

Your screen should be similar to Figure 5.23

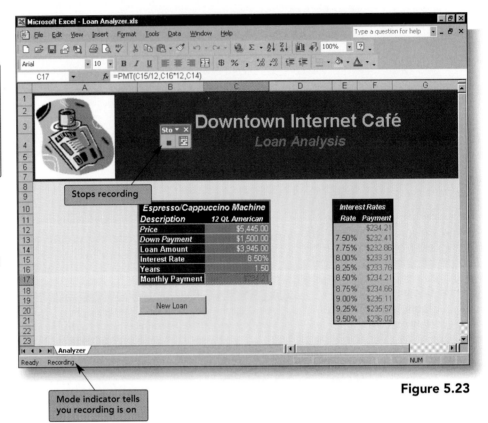

Stops recording

Mode indicator tells you recording is on

Figure 5.23

The message "Recording" is displayed in the status bar and the Stop Recording toolbar appears. Now any action you perform will be recorded as a macro.

3 ● Choose **F**ile/Page
Set**u**p.

● Open the Page tab.

● Select **L**andscape.

● Open the
Header/Footer tab.

● Click [<u>C</u>ustom Header...].

● In the **R**ight section
enter *your name*.

● Press [←Enter].

● Type the current date.

● Click [OK].

● Click [Print...].

● Click [OK].

● Click [■] Stop Recording.

Another Method

The menu equivalent is
Tools/**M**acro/**S**top Recording.

*Your printed worksheet
should be similar to that
shown here.*

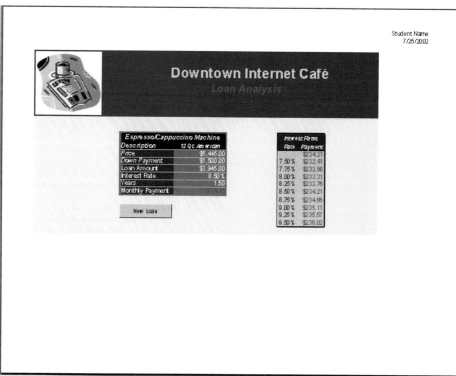

Editing a Macro

Sometimes, after recording a macro, you may want to change or customize it. You will look at the macro statements for the macro that was just recorded.

1 ● **Choose Tools/Macro/Macros.**

Another Method

The keyboard shortcut is [Alt] + [F8].

● **Select PrintAnalysis.**

● **Click** [Edit] .

Additional Information

You can delete a macro by selecting it and clicking [Delete] .

Your screen should be similar to Figure 5.24

Figure 5.24

The Visual Basic code window for the selected macro is displayed. It contains the recorded macro statements for all settings that are on by default in the page setup dialog box as well as those you changed. You can edit the macro statements just as you did when creating the command button macro. In this case, you want to add a remark statement about the purpose of the macro to the documentation. Notice that there are several blank lines that begin with an apostrophe. These are predefined as remark lines and you do not need to type the apostrophe when adding text to the line.

2 ● **On the blank line above the Keyboard Shortcut line, type Purpose: Prints the loan analysis.**

Your screen should be similar to Figure 5.25

Figure 5.25

You will test the macro next by executing it with the shortcut key you assigned.

Additional Information

You can also run the macro from within Visual Basic Editor using **R**un/**R**un Sub/UserForm or F5 .

3 ● **Close the Visual Basic window.**

● **Save the workbook again.**

● **Press** Ctrl + ⇧Shift + P.

Additional Information

The worksheet blinks while the macro is in progress.

Another Method

The menu equivalent is **T**ools/ **M**acro/**M**acros/PrintAnalysis/ **R**un.

● **Close (and save if needed) the workbook.**

The macro was executed, and the worksheet is printed a second time in landscape orientation.

Creating a Form

Your second project is to create a form that records customer monthly connection times and calculates Bonus Dollars earned by each customer. Bonus Dollars are awarded to customers based on their monthly connection time use and can be applied toward any other purchases at the Café.

---

concept 6

Form

6 A **form** is a formatted worksheet with blank spaces that can be filled in online on an individual computer or on a network, or printed and completed on paper. The steps in creating a form are the same for both purposes. However, certain elements are more appropriate for one than for the other. For example, color and shad- ing are more effective on online forms, while simplicity of design and layout is very important in printed forms. In addition, online forms can contain formulas that immediately calculate results such as totals, whereas printed forms would need to include blank spaces where the calculations would be entered manually.

The first step when creating a form is to decide what should appear on the form and what information will be entered into the form. When customers sign on to the computers, they enter their names, and the system tracks the time between sign-on and sign-off. Obtaining connection times for each customer is just a matter of checking the computers' logs. The Bonus Dollar form needs to be designed to accept input of customer connection times and to calculate Bonus Dollars earned. Although Evan wants the form to be electronic, he also wants to be able to print it out for reference.

You have already started designing the form by entering much of the text, many of the formulas, some formatting to improve the appearance, and some sample data. To see what has been done so far,

1 ● **Open the workbook file** ex05_Bonus Dollars.

● **If necessary, maximize the worksheet.**

Your screen should be similar to Figure 5.26

Customer names and sample data →

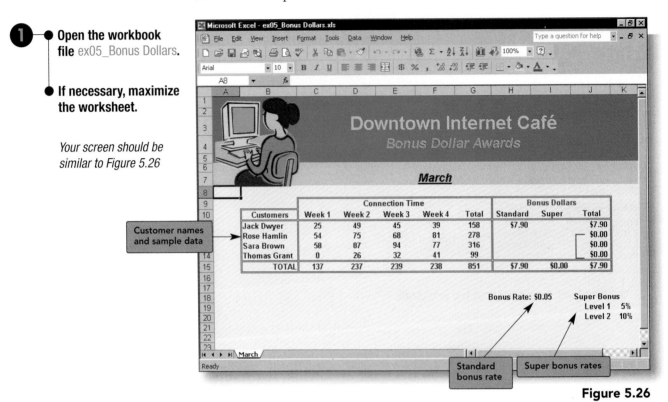

Standard bonus rate

Super bonus rates

Figure 5.26

The worksheet displays the names of four customers and their connection time in minutes for each week in columns C through F.

The last three columns will be used to calculate and display customer Bonus Dollars. The Downtown Internet Café awards Bonus Dollars based on total connection time. A Standard Bonus is applied to every customer at a rate of $.05 per minute of connection time. An additional Super Bonus is awarded at two different levels for those customers who stay connected more than 100 minutes. The bonus awards are explained in the following table.

Bonus	Award
Standard Bonus	Total connection time multiplied by $.05
Super Bonus Level 1	If total connection time is greater than 100 minutes but less than or equal to 200 minutes, Standard Bonus + 5%
Super Bonus Level 2	If total connection time is greater than 200 minutes, Standard Bonus + 10%

Naming Ranges

The formula to calculate the Standard Bonus for Jack Dwyer has already been entered.

1 ● **Move to H11.**

Your screen should be similar to Figure 5.27

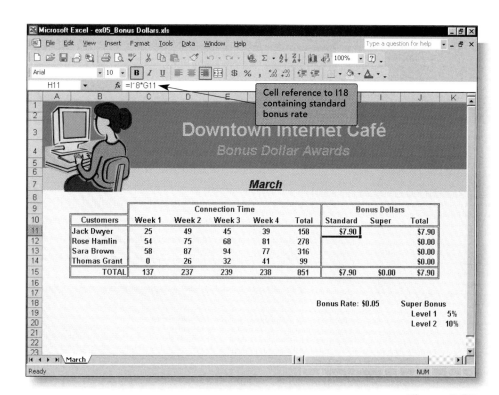

Figure 5.27

The formula references cell I18. This cell contains the Standard Bonus rate amount of $.05 per minute. To make the formula easier to read and understand, you will assign a name to this cell. A **name** is a description of a cell or range of cells that can be used in place of cell references. The name can be used any time a cell or range is requested as part of a command or in a formula or function.

2 ● **Move to I18.**

● **Choose Insert/Name/Define.**

Your screen should be similar to Figure 5.28

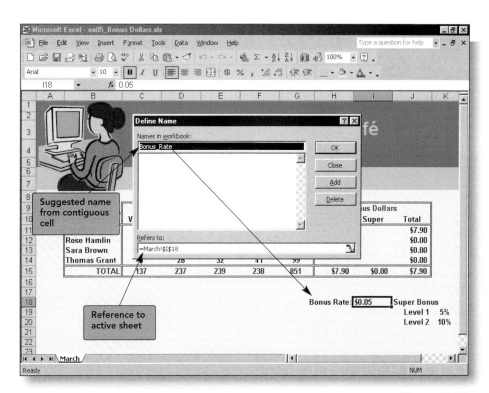

Figure 5.28

The Define Name dialog box is used to name, modify, and delete range names. In the Names in workbook text box, Excel has proposed the name Bonus_Rate. Excel automatically proposes a name for the cell or range using the contents of the active cell if it contains text, or the cell above or to the left of the active cell if the active cell does not contain text. If none of the proposed names is appropriate, you can name the range by typing the name into the text box. In this case, the proposed name is the contents of the cell to the left of the active cell. Excel replaced the blank space between the words with an underline character.

The Refers To text box displays the reference for the active cell. The reference includes the sheet name and cell reference. By default Excel makes named cell references absolute. The Names in workbook list box is empty because this worksheet does not contain any names yet. In this case, both the name and the cell reference are acceptable.

3 ● Click [OK].

Your screen should be similar to Figure 5.29

Name box displays range name rather than cell reference

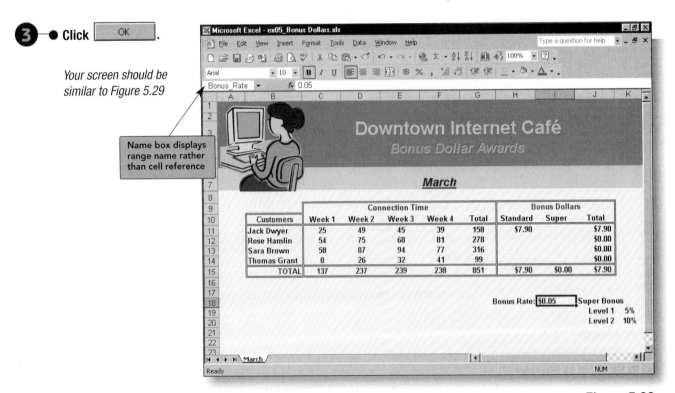

Figure 5.29

In place of the cell reference in the Name box of the formula bar, the range name is displayed.

Now you need to replace the cell reference in the formula in cell H11 with the name.

4
● Move to H11.

● Change to Edit mode.

● Select (highlight) the
cell reference I18 in
the formula.

● Choose
Insert/Name/Paste.

*Your screen should be
similar to Figure 5.30*

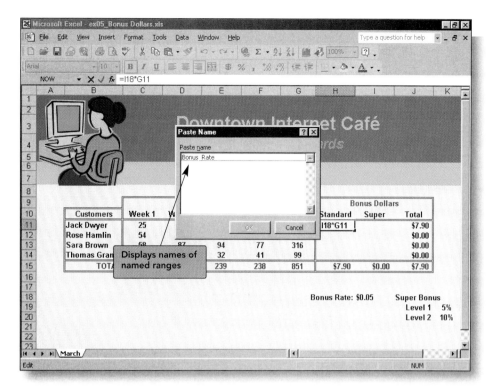

Figure 5.30

From the Paste Name dialog box you select the range name you want to use
in place of the selected cell reference.

5
● Select Bonus_Rate.

● Click [OK].

● Click Enter.

*Your screen should be
similar to Figure 5.31*

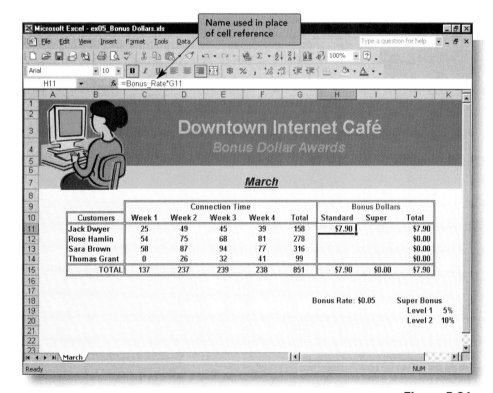

Figure 5.31

The selected range name has replaced the reference to cell I18 in the formula. Using a name makes the formula easier to understand.

Next you will name the Super Bonus levels in cells J19 and K20 that will be used in the formula to calculate the Super Bonus. You will name both cells at the same time using the labels in E19 and E20 as the names.

6 ● **Select J19 through K20.**

● **Choose Insert/Name/Create.**

Your screen should be similar to Figure 5.32

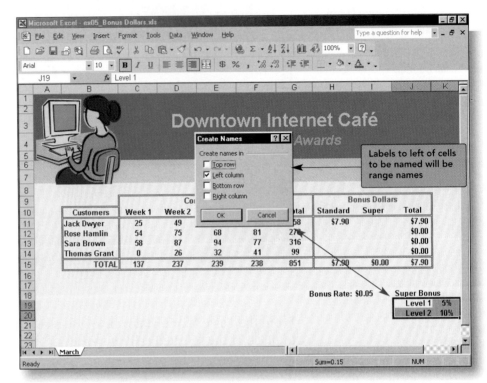

Figure 5.32

The Create Names dialog box lets you specify the location of the labels you want to use for names in relation to the cells to be named. In this case, you want to use the labels in the column to the left (K), which is the default. You will accept the default and then move to the cells to verify that the names have been created.

7 **Click** OK.

• **Move to K19 and note that Level_1 is displayed in the Name box.**

• **Move to K20 and note that Level_2 is displayed in the Name box.**

• **Save the workbook as** Bonus Dollars.

Your screen should be similar to Figure 5.33

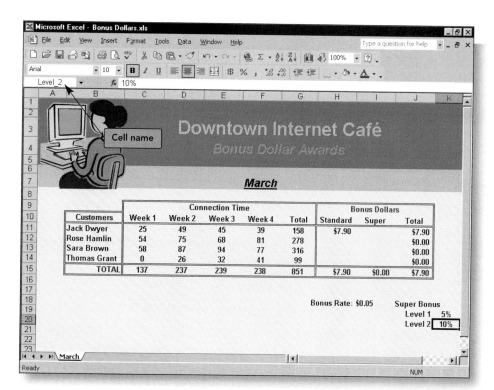

Figure 5.33

Using the IF Function

Now you are ready to enter a formula in cell I11 to calculate the Super Bonus. For any customer with more than 100 minutes of connection time, the Super Bonus is calculated using one of two levels. The highest level is for those with more than 200 minutes. Those customers receive a Super Bonus equal to 10 percent of their Standard Bonus. The other level is for those with less than or equal to 200 minutes who receive a Super Bonus equal to 5 percent of their Standard Bonus. You will use the IF function to calculate the Super Bonus.

7 The **IF function** checks to see if certain conditions are met and then takes action based on the results of the check. The syntax for this function is:

IF(logical_test,value_if_true,value_if_false)

This function contains three arguments: logical_test, value_if_true, and value_if_false. The logical_test argument is an expression that makes a comparison using logical operators. **Logical operators** are used in formulas and functions that compare numbers in two or more cells or to a constant. The result of the comparison is either true (the conditions are met) or false (the conditions are not met). The logical operators are:

Symbol	Meaning
=	Equal to
<	Less than
>	Greater than
<=	Less than or equal to
>=	Greater than or equal to
<>	Not equal to
NOT	Logical NOT
AND	Logical AND
OR	Logical OR

The logical test argument asks the question, "Does the entry in this cell meet the stated conditions?" The answer is either True (Yes) or False (No). The second argument, value_if_true, provides directions for the function to follow if the logical test result is true. The third argument, value_if_false, provides directions for the function to follow if the logical test result is false.

First you will enter the formula to calculate the discount earned for a connection time of 200 minutes or more. Then you will modify the function to include the other conditions.

1 ● Move to cell I11.

● Click f_* Insert Function.

● Select IF from the Most Recently Used or Logical Function categories.

● Click [OK].

Your screen should be similar to Figure 5.34

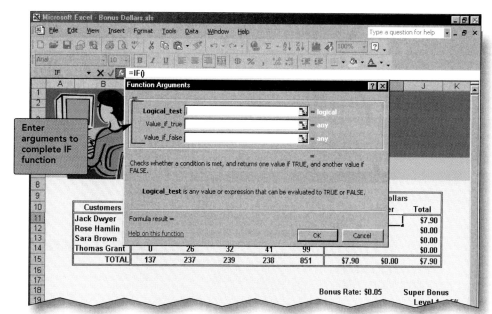

Figure 5.34

The IF Function Arguments dialog box contains three text boxes, one for each IF statement argument. The logical test is whether the total connection time for a customer is greater than 200 and the value_if_true argument provides directions for what to do if the logical test is true. In this case, the value_if_true directions are to multiply the value in cell H11 times the value in the cell named Level_2. To enter these arguments,

2 ● Type G11>200 in the Logical_test text box.

● Press [Tab⇆].

● Type Level_2*H11 in the Value_if_true text box.

Your screen should be similar to Figure 5.35

Figure 5.35

Notice that the Formula palette is already determining whether the conditions are true or false for the current customer based on the values in the referenced cells. In this case, because the value in G11 is less than 200, the logical test result is false and a Level 2 bonus would be 0.79 if true.

Next, you need to enter the value_if_false argument. It contains instructions that are executed if connection time is less than or equal to 200 minutes. If that connection time is greater than 100, then the Level_1 amount is used to calculate the Super Bonus, otherwise connection time is less than or equal to 100 and the Super Bonus is 0. To enter this condition, you include a second IF statement that will apply the Level 1 bonus. The arguments for the second IF statement are enclosed in their own set of parentheses. This is called a **nested function**.

3 ● **In the Value_if_false text box enter**
IF(G11>100,Level_1* H11,0).

Your screen should be similar to Figure 5.36

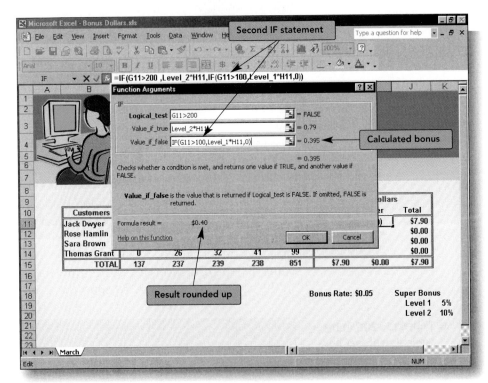

Figure 5.36

Now the calculated result is $0.395 for the current customer. The formula result will be rounded up to $0.40.

4 ● Click [OK].

Your screen should be similar to Figure 5.37

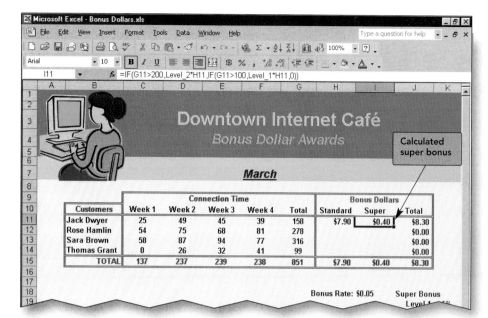

Figure 5.37

The Super Bonus for Jack Dwyer is $0.40. The IF function determined that the number in cell G11 was less than 200 but greater than 100. Therefore, the Super Bonus was calculated using Level_1, or 5 percent. Next, you will enter formulas to make these same calculations for the other three customers.

5 ● **Copy cells H11 through I11 using the fill handle to the range H12 through I14.**

● **Click cell H12 to deselect the range.**

Your screen should be similar to Figure 5.38

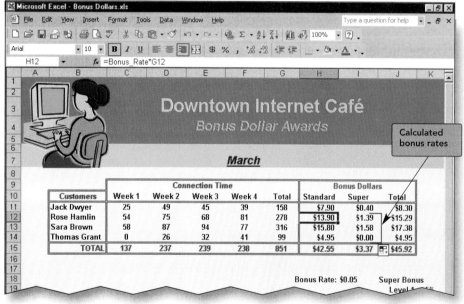

Figure 5.38

Because the named references in the copied formulas are absolute, they copied correctly. Both Rose and Sara earned Super Bonus awards of 10 percent because the values in cells G12 and G13 are greater than 200. Thomas did not earn a Super Bonus because the value in cell G14 is less than 100.

Adding a Combo Box Control

Evan really likes the layout of the form. A change needs to be made, however, to the Standard Bonus rate. During some months the bonus rate may be raised to $0.10 or $0.15 per minute. The formulas to calculate the bonuses will need to be adjusted to use the other two bonus rates during those months. You could create two additional forms that would each have a different bonus rate in cell I18. This would require that the correct form used for that month's input be based on the bonus rate for that month. A simpler way to deal with this problem is to add a combo box control to the form.

Adding controls to forms makes it easier to fill out a form and increases the accuracy of the information entered in it. This is because many of the controls can include a list of options from which the user selects. Although controls are most effectively used in online forms, they can also be used in printed forms. For example, controls such as buttons and check boxes can be printed blank and then filled in by the user.

A combo-box control displays a text box and button that will display a drop-down list with the items that can be selected. The first step in creating a combo-box control is to enter the items you want to appear in the combo-box drop-down list in a columnar range. You will enter the three bonus amounts as items to be used.

1 ● **In cells H19 through H21 enter the numbers .05, .10, and .15.**

Additional Information
Cells H19:H21 were preformatted to currency.

● **Display the Control Toolbox toolbar.**

● **If necessary, move the toolbar to the left side of your screen.**

Your screen should be similar to Figure 5.39

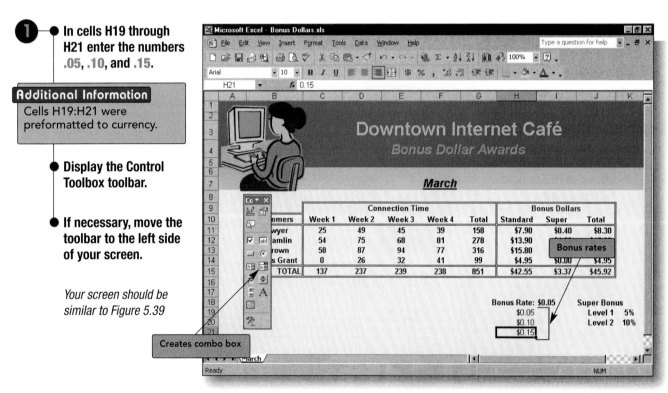

Figure 5.39

Now you are ready to add the combo box control to the form.

● Click ⊞ Combo Box on the Control Toolbox toolbar.

● Click over cell C17 to create a combo box.

Additional Information

The combo box is a selected object that can be sized or moved like any other object.

Your screen should be similar to Figure 5.40

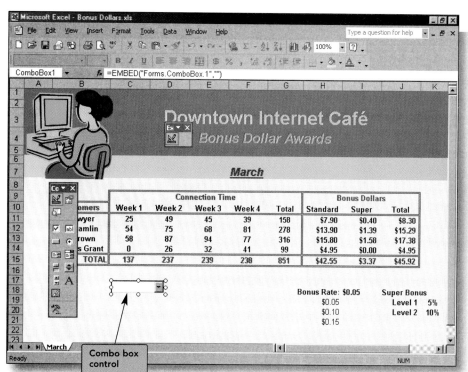

Figure 5.40

Design mode is active, so you can modify the settings associated with the selected control. You need to specify the information to be displayed in the combo-box drop-down list and the location of the cell to link the selection to. You do this by setting the properties of the combo box.

● Click 🖻 Properties (in the Control Toolbox).

● If necessary, open the Alphabetic tab.

Your screen should be similar to Figure 5.41

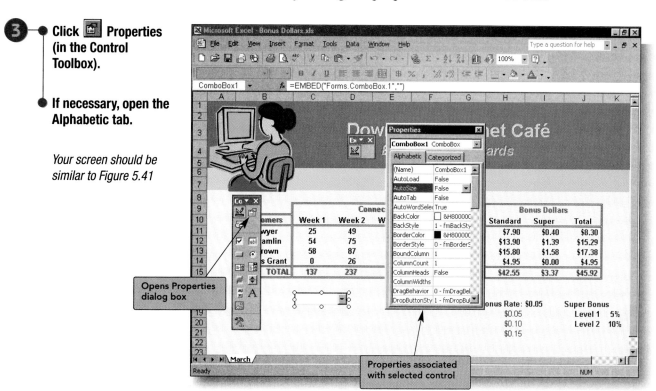

Figure 5.41

Creating a Form   **EX5.39**

The Alphabetic tab displays the properties for the selected control in alphabetic order. The ListFillRange option is used to specify the location of the cells containing the information to be displayed in the combo-box drop-down list, and the LinkedCell option is used to specify the cell to receive the selection.

4
● Scroll the list to locate the ListFillRange property box.

● Enter the range **H19:H21** as the ListFillRange.

● Enter cell **I18** as the LinkedCell.

Your screen should be similar to Figure 5.42

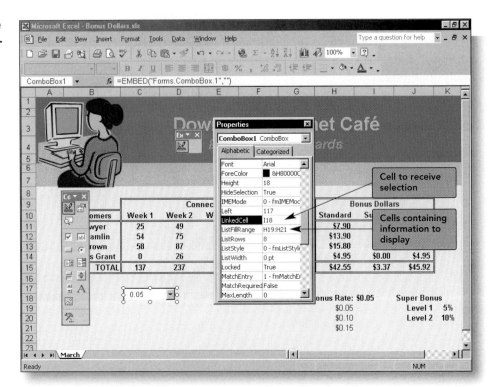

Figure 5.42

You are finished defining the properties and want to add a label next to the combo box and then try it out.

5 ● Click ☒ to close the Properties dialog box.

● Enter the label Select Bonus Rate: in cell B17 to identify the combo box.

● Reposition the combo box control as needed to align with the label (see Figure 5.43).

● Click ☒ Exit Design mode.

● Close the Control Toolbox toolbar.

● Open the combo box drop-down list.

● Select $0.15.

● Save the workbook.

Your screen should be similar to Figure 5.43

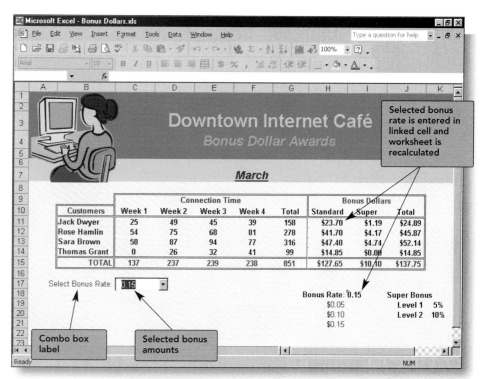

Figure 5.43

The selection you made from the combo box is entered in the bonus rate cell, I18, and the worksheet is recalculated using the new bonus rate.

Adding Comments

Now you will prepare the form to be used for entry of the same information for other months. Since someone else will most likely use the form, it is a good idea to include instructions on how to use it. Typically, these instructions are a combination of text entries and comments.

concept 8

Comments

8 **Comments** are notes attached to cells that can be used to help clarify the meaning of the data, provide documentation, or ask a question. Using comments is a good method of adding instructions that do not interfere with the appearance of the worksheet.

A comment appears as a note box attached to the cell. You can move and resize a comment box just as you would any other type of graphic object. If you move the cell that contains a comment, the associated comment box moves with it.

You will add one text entry and two cell comments that will provide the instructions for this form.

1
● Move to cell A8.

● Enter For help on how to complete this form, point to the red triangles.

● Format A8 to a font color of Dark Red and bold.

● Insert a blank row below row 8.

Your screen should be similar to Figure 5.44

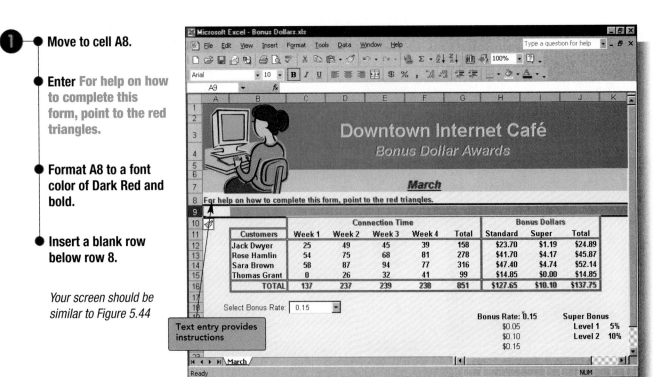

Text entry provides instructions

Figure 5.44

Next, you will add the cell comments using the Reviewing toolbar. The first comment will appear in cell F7 and will direct users to update the month.

2
● Display the Reviewing toolbar.

● If necessary, move the toolbar to the lower-right corner of the worksheet.

● Move to F7.

● Click 🗃 New Comment in the Reviewing toolbar.

Another Method
The menu equivalent is Insert/Comment.

Your screen should be similar to Figure 5.45

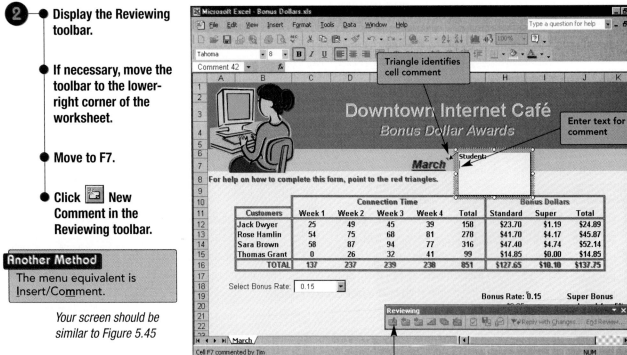

Triangle identifies cell comment

Enter text for comment

Inserts a new comment

Figure 5.45

By default, the comment box includes the user name. You will delete the text for the comment.

3 ● Select the user name and press [Delete].

● Type **Enter the month.**

● Size the comment box to fit the text.

● Click on any cell to complete the comment.

● Point to the red triangle in cell F7.

Your screen should be similar to Figure 5.46

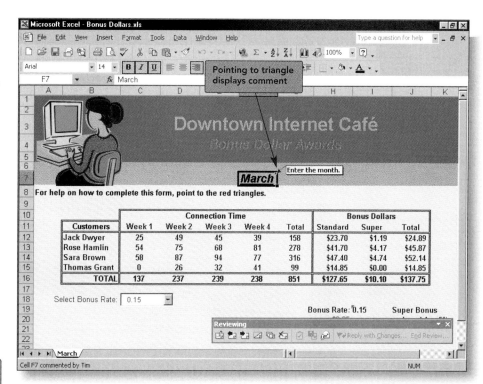

Figure 5.46

The comment is displayed in a comment text box. The second comment will be entered in cell C12.

4 ● Add a comment to C12 containing the text **Enter weekly connection times here.**

● Size the comment box to fit the text.

● Add a comment to B18 containing the text **Select this month's bonus rate.**

● Size the comment box to fit the text.

● Click 🔄 Show All Comments.

Your screen should be similar to Figure 5.47

Figure 5.47

The three comments you entered are displayed. If comments overlay one another, you can move them around just like any other graphics object. However, when you hide and redisplay the comments they return to the default location.

5 ● Click **Hide All Comments.**

Another Method

The menu equivalent, View/Comments, will display all comments or hide all displayed comments.

● **Close the Reviewing toolbar.**

● **Save the workbook.**

Your screen should be similar to Figure 5.48

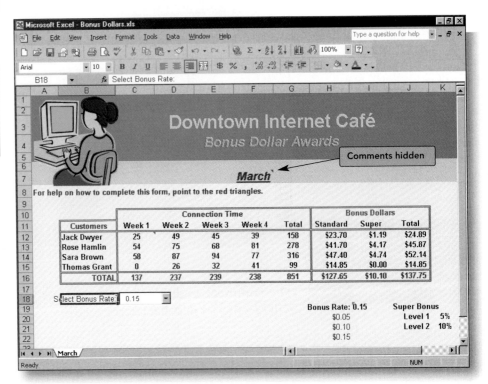

Figure 5.48

Finalizing the Form

A well-designed form is simple to use and uncluttered in design. To make the form easy to use, you will add a command button to print the output. To simplify the design you will hide non-essential items. Then you will prepare the workbook to be saved as a template to be used each month to record the customer's bonus dollar earnings. You will clear the sample data, unlock all data entry areas, and protect the worksheet. You will also add documentation to the workbook to clarify the purpose of the template.

Simplifying the Form

You will first add a command button to print the output then you will hide any non-essential information in the form to simplify its appearance.

1 ● Add a command button macro over cell E18.

● Label the button PrintForm.

● With the command button selected, record a macro to print the worksheet in landscape orientation, centered horizontally on the page. Include a custom footer that displays your name and date only.

● Exit Design Mode and close the Control Toolbox.

Your screen should be similar to Figure 5.49

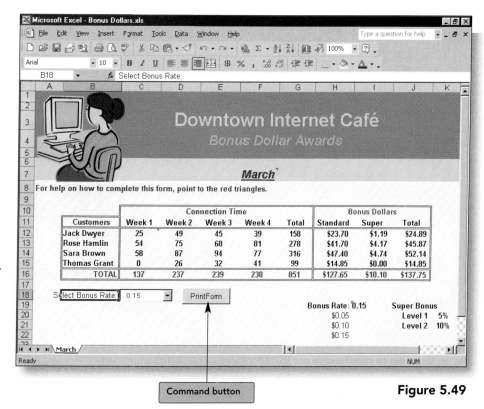

Command button

Figure 5.49

Users of this form do not need to see the list of rates and the two bonus levels. To simplify the form, you will hide this information.

2 ● Select rows 19 through 22.

Additional Information

Click the row number to quickly select an entire row.

● Choose **F**ormat/**R**ow/**H**ide.

Additional Information

To redisplay hidden rows, select the rows above and below the hidden rows and use F**o**rmat/**R**ow/**U**nhide.

Your screen should be similar to Figure 5.50

Rows 19 through 22 hidden

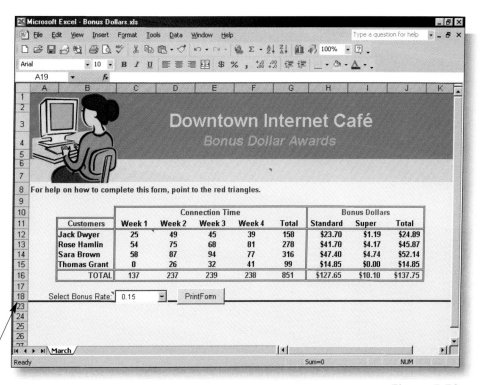

Figure 5.50

Preparing the Template

Each month the form will be used to record the customer's Bonus Dollar earnings. You need to clear the sample data and protect the worksheet. Finally, you will save it as a template file. You also want to include the file documentation so that users of the template will understand the purpose of the file.

First, you will clear the contents of the entry areas and unlock these cells for editing. Then you will protect the worksheet.

1 ● Clear the contents of cell F7 and cells C12 through F15.

● Unlock cell F7.

● Unlock the cells for weekly connection times (cells C12 through F15).

● Use <u>E</u>dit/<u>G</u>o To to move cell I19 that displays the selected bonus rate.

● Unlock cell I19.

● Protect the worksheet.

Your screen should be similar to Figure 5.51

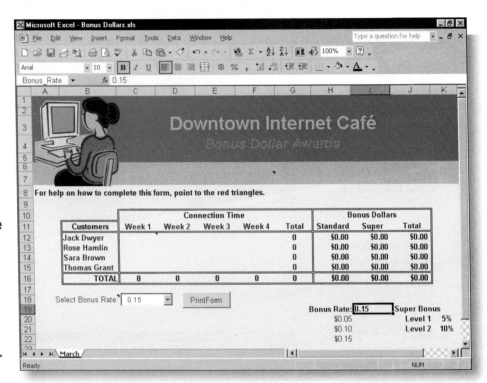

Figure 5.51

Next, you will enter basic documentation regarding the worksheet file.

2 • Choose File/Properties.

• If necessary, open the Summary tab.

• In the Subject text box, type Monthly record of connection times and bonuses.

• Enter your name into the Author text box.

• In the Comments text box type Point to the red triangles for instructions. Select the bonus amount for the month from the Bonus Rate drop-down list.

Your screen should be similar to Figure 5.52

Figure 5.52

You are now ready to save the form as a workbook template.

3 • Click OK to close the Properties dialog box.

• Move to cell A9.

• Save the workbook as a template using the file name Monthly Bonus Form to your data file location.

• Close the workbook and exit Excel.

LAB 5

Using Data Tables, Creating Macros, and Designing Onscreen Forms

Data Table (EX5.7)

A data table is a range of cells that is used to quickly calculate multiple what-if versions in one operation and to show the results of all variations together in the worksheet.

Macro (EX5.13)

A macro is a stored series of keystrokes and commands that are executed automatically when the macro is run.

Controls (EX5.14)

A control is a graphic object that is designed to help the user interact with the form.

Visual Basic Editor (EX5.16)

The Visual Basic Editor is a tool used to write and edit macros attached to Excel workbooks.

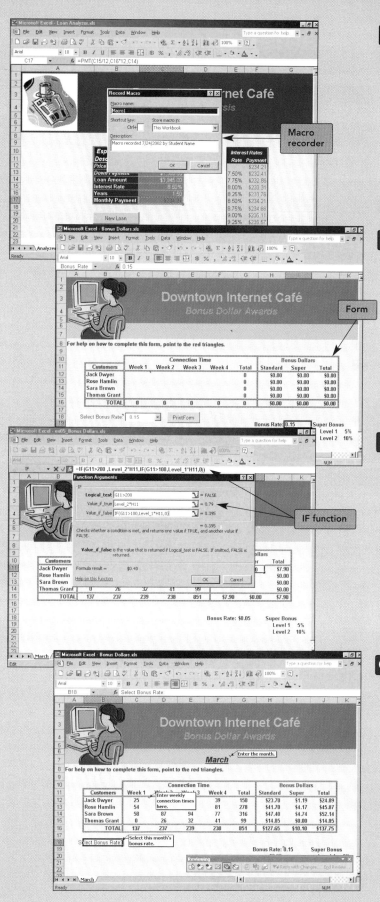

Macro Recorder   (EX5.23)

The Macro Recorder automatically creates a macro by recording a series of actions as macro commands.

Form   (EX5.27)

A form is a formatted worksheet with blank spaces that can be filled in online or on paper.

IF Function   (EX5.34)

The IF function checks to see if certain conditions are met and then takes action based on the results of the check.

Comments   (EX5.41)

Comments are notes attached to cells that can be used to clarify the meaning of the cell contents, provide documentation, or ask a question.

key terms

AutoFormat   EX5.10

column-oriented   EX5.7

comment   EX5.41

control   EX5.14

data table   EX5.7

digital signature   EX5.14

form   EX5.27

IF function   EX5.34

input cell   EX5.7

logical operator   EX5.34

macro   EX5.13

Macro Recorder   EX5.23

name   EX5.29

nested function   EX5.36

nper   EX5.6

object   EX5.16

one-variable data table   EX5.7

principal   EX5.6

property   EX5.16

pv   EX5.6

rate   EX5.6

remark statement   EX5.17

row-oriented   EX5.7

run   EX5.13

statement   EX5.16

Sub procedure   EX5.16

syntax   EX5.16

two-variable data table   EX5.7

Visual Basic Editor   EX5.16

mous skills

The Microsoft Office User Specialist (MOUS) certification program is designed to measure your proficiency in performing basic tasks using the Office XP applications. Getting certified demonstrates that you have the skills and provides a valuable industry credential for employment. After completing this lab, you have learned the following Microsoft Office User Specialist skills:

Skill	Description	Page
Formatting and Printing Worksheets	Modify row and column settings	EX5.46
	Use automated tools to format worksheets	EX5.10
Creating and Revising Formulas	Use statistical, date and time, financial, and logical functions in formulas	EX5.33
Workgroup Collaboration	View and edit comments	EX5.41

command summary

Command	Shortcut Key	Button	Action
Edit/Cle**a**r/Co**m**ments			Deletes comment in selected cell
View/**C**omments			Displays all comments or hides all displayed comments
Insert/**N**ame/**D**efine			Assigns a name you specify to a cell or range of cells
Insert/**N**ame/**P**aste			Places the selected cell or cell range name in the formula bar or lists names in the worksheet
Insert/**N**ame/**C**reate			Creates a range name using the text in cells
Insert/**C**omment			Inserts a new comment in selected cell
Insert/**E**dit Comment			Edits comment in selected cell
F**o**rmat/**R**ow/**H**ide			Hides selected rows or columns
F**o**rmat/**R**ow/**U**nhide			Displays rows and columns that were previously hidden
F**o**rmat/**A**utoformat			Applies selected table format
Tools/**M**acros/**M**acros/<Macro name>/**R**un			Runs selected macro
Tools/**M**acros/**M**acros/<Macro name>/**E**dit			Opens selected macro in Visual Basic Editor for editing
Tools/**M**acro/**R**ecord New Macro			Records a series of actions as a macro
Tools/**M**acro/**S**top Recording		▪	Stops the recording of a macro
Tools/**M**acro/**S**ecurity			Sets security level associated with macros in a workbook
Data/**T**able			Creates a data table based on specified input values and formulas
Visual Basic Editor			
File/**C**lose and Return			Closes the Visual Basic Editor window and returns to the active Excel worksheet
Run/**R**un Sub/UserForm	F5		Runs macro

lab exercises

Terminology

screen identification

In the following worksheet, several items are identified by letters. Enter the correct term for each item in the spaces that follow.

A. _____   E. _____

B. _____   F. _____

C. _____   G. _____

D. _____   H. _____

matching

Match the letter on the right to the item in the numbered list on the left.

1. digital signature _____ **a.** descriptive statements in a macro

2. macro _____ **b.** a note attached to a cell

3. nested function _____ **c.** authentication that confirms a macro

4. controls _____ **d.** rules of grammar in a Sub procedure statement

5. data table _____ **e.** a function within another function

6. remark statements _____ **f.** a stored series of keystrokes and commands

7. statements _____ **g.** information in the Visual Basic Editor

8. syntax _____ **h.** graphic objects with properties in a worksheet

9. logical operators _____ **i.** compares numbers in two or more cells or to a constant

10. comments _____ **j.** a what-if analysis in which variables are used to see the effect on formulas

multiple choice

Circle the correct response to the questions below.

1. A(n)_____ begins with a statement that starts a macro.
   a. Sub procedure
   b. property
   c. remark statement
   d. nested function

2. The _____ automatically creates a macro by recording a series of actions.
   a. Visual Basic Editor
   b. nested function
   c. Macro Reader
   d. none of the above

3. A(n)_____is a formatted worksheet with blank spaces that can be filled in online.
   a. template
   b. form
   c. object
   d. cell

4. When a macro is _____, the actions within it are performed automatically.
   a. recorded
   b. executed
   c. stored
   d. opened

5. A _____ data table can be row- or column-oriented.
   a. multivariable
   b. two-variable
   c. single-variable
   d. one-variable

6. An Excel form can contain _____.
   a. text
   b. graphics
   c. cell comments
   d. all of the above

7. A macro created with the Visual Basic Editor must be attached to a(n) _____.
   a. object
   b. command button
   c. cell
   d. control box

8. A range name must start with _____.
   a. a letter
   b. a number
   c. a backslash
   d. any of the above

9. A(n) _____ argument is an expression that makes a comparison using logical operators.
   a. if_then
   b. logical_test
   c. and_or
   d. logical_if

10. _____ are used in formulas and functions that compare numbers in two or more cells.
    a. Logical operators
    b. Function arguments
    c. Nested functions
    d. Combo boxes

true/false

Circle the correct answer to the following questions.

1.	When a macro is executed the stored actions are performed automatically.	True	False
2.	The properties of controls cannot be changed or customized.	True	False
3.	Comments are attached to functions.	True	False
4.	A form created in Excel can only be used online.	True	False
5.	The result of an IF argument is either true or false.	True	False
6.	High security automatically disables macros if they are not digitally signed.	True	False
7.	A range name can only include letters and numbers.	True	False
8.	An apostrophe identifies a statement as a remark.	True	False

9. The IF function requires six arguments.　　　　True　　　False

10. The only way to execute a macro is to use a command button.　　　True　　　False

Concepts

fill-in questions

Complete the following statements by filling in the blanks with the correct terms.

1. A range _____ can consist of any combination of 255 characters.

2. _____ are used in formulas and functions that compare values in two or more cells.

3. Excel uses the _____ computer programming language for macros.

4. A _____ appears as note box attached to a cell.

5. An _____ is a cell in which a list of values is substituted to see the resulting effect on the related formulas.

6. The steps in creating a(n)_____ are the same for online or paper completion.

7. The _____ can be used any time a cell or range is requested.

8. A(n)_____ control displays a text box and a button that will display a drop-down list.

9. The _____ function checks to see if certain conditions are met and takes actions based on the results.

10. Graphic objects that are designed to help the user interact with the worksheet are called _____.

discussion questions

1. Discuss different ways in which a data table can be used. When would you use a one-variable data table? When would a two-variable table be more appropriate?

2. Discuss some spreadsheet functions that you could automate with a macro. Would it be more appropriate to use the Visual Basic Editor or the Macro Recorder to create each of these macros?

3. Discuss what range names are and when it is appropriate to use them. Give some examples.

Hands-On Exercises

rating system
★ Easy
★★ Moderate
★★★ Difficult

step by step

Animal Rescue Foundation Volunteer Rewards

★ 1. After viewing the revenue analysis you provided (Lab 4, Step by Step, 5), Samuel Johnson and the other Animal Rescue Foundation board members have begun the budget planning for the next year. They have realized that daily operation of the agency depends on the volunteers. To repay them for their time, the board has decided to implement a rewards program with some of the budget surpluses you have anticipated. You have been asked to create a worksheet to track the number of hours people have worked and determine their award level. Your completed worksheets should be similar to the one shown here.

a. Open the workbook file ex05_ARF Volunteers. Enter the data shown below into the worksheet.

Row		Col B	Col C	Col D	Col E
33	Pennington, Neil	75	62	8	79
34	Wilson, Aaron	35	40	23	39
35	Tranthorn, Ellie	27	35	19	12
36	Clark, Jamel	61	30	28	58
37	Ferguson, Robby	99	12	0	43
38	Carey, Ronnie	105	42	50	103

Student Name   September 8, 2002

Animal Angels Volunteers

	1st Qtr	2nd Qtr	3rd Qtr	4th Qtr	Average	Total	Level
Bell, Patricia	45	34	102	235	104	416	1
Carey, Ronnie	105	42	50	103	75	300	1
Carver, Kathi	30	83	3	3	29.75	119	3
Chorley, Besty	68	2	235	96	100.25	401	1
Clark, Jamul	61	30	28	58	44.25	177	3
Cody, Martin	28	66	6	45	36.25	145	3
Dickson, Diane	70	18	88	27	50.75	203	2
Edwards, Mike	12	20	61	28	30.25	121	3
Ferguson, Robby	99	12	0	43	38.5	154	3
Forester, Kimberly	30	63	34	44	42.75	171	3
Franklin, Stacey	57	98	93	80	82	328	1
Fulton, Anne	12	18	68	122	55	220	2
Garcia, Maria	5	23	61	36	31.25	125	3
Gatens, Chris	0	100	58	85	60.75	243	2
Henderson, James	9	76	51	60	49	196	3
Ingram, Helen	29	12	33	12	21.5	86	0
Isbell, Sonya	46	65	47	3	40.25	161	3
Johnson, Thaman	3	30	20	6	14.75	59	0
Jones, April	70	83	38	79	67.5	270	2
Kelly, William	12	76	63	94	61.25	245	2
Kettonhoeffer, Bill	4	59	57	8	32	128	3
Kullman, Rodney	28	30	35	16	27.25	109	3
La Paglia, Sally	39	10	12	134	48.75	195	3
Lee, Su	56	6	5	0	16.75	67	0
Legge, Cristan	3	81	73	34	47.75	191	3
Lopez, Andrew	86	34	5	156	70.25	281	2
Marcus, Danielle	3	19	24	2	12	48	0
Merwin, Michael	44	9	95	37	46.25	185	3
Nelson, Faith	9	112	6	0	31.75	127	3
Pennington, Neil	75	62	8	79	56	224	2
Peterson, Tracey	83	3	165	0	62.75	251	2
Pierce, Kai	6	98	4	75	45.75	183	3
Tranthorn, Ellie	27	39	19	12	24.25	97	0
Wilson, Aaron	35	40	23	39	34.25	137	3

b. Sort the list in ascending order by name.

c. Enter formulas to calculate the average and total hours for the year in columns F and G.

d. Enter the labels Star Level 1, Star Level 2, and Star Level 3 right-aligned in cells I40 through I42. In cells J40 through J42, enter 300, 200, 100 as the award levels.

e. Use the Name Range command to name the values for the star levels.

f. In cell H5 enter the following formula to calculate the award level for the volunteers: IF(G5>=Star_Level_1,1,IF(G5>=Star_Level_2,2,IF(G5>=Star_Level_3,3,0))).

g. Change the value in cell B5 to 450 and then to 0 to check the formula. Return the value to 235. Copy the formula down the column.

h. Select the entire worksheet excluding the star values. Enter your name and the current date in a header, center the worksheet horizontally.

i. Print the selection. Save the workbook as ARF Bonus Awards.

Grade Book Maintenance

★ ★ **2.** You are a graduate assistant and have been assigned to work for a university professor. You are responsible for maintaining the grade book and have decided to create a worksheet that will calculate the students' final grades. You started the workbook by entering the row and column labels and the points earned for a sample set of students in four categories. You need to add formulas that will total the students' points on a summary worksheet and then use this new total to calculate the grade for the course. Your completed workbook should be similar to that shown here.

a. Open the file ex05_Grades.

b. Set cell D6 of the Summary sheet equal to the total on the Homework sheet (H6). Copy the formula down the column to insert the total homework points for all the students in the Summary sheet.

c. Repeat this step for the Projects, Quizzes, and Exams columns.

d. Enter a formula in row H of the Summary sheet to calculate the students' total points for the four categories.

Grade Book for Spring 2003

ID #	Last Name	First Name	Homework	Projects	Quizzes	Exams	Total	Percent	Letter
003874	Altiveros	Elaine	93	312	34	215	654	79.27%	C
004875	Brown	Stephanie	102	340	48	283	773	93.70%	A
000606	Colburn	Melissa	78	309	31	165	583	70.67%	C
009690	Davis	Kylie	110	331	51	275	767	92.97%	A
000943	Douglas	Mary	74	290	29	235	628	76.12%	C
002773	Dwyer	Jen	113	326	42	272	753	91.27%	A
009873	Gott	Linda	65	278	29	248	620	75.15%	C
007747	Hardy	Thomas	68	252	27	233	580	70.30%	C
002981	Hobson	Scott	110	329	42	282	763	92.48%	A
002637	Holt	Michelle	71	287	29	263	650	78.79%	C
002779	Jackson	Nicholas	103	340	48	281	772	93.58%	A
004994	Lopez	Marlene	78	302	29	198	607	73.58%	C
001572	Meese	Theresa	75	262	26	214	577	69.94%	C
004919	Mittelstadt	Jennifer	81	293	30	214	618	74.91%	C
003789	Oestreich	Kenneth	108	319	37	227	691	83.76%	B
002563	Pawlowski	Helen	57	232	26	202	517	62.67%	D
001326	Plumm	Kelly	109	320	41	265	735	89.09%	B
004662	Reboton	Erin	113	321	44	272	750	90.91%	A
002679	Riley	Russell	96	312	35	235	678	82.18%	B
000983	Shumacker	Michael	99	317	41	223	680	82.42%	B
00/503	Smith	Shawn	85	311	34	249	679	82.30%	B
007843	Steele	Blaine	105	318	39	243	705	85.45%	B
006472	Williamson	Paul	77	246	24	220	567	68.73%	D

| Total Points Possible: | | | 120 | 345 | 60 | 300 | 825 | | |

Student Name
9/2/2001 12.18

e. Name cell H30 **Points_Possible**. Enter the formula **=H6/Points_Possible** in cell I6. Copy the formula down the column for the other students. Apply the percentage format with two decimal places.

f. Enter the following IF statement in cell J6
=IF(I6>0.899,"A",IF(I6>0.799,"B",IF(I6>0.699,"C",IF(I6>0.599,"D",E)))). You can use the insert function feature or type the IF statement directly into the cell. Copy the IF statement down the column for the other students.

g. Enter your name and the current date using the NOW function below the worksheet data.

h. Preview the Summary worksheet. Make any necessary formatting changes. Remove the header from the worksheet. Set the orientation to landscape.

i. Horizontally center the worksheet. Save the workbook as Gradebook and print the worksheet.

Wilson Electronics Financial Analysis

★ ★ **3.** You have been hired as a salesperson for the Wilson Electronics Company. You want to be able to give your customers up-to-date and accurate information on the cost of high end electronics you sell. Many times customers have financing issues that are easily answered with what-if analysis on the terms of the payment plans you can give them. To automate the process, you plan to use a data table containing the model information and a table to calculate the different payments. The completed worksheet will be similar to the one shown here.

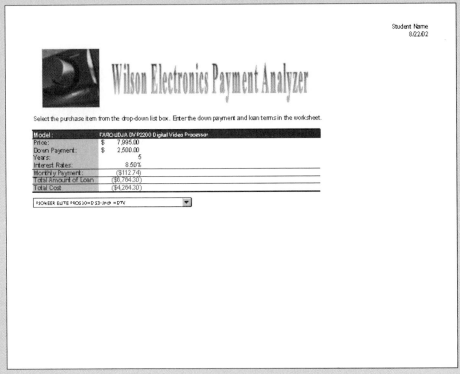

a. Open the file ex05_Electronics Analyzer.

b. Instead of typing in the model and price of the item each time, you want to be able to choose it from a drop down list that links to a data table. The information for the data table has already been created in cells C24 through D41. Enter the number **1** in cell C23. You will use the Choose function. In cell B12 enter **=CHOOSE(C23,D25, D26,D27,D28,D29, D31,D32,D33,D35, D36,D38,D39,D40,D41)** to select the items in the data table based on the number entered in cell C23.

c. Create a similar choose function in cell B13 to display the price associated with each item.

d. Enter sample data for the down payment of **$500** in cell B14, **2** for the years in cell B15, and **.0725** for the interest rate in cell B16.

e. Enter the payment function **=PMT(B16/12,B15*12,B13-B14)** in cell B17. To calculate the total amount of the loan, enter the formula **= B17*(B15*12)**. To calculate the total cost, enter the formula **=B14-B14**.

f. To see how the calculator works, enter 8 in cell C23.

g. Since each customer orders a different item, you would like to create a combo box that will allow you to quickly select the item rather than have to type the reference number in the cell. Using the Forms toolbar Combo Box button, create a combo box below cell D6. Set the Link Cell to C23 and the input range to **D24 through D41**.

h. Hide the Forms toolbar. Adjust the size and placement of the combo box and display it below the form data. Select an item from the combo box list.

i. Hide rows 18 though 36.

j. Apply an AutoFormat to enhance the worksheet. Adjust the column widths and layout as necessary. If necessary, change the alignment of cell B12 to left aligned

k. In cell A10, enter directions on how to use the form. Include cell comments to inform the user how to use the form.

k. To see how the worksheet works, enter the following for changing variable values:

Select	Pioneer Elite PRO510HD 53-inch TV
Down payment:	2,500
Years:	5
Interest Rate:	.085

l. Include your name and the current date in a header and print the worksheet in landscape orientation. Save the worksheet as Electronics Analyzer.

Currency Exchange Calculator

★ ★ **4.** You work for Johnson & Scannell, an investment company that handles a lot of foreign accounts.
★ The company does a lot of currency exchanging and you would like to create a worksheet that will help employees quickly calculate the conversion. You have already created a worksheet that has the calculations for U.S. dollars to Canadian dollars. So that the worksheet works for any type of foreign currency, you will create a command button to ask the user to input the country's currency, the current exchange rate, and the U.S. dollar amount. The completed Exchange Rate worksheet and Visual Basic code window will be similar to the ones shown here.

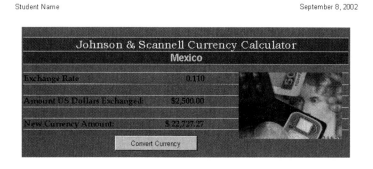

a. Open the Excel workbook file ex05_Currency Exchange. Open the Control Toolbox toolbar and create a command button positioned as shown in the example. Edit the command button to display the words Convert Currency.

b. Start the Visual Basic Editor to create the Command Button macro.

```
'Used to calculate US dollars to a different currency
'Written by Student Name
'Last Modified Current Date
'Run from Currency worksheet by clicking the Convert Currency button
'User enters the country, exchange rate from US dollars and the amount of US currency


Private Sub CommandButton1_Click()
    Sheets("Currency").Select
    Range("A3,B5,B7").Select
    Selection.ClearContents
    Range("A3").Value = InputBox("What country's currency?", "Enter")
    Range("B5").Value = InputBox("What is today's exchange rate from dollars?", "Enter")
    Range("B7").Value = InputBox("How much US money do you want to exchange?", "Enter")
    Range("A1").Select

End Sub
```

c. Enter the following remarks above the Sub procedure header:

'Used to calculate US dollars to a different currency
'Written by [Student Name]
'Last Modified [Current Date]
'Run from Currency worksheet by clicking the Convert New Currency button
'User enters the country, exchange rate from US dollars, and the amount of US currency

d. Inside the Sub and End Sub statements enter the following:

```
Sheets("Currency").Select
Range("A3,B5,B7").Select
Selection.ClearContents
Range("A3").Value = InputBox("What country's currency?", "Enter")
Range("B5").Value = InputBox("What is today's exchange rate from dollars?", "Enter")
Range("B7").Value = InputBox("How much US money do you want to exchange?", "Enter")
Range("A1").Select
```

e. Print the text in the code window and close the Visual Basic window. Exit design mode and close the Control Toolbox toolbar.

f. If necessary, change your macro security level to medium.

g. Click the command button and enter the following to check the accuracy of your command button. (The calculator should return $803.57.)

Country: Australia
Rate: $0.56
US Money: $450.00

h. Enter your name and the current date in a header and print the worksheet showing the exchange of Mexican pesos.

j. Save the workbook as Currency Converter.

Adventure Travel Tours Package Analysis

★ ★ **5.** Adventure Travel Tours agents work hard to sell travel packages. To give their customers the best
★ possible fares, ATT agents make reservations based on group rates. Because the rates are
calculated as a percentage of the previous year's sales, you would like to create a worksheet that
will show the effects of a change in sales from –5 to 10 percent. The completed Adventure Travel
Sales worksheet will be similar to the one shown here.

a. Open the file ex05_ATT Sales. Enter
functions to calculate the totals.

b. Enter the values –5% to 10% at 1% increments starting in K4 to be used for
the values in a combo box.

c. Create a combo box that contains
these values and display the combo
box over cell C13. Link the combo
box to cell J5. Enter the label Increase
Percentage in cell A13.

d. Copy cells A3 to F11 to cell A15.
Change the title in row 15 to Number
of Packages Needed in 2003. Merge the
title over the data.

e. In cell B18 enter the formula
=B6*(1+J5). Copy the formula
through the cell range B18:E22.

f. Adjust the formatting as needed to
make the worksheet attractive.

g. Enter comments to tell the user how
to use the worksheet.

h. Hide columns J and K. Set the percentage increase to 3%.

i. Enter your name and the current date
in a header, center the worksheet horizontally and print the worksheet.

j. Save the workbook as ATT Sales2.

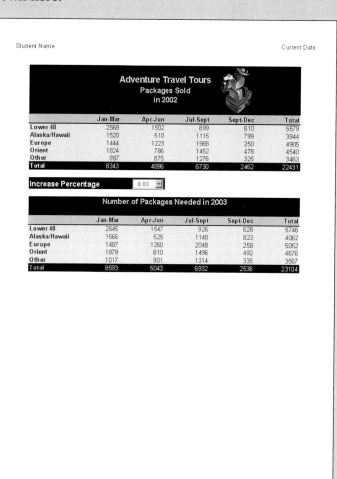

On Your Own

Creating a Personal Macro Library

★ **1.** In a blank new worksheet, use the Macro Recorder to record five macros for procedures that you use frequently and for which using a macro would save you time. For example, you may want to create a macro to modify the contents of the selected cell to 16 points, a selected font style, bold, and centered. Make sure that the macros are available to other open worksheets by using the Tools/Macros/Macros command. Add descriptions of the macros in the worksheet. Put the macro shortcut keys you assigned in cell comments. Enter your name and the current date in the worksheet. Test your macros by opening a new workbook and running the macros. Save the file as Macros and print both the macro and new worksheet.

401K Analysis

★ ★ **2.** The company you work for will contribute 3 percent of your gross pay to an individual retirement account (IRA). You can add up to another 15 percent of your gross pay to the same IRA. Create a worksheet with the following columns: Gross Wages, Employer Contribution, My Contribution, and Total Contribution. Enter your gross wages and create a formula to calculate the company contribution. In a column to the right, enter the numbers 0 to 10. Format them as percentages. Create a combo box that uses the percentages and calculates your contribution for the My Contribution column. Total the contributions. Use the combo box to see how much of your gross pay you can contribute to the IRA. Select the value you think is most appropriate for you. Enter your name and the current date in the worksheet. Save the file as My 401K and print the worksheet.

Furniture Purchase Analysis

★ ★ **3.** You have been furniture shopping for family room furniture and have your decision down to three groupings from different stores. Part of your decision is what the monthly payments will be based on the terms offered at the stores. The three stores offer different interest rates over a 3-year payment period. Using the information shown below and the features you learned in this lab, create a workbook to calculate the monthly payments for different interest rates. Use an AutoFormat to enhance the appearance of the worksheet. Save it as Furniture Loan Analysis. Print the analysis for the furniture grouping you want to purchase. Include your name and the current date in a header.

	Store 1	Store 2	Store 3
Purchase Total	$15,975	$22,320	$18,470
Down payment	$1,500	$2,000	$1,000
Interest rate	12%	8.5%	9%

Sports Company Credit Card Incentives

★ ★ **4.** The Sports Company has decided to offer its own credit card. As an incentive to get employees to
★   promote the card, the company offers to give employees $1.00 for each card application they file.
If an employee files 25 or more applications, a bonus is added. Create a worksheet for four
employees that tracks the number of applications filed per week. Total the number of applications
by employee and for the month. Calculate the amount the employee earned by multiplying the
total by $1.00. Use a linking cell for the $1.00 bonus value so that you can increase or decrease it
to see the effect. Use an IF statement to calculate a 10 percent bonus for employees who file 25
applications, and a 20 percent bonus for employees who file 50 or more applications. Create a
combo box with $1.00, $1.50, and $2.00 in it. Unlock the data entry cells in the worksheet. Protect
the worksheet. Select the $2.00 bonus amount. Enter your name and the current date in a header
of the worksheet. Apply an AutoFormat of your choice to enhance the sheet. Save the file as Sports
Company Credit Card and print the worksheet.

★ ★ Speeding Fine Calculator

★ **5.** You have been hired to work for the local traffic court. Create a worksheet that the clerks can use
to calculate the amount of a speeding ticket. The worksheet should contain the following
information: actual speed limit, speed offender was traveling, and number of tickets offender has
received. The worksheet should calculate miles above speed limit, cost of ticket ($10.00 for each
mile), court costs ($53.20), and additional charges ($20.00 for each offense). Use the Visual Basic
Editor window and write the statements to ask the clerk to enter the actual speed limit, the speed
offender was traveling, and number of tickets. Calculate the cost of the speeding ticket. Apply an
AutoFormat of your choice to enhance the sheet. Enter your name and the current date in a
header of the worksheet. Save the file as Speeding Fines and print the worksheet.

On the Web

Personal Computer Comparison Shopping

You are interested in buying a computer. Use the Internet to find prices for similar features for
computers manufactured by different companies. Using the features you learned in this tutorial, create
a worksheet that allows you to compare multiple computers on the same worksheet. Use a combo box
to change the loan interest rate you have to pay for financing the purchase. Link the down payment,
number of years, and interest rates to cells that can vary. Format the worksheet in an attractive
manner. Enter your name and the current date in a header and print the worksheet. Save the workbook
as Computer Comparisons.

Creating and Using Lists and Web Pages

LAB 6

objectives

After completing this lab, you will know how to:

1.	Create a list.
2.	Use a data form to add records.
3.	Create and use hyperlinks.
4.	Save a workbook in a new folder.
5.	Find and Replace information.
6.	Sort data.
7.	Filter records.
8.	Print selected areas.
9.	Save a worksheet as a Web page.

Creating a list is useful for organizing related information.

Using a data form speeds up entering and locating records in a list.

Sorting the information in a list displays the information you need in the specified order, alphabetically, numerically or by date.

Downtown Internet Café

The form you created to track the Downtown Internet Café's customer Internet connection times and Bonus Dollar awards is working quite well. Evan would now like to have a separate worksheet that contains the café customers' contact information so that he can use it to send out the Bonus Dollars discount coupons. This type of information can be entered into a worksheet as a list. While using Excel to create the list, you will learn about locating, modifying, ing, sorting, and filtering records in the list.

Now you have two workbooks containing data pertaining to

the Downtown Internet Café customers. To make it easier to work with the two workbooks, you will create a hyperlink in one workbook to open the other workbook. You will also save them to a separate folder.

The second project Evan has asked you to look into is to make the Bonus Dollars worksheet available to customers on the Web site to check their award status. To do this you will convert it to a Web page. A printout of a filtered list and the Bonus Dollars Web page are shown on the preceding page.

© Corbis

concept overview

The following concepts will be introduced in this lab:

1	**List**	A list or database is an organized collection of related information that is entered into a series of worksheet rows and columns.
2	**Find and Replace**	The Find and Replace feature helps you quickly find specific information and automatically replace it with new information.
3	**Sort**	You can sort data in a specified sequence, alphabetically, numerically, or by date.
4	**Filter**	A filter is a restriction you place on records in a list to quickly isolate and display a subset of records.
5	**Web Page**	A Web page is a document that can be used on the World Wide Web (WWW) and displayed in a browser.

Creating a List

You want to create an Excel worksheet that will contain the café's customer contact information and Internet connection times. In order to manipulate the data the way you want to, you decide to format this worksheet as a list.

concept 1

List

1 A **list** or **database** is an organized collection of related information that is entered into a series of worksheet rows and columns. Each row contains a **record**, which is all the information about one person, thing, or place. Each column is a **field**, which is the smallest unit of information about a record.

The first row in a list must contain column labels that serve as field names. A **field name** is a descriptive label used to identify the data stored in the field. The field names are used to create reports and find and organize data stored in the list. All other contiguous rows contain the records. The area containing the records is called the **list range**.

You have already entered many of the field names to create the structure for the list and have saved it in a workbook file named Customer List.

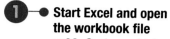

1 → **Start Excel and open the workbook file** ex06_Customer List.

Your screen should be similar to Figure 6.1

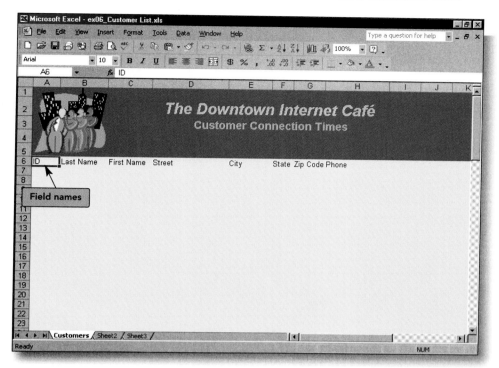

Figure 6.1

Additional Information

If you use the same combination of formats frequently, you may want to define the combination as a style by assigning it a name using Format/Style. Then it can be quickly applied like any other style. Styles can be deleted just as easily by selecting the style name and clicking Delete.

Row 6 contains the field names for the customer information that will be entered in the list.

Defining Field Names

You decide to change the phone field to a field for each customer's e-mail address. Additionally, you still need to add field names for the months that will be used to record the monthly connection times for each customer. In addition, it is a good idea to use formatted column labels for field names to help differentiate the labels from the data in the list. You will center, bold, and add a blue fill color to all the field name labels.

1 Replace the entry in H6 with **E-mail**.

Additional Information
Field names must be text entries.

● Enter **Jan** in cell I6.

● Drag the fill handle of cell I6 to extend the range through December (cell T6).

● Center, bold, and add the Pale Blue fill to the entire range A6 through T6.

● Move to A6.

Your screen should be similar to Figure 6.2

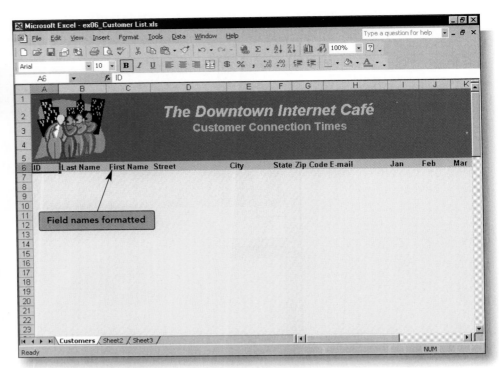

Figure 6.2

You are now ready to begin entering the information for the first record in row 7.

Entering Records

You have the customer information and connection time data for the first two months of the year and want to enter this information into the list range. The first record in the list must begin in the row immediately below the row of field names. Although you can enter the record information by typing it directly in the cells, Excel includes a special form, called a **data form**, that makes it easy to enter database records. Excel generates the data form from the field labels. When using the data form, the cell selector must be on any cell in the row containing the field labels in order to identify the location of the labels.

1 ● Choose **D**ata/F**o**rm.

● Click [OK] to use the first row in the selection as the labels.

Your screen should be similar to Figure 6.3

Figure 6.3

Notice that the Data Form dialog box has the name of the worksheet as its title and the column labels as its field names. In the text box to the right of each label, you enter the record information for that field.

When entering the data in a list, it is important that the data are entered consistently. For example, if you abbreviate the word "Street" as "St", it should be abbreviated in the same way for each record where it appears. Also be careful not to include blank spaces before or after an entry as this can cause problems when trying to locate information in the list. When a field entry is complete, use [Tab ⇥] to move to the next field entry box or click on the box you want to move to. Use [⇧ Shift] + [Tab ⇥] to move to a previous box. Do not use the [↓] and [↑] keys to move within the data form as this will display the next or previous record or a blank new form.

2 → Enter the information shown to the right for the first record.

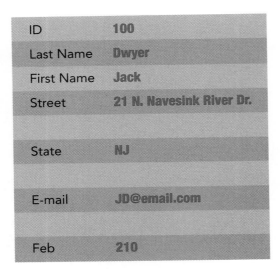

ID	100
Last Name	Dwyer
First Name	Jack
Street	21 N. Navesink River Dr.
State	NJ
E-mail	JD@email.com
Feb	210

HAVING TROUBLE?

If you press ↓ a new record form is displayed. Press ↑ or Find Prev to return to the previous record.

Additional Information

Connection time is recorded in minutes.

Your screen should be similar to Figure 6.4

Figure 6.4

The data for the first record is complete. You will add it to the list and display another blank entry form to add the information for another record. You will add three more records and then you will close the data form.

3 ● Click [New].

Another Method

You can also press Enter or ↓ to move to a new entry form if you are on the last record.

● Enter the information shown to the right for the next three records.

Additional Information

While you are adding a record, you can make changes and correct mistakes. You can also undo all changes by clicking [Restore], as long as you do it before clicking [New] or closing the data form.

	Record 2	Record 3	Record 4
ID	101	102	103
Last Name	Hamlin	Brown	Thomas
First Name	Rose	Sara	Grant
Street	7 Church St.	1005 First Ave.	159 Branch Ave.
City	Dayton	Albany	Red Bank
State	OH	NY	NJ
Zip	73094	20203	07730
Phone	RH@email.com	SB@email.com	GT@email.com
Jan	270	299.5	38
Feb		330	62

● Click [Close].

● Best-fit the Street column width so that the entire data entry is visible.

● Move to G.

Your screen should look similar to Figure 6.5

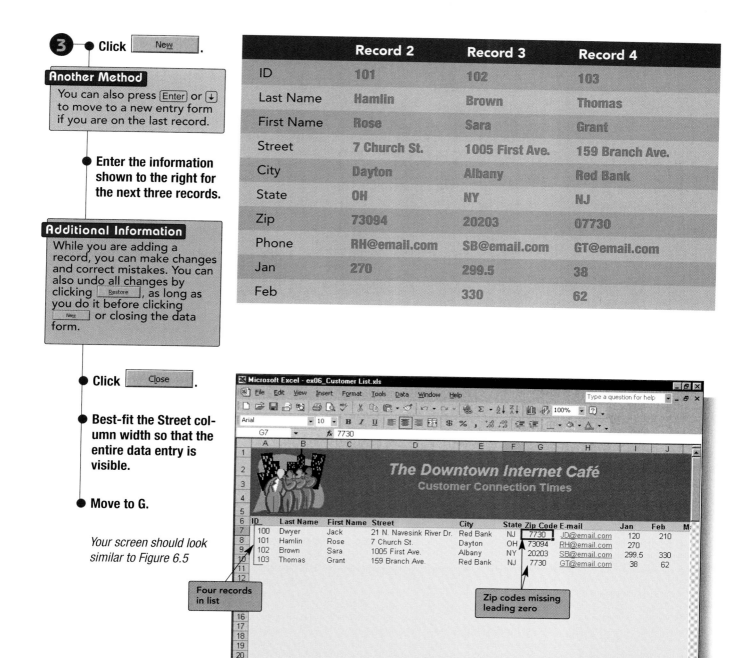

Four records in list

Zip codes missing leading zero

Figure 6.5

The field information for the first four records is displayed in the list range.

Editing Records

Notice that the zip codes for the first and last records do not display the leading zero (07730). This is because Excel drops leading zeros for numeric data. Since this field will not be used in calculations, you can change the format for the field to text so that numeric entries will appear as entered. Since you will be adding many more records to the database, you will extend the format for this field beyond the records that are currently entered.

- Select the range G7 through G30.

- Choose **F**ormat/C**e**lls.

- Open the Number tab.

- Select Special from the **C**ategory list.

Your screen should look similar to Figure 6.6

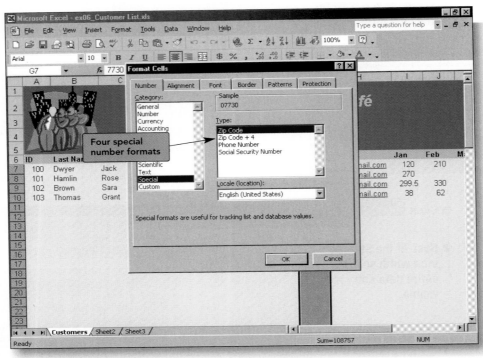

Figure 6.6

There are four special formats that are designed particularly for use in lists where numeric data is frequently entered but not used for calculations. You want to format the selection to the standard zip code format.

- From the **T**ype list box, select Zip Code

- Click OK .

Your screen should look similar to Figure 6.7

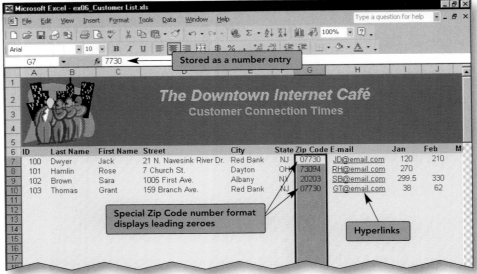

Figure 6.7

The number entries appear as they were entered because they are formatted as a special number entry. However, the entries are stored as numbers without the zero.

Working with Hyperlinks

Notice the addresses in the E-mail column are underlined and in blue. This is because they were automatically identified as an e-mail address and formatted as a hyperlink. A **hyperlink** is a connection to a location in the current document, in another document, or to a Web site. It allows the user to jump to the referenced location by clicking on the hyperlink text when reading the document on the screen.

Another Method

You can also use Tools/ Autocorrect Options and clear the "Internet and network paths with hyperlinks" option in the AutoFormat As You Type tab.

The automatic identification of Internet or network paths and the conversion to hyperlinks is a feature common to all Office programs. Sometimes you may not want the item to be automatically formatted as a hyperlink. You can turn off this feature using **S**top Automatically Creating Hyperlink from the 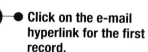 AutoCorrect Options button menu. You can also remove the hyperlink autoformatting from an individual cell by selecting **R**emove Hyperlink from the shortcut menu.

Using a Hyperlink

In this case, clicking on the hyperlink opens a new e-mail message window to allow you to send a message to the address. You think this would be a pretty convenient method of notifying customers of special sales as well as their Bonus Dollar status.

1 ● **Click on the e-mail hyperlink for the first record.**

Additional Information

The mouse pointer appears as 🖑 when pointing to a hyperlink.

Your screen should be similar to Figure 6.8

Clicking e-mail address hyperlink opens New Message window

HAVING TROUBLE?

Your new message window may be different than shown depending on the e-mail program on your system.

Figure 6.8

The new message window for the e-mail application on your system opens and is already addressed to the selected address. You will learn more about e-mailing in the Working Together 2 lab.

To select a cell containing a hyperlink without activating the hyperlink, click and hold on the cell until the mouse pointer changes to ✛ to indicate it will select the cell rather than jumping to the hyperlink destination.

2 ● Click ✕ Close to close the New Message window.

● If necessary, click No to discard the message.

● Point to cell H8.

Additional Information

A ScreenTip appears when you point to a hyperlink with instructions on how to follow a link or select the cell.

● Click and hold on cell H8.

Your screen should look similar to Figure 6.9

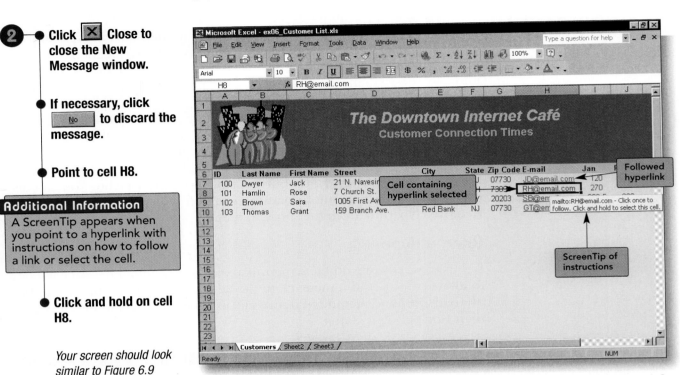

Figure 6.9

The cell containing the hyperlink is now selected and can be edited as needed. Notice that the color of the hyperlink you used in cell H7 is purple and the color of the hyperlink in the other cells is the default color of blue. The change in color indicates the link has been followed.

Creating a Hyperlink between Workbooks

Now that you see how convenient the hyperlink will be, you decide to add a hyperlink from the customer list worksheet to the Bonus Dollars workbook (created in Lab 5. Adding this hyperlink will make it easy to switch to the appropriate sheet in the Bonus Dollars workbook and copy the customers' total monthly connection times into the list. You will link to the Bonus Dollars workbook file and will display the hyperlink in cell K5, above the March column of data.

1 ● Move to K5.

● Click 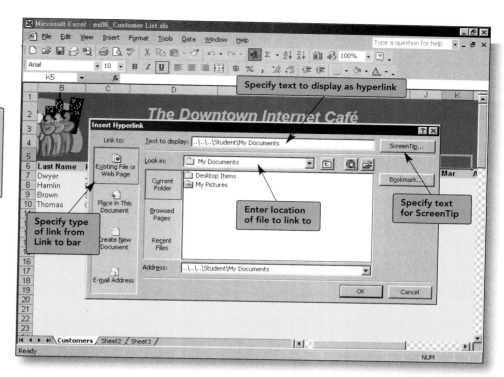 **Insert Hyperlink**

Another Method
The menu equivalent is Insert/Hyperlink and the keyboard shortcut is Ctrl + K. You can also select Hyperlink from a cell's shortcut menu.

Your screen should be similar to Figure 6.10

Figure 6.10

From the Insert Hyperlink dialog box, you first need to specify the type of link from the Link to bar. The four options are described below.

Option	Effect
E**x**isting File or Web Page	Creates a link in an existing Web page or file
Pl**a**ce in This Document	Creates a link to a place in the active file
Create **N**ew Document	Creates a link to a file that you have not created yet
E-**m**ail Address	Creates a link that allows users to create an e-mail message with the correct address in the To line

You want to create a link to a location in another workbook file.

2 ● If necessary, select Existing File or Web Page from the Link to bar.

● Specify the location of your Excel solution files in the Look in location.

● Select Bonus Dollars from the file list.

Next, you want to enter the text that the hyperlink will display in the work-sheet. If you do not enter anything in the "Text to Display" box, the hyper-link automatically displays the path of the linked file. You will also put instructions in the hyperlink ScreenTip.

3 ● Replace the entry in the Text to Display text box with March.

● Click ScreenTip... .

● Type Click to open the March Bonus Dollars worksheet.

● Click OK .

Your screen should be similar to Figure 6.11

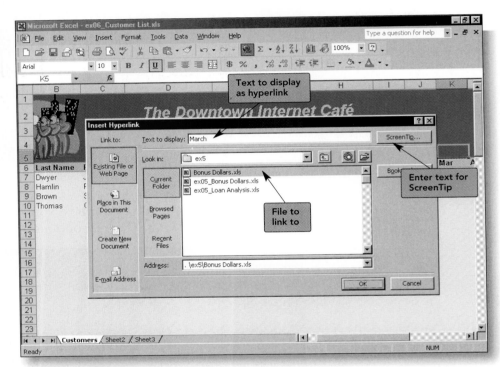

Figure 6.11

In the future, as you record each month's bonus dollar awards using the Monthly Bonus Form template, you plan to maintain the completed monthly worksheets in a single workbook file. When the workbook contains many worksheets, you will want to make sure that the user is taken directly to the worksheet containing the data for the appropriate month. To do this, you cre-ate a bookmark to that location in the linked workbook file.

4 ● Click [Bookmark...].

● If necessary, click [Enable Macros].

Your screen should be similar to Figure 6.12

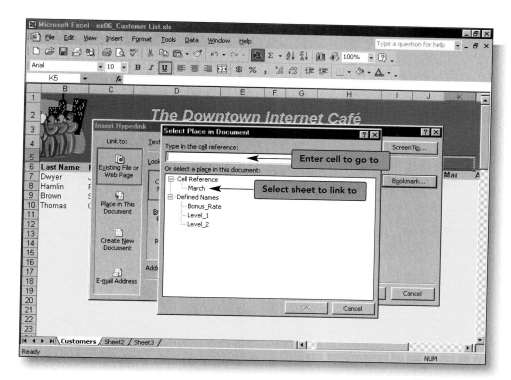

Figure 6.12

In the Select Place in Document dialog box you select a specific location to which you want the user to be taken in the linked document. The list box displays a tree diagram showing the outline of the information in the workbook and named ranges. From the outline, you select the location to which you want to link. In this case, you want the cell pointer positioned on the first customer's total connection time data (G12).

5 ● Select March in the Cell Reference list.

● In the Type in the Cell Reference text box, enter **G12**.

● Click [OK] to close the Select Place in Document dialog box.

● Click [OK] to close the Insert Hyperlink dialog box.

● Point to cell K5.

Your screen should be similar to Figure 6.13

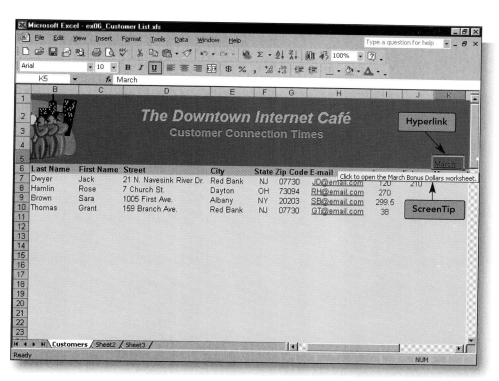

Figure 6.13

The text you entered for the hyperlink is displayed in the cell. It appears underlined and in the default hyperlink colors. The ScreenTip displays the text you entered. Because the hyperlink text is difficult to see, you will first change the text color and bold the entry. Then you will use the hyperlink.

6 ● Change the font color of cell K5 to dark gold and bold.

● Click on the hyperlink.

● If necessary, click Enable Macros **.**

Your screen should be similar to Figure 6.14

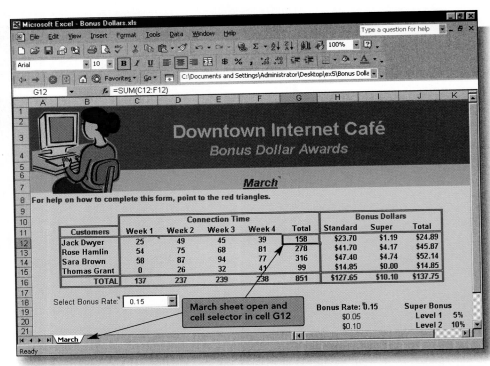

Figure 6.14

The Bonus Dollars workbook is open and the cell selector is in the location you specified as the bookmark. The user can now copy the customer monthly Internet connection totals from the Bonus form to the Customers worksheet.

Once both workbooks are open, you can switch back and forth between them or tile the two workbooks so that you can see them both simultaneously. You will tile the windows and copy the March total values into the list.

7 Choose Window/**A**rrange/**T**iled

• Scroll the Bonus Dollars sheet to display column G.

• Copy the total values in cells G12:G15.

• Scroll the Customer List worksheet to see column K.

• Paste the copied values into cells K7:K10.

• From the 📋 Paste Options button, select **V**alues only.

Your screen should be similar to Figure 6.15

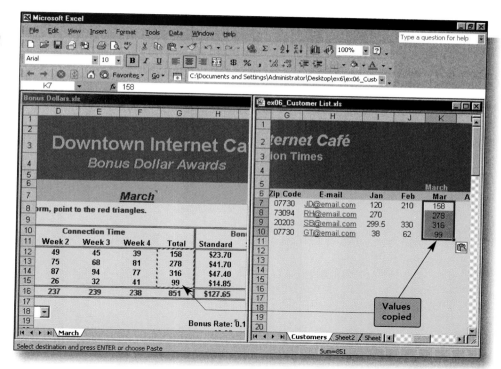

Figure 6.15

Saving to a New Folder

Since the workbooks you have been creating recently are to track customer information, you decide to save them in a separate folder from the rest of the café's financial workbooks. You will save the ex06_Customer List file as Customer1 to a new folder named Café Customers.

1 Choose **F**ile/Save **A**s.

• Type **Customer1** as the File name.

• If necessary, change the location to where you save your files.

• Click 📁 Create New Folder in the Save As dialog box.

Your screen should be similar to Figure 6.16

Figure 6.16

The New Folder dialog box enables you to create and name a new folder.

② ● Type **Café Customers** in the Name text box.

● Click [OK].

● Click [Save].

Your screen should be similar to Figure 6.17

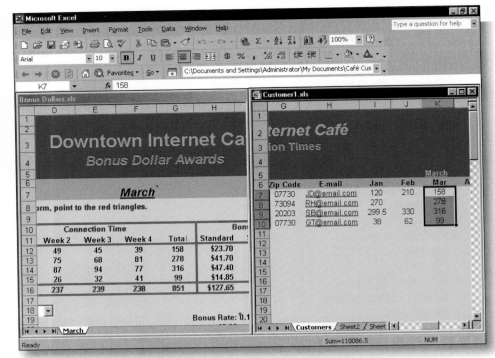

Figure 6.17

The Customer1 workbook is saved in the new folder.

③ ● Save the Bonus Dollars **workbook to the new folder.**

● Close the Bonus Dollars **workbook.**

● Close the Customer1 **workbook.**

● Turn off the display of the Web toolbar.

Finding and Replacing Information

You have continued to work on the café customer list by adding additional records. You will open the workbook file and continue working on the list.

1 ● Open the workbook
file ex06_Customers2.

● Maximize the window.

● Use the data form to
add your data to the
list as a new record
using ID number **999**.
Enter connection times
of **210**, **270**, and **240**
for the Jan, Feb, and
Mar fields. All other
information can be
fictitious.

● Close the data form.

● Scroll to see your
record in row 40.

*Your screen should be
similar to Figure 6.18*

	A	B	C	D	E	F	G	H	I	J
21	114	Morgan	Dan	564 S. Lemon Dr.	Red Bank	NJ	07730	DM@email.com	115	95
22	115	Lopez	Mina	4290 E. Alameda Dr.	Long Branch	NJ	07735	ML@email.com	190	120
23	116	Sitzman	Georgia	94 Evergreen Ave.	Albany	NY	20203	GS@email.com	210	245
24	117	Merwin	Adda	947 S. Forest	St. Paul	MN	47088	AM@email.com	300	
25	118	Switzer	Jon	32 W. Orange St.	Winfield	IL	60790	JS@email.com		60
26	119	Bloomquist	William	43 Kings Rd.	Little Silver	NJ	07739	WB@email.com	175	120
27	120	Brett	Anna	23 Suffolk Ln.	Holmdel	NJ	07734	AB@email.com	150	267
28	121	Shoemaker	Wendy	858 E. Mt. Aire Ct.	Poughkipsie	NY	12590	WS@email.com		89
29	122	Facqur	Daniel	5832 Fremont St.	Long Branch	NJ	07735	DF@email.com	150	150
30	123	Simson	Marge	432 Tercera Dr.	E. Aurora	NY	14052	MS@email.com	90	150
31	124	Briggs	Scott	45 E. Camelback Rd.	Scottsdale	AZ	85230	SB@email.com	110	150
32	125	Howard	Karen	9423 S. Forest Ave.	Hartford	CT	31922	KH@email.com		270
33	126	Lawrence	Nichol	433 S. Gaucho Dr.	Holmdel	NJ	07734	NL@email.com	300	
34	127	Robertson	Kirk	832 S. William Ave.	Poughkipsie	NY	12590	KR@email.com	89	110
35	128	Falk	Nancy	9483 W. Island Dr.	Long Branch	NJ	07735	NF@email.com	270	210
36	129	Brown	Jill	4344 W. Gala Ln.	Rochester	NY	14892	JB@email.com	235	145
37	130	Ingles	Raya	8432 N. Cimarron	Scottsdale	AZ	85230	RI@email.com	360	268
38	131	Roman	Anita	2348 S. Bala Dr.	St. Paul	MN	47088	AR@email.com	30	55
39	132	Matsumoto	Scott	34 S. Onza Ave.	Mesa	AZ	85202	SM@email.com	120	90
40	999	Name	Student	850 S. River Dr.	Tempe	AZ	85201	SN@email.com	210	270

New record

Figure 6.18

As you look over the records in the list and check the information against
the customer registration information, you notice that the address for one
of the café's customers, Frank Liston, was entered incorrectly. The street
address should be 3021 Ash St. instead of 302. You have also been notified
of a zip code change; 07730 is now 07732. Also, the January connection
time for Jill Brown should be 135, not 235.

You could correct the data just by changing the appropriate cells directly
on the worksheet. However, the larger your list becomes, the more difficult
it will be to find the data you want to modify. Therefore, you'll practice
using the other data location and modification methods to make the necessary changes.

concept 2

Find and Replace

2 The **Find and Replace** feature helps you quickly
find specific information and automatically replace it with new information. The Find command
locates all occurrences of the text or numbers you
specify. The Replace command is used with the
Find command to locate the specified entries
and replace the located occurrences with the re-

placement text you specify. You can also find
cells that match a format you specify and replace
the format with another. Finding and replacing
data and formats is both fast and accurate, but
you need to be careful when replacing that you
do not replace unintended matches.

Finding Information

First, you will locate and correct the incorrect data using the Find command. This command can be used to locate data in any type of worksheet, not just in a list.

1 ● **Choose Edit/Find.**

Another Method
The keyboard shortcut is Ctrl + F.

● **If necessary, click** Options >> **to display the additional search options.**

Your screen should be similar to Figure 6.19

Figure 6.19

In the Find and Replace dialog box, you enter the information you want to locate in the Fi**n**d what text box. It must be entered exactly as it appears in the worksheet.

The additional options in the Find dialog box can be combined in many ways to help locate information. They are described in the table below.

Option	Effect
Within	Searches the active worksheet or workbook.
Search	Specifies the direction to search in the worksheet: By Columns searches down through columns and By Rows searches to the right across rows.
Look in	Looks for a match in the specified worksheet element; formulas, values, comments.
Match case	Finds words that have the same pattern of uppercase letters as entered in the Find what text box. Using this option makes the search **case sensitive**.
Match entire cell contents	Looks for an exact and complete match of the characters specified in the Find what text box.
Format	Used to specify a cell format to locate and replace. A sample of the selected format is displayed in the Preview box.

To enter the address to find and to search using the default options,

2 ● Type **302 ash** in the **Find** what box.

Additional Information
Because the Match Case option is not selected, Find will look for an exact match regardless of whether the characters are uppercase or lowercase.

● Click **Options <<** to hide the additional search options.

● Click **Find Next**.

Your screen should be similar to Figure 6.20

Additional Information
Clicking **Find All** displays all text or format matches in a list. Selecting an item from the list moves the cell selector to the cell containing the entry.

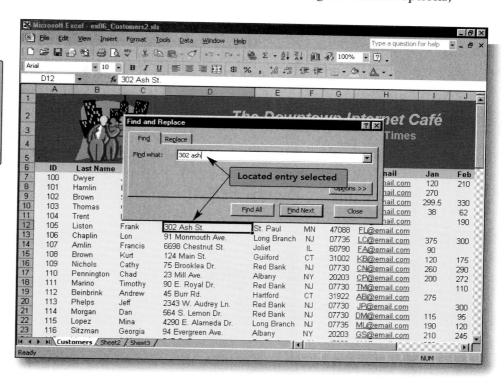

Figure 6.20

The cell containing this entry is located and displayed. You can now edit the cell to display the correct address information.

3 ● Double-click on the cell.

● Change the address to **3021 Ash St.**

Your screen should be similar to Figure 6.21

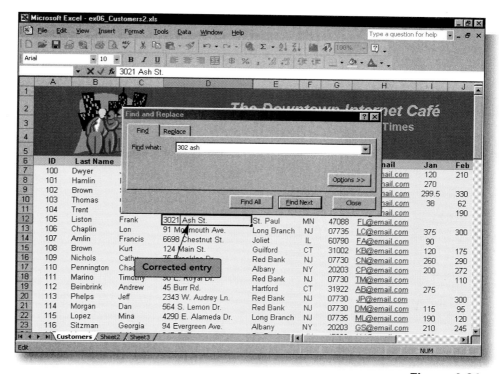

Figure 6.21

Replacing Information

Next, you'll use the Replace command to update the zip code. Once again, this command can be used on any type of worksheet to change cell data. The replacement text must be entered exactly as you want it to appear.

1 ● Open the Replace tab.

Another Method

The menu equivalent is Edit/Replace and the keyboard shortcut is Ctrl + H.

● Type 7730 in the Find what box.

Additional Information

You do not enter the leading zero in the zip code to find because the values are stored without the zero.

● Type 07732 in the Replace with box.

● Click Find Next .

● Click Replace .

Your screen should be similar to Figure 6.22

Figure 6.22

The original zip code entry is replaced with the new zip code. The program immediately continues searching and locates a second occurrence of the entry. You decide the search is locating the values accurately and that it will be safe to replace all finds with the replacement value.

2 — Click [Replace All].

— Click [OK].

— Click [Close].

Your screen should be similar to Figure 6.23

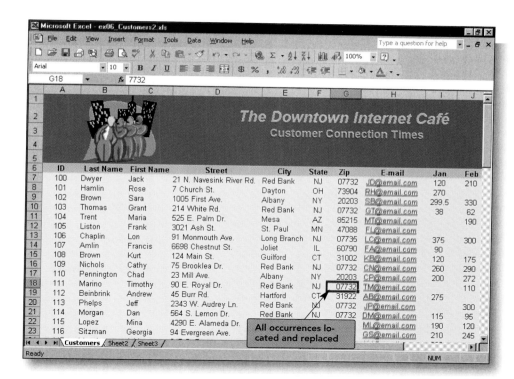

Figure 6.23

All matches are replaced with the replacement text and the dialog box is closed. It is much faster to use Replace All than to confirm each match separately. However, exercise care when using Replace All because the search text you specify might be part of another word and you may accidentally replace text you want to keep.

Using the Data Form to Locate and Change Data

Since the data you are working with has been defined as a database list, you can also use the Data Form to find and modify records. You'll use this method to make the final change to your data, correcting the connection time for Jill Brown.

1 ● Choose **D**ata/F**o**rm.

● Click [**Criteria**] .

*Your screen should be
similar to Figure 6.24*

Blank data form
used to enter
criteria to locate

Figure 6.24

A blank data form is displayed in which you can enter the **criteria** or conditions for the record to meet in order to be located. The more precise and unique the criteria you enter, the fewer matches will be located. In this case, you'll enter the customer's last name, Brown, to locate and display the record for Jill Brown.

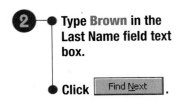

2 ● Type **Brown** in the
Last Name field text
box.

● Click [Find **N**ext] .

*Your screen should be
similar to Figure 6.25*

First record
located with a last
name of Brown

Figure 6.25

Additional Information

You could refine the search by entering additional information in other fields, such as Jill in the First name field; then only records meeting all criteria will be located.

The first located record with a last name of Brown, Sara Brown, is displayed in the data form. Because there are several records with a last name of Brown, the located record is not the record you want to edit. You want to find the record for Jill Brown.

3 ● Click [Find Next] two more times until Jill Brown's record is displayed.

● Double-click the Jan field text box to highlight the current value, 235.

● Type **135**.

● Click [Close].

● Scroll the list to see Jill Brown's record in row 36.

Your screen should be similar to Figure 6.26

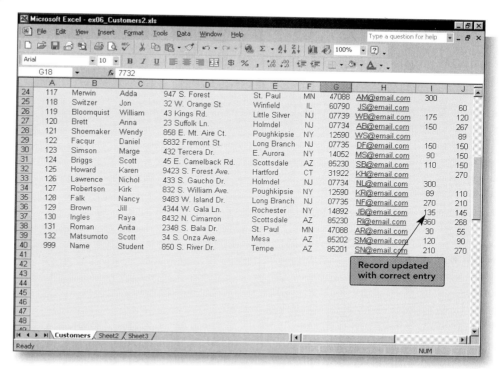

Figure 6.26

The record for Jill Brown is updated and now contains the correct value, 135, in the January connection time field.

Now that your data entries are error-free, you're ready to move on to sorting the data in a logical order.

Sorting Data

Currently, the records in the list are in the order in which you entered them. However, you feel that they would be easier to work with if they were displayed in alphabetical order by last name. To do this, you can sort the records in the list.

Sort

3 You can **sort** data in a specified sequence, alphabetically, numerically, or by date. Sorting data often helps you find specific information quickly. The data in a worksheet can be sorted into ascending (A to Z, 1 to 9, earliest date to most recent date) or descending (Z to A, 9 to 1, most recent date to earliest date) order. When you sort, Excel rearranges the rows, columns, fields, or individual cells according to the sort order you specify.

A single sort operation can be based on up to three columns or fields of data. When a sort is done on more than one column or field, it is called a **multilevel sort**. For example, if you wanted to rearrange a list of employee data to begin with those who have worked for the company the longest, you could sort it in ascending order by date and then by name.

Sorting on a Single Field

For the first sort, you want the records arranged in ascending alphabetical order by last name. The cell selector needs to be in any cell in the field to be sorted.

1 ● **Move to cell B7.**

● **Click** **Sort Ascending.**

Your screen should be similar to Figure 6.27

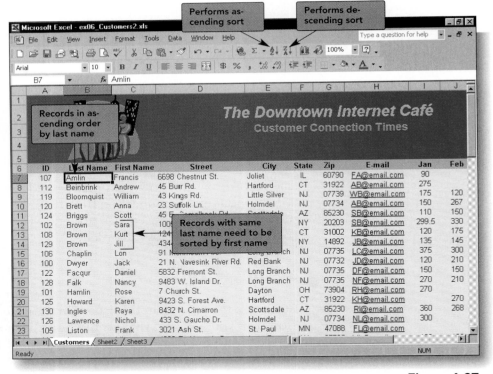

Figure 6.27

The records in the database range are rearranged to display in ascending alphabetical order by last name. However, notice that although the records for Sara, Kurt, and Jill Brown are sorted correctly by last name, they are not sorted correctly by first name.

Sorting on Multiple Fields

You want the records that have the same last name to be further sorted by first name. To do this, you will perform a multilevel sort.

1 ● Choose **D**ata/**S**ort.

Your screen should be similar to Figure 6.28

Figure 6.28

A multilevel sort uses the first field name selected in the Sort By section of the dialog box as the primary sort field; all other fields are sorted in order after the primary sort is performed. The Sort By text box correctly displays the name of the field on which the primary sort will be performed. Additionally, because the default setting is Ascending sort order, this option does not need to be changed. You need to specify the secondary sort field as the First Name field.

2 ● Select First Name from the first **Then by** drop-down list.

Your screen should be similar to Figure 6.29

Figure 6.29

Sorting Data   **EX6.27**

Excel 2002

When a sort is performed, Excel assumes that you want all data except the uppermost row contained in contiguous rows and columns surrounding the selected cell to be sorted. The first row is not included in the sort range because the default setting assumes that the first row contains column labels or field names that you do not want included in the sort. If your data did not include a column label or field name as the first row in the range, you would need to choose the No header ro**w** option to change the setting to include this row in the sort. Since this worksheet includes field names in the first row, the Header **r**ow option is correctly specified already.

3 ● Click [OK].

● Save the changes you have made to this workbook as Customers2 **to the Café Customers folder.**

Your screen should be similar to Figure 6.30

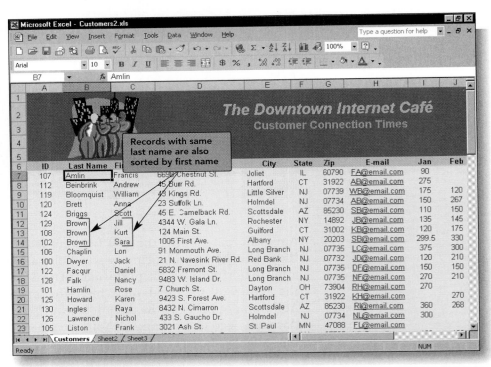

Figure 6.30

The records are now in sorted order first by last name and second by first name within same last names. As you can see, sorting is a fast, useful tool. The original sort order remains in effect until you replace it with a new sort order. If the order in which you enter records in a list is important, include a field for a unique record number. Then you can return to the entry order by sorting on the number field.

Filtering Data

Evan has informed you that he is sending out "valued customer" e-mail notes to the in-state customers who have been connecting at the café since the beginning of the year. He has asked you for a printout of the connection times and e-mail address information for those customers. Rather than creating a separate worksheet, you can filter the database range in the current worksheet to show only the requested records.

Filter

4 A **filter** is a restriction you place on records in the list to quickly isolate and display a subset of records. A filter is created by specifying a set of limiting conditions, or criteria, that you want records to meet in order to be displayed. A filter is ideal when you want to display the subset for only a brief time and then return immediately to the full set of records. You can print the filtered records as you would any worksheet. A filter is only temporary, and all records are redisplayed when you remove the filter.

Unlike the Sort feature, the Filter feature does not rearrange a list. It just temporarily hides rows that do not meet the specified criteria. Data in a filtered list can be edited, formatted, charted, or printed.

Filtering on a Single Criteria

You will filter the list to display only NJ residents first.

1 ● **Choose**
Data/Filter/AutoFilter.

Your screen should be similar to Figure 6.31

Drop-down list used to select filter criteria

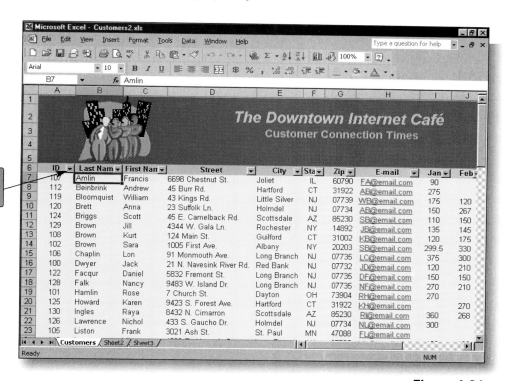

Figure 6.31

Drop-down list arrows appear next to each field name. These enable you to select the field or fields and field criteria you want to use to filter the list. The first criterion you want the records in your database range to meet is in the State field.

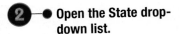

2 Open the State drop-down list.

Your screen should be similar to Figure 6.32

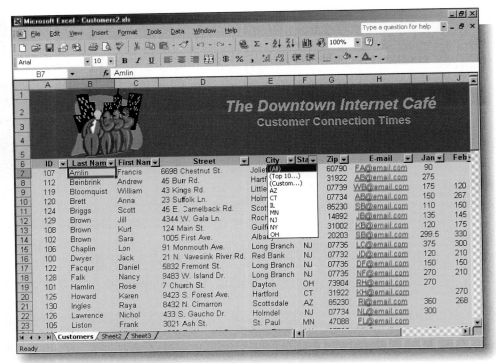

Figure 6.32

The drop-down list contains the current values in the field. In addition, you can select from these options:

Option	Effect
(All)	Displays all records regardless of the value in this field
(Top 10)	Displays the records with the highest values in this field
(Custom)	Used to specify ranges of values that a record must meet to be displayed
(Blanks)	Displays only those records that do not contain a value in this field
(NonBlanks)	Displays only those records that contain a value in this field

You want to specify that only records that have a state value of NJ are displayed.

3 ● Choose NJ from the drop-down list.

Your screen should be similar to Figure 6.33

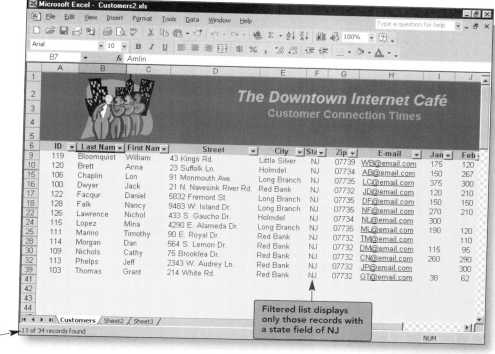

Number of records in filtered list

Filtered list displays only those records with a state field of NJ

Figure 6.33

Only those records for customers in New Jersey are displayed. However, not all of these customers have been online at the café all three months. Therefore, you want to specify further criteria to accept only "nonblanks" in the month field.

4 ● Open the Mar drop-down list.

● Choose (NonBlanks).

● In a similar manner, choose (NonBlanks) for January and February.

Your screen should be similar to Figure 6.34

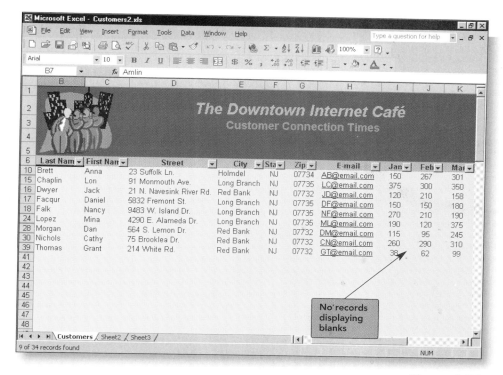

No records displaying blanks

Figure 6.34

Only the records that meet the specified criteria are displayed.

Creating a Custom Filter

You would also like to see the same information for the other out-of-state customers. To do this, you could change the State criteria and print each filter result. However, a faster way is to create a custom filter for the State field.

1 ● **From the State drop-down list, select (Custom...).**

Your screen should be similar to Figure 6.35

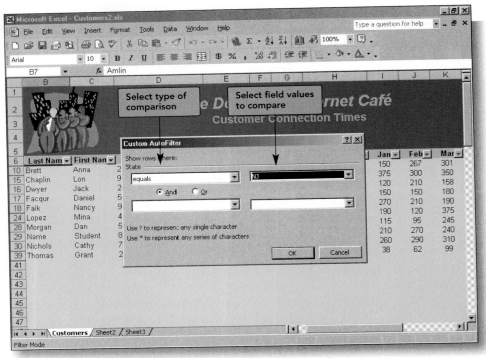

Figure 6.35

The Custom AutoFilter dialog box is used to specify a filtering operation that makes comparisons between two values. The type of comparison to make is specified in the box on the left, and the value to compare to is specified in the box on the right. You can include a second set of criteria by selecting the **A**nd or **O**r options and specifying the settings in the lower row of boxes. The AND and OR operators are used to specify multiple conditions that must be met for the records to display in the filtered list. The AND operator narrows the search, because a record must meet both conditions to be included. The OR operator broadens the search, because any record meeting either condition is included in the output.

· You want to display records for all states except New Jersey.

2 From the box on the left, select Does Not Equal from the drop-down list of operations.

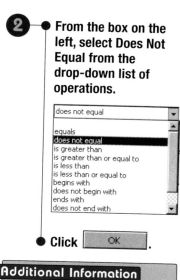

Click [OK].

Additional Information
Your record may appear in the filtered list if your state field entry is not NJ.

Your screen should be similar to Figure 6.36

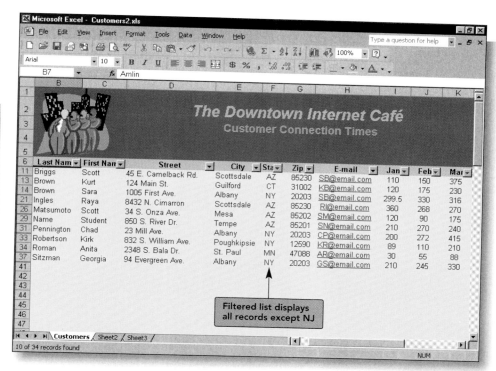

Figure 6.36

Now the filtered list displays records for all states except New Jersey that have connection time usage in all three months. As expected, only a few out-of-state customers meet this requirement.

Printing Selected Areas

You are finished filtering the data, and you've got the information Evan requested. However, you do not want the worksheet printout to include the months that do not yet have any connection data in them, so you will set a **print area** that specifies the area of the worksheet to print. The print area can be one or more ranges of cells.

Setting a Print Area

You will include only the list fields through March. To define a print area, you first select the cell range that you want to print.

1
- Select NJ from the AutoFilter drop-down list to display the NJ records again.

- Select A6 through column K of the last row of displayed records.

- Choose <u>F</u>ile/Print Area/<u>S</u>et Print Area.

Your screen should be similar to Figure 6.37

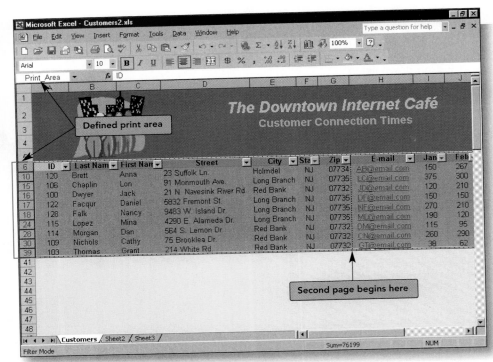

Figure 6.37

A print area is highlighted and a page break line shows where the selected range will print on a second page. You need to change the orientation to landscape so that the range will print on one page.

2
- Click ▣ Print Preview.

- Change the worksheet orientation to Landscape.

- Add a right-aligned header that displays **your name** and the **current date**, on a single line.

- If necessary, click Zoom to view the whole page.

Your screen should be similar to Figure 6.38

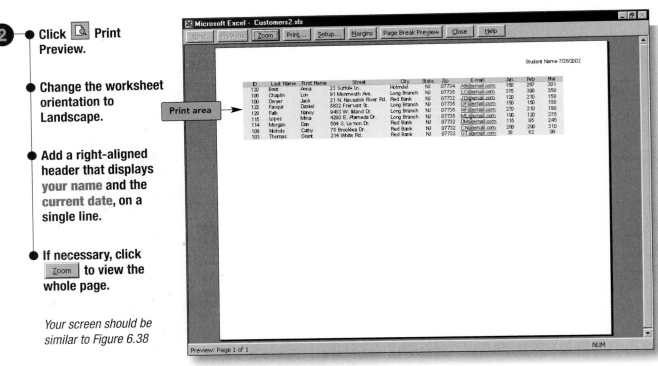

Figure 6.38

The preview window displays only the information contained in the defined print area. The print area is saved with the worksheet and will be used automatically whenever you print the worksheet.

Printing Nonadjacent Ranges

However, as you look at the preview, you realize Evan will not need the address information either, since the promotion is being sent by e-mail. You want to print the name fields and the e-mail address and connection time fields only. To do this, you select a range to print and use the Selection option in the Print dialog box to specify a temporary print area.

1 ● Close the preview window.

● Select A6 through the last row of records in column C and H6 through the last row of records in column K.

> **HAVING TROUBLE?**
> Hold down Ctrl to select nonadjacent ranges.

● Choose File/Print/Selection.

● Click Preview.

● Scroll down to see the second page.

Your screen should be similar to Figure 6.39

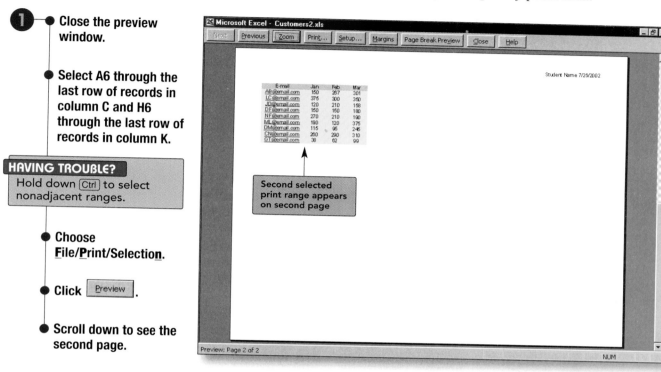

Figure 6.39

The first selection appears on the first page and the second selection on the second page. Each nonadjacent selection begins printing on a new page. To fix this, you need to hide the columns you do not want to print and then define a single print range.

2 ● Close the preview window.

● Select and hide columns D through G.

HAVING TROUBLE?
Use Format/Column/Hide to hide the selected columns.

● Select A6 through K39.

● Click 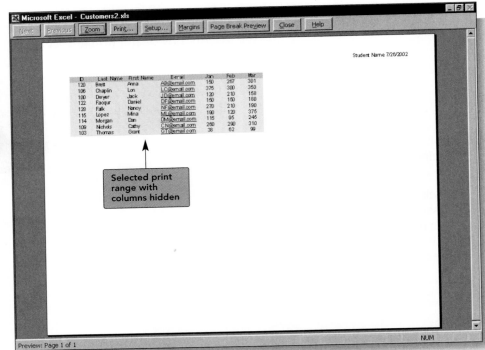 Print Preview.

Your screen should be similar to Figure 6.40

Figure 6.40

Finally, the printout is how you want it to appear, except you no longer need to use landscape orientation.

3 ● Change the orientation to Portrait.

● Center the worksheet horizontally on the page.

● Print the worksheet.

Additional Information
The AutoFilter drop-down buttons do not print.

Evan now has the information in the printout that he needs.

Clearing Print Areas

You can now unhide the columns and remove the AutoFilter from the database range and continue working on it.

1 ● **Unhide the columns.**

● **Choose Data/Filter/AutoFilter.**

● **Move to cell A7.**

Your screen should be similar to Figure 6.41

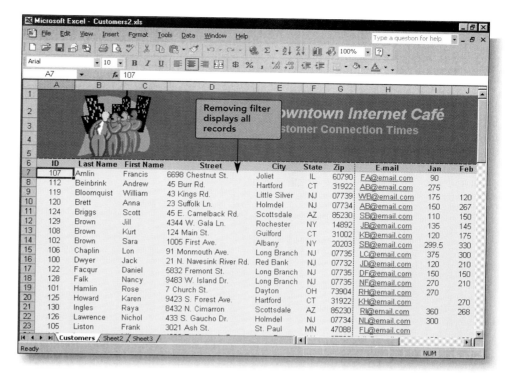

Figure 6.41

The filter is removed and all records are again displayed. The dotted lines indicate where a page break will occur when the worksheet is printed using the defined print area. Since the print area did not work for the data you wanted to print, you will remove it.

2 ● **Choose File/Print Area/Clear Print Area.**

● **Save the workbook.**

Your screen should be similar to Figure 6.42

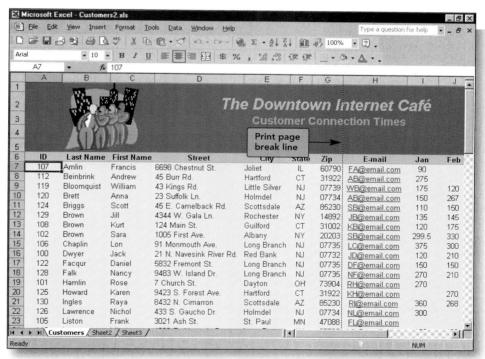

Figure 6.42

The single page break line indicates where the second page would begin if the entire worksheet were printed in portrait orientation.

Creating a Web Page

The second project Evan has asked you to look into is to make the Bonus Dollars worksheet available to customers on the Café's Web site so that they can check their award status. To do this, you will convert the Excel worksheet to a Web page.

---

concept 5

Web Page

5   A **Web page** is a document that can be used on the World Wide Web (WWW) and displayed in a browser. A **browser** is a program that connects to remote computers and displays the Web pages you request. The browser interprets the HTML commands that are included in the Web page in order to know how to display the page contents. **HTML (Hypertext Markup Language)** is a programming language used to create Web pages. HTML commands control the display of information on a page, such as font colors and sizes, and how an item will be processed. HTML also allows users to click on hyperlinks and jump to other locations on the same page, other pages in the same site, or to other sites and locations on the WWW.

Previewing the Web Page

Note: This section of the lab assumes that a Web browser is installed on your computer.

You have made several changes to the worksheet that were needed before it could be used on the Web. You replaced the Customer name with the ID number and removed the Select Bonus Rate combo box and the Print Command button from the form.

1 ● **Open the workbook file** ex06_Bonus Dollars Web.

Your screen should be similar to Figure 6.43

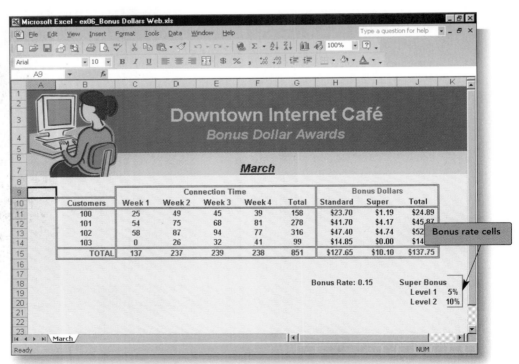

Figure 6.43

The only information remaining below the form are the Bonus Rate cells used to calculate the Bonus Dollars. Before you convert the worksheet, you want to preview how it will look first.

2 ● **Choose File/Web Page Preview**

● **Maximize the browser window.**

Your screen should be similar to Figure 6.44

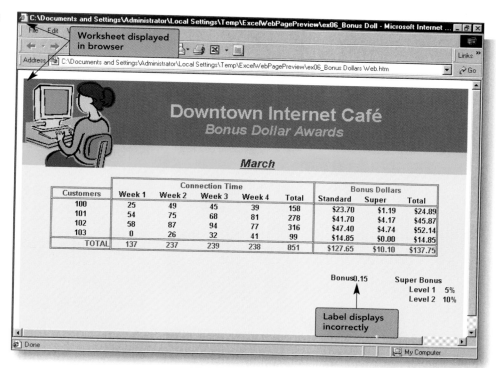

Figure 6.44

The browser opens on your system and displays the worksheet. The name of the worksheet appears in the browser window title bar. Most of the information looks pretty good, except for the display of the Bonus Rate label.

Saving the Worksheet as a Web Page

You will go ahead and convert the worksheet to a Web page and then make the needed adjustments.

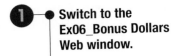

1 ● Switch to the Ex06_Bonus Dollars Web window.

HAVING TROUBLE?
Click on the appropriate button in the taskbar to display the worksheet or press [Alt] + [Tab] to display the previously viewed window.

● Choose **File/Save as Web Page.**

Your screen should be similar to Figure 6.45

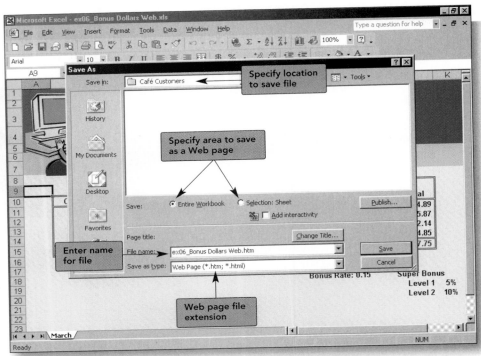

Figure 6.45

Additional Information
You can also preselect a range to use as the area to save as a Web page.

In the Save As dialog box, enter a name for the Web page file, choose the location where you want the file saved, and specify whether you want to use the entire workbook or just the current selection as your Web page contents. The default file name is the same as the workbook file name with the Web page file extension of .htm or html. Excel converts a worksheet to a Web page by adding hypertext markup language (HTML) coding to the document. You can also add a title to your Web page from this dialog box. You will specify the current worksheet as the contents for the Web page.

2

- Select Selection:Sheet.

- Change the file name to **March Bonus Dollars**.

- Specify the Café Customers folder as the location to save the file.

- Click ⟨ Save ⟩.

Your screen should be similar to Figure 6.46

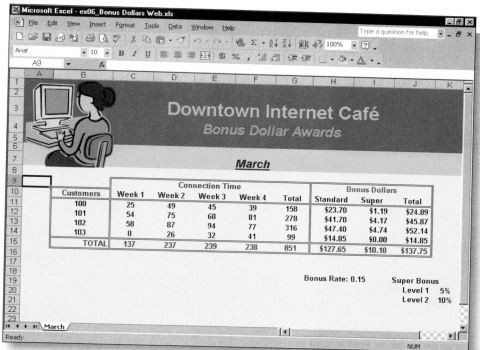

Figure 6.46

Next, you will make the changes to the Bonus Rate cell so that it displays correctly and then preview the Web page to check how it looks again.

3

- Move the contents of cell H18 to G18.

- Left-align the entry.

- Fix the fill color of cell H18.

- Format cell I18 as Currency with two decimal places.

- Choose **File/Web** Page Preview.

Your screen should be similar to Figure 6.47

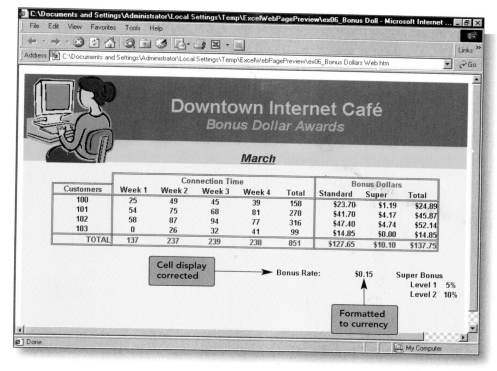

Figure 6.47

The revised worksheet is displayed in your browser window. You like the way this looks and need to resave the changes you made to the worksheet to update the Web page file.

- Close the browser application.

- Choose File/**S**ave as Web Page.

- Select R**e**publish:Sheet.

- Click [**S**ave].

- Close all open workbooks without saving changes and exit Excel.

Using Supporting Folders

Each Web page you create has a folder that contains all the elements on the page, such as images and hyperlinks.

You will use the Windows Exploring window to see the Web page and folder that were created.

- Open the Exploring window.

HAVING TROUBLE?
Select E**x**plore from the My Computer icon shortcut menu.

- Change the location to the location where you saved the Web page.

- Select the March Bonus Dollars.htm **file.**

Your screen should be similar to Figure 6.48

Figure 6.48

The Web page file and its supporting folder are saved in the Café Customers folder. By default, the name of the supporting folder is the name of the Web page plus an underscore (_) and the word "files." All supporting files, such as those for bullets, graphics, and background are contained in the supporting folder. Any graphics that were added to the page that were not already JPEG or GIF files are converted to that format. To see the files in the supporting folder,

2 ● **Open the** March Bonus Dollars_files **folder.**

● **If necessary, expand the Name column to fully display the file names.**

Your screen should be similar to Figure 6.49

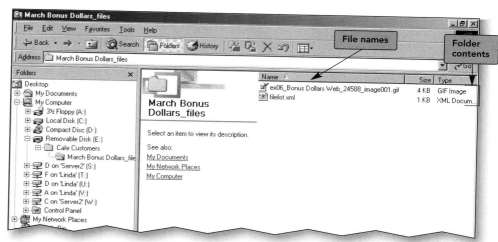

Figure 6.49

The Web page contains one graphic element. The graphic has been renamed "image001."

When you move your files to place on a server, you need to include the HTML file and the associated supporting folder that contains all the elements on the page. If this folder is not available when the associated HTML page is loaded in the browser, the graphic elements will not be displayed.

3 ● **Close the Exploring window.**

Discussion Comments

When working with a Web page or other Office file that can be opened with a browser, the **Web discussion** feature can be used. This feature allows users to attach comments to the document that can be read and responded to by all reviewers. The **discussion comments** are stored in a database on a discussion server and appear with the document. A **discussion server** is a computer that stores discussion text and information about the location of the file being discussed. The file must be available on the discussion server or another server location for access by all reviewers.

concept summary

LAB 6

Creating and Using Lists and Web Pages

List (EX6.4)

A list or database is an organized collection of related information entered in sequential rows and columns.

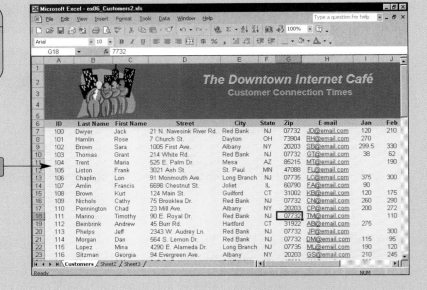

Find and Replace (EX6.19)

The Find and Replace feature helps you quickly find specific information and automatically replace it with new information.

lab review

Creating and Using Lists and Web Pages

key terms

browser   EX6.38
case sensitive   EX6.20
criteria   EX6.24
data form   EX6.6
database   EX6.4
discussion comments   EX6.43
discussion server   EX6.43

field   EX6.4
field name   EX6.4
filter   EX6.29
Find and Replace   EX6.19
HTML (Hypertext Markup Language)   EX6.38
hyperlink   EX6.11

list range   EX6.4
list   EX6.4
multilevel sort   EX6.26
print area   EX6.33
record   EX6.4
sort   EX6.26
Web Page   EX6.38

mous skills

The Microsoft Office User Specialist (MOUS) certification program is designed to measure your proficiency in performing basic tasks using the Office XP applications. Getting certified demonstrates that you have the skills and provides a valuable industry credential for employment. After completing this lab, you have learned the following Microsoft Office User Specialist skills:

Skill	Description	Page
Working with cells and cell data	Find and replace cell data and formats	EX6.19
	Work with a subset of data by filtering lists	EX6.29
Managing Workbooks	Manage workbook files and folders	EX6.17
Formatting and Printing Workbooks	Modify page setup options for worksheets	EX6.33
	Preview and print worksheets and workbooks	EX6.34
Workgroup Collaboration	Convert worksheets into Web pages	EX6.38
	Create hyperlinks	EX6.11
	View and edit comments	EX6.43

command summary

Command	Shortcut Key	Button	Action
File/Save as Web Page			Creates a Web page from the entire active workbook or the current worksheet selection
File/Web Page Preview			Displays the active workbook as a Web page in the browser without actually publishing it
File/Print Area/Set Print Area			Sets area of worksheet to be printed
File/Print Area/Clear Print Area			Clears print area
Edit/Find	Ctrl + F		Searches for a specified entry
Edit/Replace	Ctrl + H		Searches for a specified entry and replaces it with another specified entry
Insert/Hyperlink	Ctrl + K		Inserts a new hyperlink or modifies the selected hyperlink
Insert/Hyperlink/Remove Link			Removes hyperlink settings from selected cell
Tools/AutoCorrect Options/ AutoFormat As You Type/ Internet and network paths with hyperlinks			Turns on/off feature to automatically format Internet and network paths as hyperlinks
Format/Cells/Category/Special			Applies the selected special format to the number entries
Data/Sort			Arranges data alphabetically, numerically, or by date
Data/Filter/AutoFilter			Displays records based on specified criteria
Data/Form			Displays a data form dialog box for record entry and modification

Terminology

screen identification

In the following worksheet, several items are identified by letters.
Enter the correct term for each item in the spaces that follow.

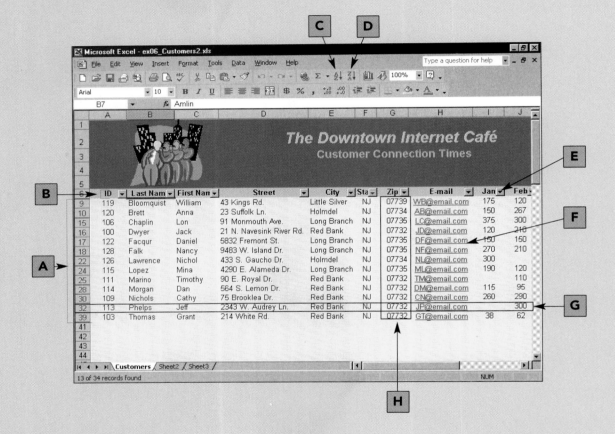

A. _____   E. _____

B. _____   F. _____

C. _____   G. _____

D. _____   H. _____

matching

Match the letter on the right to the item in the numbered list on the left.

1. Web page   _____ **a.** a connection to a location in another document

2. field   _____ **b.** displays a subset of records according to specified criteria

3. descending   _____ **c.** Web page programming language

4. filter   _____ **d.** Z to A order

5. list   _____ **e.** displayed in each row of a list

6. sort   _____ **f.** used to enter information in a list

7. hyperlink   _____ **g.** a document that can be displayed in a browser

8. record   _____ **h.** the smallest unit of information about a record

9. data form   _____ **i.** organizes data in a specified sequence

10. HTML   _____ **j.** a database

multiple choice

Circle the correct response to the questions below.

1. A _____ is one unit of information in a list.
   a. field
   b. record
   c. sort
   d. database

2. The _____ from the list appear as the column labels in a data form.
   a. record names
   b. column letters
   c. field names
   d. cell references

3. The sort feature lets you sort up to _____ fields in a list at a time.
   a. 2
   b. 1
   c. 3
   d. 4

4. The _____ option in a filter field drop-down list enables you to specify ranges of values that the record must meet to be displayed.
   a. Criteria
   b. Range
   c. Values
   d. Custom

5. The quickest way to locate a record in a large list is to use the _____ feature.
   a. Find
   b. Criteria
   c. Replace
   d. Sort

6. A sort that is performed on more than one column or field is called a:
   a. multiple sort
   b. advanced sort
   c. multi-level sort
   d. selective sort

7. Use a _____ to quickly jump to another location in a document.
   a. Web page
   b. hyperlink
   c. browser
   d. filter

8. The programming language used in Web pages is:
   a. HTLM
   b. HTXT
   c. HTML
   d. HXLS

9. To locate and change data in a list, use the_____.
   a. Find command
   b. Replace command
   c. Data form
   d. All of the above

10. To print nonadjacent ranges on the same page,
    a. move the columns between the areas you do not want to print and select the range
    b. select the nonadjacent ranges and print the selections
    c. define a print area
    d. hide the columns between the areas you do not want to print and select the range

true/false

Circle the correct answer to the following questions.

1. You can erase any changes you made to a record in the data form by clicking
   [↩▾], as long as you do it before proceeding to the next record or closing
   the dialog box.   True   False
2. A browser is used to display Web pages.   True   False
3. A print area is saved with the worksheet.   True   False
4. A data form cannot be used to locate records.   True   False
5. A sort displays a subset of records.   True   False
6. A filter rearranges data according to the criteria you specify.   True   False
7. A discussion comment is saved with the worksheet.   True   False

8. Field names are entered in the first row of a list. True False
9. Nonadjacent ranges can only be printed on separate pages. True False
10. You must first create a new folder in Windows Explorer before you can save a workbook in it. True False

Concepts

fill-in questions

Complete the following statements by filling in the blanks with the correct terms.

1. Converting a worksheet to a Web page changes the file type to _____.

2. A _____ is used to enter records into a list.

3. _____ adds drop-down lists to the field names in a list.

4. _____ a list to display records in a specified order.

5. _____ order displays records in Z to A alphabetical order.

6. Apply a _____ to a list to display a subset of records.

7. The two types of filter functions are _____ and _____.

8. Define a _____ to print the same selection each time you print the worksheet.

9. Use a _____ to specify operations that make comparisons between two values.

10. A _____ folder is created when you save a worksheet as a Web page.

discussion questions

1. Discuss different ways that an Excel list can be used.

2. Discuss the differences between the AutoFilter function and the Custom Filter function. When would you use AutoFilter? When would the custom filter be more appropriate?

3. Discuss how a worksheet is converted to a Web page and used.

Hands-On Exercises

step by step

Kodiak Construction Database

★ 1. The Kodiak Construction Company uses an Excel list to keep track of jobs for the year and the permit fees paid on them. They have asked you to do some analysis on the data so that they can better see trends and make any needed adjustments. Your completed analysis of the list will be similar to the one shown on the facing page.

   a. Open the workbook file ex06_Kodiak Database.
   b. Format the Phone field using the special phone number format.
   c. You have been given invoices for three new jobs. Using the data form, enter the following three new records into the database.

Job Number	04025	04026	04027
Date	04/23/04	04/26/04	04/28/04
Category	Residential	Residential	Commercial
Site Address	2983 Club House Dr	20234 Midway Ave	467 Broadway Rd
Contact	Leware, Edward	Williams, Gary	Student Name
Phone	555-1763	555-0031	555-2763
Permit Fees	$55.00	$350.00	$1,075.00

   d. Close the data form and scroll to the end of the list.
   e. The Accounting department has requested a list of jobs whose permit fees were more than $1000. Filter the database to display these records only. Print the filtered list in landscape orientation, centered horizontally.
   f. Marketing has also requested a copy of the job list sorted by category. Sort the list on Category. Print all the fields except the Permit Fees field.
   g. Change the layout to Portrait and include your name and the current date in the header.
   h. Save the workbook as Kodiak Database Update.

Job Number	Date	Category	Site Address	Contact	Phone
30055	01/11/04	Commercial	420 McCormick Dr	Forester, Kimberly	555-7521
09851	01/12/04	Commercial	639 Bear Claw Rd	Paul, Timothy	555-2454
98374	01/15/04	Commercial	33 Arrowhead Rd	Vaughn, James	555-7483
00983	02/13/04	Commercial	5623 Scott Dr	Anderson, Tom	555-2734
34592	02/16/04	Commercial	7020 Green Valley Way	Merwin, Michael	555-6853
46191	03/07/04	Commercial	23418 Placer Cr	Carothers, Daryl	555-1324
30141	03/09/04	Commercial	2351 Live Oak Dr	Ross, Cathy	555-4314
09834	03/10/04	Commercial	4512 Brandling Ave	Stansbury, Thomas	555-1287
00123	04/07/04	Commercial	41523 Mount Marapai Rd	Kenson, Lois	555-0267
92364	04/10/04	Commercial	1873 Rosser St	Young, Luanne	555-0153
15623	04/18/04	Commercial	90842 Rolling Ridge Ave	Davis, Dorothy	555-0931
04027	04/28/04	Commercial	467 Broadway Rd	Name, Student	555-2763
98753	01/04/04	Residental	3200 Sunflower Dr	Jones, April	555-3443
00083	01/06/04	Residental	11440 N Deer Hill	Sierra, Judy	555-7464
03652	01/06/04	Residental	2154 Congress Ave	Kelly, William	555-7674
98345	01/12/04	Residental	78343 Honzon Rd	Henderson, James	555-4245
28974	01/12/04	Residental	2489 Green Brier Pkwy	Thomas, Susanne	555-9313
89120	01/17/04	Residental	2873 Pinnacle Pass	Carilisi, Sarah	555-2384
00095	02/10/04	Residental	2983 E Hwy 78	Mattson, Linda	555-2938
12654	02/13/04	Residental	1024 Gurley Peaks	Staley, Jeff	555-1982
09852	02/23/04	Residental	934 Hillside Dr	Richards, Mike	555-2094
22523	02/28/04	Residental	12004 Upper Sky Pkwy	Rhodes, Edna	555-1983
22083	03/23/04	Residental	845 Willow Creek Rd	Eaton, Gloria	555-1236
00376	03/30/04	Residental	5637 Hilltop Rd	Boyer, Keith	555-1828
04025	04/23/04	Residental	2983 Club House Dr	Leware, Edward	555-1763
04026	04/26/04	Residental	20234 Midway Ave	Williams, Gary	555-0031

Job Number	Date	Category	Site Address	Contact	Phone	Permit Fees
98374	01/15/04	Commercial	33 Arrowhead Rd	Vaughn, James	555-7483	$ 3,300.00
00983	02/13/04	Commercial	5623 Scott Dr	Anderson, Tom	555-2734	$ 9,830.00
34592	02/16/04	Commercial	7020 Green Valley Way	Merwin, Michael	555-6853	$ 2,240.00
09852	02/23/04	Residental	934 Hillside Dr	Richards, Mike	555-2094	$ 1,500.00
46191	03/07/04	Commercial	23418 Placer Cr	Carothers, Daryl	555-1324	$ 7,522.00
09834	03/10/04	Commercial	4512 Brandling Ave	Stansbury, Thomas	555-1287	$ 10,023.00
00123	04/07/04	Commercial	41523 Mount Marapai Rd	Kenson, Lois	555-0267	$ 8,700.00
04027	04/28/04	Commercial	467 Broadway Rd	Name, Student	555-2763	$ 1,075.00

Wilson Electronics Employee Database

★ **2.** Part of your job in the Personnel department at Wilson Electronics is to maintain the employee sales database. Recently, in order to boost sales, the company has been running a rewards program for their employees based on sales performance. In addition to the standard database maintenance, you have been asked to examine the employee database and determine the appropriate rewards. Your completed analysis and update of the database should be similar to that shown here.

a. Open the file ex06_Wilson Employees.

b. The employee data for several new employees has not been included in the database. Use the data form to enter the records shown below.

Employee #	Last Name	First Name	Department	Total Sales
45925	Phillips	Jennifer	Audio	$752.98
08420	Schwartz	Grant	Small Appliances	$1230.79
64301	Thurman	Andy	Electronics	$1951.50
00345	Wood	Cyrus	Computers	$5,450.97

c. Apply an ascending sort to the Last Name column to alphabetize your list.

d. As you work with the database, you realize that a change in department structure has not yet been included. The Large Appliances department has been restructured and is now called Kitchen and Home. Use Find and Replace to make this change to the file.

e. There have been some personnel changes since the last database update. Eugene Radden and Tony Patel are no longer with the company. Find and remove their records from the database. Joann Keifer recently got married. Change her last name to **Hancock**.

f. You have finished making the necessary changes to the database and can now begin your analysis. Use a multilevel sort to display the records first by department and then by last name.

g. Now that you have the data organized, you need to filter the records to determine which employees have earned rewards. There are two awards levels. Those who have sales of at least $2000 receive $75, those with sales of at least $4000 receive $150. Use AutoFilter and apply a custom filter to determine those employees whose sales are greater than or equal to $2000 but less than $4000. Copy this filtered sheet to a new sheet and name it **Bonus Winners**. Best Fit columns.

h. Use AutoFilter on the Employee Sales sheet and apply a custom filter to determine those employees whose sales are greater than or equal to $4000. Copy this information to the Bonus Winners sheet below the other information separated by a blank row.

i. Apply an AutoFormat of your choice to the new sheet. Change the subtitle to **Level 1 Bonus Winners**.

j. Insert the copy of the title and field name above the second group of records. Best Fit the columns. Change the subtitle to **Level 2 Bonus Winners**.

k. You need to print the list of winners to post in the break room, but some of the information included in your new sheet is confidential. Define a print area to include only the employees' last and first names and their department.

l. Adjust the formatting so that the printout will include the title information and graphic. Print the Bonus Winners worksheet with your name and the current date centered on a separate line in a header. Center the worksheet horizontally.

m. Remove the filter from the sales worksheet. Save your completed workbook as **Wilson Employee Rewards**.

Lifestyle Fitness Club Employee Database

★ ★ **3.** You work in Human Resources at the Lifestyle Fitness Club. One of your duties includes maintaining an Excel database of employee information. Your supervisor requested some payroll information that will be used to determine pay raises. You have been asked to provide an analysis of jobs and pay rates. Your completed analysis will be similar to the one shown here.

a. Open the file ex06_LFC Database.

b. Using the data form, enter a new record into the database. Use your name as the employee. Enter **9999** as your employee number, the current date as the Hire Date, **Sales Associate** as your job title, **10.00** as your pay rate and **20** as your Hours.

c. Use the data form to edit the entry for Kimberly Kieken. Her last name is now **Larson**.

d. Sort the list to display the records by pay rate first, job title second, and hire date third. Filter the list to exclude records with a pay rate of salary. Add your name and the current date to the footer. Print the sorted list in landscape orientation.

e. Filter the list again to display only those records with a hire date before November 2000. Print the filtered sheet.

f. Remove the filter.

g. Save your completed workbook as LFC Analysis.

Adventure Travel Tours Client Database

★ ★ **4.** As a travel agent at Adventure Travel Tours you maintain an Excel database of your clients. You
★   have recently created several new tour packages and would like to inform your clients about them.
        Your database includes information about where customers have traveled in the six areas your
        new packages cover. You would like to target those who have already traveled in the new areas of
        your packages. Some of your completed worksheets will be similar to those shown here.

a. Open the file ex06_ATT Client List.

b. Merge and center **Your Name Client List** under the company name at the top of the worksheet. Increase the font size to 14 and apply the same font color as the main title.

c. The data for one of your clients has changed since you last worked with the workbook. Use the data form to locate the record for Debby Shaw. Change her e-mail address to **debby_shaw@ mail.com**.

d. One of your new packages is a tour of Indonesia. Filter the list to display those clients who have traveled to Indonesia in the past. Insert a new sheet and name it **Indonesia Tour**. Copy the filter results (including the title) to the new sheet. Best Fit the columns. Change the title to **Indonesia Tour**.

e. Print the Indonesia Tour sheet centered horizontally in landscape orientation.

f. You have another tour package that explores the Mediterranean and then ventures into Africa. You need to display a list of clients who have traveled to Africa and Europe. In the Client List sheet, display all the records in the Indonesia category again. First filter for those who have traveled to Europe. Then filter the list to determine which of those clients have traveled to Africa.

h. Insert a new sheet titled **Mediterranean Tour**. Copy the filtered Client List sheet to the new sheet. Best Fit the columns. Change the title to **Mediterranean Tour**. Print the Mediterranean Tour sheet centered horizontally in landscape orientation.

i. Return to the Client List sheet and remove the filter. Save your completed worksheet as ATT Client List2.

Animal Rescue Foundation Donation Inventory

★ ★
★ **5.** The Animal Rescue Foundation relies on donations to furnish foster homes with the supplies they need. They have started to record the donation information in an Excel workbook so that they can keep an inventory of goods. You have been asked to update and maintain this inventory and furnish the board of directors with an inventory that calls attention to supply shortages. The directors have also asked you to create a Web page so that foundation members can see the inventories and make donations accordingly. Your completed worksheets should be similar to those shown here.

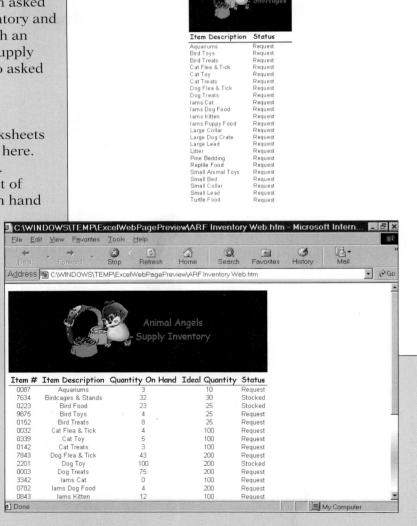

a. Open the file ex06_ARF Inventory.

b. The inventory consists of a list of items showing the quantity on hand and the desired quantity. You need to add a column that will identify the need status of each item. Add the label **Status** in cell E9. Adjust the formatting as needed.

c. In order to indicate a need for an item, you will enter a formula that will calculate when an item's on-hand amount is less than half of the ideal amount, and display either stocked or request based on the determination. Enter the formula **=IF(C10<(D10/2), "Request","Stocked")** in cell E10. Copy the formula to the rest of the cells in that column.

d. You now have a list that displays which items need to be restocked. Now you need to print a list of low stock items for the board. Display only those items with "Request" status.

e. The board does not need most of the information in the sheet. They would like a list with the item description and the status. Hide columns A, C, and D. Add the title **Inventory** in cell E2 and **Shortages** in E3. Apply formatting of your choice. Preview the sheet. Add your name and the current date to a custom header and print the sheet centered horizontally.

f. Unhide the columns. Delete the titles in cells E2 and E3. Remove the AutoFilter. Save your completed workbook as ARF Inventory2.

g. You have been asked to create a Web page with the inventory information. Preview the Web page. Fix and enhance the formatting of the sheet as needed.

h. Save the Supply Inventory as a Web page called ARF Inventory Web.

i. Create a folder named ARF Inventory to contain the workbook files.

on your own

Statters Suppliers Database

★ 1. Statters Office Supply needs you to create a database to hold supplier information such as company name, location, sales representative, product category (such as paper, furniture, computers, small electronics, and so on). Enter a list of at least 20 records in an Excel worksheet with the appropriate fields. Format the worksheet in an attractive manner. Sort the list by the supplier's state. Filter the list to display suppliers of the same category of product. Enter a function to count the number of records and include an appropriate label. Print the filter results with your name and the current date as a header. Save the workbook as Statter's Suppliers.

Kids Express Inventory Analysis

★★ 2. The Kids Express Toy Company needs help with its inventory. Create a worksheet that has 20 inventory records. The records should contain a product identification number, description, wholesale distributor, wholesale price, retail price, and quantity on hand. Format the worksheet in an attractive manner. Sort the records by distributor. Filter the records to display a selected distributor and total the quantity on hand for that distributor. Enter your name and the current date as a header to the filter results and print them. Filter the list next to find all items with a retail price higher than a selected value. Enter your name and the current date as a header to the filter results and print them. Save the workbook as Toy Inventory.

Baseball League Roster

★ ★ **3.** You have a summer internship working in your town's community activities department. You have been asked to create a database of players enrolled in the summer baseball program in order to divide them into the various teams. Create a database that lists the players' name, address, phone number, age, and position. Format the worksheet in an attractive manner. Enter 30 records in the list. Include your name as one of the records and a position of pitcher. Sort the database by player name, position, and age. Filter the list to show only pitchers. Enter your name and the current date as a header to the worksheets. Print the filter results. Save the workbook as Summer Baseball League.

Cleaning Service Customer List

★ ★ **4.** Desert Rescue Cleaning wants to keep track of its customers with an Excel worksheet database. Create a worksheet database that includes the customers' ID number, cleaning address with suite or apartment number, contact name, phone number, and square footage. Format the worksheet in an attractive manner. Enter 15 records into the database. Enter your name as the contact for the first record. Sort the database contact name. Filter the list to display only those records with a square footage larger than a specified value. Enter functions to display the minimum and maximum square footage values. Include appropriate labels. Enter your name and the current date as a header to the worksheets. Print the filter results. Save the workbook as Cleaning Company Customers.

★ ★ **5.** After analyzing your budget to see if you will have enough money to take a trip over spring break
★ (step-by-step exercise 3 of Lab 4), you tell your friends about the results. They would also like to analyze their budgets. To make the worksheet available to your friends, you decide to create a template of the worksheet and make it available on your Web site for them to use. Clear out your personal data to create the template and preview it as a Web page. Make any necessary adjustments to the worksheet and then save it as an interactive Web page as Budget Analysis. Try out the worksheet to make sure it works in the browser and modify again as needed. Print the blank worksheet in the browser.

You decide to convert your Stock Analysis worksheet (On Your Web, Lab 4) to a Web page for use by your friends. Clear out your stock data to create the template and preview it as a Web page. Make any necessary adjustments to the worksheet so that it displays correctly in the browser. Include instructions on how to use the worksheet. Include a link to a Web site that provides stock information. Save the worksheet as an interactive Web page as Stock Analysis Web. Try out the worksheet to make sure it works in the browser and connects you to the stock Web site. Modify it again as needed. Print the blank worksheet in the browser with your name in a header.

Case Study

The Downtown Internet Café

The first project you are working on is to send Evan a copy of the Customers2 workbook to look at and make changes to as needed. You will send it to him for review by e-mail. When it is returned to you, you will review the suggested changes and update the workbook with the necessary changes.

The second project you are working on is to check the inventory on hand of certain items. If some items are overstocked, you plan to run a special on them. This information is maintained in an Access database table. You plan to import the table into Excel to quickly analyze the inventory numbers.

Sending a workbook out for review allows multiple users to make changes to the workbook

Importing data from Access allows you to analyze the list information using Excel.

Reviewing a Workbook

Microsoft Office XP makes it easy to work with others to develop and use workbooks. You can send a workbook or other document for review so that the recipients can add comments and make changes to it. As the reviewed documents are sent back to you, you can combine them with your original copy of the document, and then use the reviewing tools to accept or reject the changes.

Sending the Workbook for Review

Note: You will need the Customers2 file you saved at the end of Lab 6.

Now you will send the Customers2 workbook to Evan via e-mail to review.

1 ● **Open the workbook file Customers2 from your Café Customers folder.**

● **Choose File/Send to/Mail Recipient (for Review).**

Your screen should be similar to Figure 1

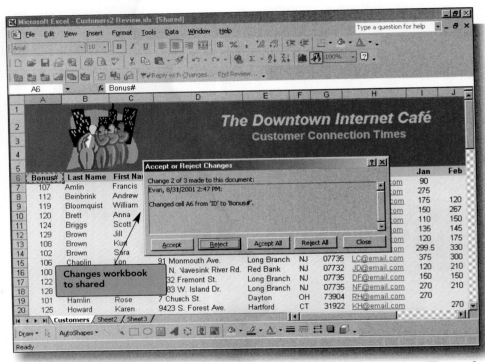

Figure 1

An informational message is displayed notifying you that the workbook status needs to be changed to shared in order to track reviewers' comments. Initially, a workbook's status is **exclusive,** which allows only one user the capability to edit the workbook at one time. A **shared workbook** allows multiple users to make changes to the workbook at the same time.

Additional Information

You can also make a workbook shared using **T**ools/Share Workbook/**A**llow changes by more than one user.

---

2 ● Click [Yes].

● Save the workbook as Customers2 Review **in the Café Customers folder.**

● Click [Save].

Your screen should be similar to Figure 2

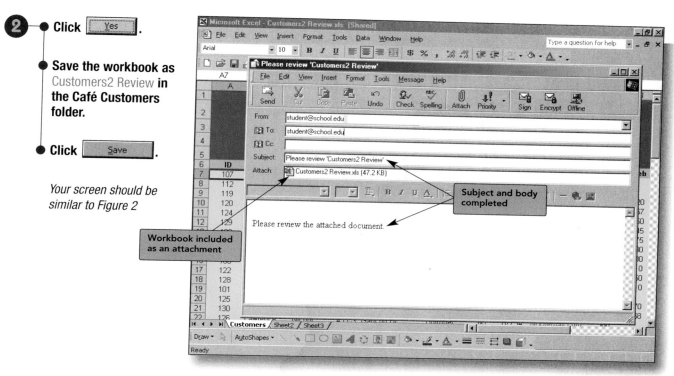

Figure 2

The new e-mail message window is displayed. Because the command to send the workbook by e-mail was to send it for review, the subject and body of the message already include appropriate information. The workbook is included as an attachment to the e-mail message.

3 ● In the To field, enter your e-mail address.

● Below the body of the e-mail, type your name.

● Click [Send].

● Close the workbook.

Combining Reviewed Workbooks

A short while later, while checking your e-mail for new messages, you see that Evan has returned the workbook with his changes. You have downloaded the attachment and saved it using a different file name to the same folder. Now you want to review the suggested changes.

When you receive reviewers' comments, the easiest way to review them is to merge the reviewed copy with the original.

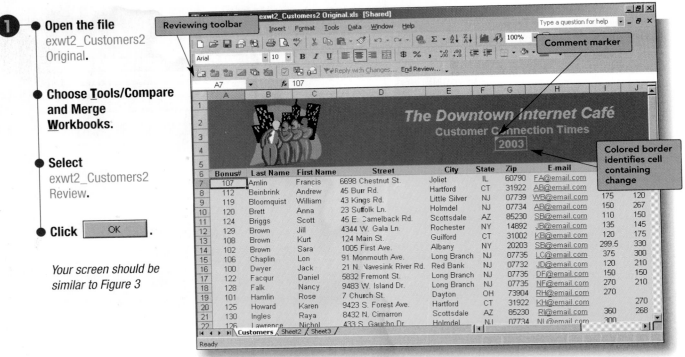

1 ● **Open the file**
exwt2_Customers2
Original.

● **Choose Tools/Compare**
and Merge
Workbooks.

● **Select**
exwt2_Customers2
Review.

● **Click** [OK] .

Your screen should be
similar to Figure 3

Figure 3

Additional Information

If all the reviewers are using Outlook, Excel 2002 will prompt you to combine the reviewed workbook with the original when you open the workbook.

Additional Information

If there are multiple reviews, each reviewer's changes are identified with different colors.

The changes from Evan's reviewed workbook are combined with and displayed in the original worksheet. The Reviewing toolbar is automatically displayed.

Viewing Changes

The changes that are made in a shared workbook are maintained in a separate **History worksheet**. The **change history** is also displayed directly on the worksheet using onscreen highlighting. Cells that contain changes are identified with a colored border and comment marker. The change history includes information about who made the change, the date of the change, and the data that were changed.

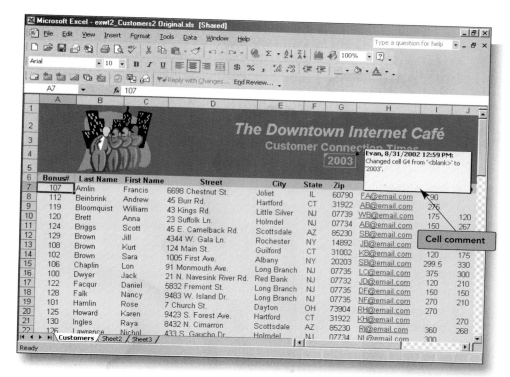

Figure 4

Cell comments containing the change history for that cell are automatically added to the worksheet whenever the reviewer makes a change. In this case, Evan changed the column label from ID to Bonus #. Next, you will look at the History worksheet of all changes.

2 ● **Choose Tools/Track Changes/Highlight Changes.**

Your screen should be similar to Figure 5

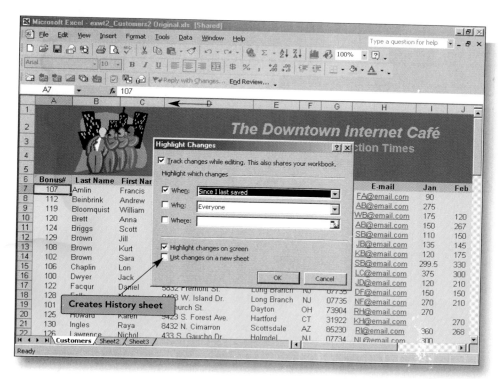

Figure 5

From the When check box, you can enter a date to specify an interval of elapsed time or to review all changes that have not been reviewed yet. The Who check box is used to specify that you want to review changes made by specific persons and the Where check box is used to specify that you want to see changes made to a specific range of cells.

3 ● **If necessary, select the When check box.**

● **Select All from the When drop-down list.**

● **If necessary, clear the Who and Where check boxes.**

● **Select List changes on a new sheet.**

● **Click** OK .

Your screen should be similar to Figure 6

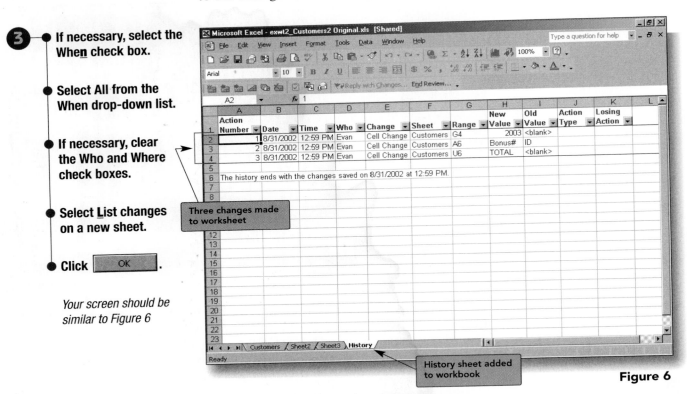

Three changes made to worksheet

History sheet added to workbook

Figure 6

A temporary History sheet has been inserted in the workbook and opened. You can quickly see that Evan made three changes to the worksheet. You can also use the filter arrows next to the column labels to isolate specific changes. Using the History sheet is particularly useful when there are many reviewers and a lot of changes to track.

Reviewing Changes

You want to review the changes in the worksheet one by one and make a decision as to whether to accept or reject each change.

1 Switch to the Customers sheet.

● Choose **Tools/Track Changes/Accept or Reject Changes**

Your screen should be similar to Figure 7

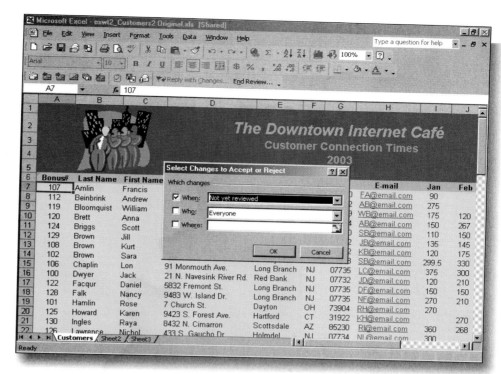

Figure 7

Again, you specify the When, Who, and Where settings. You want to review all changes made by everyone in the entire worksheet.

2 ● Click **OK**.

Your screen should be similar to Figure 8

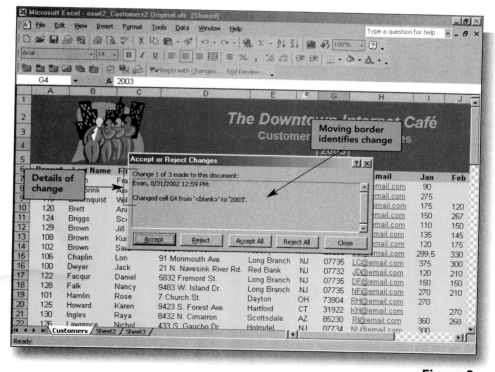

Figure 8

The first change that was made is the addition of the date in cell G4. The change is identified with a moving border. Because Evan entered the wrong date, you will reject it.

3 ● Click [Reject].

Your screen should be similar to Figure 9

Next change identified

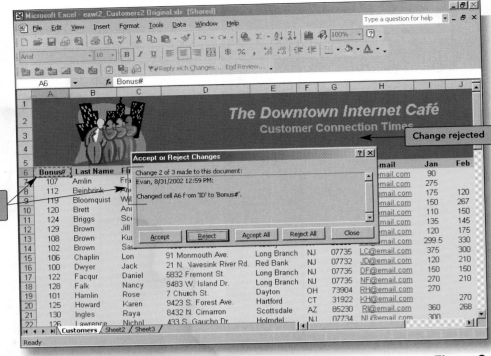

Figure 9

The change is deleted and the next change is identified. You will accept this change.

4 ● Click [Accept].

HAVING TROUBLE?
If necessary, move the dialog box to see the identified change.

Your screen should be similar to Figure 10

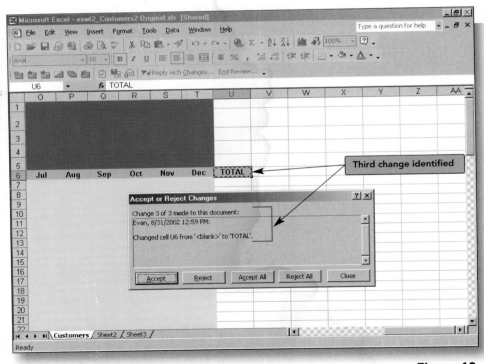

Figure 10

No change is made because the change was already included in the worksheet when the files were merged. The last change is identified. Again you will accept this change.

5 ● Click [Accept].

● Save the workbook as
Customers2 Final **to the
Customers folder.**

*Your screen should be
similar to Figure 11*

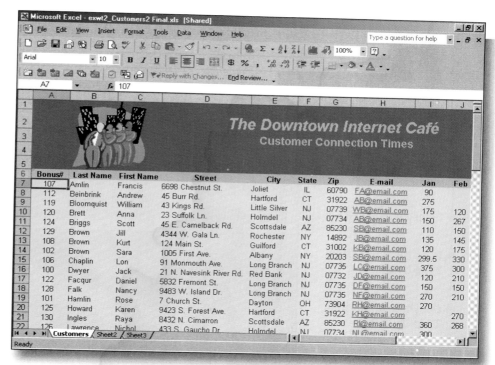

Figure 11

The History sheet was removed when you started the process of reviewing
changes. To see how the History worksheet has been updated to reflect your
decisions, you need to recreate the worksheet.

6 ● **Choose Tools/Track
Changes/Highlight
Changes.**

● **Choose List changes
on a new sheet.**

● Click [OK].

● **Scroll the window to
the right.**

*Your screen should be
similar to Figure 12*

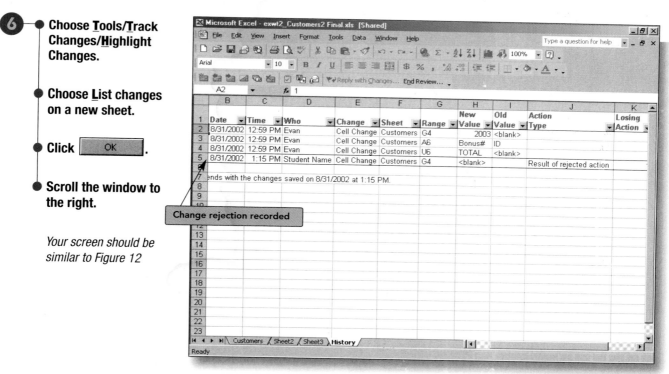

	Date	Time	Who	Change	Sheet	Range	New Value	Old Value	Action Type	Losing Action
2	8/31/2002	12:59 PM	Evan	Cell Change	Customers	G4	2003	<blank>		
3	8/31/2002	12:59 PM	Evan	Cell Change	Customers	A6	Bonus#	ID		
4	8/31/2002	12:59 PM	Evan	Cell Change	Customers	U6	TOTAL	<blank>		
5	8/31/2002	1:15 PM	Student Name	Cell Change	Customers	G4	<blank>		Result of rejected action	

The list ends with the changes saved on 8/31/2002 at 1:15 PM.

Change rejection recorded

Figure 12

The History worksheet has recorded the rejection action in the Action Type column for cell G4. Accepted actions are not noted, as they were already incorporated into the worksheet when it was merged.

Ending the Review

To complete the worksheet, you will enter the correct date in G4 and format the TOTAL column.

1
- **Switch to the Customers sheet.**

- **Enter 2002 in cell G4.**

- **Copy the format from T1 to U1:U5.**

- **Copy the format from T7 to U7:U59.**

- **Click anywhere to deselect the column.**

Your screen should be similar to Figure 13

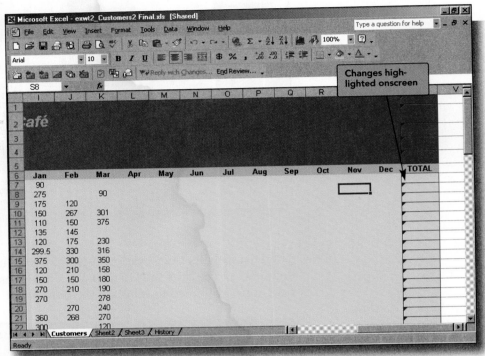

Figure 13

Because the track changes feature is still on for the workbook, your changes are identified onscreen.

Now that you have reviewed all the comments, you want to end the review process.

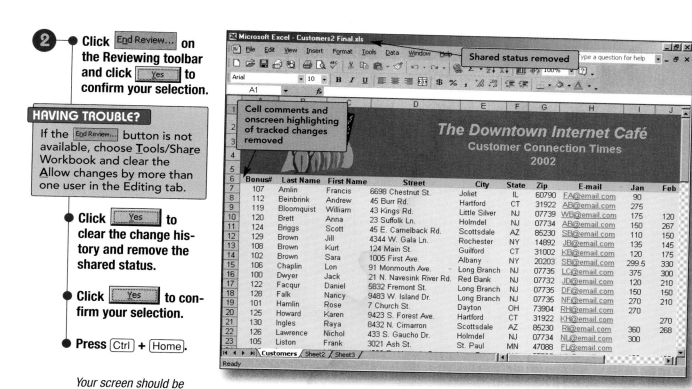

2 Click [End Review...] on the Reviewing toolbar and click [Yes] to confirm your selection.

HAVING TROUBLE?
If the [End Review...] button is not available, choose Tools/Share Workbook and clear the Allow changes by more than one user in the Editing tab.

● Click [Yes] to clear the change history and remove the shared status.

● Click [Yes] to confirm your selection.

● Press Ctrl + Home.

Your screen should be similar to Figure 14

Figure 14

The onscreen highlighting of tracked changes is removed. When the review process is over, you cannot combine any more reviewed workbooks with your original workbook.

3 ● Preview the worksheet.

● Change the orientation to landscape.

● Set the print area as A1:K39.

● Print the worksheet using the print area settings.

● If necessary, close the Reviewing toolbar.

● Save and close the workbook file.

Your printed output should be similar to that shown here.

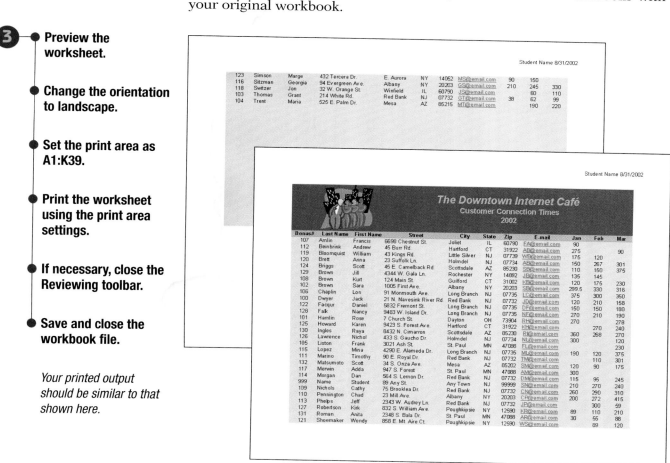

Importing Data

The other project you are working on is to check the inventory on hand of certain items. If some items are overstocked, you plan to run a special on them. This information is maintained in an Access database table. You will import the table into Excel to quickly analyze the inventory numbers.

Importing Access Table Data to Excel

Importing converts external data that have been saved in another format into a format that can be used by the application. **External data** is data that are stored outside the application, in this case Excel, such as a database or text file.

You want to import the data from the Vendors table of the Café Supplies Access database to an Excel workbook so that you can perform additional mathematical analysis on the data.

1 • Click ☐ New.

• Choose **D**ata/Import External **D**ata/Import **D**ata

• Select exwt2_Café Supplies.mdb **from your data file location.**

• Click Open ▾.

• Select the Vendors table from the Select Table dialog box.

• Click OK.

Your screen should be similar to Figure 15

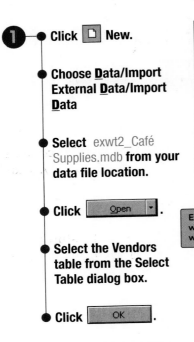

Figure 15

Next, you need to specify where you want the data inserted. The default selection, cell A1, in the worksheet is appropriate. When specifying the location, be careful to select an area that is empty below and to the right of the selected cell so that data you want to keep are not overwritten.

2 **Click** OK .

Your screen should be similar to Figure 16

Access table converted to an Excel list →

Records

Field names

Figure 16

The database table is converted to an Excel list with the field names in the first row of the worksheet and the records beginning in row 2. The column heads and column widths are formatted as they appeared in the Access table.

Analyzing the List

Now the data can be manipulated using Excel commands and features. You want to find out how much coffee is on hand to determine what coffee specials to offer next week.

1 ● Choose **Data/Filter/AutoFilter**.

● From the Vendor Name field select Better Beverages, Inc.

● Calculate the total coffee on hand in cell C34.

● Enter, bold, and right-align the label **Total** in cell B34.

Your screen should be similar to Figure 17

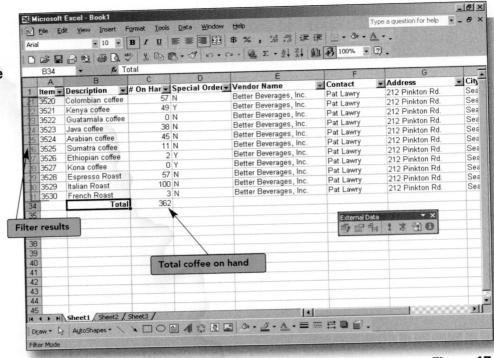

Figure 17

You can now easily see that the Italian Roast coffee quantity on hand is very high and decide to offer a special on that item. At the same time, you need to order several coffees whose quantity is very low. You will print out the filtered list for Evan to confirm your ordering decisions.

2 ● Select the range A1:C34.

● Specify this range as the selection to print and then preview the worksheet.

● Center the worksheet horizontally.

● Enter your name and the current date right-aligned on separate lines in a custom header.

● Print the worksheet.

Your printed output should be similar to that shown here.

Item #	Description	# On Hand
3520	Colombian coffee	57
3521	Kenya coffee	49
3522	Guatamala coffee	0
3523	Java coffee	38
3524	Arabian coffee	45
3525	Sumatra coffee	11
3526	Ethiopian coffee	2
3527	Kona coffee	0
3528	Espresso Roast	57
3529	Italian Roast	100
3530	French Roast	3
	Total	362

Now that you have the information you need, you will remove the filter and save the workbook.

3 ● **Remove the filter.**

● **Close the External Data toolbar.**

● **Save the worksheet as** Café Supplies**.**

● **Exit Excel.**

Working Together 2: Reviewing a Workbook and Importing Access Data

key terms

change history   EXWT2.4

exclusive   EXWT2.2

export   EXWT2.12

external data   EXWT2.12

History worksheet   EXWT2.4

import   EXWT2.12

shared workbook   EXWT2.2

command summary

Command	Action
File/Sen**d** to/Mail Re**c**ipient (for Review)	Sends the active workbook as an attachment to an e-mail message and sets up the file for review
Data/Import External **D**ata/Import **D**ata	Imports data from an external source into a worksheet
Tools/Sha**r**e Workbook/**A**llow changes by more than one user	Changes workbook status to shared or exclusive
Tools/**T**rack Changes/**A**ccept or Reject Changes	Sequentially moves to each tracked change and lets you decide to accept or reject each
Tools/**T**rack Changes/**H**ighlight Changes/ **L**ist changes on a new sheet	Displays a separate History sheet of all tracked changes
Tools/Compare and Merge **W**orkbooks	Combines workbooks sent to review

Hands-On Exercises

step by step

rating system

★ Easy

★★ Moderate

★★★ Difficult

★★ **1.** You have completed the analysis of projected donations for the next year for the Animal Rescue Foundation. Now you want to send the workbook to Mary Munson, the Fund Raising Administrator, for review and comments. The revised analysis is shown here.

    a. Start Excel and open the workbook file ARF Analysis (from Lab 4, exercise 5).

    b. Send the workbook by e-mail for review to a classmate with the file name of ARF Analysis Review. In the body of the e-mail, ask your classmate to make the changes shown below to the workbook and to use the Reply with Changes option to send the workbook back to you.

Student Name   9/04/02

Animal Rescue Foundation

Analysis and Projections

	2001 Income	5% Increase	10% Increase	10% Decrease	5% Decrease	Current Scenario
Annual Memberships	$54,834	$57,576	$60,317	$49,351	$52,092	$54,834
Phone Solicitation	$6,400	$6,720	$7,040	$5,760	$6,080	6,400
Corporate Donations	$45,000	$47,250	$49,500	$40,500	$42,750	45,000
Raffle Tickets	$2,894	$3,039	$3,183	$2,605	$2,749	2,894
Pet Shows	$16,000	$16,800	$17,600	$14,400	$15,200	16,000
Other	$24,000	$25,200	$26,400	$21,600	$22,800	24,000
Total	$149,128	$156,584	$164,041	$134,215	$141,672	$149,128

Sheet	Cell	Change
Spring/Summer	D3	Current year
	D3	Current year
Fall/Winter	C10	5000
Analysis	A3	Add [Current year] – [Next year] to the subtitle

    c. When you receive the reply, save the reviewed workbook as ARF Analysis Review2. Merge the reviewed and original workbooks.

    d. Track the changes and accept all changes except the change to cell C10.

    e. Save the workbook as ARF Analysis2 and print the Analysis worksheet.

★★ **2.** After developing the worksheet to show the effects of a change in sales from –5 to 10 percent for Adventure Travel Tours, you want the manager to review it. You will send it to the manager by e-mail and then respond to the changes. The revised Adventure Travel Sales worksheet will be similar to the one shown here.

a. Start Excel and open the workbook file ATT Sales2 (from Lab 5, exercise 5).
b. Unprotect the worksheet.
c. Send the workbook by e-mail for review to a classmate with the file name of ATT Sales Review. In the body of the e-mail, ask your classmate to make the changes shown below to the workbook and to use the Reply with Changes option to send the workbook back to you.

Cell	Change
C3	in 2002
E8	1250
E10	725
A15	Packages Needed in 2003

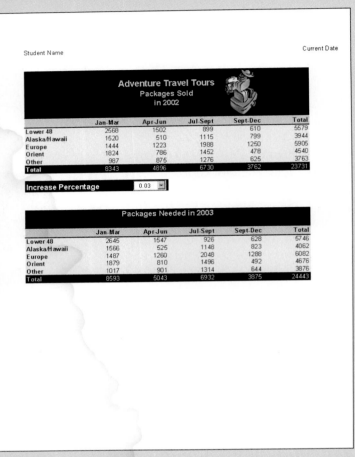

d. When you receive the reply, save the reviewed workbook as ATT Sales Review2. Merge the reviewed and original workbooks.
e. Track the changes and accept all changes except the change to cell E10. Create a History sheet.
f. Change the value in E10 to 625.
g. Save the workbook as ATT Sales3 and print the worksheet and History sheet.

★★ **3.** Alice works at the Decorator's Resource Gallery. An invoice for a garden themed office has arrived. The decorator has requested the prints all be by the same artist. Alice believes Bassett prints will be ideal. She needs to find out the number of prints by Basset in stock. To do this, she plans to use the information in the Access Gallery Database file and analyze it using Excel.

a. Open a blank workbook in Excel.

b. Import the Vendor table from the exwt2_Decorator's Resource Gallery file.

c. Filter the list to display the artist Bassett only.

d. Total the Quantity column. Include a label for the total value. Add the title **Decorator's Resource Gallery: Artist Inventory** above the data. Apply formatting of your choice.

e. Print the filtered list. Include your name and the date in a header.

f. Remove the filter and save the workbook as Artist Inventory.

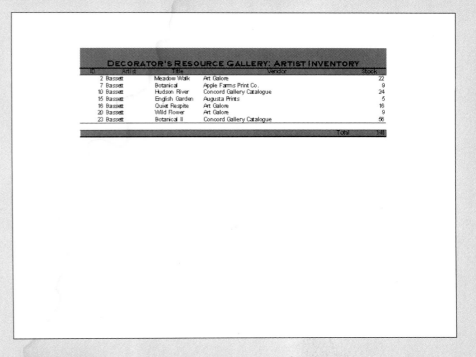

ID	Artist	Title	Vendor	Stock
2	Bassett	Meadow Walk	Art Galore	22
7	Bassett	Botanical	Apple Farms Print Co.	9
10	Bassett	Hudson River	Concord Gallery Catalogue	24
15	Bassett	English Garden	Augusta Prints	5
16	Bassett	Quiet Respite	Art Galore	16
20	Bassett	Wild Flower	Art Galore	9
23	Bassett	Botanical II	Concord Gallery Catalogue	56
			Total	141

Command Summary

Command	Shortcut	Button	Action
File/**O**pen <file name>	Ctrl + O		Opens an existing workbook file
File/**C**lose		X	Closes open workbook file
File/**S**ave <file name>	Ctrl + S		Saves current file on disk using same file name
File/Save **A**s <file name>			Saves current file on disk using a new file name
File/Save as Web Page			Creates a Web page from the entire active workbook or the current worksheet selection.
File/We**b** Page Preview			Displays the active workbook as a Web page in the browser without actually publishing it
File/Prin**t** Area/**S**et Print Area			Sets area of worksheet to be printed
File/Prin**t** Area/**C**lear Print Area			Clears print area
File/Se**n**d to/**M**ail Recipient			Sends the active document to the e-mail recipient.
File/Page Set**u**p/Page/**L**andscape			Changes orientation to landscape
File/Page Set**u**p/Header/Footer			Adds header and/or footer
File/Print Pre**v**iew			Displays worksheet as it will appear when printed
File/**P**rint	Ctrl + P		Prints a worksheet
File/**P**rint/Entire Workbook			Prints all the sheets in a workbook
File/Proper**t**ies			Displays information about and documents the workbook
File/E**x**it		X	Exits Excel 2002
Edit/**U**ndo	Ctrl + Z		Undoes last editing or formatting change
Edit/**R**edo	Ctrl + Y		Restores changes after using Undo
Edit/**C**opy	Ctrl + C		Copies selected data to Clipboard
Edit/**P**aste	Ctrl + V		Pastes selections stored in Clipboard
Edit/Paste **S**pecial			Inserts the object as an embedded object
Edit/Paste **S**pecial/Paste **L**ink			Creates a link to the source document
Edit/Lin**k**s			Modifies selected link
Edit/Linked **O**bject/**E**dit Link			Modifies selected linked object
Edit/Fi**l**l			Fills selected cells with contents of source cell
Edit/Clear/**C**ontents	Delete		Clears cell contents

Command	Shortcut	Button	Action
Edit/Clear/Comments		🗔	Deletes comment in selected cell
Edit/Delete/Entire row			Deletes selected rows
Edit/Delete/Entire column			Deletes selected columns
Edit/Delete/Shift Cells Left			Deletes selected cells and shifts remaining cells to left
Edit/Delete/Shift Cells Up			Deletes selected cells and shifts remaining cells up
Edit/Move or Copy Sheet			Moves or copies selected sheet
Edit/Find	Ctrl + F		Searches selected cells for a specified value
Edit/Replace	Ctrl + H		Searches for a specified value and replaces it with another specified value
Edit/Delete Sheet			Deletes selected sheets from a workbook.
View/Toolbars			Displays or hides selected toolbar
View/Comments		🗔	Displays all comments or hides all displayed comments
View/Zoom		100% ▾	Changes magnification of window
Insert/Cells/Shift Cells Right			Moves existing cells to the right when you insert new cells
Insert/Cells/Shift Cells Down			Moves existing cells down when you insert new cells
Insert/Copied Cells			Inserts row and copies text from Clipboard
Insert/Rows			Inserts a blank row
Insert/Columns			Inserts a blank column
Insert/Chart		📊	Inserts chart into worksheet
Insert/Function	⇧Shift + F3	ƒ✱	Inserts a function
Insert/Name/Define			Assigns a name you specify to a cell or range of cells
Insert/Name/Paste			Places the selected cell or cell range name in the formula bar or lists names in the worksheet
Insert/Name/Create			Creates a range name using the text in cells
Insert/Comment		🗔	Inserts a new comment in selected cell
Insert/Edit Comment		🗔	Edits comment in selected cell
Insert/Object			Inserts an entire file as an embedded object.
Insert/Hyperlink	Ctrl + K		Inserts a new hyperlink or modifies the selected hyperlink
Insert/Hyperlink/Remove Link			Removes hyperlink settings from selected cell
Insert/Picture/From File			Inserts picture at insertion point from disk
Format/Cells/Number/Currency			Applies Currency format to selection
Format/Cells/Number/Accounting		$	Applies Accounting format to selection

Command	Shortcut	Button	Action
Format/Cells/Number/Date			Applies Date format to selection
Format/Cells/Number/Percent		%	Applies Percent format to selection
Format/Cells/Number/Decimal places		⬚ ⬚	Increases or decreases the number of decimal places associated with a number value
Format/Cells/Alignment/Horizontal/ Left (Indent)		▤	Left-aligns entry in cell space
Format/Cells/Alignment/Horizontal/ Center		▤	Center-aligns entry in cell space
Format/Cells/Alignment/Horizontal/ Right		▤	Right-aligns entry in cell space
Format/Cells/Alignment/Indent/1		▤	Indents cell entry one space
Format/Cells/Alignment/Horizontal/ Center Across Selection		▦	Centers cell contents across selected cells
Format/Cells/Font			Changes font and attributes of cell contents
Format/Cells/Font/Font Style/Bold	Ctrl + B	B	Bolds selected text
Format/Cells/Font/Font Style/Italic	Ctrl + I	I	Italicizes selected text
Format/Cells/Font/Underline/Single	Ctrl + U	U	Underlines selected text
Format/Cells/Font/Color		A ▾	Adds color to text
Format/Cells/Patterns/Color		◩ ▾	Adds color to cell background
Format/Row/Height			Changes height of selected row
Format/Row/Hide			Hides selected rows or columns
Format/Row/Unhide			Displays rows and columns that were previously hidden
Format/AutoFormat			Applies selected table format
Format/Column/Width			Changes width of columns
Format/Column/AutoFit Selection			Changes column width to match widest cell entry
Format/Sheet/Rename			Renames sheet
Format/Style			Applies selected style to selection
Format/Style/Style name/Currency			Applies currency style to selection
Format/Style/Style name/Percent		%	Changes cell style to display percentage
Format/Selected Data Series/ Data Labels	Ctrl + 1		Inserts data labels into chart
Format/Selected Legend	Ctrl + 1	▤	Changes legend
Format/Selected Chart Title	Ctrl + 1	▣	Changes format of selected chart title
Format/Selected Data Series	Ctrl + 1	▣	Changes format of selected data series
Format/Selected Object		▣	Changes format of embedded objects
Chart/Chart Type		▣ ▾	Changes type of chart
Chart/Chart Options			Adds options to chart

Command	Shortcut	Button	Action
Chart/Location			Moves chart from worksheet to chart sheet
Tools/Share Workbook/Allow changes by more than one user			Changes workbook status to shared or exclusive
Tools/Track Changes/Accept or Reject Changes			Sequentially moves to each tracked change and lets you decide to accept or reject each
Tools/Track Changes/Highlight Changes/List changes on a new sheet			Displays a History sheet of all tracked changes
Tools/Compare and Merge Workbooks			Combines workbooks sent to review
Tools/Protection/Protect Sheet sheet's contents			Prevents unauthorized users from changing a
Tools/Scenarios			Creates and saves sets of data used to perform what-if analyses
Tools/Formula Auditing/ Show Auditing Toolbar			Displays auditing toolbar
Tools/Solver			Calculates a formula to achieve a given value by changing one of the variables that affects formulas.
Tools/Macro/Macros	Alt + F8		Runs, edits, or deletes selected macro
Tools/Macro/Record New Macro			Records a series of actions as a macro
Tools/Macro/Stop Recording			Stops the recording of a macro
Tools/Macro/Security			Sets security level associated with macros in a workbook
Tools/Spelling	F7	ABC✓	Spell-checks worksheet
Tools/Goal Seek			Adjusts value in specified cell until a formula dependent on that cell reaches specified result
Tools/Formula Auditing/ Show Watch Window			Opens the Watch Window toolbar
Tools/AutoCorrect Options/ AutoFormat As You Type/Internet and network paths with hyperlinks			Turns on/off feature to automatically format Internet and network paths as hyperlinks
Data/Sort		⫬↓	Arranges selected data alphabetically, numerically, or by date
Data/Filter/AutoFilter			Displays items based on selections in a list or database range
Data/Filter/Show All			Redisplays all records after a filter operation has been performed
Data/Form			Displays a data form dialog box for record entry and modification
Data/Table			Creates a data table based on specified input values and formulas
Data/Import External Data/Import Data			Imports data from an external source into a worksheet

Command	Shortcut	Button	Action
Window/**A**rrange			Arranges open windows side-by-side, vertically, horizontally, or tiled.
Visual Basic Editor			
File/**C**lose and Return			Closes the Visual Basic Editor window and returns to Microsoft Excel to the active Excel worksheet
Run/Run sub/Userform	F5		Runs macro
Window/Un**f**reeze Panes			Unfreezes window panes
Window/**F**reeze Panes			Freezes top and/or leftmost panes
Window/**S**plit			Divides window into four panes at active cell
Window/Remove **S**plit			Removes split bar from active worksheet

Glossary of Key Terms

3-D reference   A reference to the same cell or range on multiple sheets in the same workbook.

3-D shape   A line, AutoShape, or freeform drawing object that has a three-dimensional effect applied to it.

absolute reference   A cell or range reference in a formula whose location remains the same (absolute) when copied. Indicated by a $ character entered before the column letter or row number or both.

active cell   The cell displaying the cell selector that will be affected by the next entry or procedure.

active pane   The pane that contains the cell selector.

active sheet   A sheet that contains the cell selector and that will be affected by the next action.

active workbook   The workbook that contains the cell selector and that will be affected by the next action.

adjacent range   A rectangular block of adjoining cells.

adjustable cell   In Solver, the cell or cells whose values will be changed in order to attain the value set in the target cell.

alignment   The vertical or horizontal placement and orientation of an entry in a cell.

area chart   A chart that shows trends by emphasizing the area under the curve.

argument   The data used in a function on which the calculation is performed.

arrange windows   The arrangement of multiple open workbook windows on the screen   tiled, cascade, horizontally, or vertically.

AutoFill   Feature that logically repeats and extends a series.

autoformat   A built-in combination of formats that can be applied to a range.

automatic recalculation   The recalculation of a formula within the worksheet whenever a value in a referenced cell in the formula changes.

browser   A program that connects you to remote computers and displays the Web pages you request.

cascade   The window arrangement that displays one workbook window on top of the other, cascading down from the top of the screen.

case sensitive   The capability to distinguish between uppercase and lowercase characters.

category-axis   Another name for the X-axis of a chart.

category-axis title   A label that describes the X-axis.

category name   Labels displayed along the X-axis in a chart to identify the data being plotted.

cell   The space created by the intersection of a vertical column and a horizontal row.

cell selector   The heavy border surrounding a cell in the worksheet that identifies the active cell.

change history   Information in a shared workbook that is maintained about changes made to the worksheet.

chart   A visual representation of data in a worksheet.

chart gridlines   Lines extending from the axis lines across the plot area that make it easier to read and evaluate the chart data.

chart object   One type of graphic object that is created using charting features included in Excel 2002. A chart object can be inserted into a worksheet or into a special chart sheet.

chart title   Appears at the top of a chart and is used to describe the contents of the chart.

ClipArt   A collection of graphics that is usually bundled with a software application.

column   A vertical block of cells one cell wide in the worksheet.

column letters The border of letters across the top of the worksheet that identifies the columns in the worksheet.

column-oriented In a data table, the orientation of the data in a table down a column as opposed to across a row (row-oriented).

combination chart A chart type that includes mixed data markers, such as both columns and lines.

comment Notes attached to cells that can be used to help clarify the meaning of the data, provide documentation or ask a question.

constant A value that does not change unless you change it directly by typing in another entry.

control Graphic objects that are designed to automate the process of completing information in a worksheet.

copy area The cell or cells containing the data to be copied.

custom dictionary An additional dictionary you create to supplement the main dictionary.

criteria A set of limiting conditions that you want records to meet in order to be displayed.

data form A special form that makes it easy to enter records in a list.

data labels Labels for data points or bars that show the values being plotted on a chart.

data marker Represents a data series on a chart. It can be a symbol, color, or pattern, depending upon the type of chart.

data series The numbers to be charted.

data table A type of what-if analysis where one or more variables are changed to see the effect on the formula or formulas that include these variables.

database An organized collection of related information consisting of fields and records. Also called a list in Excel.

date numbers The integers assigned to the days from January 1, 1900, through December 31, 2099, that allow dates to be used in calculations.

dependent cell The cell that receives the linked data.

dependent workbook The workbook file that receives the linked data.

default Initial program settings.

destination The cell or range of cells that receives the data from the copy area or source.

destination file A document in which a linked object is inserted.

destination document The workbook file in which a linked object is inserted.

digital signature An electronic encryption-based stamp of authentication.

discussion comments Comments that are attached to a document and stored on a discussion server so they can be read and responded to by multiple reviewers.

discussion server A computer that stores discussion text and information about the file being discussed.

drawing object Object consisting of shapes such as lines and boxes that can be created using features on the Drawing toolbar.

embed Information inserted into a destination file of another application that becomes part of this file but can be edited within the destination file using the server application.

embedded chart A chart that is inserted into another file.

embedded object Information inserted into a destination file of another application that becomes part of this file but can be edited within the destination file using the server application.

exclusive Workbook status that allows editing by only one user at a time.

explode To separate a wedge of a pie chart slightly from the other wedges in the pie.

export To save data in another format so that it can be used in an application other than the application in which it was created.

external data Data that is created in another application.

external reference formula A formula that creates a link between workbooks.

field A single category of data in a list, the values of which appear in a column of a worksheet.

field name A label used to identify the data stored in a field.

fill handle A small black square located in the lower-right corner of the selection that is used to create a series or copy to adjacent cells with a mouse.

filter   A restriction placed on records in a database to temporarily isolate a subset of records.

Find and Replace   Feature that quickly finds and automatically replaces specific information with new information.

font   The typeface, type size, and style associated with a worksheet entry that can be selected to improve the appearance of the worksheet.

footer   A line (or several lines) of text that appears at the bottom of each page just above the bottom margin.

form   A formatted worksheet that is designed to be completed by filling in data in the blank spaces.

format   Formats are settings that affect the display of entries in a worksheet.

Formatting toolbar   A toolbar that contains buttons used to change the format of a worksheet.

formula   An entry that performs a calculation.

Formula bar   The bar near the top of the Excel window that displays the cell contents.

freeze   To fix in place on the screen specified rows or columns or both when scrolling.

function   A prewritten formula that performs certain types of calculations automatically.

Goal Seek   Tool used to find the value needed in one cell to attain a result you want in another cell.

graphic   A non-text element or object, such as a drawing or picture that can be added to a document.

group   An object that contains other objects.

header   A line (or several lines) of text that appears at the top of each page just below the top margin.

heading   Row and column entries that are used to create the structure of the worksheet and describe other worksheet entries.

History worksheet   A worksheet that displays the history of tracked changes in a worksheet.

horizontal   The window arrangement that displays one open workbook window above the other.

HTML (HyperText Markup Language)   A programming language whose commands are interpreted by the browser software you are using and which controls how the information on a Web page is displayed.

hyperlink   A special type of link that provides a shortcut or jump to another location in the same or different workbook, to a document in a different application, or to a document on a Web site.

IF function   A function that checks to see if certain conditions are met and then takes action based upon the results of the check.

import   To bring in external data for use in a worksheet.

input cell   A cell in which a list of values is substituted to see the resulting effect on the related formulas. Input values can be listed down a column (column-oriented) or across a row (row-oriented).

landscape   The orientation of the printed document so that it prints sideways across the length of the page.

legend   A brief description of the symbols used in a chart that represent the data ranges.

line chart   A chart that represents data as a set of points along a line.

link   A relationship created between files that allows data in the destination file to be updated automatically when changes occur in the source file.

linked object   Information created in a source file from one application and inserted into a destination file of another application while maintaining a link between files.

list   An organized collection of related information consisting of fields and records. Also called a database.

list range   The area of the worksheet containing the records in a list.

live link   A linked object that automatically reflects in the destination document any changes made in the source document when the destination document is opened.

logical operator   Symbols used in formulas that compare values in two or more cells.

macro   A stored series of keystrokes and commands. When the macro is executed or run, the stored actions are performed automatically

Macro Recorder   A tool used to create a macro by recording a series of actions as macro statements as they are performed.

main dictionary   The dictionary included with Office XP.

margins   The blank space around the edge of the paper.

merged cell   A cell made up of several selected cells combined into one.

minimal recalculation   The recalculation of only the formulas in a worksheet that are affected by a change of data.

mixed reference   A cell address that is part absolute and part relative.

multilevel sort   A sort on more than one column or field.

name   A description of a cell or range that can be used in place of cell or range references.

name box   The area located on the left side of the formula bar that provides information about the selected item such as the reference of the active cell.

nested function   A second argument in a function that is enclosed within its own set of parentheses.

nonadjacent range   Cells or ranges that are not adjacent but are included in the same selection.

nper   The argument in the PMT function that is the total number of payments.

number   A cell entry that contains any of the digits 0 to 9 and any of the special characters + = ( ) , . / $ % Σ =.

number formats   Affect how numbers look onscreen and when printed.

object   An element such as a text box that can be added to a workbook and that can be selected, sized, and moved. In Visual Basic, the *object* is the item that the statement will affect (such as a cell, cell range, worksheet, or workbook). The object is enclosed in parentheses and surrounded by quotes.

one-variable data table   A data table can contain one or more formulas and each formula refers to one input cell.

operand   A value on which a numeric formula performs a calculation.

operator   Specifies the type of calculation to be performed.

order of precedence   Order in which calculations are performed and can be overridden by the use of parentheses.

pane   A division of the worksheet window, either horizontal or vertical, through which different areas of the worksheet can be viewed at the same time.

password   A secret code that prevents unauthorized users from turning off protection.

paste area   The cells or range of cells that receive the data from the copy area or source.

picture   An illustration such as a scanned photograph.

pie chart   A chart that compares parts to the whole. Each value in the data range is a wedge of the pie (circle).

plot area   The area of the chart bounded by the axes.

point   Measure used fot height of type; one point equals 1/72 inch.

portrait   The orientation of the printed document so that it prints across the width of the page.

principal   In the PMT function, the principal or *pv* argument is the amount of the loan.

print area   A defined range that is saved with the worksheet and printed by default.

property   In Visual Basic Editor, the property is the action you want to perform on the object. The property consists of reserved words that have special meaning and direct Excel to perform the specified action.

protection   A worksheet feature that prevents users from making changes to data and formats.

pv   The argument in the PMT function that is the amount of the loan. Also called the principal.

range   A selection consisting of two or more cells in a worksheet.

range name   A descriptive name assigned to a cell or range of cells.

rate   In the PMT function, the rate argument is the interest rate of the loan.

record   A row of a database or list consisting of a group of related fields.

reference   The column letter and row number of a cell.

relative reference   A cell or range reference that automatically adjusts to the new location in the worksheet when the formula is copied.

remark statement   Descriptive statement lines in a macro that are not executed.

row   A horizontal block of cells one cell high in the worksheet.

row numbers   The border of numbers along the left side of the worksheet that identifies the rows in the worksheet.

row-oriented   In a data table, the orientation of the data in a table across a row as opposed to down a column (column-oriented).

run   To execute the commands stored in the macro.

sans serif font   A font, such as Arial or Helvetica, that does not have a flair at the base of each letter.

scenario   A named set of input values that you can substitute in a worksheet to see the effects of a possible alternative course of action.

selection handles   Small boxes surrounding a selected object that are used to size the object.

selection rectangle   Border around selected object indicating it can be sized or moved.

series formula   A formula that links a chart object to the source worksheet.

serif font   A font, such as Times New Roman, that has a flair at the base of each letter.

shared workbook   A workbook that is set up for use by multiple people at the same time.

sheet reference   Used in references to other worksheets and consists of the name of the sheet enclosed in quotes and is separated from the cell reference by an exclamation point.

sheet tab   On the bottom of the workbook window, the tabs where the sheet names appear.

sizing handle   Box used to size a selected object.

Solver   A tool that is used to perform what-if analyses to determine the effect of changing values in two or more cells, called the adjustable cells, on another cell, called the target cell.

source   The cell or range of cells containing the data you want to copy.

source file   The document that stores the data for the linked object.

source cell   The cell or range of cells containing the data you want to copy.

source document   The document that stores the data for the linked object.

source workbook   The workbook file that supplies linked data.

sort   To rearrange the records in a list in ascending or descending alphabetical order.

Spelling Checker   Feature that locates misspelled words and proposes corrections.

spreadsheet   A rectangular grid of rows and columns used to enter data.

stack   The order in which objects are added in layers to the worksheet.

stacked-column chart   A chart that displays the data values as columns stacked upon each other.

Standard toolbar   A toolbar that contains buttons used to complete the most frequently used menu commands.

statement   The types of information you enter into the Visual Basic Editor are called statements.

style   A named combination of formats that can be applied to a selection.

Sub procedure   In Visual Basic Editor, a Sub procedure begins with a statement that starts the macro and ends with one that closes the macro (an End Sub statement). Sub procedures can also include remarks about the macro (such as its name and purpose) and functions (such as returning values to the procedure).

syntax   Rules of structure for entering all Visual Basic statements.

tab scroll buttons   Located to the left of the sheet tabs, they are used to scroll sheet tabs right or left.

target cell   In Solver, the cell you set to the value that you want to be attained.

task pane   A pane that provides quick access to features as you are using them.

template   A workbook file that contains predesigned worksheets that can be used as a pattern for creating other similar sheets in new workbooks. It has an .xlt file extension.

text   A cell entry that contains text, numbers, or any other special characters.

text box   A rectangular object in which you type text.

thumbnail   Miniature images displayed in the Clip Organizer.

tiled   A window arrangement in which open workbook windows are displayed one after the other in succession, across and down the screen.

title   In a chart, descriptive text that explains the contents of the chart.

two-variable data table   A data table that uses only one formula that refers to two different input cells, one column-oriented and one row-oriented. The purpose of this table is to show the resulting effect on the formula when the values in both of these cells are changed.

typeface   The appearance and shape of characters. Some common typefaces are Roman and Courier.

value axis   Y axis of a chart that usually contains numerical values.

value axis title   A label that describes the values on the Y axis.

variable   The resulting value of a formula that changes if the data it depends on changes.

vertical   The window arrangement in which open workbook windows are displayed side by side.

Visual Basic Editor   A programming application used to write and edit macros attached to Excel workbooks.

Web discussion   A review feature that allows users to attach comments to a file that can be read and responded to by all reviewers.

Web page   A document that can be used on the World Wide Web (WWW) and is displayed in a browser.

what-if analysis   A technique used to evaluate what effect changing one or more values in formulas has on other values in the worksheet.

word wrap   Feature that automatically determines when to begin the next line of text.

workbook   The file in which you work and store sheets created in Excel 2002.

workbook window   A window that displays an open workbook file.

worksheet   Similar to a financial spreadsheet in that it is a rectangular grid of rows and columns used to enter data.

X-axis   The bottom boundary line of a chart.

Y-axis   The left boundary line of a chart.

Z-axis   The left boundary line of a 3-D chart.

Supplied/Used file	Created/Saved As
Lab 1	
ex01_Forecast2	Forecast
ex01_Internet (graphic)	Forecast3
Step by Step	
1. ex01_Improvements	Park Improvements
2. ex01_New Positions	Jobs
3. ex01_Poverty Level	Poverty Level
ex01_Family (graphic)	
4. ex01_IT Salaries	IT Salaries
ex01_Disks (graphic)	
5. ex01_Springs Budget	Springs Projected Budget
On Your Own	
1.	Class Grades
2.	Personal Budget
3.	Weekly Sales
4.	Job Analysis
5.	Membership
On the Web	
1.	Spreadsheet Design
Lab 2	
ex02_Café Sales	Café Sales Charts
Step by Step	
1. ex02_Real Estate Prices	Real Estate Charts
2. ex02_Tiger Data	Tiger Charts
3. ex02_Birds	Bird Observations
4.	Youth Sport Charts

Supplied/Used file	Created/Saved As
5. ex02_Higher Education	Higher Education Charts
On Your Own	
1. ex02_Job Market	Seminar
2.	Grades
3.	Stocks
4.	Statistics
5.	Insurance
Lab 3	
ex03_First Quarter Forecast	Forecast4
ex03_Annual Forecast	Annual Forecast Revised
Step by Step	
1. ex03_Sandwich Shop	Sandwich Shop2
2. ex03_West Income Statement	West Income Statement2
3. ex03_Time Sheets	Time Sheets2
4. ex03_Grade Report	Grade Report2
5. ex03_Springs Forecast	Springs Forecast2
6. ex03_African Safari	African Safari2
On Your Own	
1. Personal Budget (from Lab 1)	Personal Budget2
2.	Art Expenses
3.	Stock Analysis
On the Web	
1.	My Business
Working Together	
exwt1_Sales Forecast Memo	Sales Forecast Memo Linked
Cafe Sales Charts (from Lab 2)	Cafe Sales Charts Linked
exwt1_Forecast Memo	Second Quarter Forecast
Annual Forecast Revised (from Lab 3)	
Practice Exercises	
1. exwt1_Rescue Memo	Rescue Memo Linked
exwt1_Contributions	Contributions2
2. exwt1_Tour Status Report	March Status Report
exwt1_Adventure Travel Monthly	Adventure Travel Monthly2

Supplied/Used file	Created/Saved As
3. exwt1_Hotel Memo	Hotel Memo2
exwt1_Hotel Data	
Lab 4	
ex04_Revised Annual Forecast	2002 Forecast
	Forecast Template.xlt
	2003 Forecast
Step by Step	
1. ex04_West Side Income	West Side Income.xlt
	West Side Income1
2. ex04_Travel Analysis	ATT Analysis Template
	ATT Revenue Analysis
	ATT Revenue Analysis2
3. ex04_Personal Budget	Personal Budget2
4. ex04_School GPA	GPA Analysis
5. ex04_ARF Contributions	ARF Analysis
On Your Own	
1.	LFC Revenue Analysis
2.	LocalNet Projections
3.	Spring Break Analysis
4.	Art Equipment Analysis
5.	Expansion Projections
On the Web	
1.	Stock Analysis
Lab 5	
ex05_Loan Analysis	Loan Analysis
ex05_Bonus Dollars	Loan Analyzer
	Bonus Dollars
	Monthly Bonus Form.xlt
Step by Step	
1. ex05_ARF Volunteers	ARF Bonus Awards
2. ex05_Grades	Gradebook
3. ex05_Electronics Analyzer	Electronics Analyzer
4. ex05_Currency Exchange	Currency Converter
5. ex05_ATT Sales	ATT Sales2

Supplied/Used file	Created/Saved As
On Your Own	
1.	Macros
2.	My 401K
3.	Furniture Loan Analysis
4.	Sports Company Credit Card
5.	Speeding Fines
On the Web	
1.	Computer Comparisons
Lab 6	
ex06_Customer List	Customer1
Bonus Dollars (from Lab 5)	Bonus Dollars (in Café Customers folder)
ex06_Customers2	Customers2
ex06_Bonus Dollars Web	March Bonus Dollars.htm
Step by Step	
1. ex06_Kodiak Database	Kodiak Database Update
2. ex06_Wilson Employees	Wilson Employee Rewards
3. ex06_LFC Database	LFC Analysis
4. ex06_ATT Client List	ATT Client List2
5. ex06_ARF Inventory	ARF Inventory2
	ARF Inventory Web
On Your Own	
1.	Statter's Suppliers
2.	Toy Inventory
3.	Summer Baseball League
4.	Cleaning Company Customers
5.	Budget Analysis
On the Web	
1. Stock Analysis	StockAnalysis.Web
Working Together 2	
Customers2 (from Lab 6)	Customers2 Review (in Café Customers folder)
exwt2_Customers2 Original	Customers2 Final (in Café Customers folder)
exwt2_Customers2 Review	
exwt2_Café Supplies.mdb	Café Supplies

Supplied/Used file	Created/Saved As
Step by Step	
1. ARF Analysis	ARF Analysis Review
	ARF Analysis Review2
	ARF Analysis2
2. ATT Sales2	ATT Sales Review
	ATT Sales Review2
	ATT Sales3
3. exwt2_Decorator's Resource Gallery	Artist Inventory

MOUS Skills

Excel Core Certification

Standardized Coding Number	Activity	Lab Exercises			
		Lab	Page	Step By Step	On Your Own
Ex2002-1	**Working with Cells and Cell Data**				
Ex2002-1-1	Insert, delete, and move cells	1	1.36,1.37,1.53	1,2,3,4,5	1,2,3,4,5
		3	3.14	1,2,3,4,5	1,2,3,4,5
		4	4.41		
Ex2002-1-2	Enter and edit cell data including text, numbers,and formulas	1	1.15–1.23,1.39, 1.42,1.59	1,2,3,4,5	1,2,3,4,5
Ex2002-1-3	Check spelling	3	3.4	1,5,6	
Ex2002-1-4	Find and replace cell data and formats	3	3.31		
Ex2002-1-5	Use automated tools to filter lists	6	6.19,6.29	1,2,3,4,5	1,2,3,4,5
Ex2002-2	**Managing Workbooks**				
Ex2002-2-1	Manage workbook files and folders	1	1.28	1,2,3,4,5	1,2,3,4,5
		4	4.16	1,2	1
		6	6.17	5	
Ex2002-2-2	Create workbooks using templates	1	1.5		
		4	4.9–4.18	1,2	1
Ex2002-2-3	Save workbooks using different names and file formats	1	1.26	1,2,3,4,5	1,2,3,4,5
		4	4.16	1,2	1
		6	6.17		
Ex2002-3	**Formatting and Printing Worksheets**				
Ex2002-3-1	Apply and modify cell formats	1	1.54–1.60	1,2,3,4,5	1,2,3,4,5
Ex2002-3-2	Modify row and column settings	1	1.48	1,2,3,4,5	
		3	3.35	1,2,3,4,5	
		5	5.46	3	
Ex2002-3-3	Modify row and column formats	1	1.24–1.26,1.49	1,2,3,4,5	
Ex2002-3-4	Apply styles	1	1.61	1,2,3,4,5	
Ex2002-3-5	Use automated tools to format worksheets	5	5.10	2,3	2,3,4,5
Ex2002-3-6	Modify Page Setup options for worksheets	2	2.51	1,2,3,4,5	
		3	3.44,3.47	1,2,3,4,5,6	
		6	6.33,6.34	1,2,3,4,5	1,2,3,4,5
Ex2002-3-7	Preview and print worksheets and workbooks	1	1.69	1,2,3,4,5	1,2,3,4
		6	6.33	1,2,3,4,5	1,2,3,4,5

Standardized Coding Number	Activity	Lab Exercises			
		Lab	Page	Step By Step	On Your Own
Ex2002-4	**Modifying Workbooks**				
Ex2002-4-1	Insert and delete worksheets	3	3.27	1,3,4,5,6	2,3,4
Ex2002-4-2	Modify worksheet names and positions	3	3.20,3.27	1,3,4,5,6	2,3,4
Ex2002-4-3	Use 3-D references	3	3.24	1	
Ex2002-5	**Creating and Revising Formulas**				
Ex2002-5-1	Create and revise formulas	1	1.39,1.41,1.46		
		3	3.11,3.14	1,2,3,4,5,6	1,2,3,4
Ex2002-5-2	Use statistical, date and time, financial, and logical functions in formulas	1	1.42	1,2,3,4,5	1,2,3,4
		3	3.11	1,2,3,4,5,6	1,2,3,4
		4	4.39	1	
		5	5.33	1,2,3,4,5	1,2,3,4,5
Ex2002-6	**Creating and Modifying Graphics**				
Ex2002-6-1	Create, modify, position, and print charts	2	2.7–2.22,2.49	1,2,3,4,5	1,2,3,4,5
Ex2002-6-2	Create, modify, and position graphics	1	1.65–1.68	1,2,3,4,5	5,On the Web
Ex2002-7	**Workgroup Collaboration**				
Ex2002-7-1	Convert worksheets into Web pages	6	6.38	5	5,On the Web
Ex2002-7-2	Create hyperlinks	6	6.12		
Ex2002-7-3	View and edit comments	5	5.41	3,5	

Reference 2: MOUS Skills

www.mhhe.com/oleary

Index

####, EX3.8
#DIV/0!, EX3.8
#N/A, EX3.8
#NAME?, EX3.8
#NULL!, EX3.8
#NUM!, EX3.8
#REF!, EX3.8
#VALUE!, EX3.8

<, EX5.34
<=, EX5.34
<>, EX5.34
=, EX5.34
>, EX5.34
>=, EX5.34

=Sheet1!A1+Sheet2!B2, EX3.24
=Sheet2!B17, EX3.24
=SUM(Sheet1!H6:K6), EX3.24
=SUM(Sheet1:Sheet4!H6), EX3.24
=SUM(Sheet1:Sheet4!H6:K6), EX3.24

ABS, EX1.42
ABS key, EX3.16
Absolute references, EX3.14-EX3.18
Accounting format, EX1.60
Active cell, EX1.7
Active sheet, EX1.8
Active workbook, EX4.19
Add Scenario dialog box, EX4.28
Add Watch dialog box, EX3.38
Adjacent range, EX1.33
Adjustable cells, EX4.6
Aligning sheet on page, EX2.51
Alignment, EX1.49-EX1.51
Analyzing the worksheet, EX4.4-EX4.9
AND, EX1.43, EX5.34

Answer report, EX4.8, EX4.9
Area charts, EX2.5, EX2.20
Argument, EX1.42
Arial, EX1.54
Arithmetic operations, EX1.39
Arrange windows, EX4.20
Arrows, EX2.38, EX2.39
AutoCorrect, EX1.20, EX1.21
AutoFill, EX3.22
AutoFit, EX1.25
Autoformat, EX5.10-EX5.12
AutoFormat dialog box, EX5.11
AutoRecover, EX1.26
AutoSum button, EX1.43
AVERAGE, EX1.42
Backspace key, EX1.16, EX1.18
Bar charts, EX2.5, EX2.20
Bitmap files, EX1.65
.bmp files, EX1.65
Bold, EX1.56
Browser, EX6.38
Bubble charts, EX2.5, EX2.31
Bubble size, EX2.31

Caps Lock, EX1.19
Cascaded windows, EX4.20
Case sensitive, EX6.20
Category-axis title, EX2.6
Category names, EX2.6
Cell, EX1.7
Cell alignment, EX1.49-EX1.51
Cell reference. *See* Reference
Cell selector, EX1.7
Center Section, EX3.48
Centering across a selection, EX1.53
Changing worksheet data, EX2.34, EX2.35
Character effects, EX1.56